The *topos* of Divine Testimony in Luke-Acts

The *topos* of Divine Testimony in Luke-Acts

JAMES R. MCCONNELL JR.

◈PICKWICK *Publications* • Eugene, Oregon

THE *TOPOS* OF DIVINE TESTIMONY IN LUKE-ACTS

Copyright © 2014 James R. McConnell Jr. All rights reserved. Except for brief quotations in critical publications or reviews, no part of this book may be reproduced in any manner without prior written permission from the publisher. Write: Permissions, Wipf and Stock Publishers, 199 W. 8th Ave., Suite 3, Eugene, OR 97401.

Pickwick Publications
An Imprint of Wipf and Stock Publishers
199 W. 8th Ave., Suite 3
Eugene, OR 97401

www.wipfandstock.com

ISBN 13: 978-1-62032-755-5

Cataloguing-in-Publication data:

McConnell, James R., Jr.

The *topos* of divine testimony in Luke-Acts / James R. McConnell Jr.

xii + 322 pp. ; 23 cm. Includes bibliographical references and index.

ISBN 13: 978-1-62032-755-5

1. Bible. Luke—Criticism, interpretation, etc. 2. Bible. Acts—Criticism, interpretation, etc 3. Word of God (Christian theology)—Biblical teaching. 4. Authority—Religious aspects—Christianity—Biblical teaching. I. Title.

BS2589.6 H62 M26 2014

Manufactured in the U.S.A.

To Susan, Luke and Mary, Evan, and Molly:

Εὐχαριστῶ τῷ θεῷ μου πάντοτε περὶ ὑμῶν
ἐπὶ τῇ χάριτι τοῦ θεοῦ τῇ δοθείσῃ ὑμῖν ἐν Χριστῷ Ἰησοῦ

1 Corinthians 1:4

Contents

Acknowledgments   ix

Abbreviations   x

1. Introduction   1
2. The *topos* of Divine Testimony and its Application in Ancient Speeches and Treatises   23
3. The *topos* of Divine Testimony through Utterances in Hellenistic Narratives   74
4. The *topos* of Divine Testimony through Utterances in Luke-Acts   121
5. The *topos* of Divine Testimony through Deeds in Hellenistic Narratives   177
6. The *topos* of Divine Testimony through Deeds in Luke-Acts   227
7. Conclusion   265

Bibliography   279

Scripture Index   301

Ancient Writers Index   311

Acknowledgments

I WOULD BE REMISS not to recognize those without whom this project would have been impossible. Dr. Mikeal Parsons has been an outstanding mentor, teacher, supervisor, and friend; to him I am especially grateful for opening my eyes to the world of ancient rhetoric and narrative criticism, and for encouraging me to pursue publication of this work. This book would not exist without his help. I am thankful to Dr. Charles Talbert and Dr. David Jeffrey for their willingness to serve on my dissertation committee and for always providing such timely and insightful critique of my work. Of course, any errors in this volume are solely my responsibility.

But it is to my family that I owe the largest debt of gratitude. My wife, Susan, and children, Luke (and now Mary), Evan, and Molly, have exhibited incredible flexibility in allowing their lives to be interrupted and move across the country (and, in some cases, back again!) so that I might pursue the calling to minister to students through theological education. They have demonstrated great patience in allowing me the time I needed for my studies and research, and they have never failed to support and encourage me along the way. I am truly blessed beyond measure by my children and by my wife, who daily models and practices sacrificial love.

Abbreviations

ABBREVIATIONS FOR BIBLICAL BOOKS, ancient sources, and secondary sources referenced in this study have been adapted from *The SBL Handbook of Style* (Peabody, MA: Hendrickson, 1999).

AB	Anchor Bible
AJBI	*Annual of the Japanese Biblical Institute*
AJP	*American Journal of Philology*
AJT	*American Journal of Theology*
ANRW	*Aufstieg und Niedergang der römischen Welt: Geschichte und Kultur Roms im Spiegel der neueren Forschung*
BBR	*Bulletin for Biblical Research*
BDAG	Bauer, W., F. W. Danker, W. F. Arndt, and F. W. Gingrich. *Greek-English Lexicon of the New Testament and Other Early Christian Literature*. 3rd ed. Chicago, 1999
Bib	*Biblica*
BN	*Biblische Notizen*
BRev	*Bible Review*
BSac	*Bibliotheca sacra*
BZ	*Biblische Zeitschrift*
BZNW	*Beihefte zur Zeitschrift für die neutestamentliche Wissenschaft*
CBET	Contributions to Biblical Exegesis and Theology
CBQ	*Catholic Biblical Quarterly*
CJ	*Classical Journal*
Colloq	*Colloquium*
CQ	*Classical Quarterly*
CurTM	*Currents in Theology and Mission*

Abbreviations

EKKNT	Evangelisch-katholischer Kommentar zum Neuen Testament
ETL	*Ephemerides theologicae lovanienses*
EvT	*Evangelische Theologie*
ExpTim	*Expository Times*
HSCP	*Harvard Studies in Classical Philology*
HTKNT	Herders theologischer Kommentar zum Neuen Testament
HTR	*Harvard Theological Review*
Int	*Interpretation*
JBL	*Journal of Biblical Literature*
JES	*Journal of Ecumenical Studies*
JRS	*Journal of Roman Studies*
JSNT	*Journal for the Study of the New Testament*
JSNTSup	Journal for the Study of the New Testament: Supplement Series
JSOT	*Journal for the Study of the Old Testament*
JTS	*Journal of Theological Studies*
LASBF	*Liber annuus Studii biblici franciscani*
LB	*Linguistica Biblica*
LCL	Loeb Classical Library
L&N	*Greek-English Lexicon of the New Testament: Based on Semantic Domains*. Edited by J. P. Louw and E. A. Nida. 2nd ed. New York, 1989
LXX	Septuagint
NAC	New American Commentary
Neot	*Neotestamentica*
NIGTC	New International Greek Testament Commentary
NovT	*Novum Testamentum*
NovTSup	Supplements to Novum Testamentum
NRSV	New Revised Standard Version
NRTh	*La nouvelle revue théologique*
NTS	*New Testament Studies*

Abbreviations

ProEccl	*Pro ecclesia*
PRSt	*Perspectives in Religious Studies*
RCT	*Revista catalana de teología*
ResQ	*Restoration Quarterly*
RevExp	*Review and Expositor*
RevScRel	*Revue des sciences religieuses*
RSR	*Recherches de science religieuse*
SBLDS	Society of Biblical Literature Dissertation Series
SBLSP	*Society of Biblical Literature Seminar Papers*
SBT	Studies in Biblical Theology
SJT	*Scottish Journal of Theology*
SNTSMS	Society for New Testament Studies Monograph Series
SNTSU	Studien zum Neuen Testament und seiner Umwelt
SP	Sacra pagina
STRev	*Sewanee Theological Review*
TBei	*Theologische Beiträge*
Them	*Themelios*
TJ	*Trinity Journal*
TJT	*Toronto Journal of Theology*
TynBul	*Tyndale Bulletin*
TZ	*Theologische Zeitschrift*
VF	*Verkündigung und Forschung*
WBC	Word Biblical Commentary
WMANT	Wissenschaftliche Monographien zum Alten und Neuen Testament
WUNT	Wissenschaftliche Untersuchungen zum Neuen Testament
WW	*Word and World*
ZNW	*Zeitschrift für die neutestamentliche Wissenschaft und die Kunde der älteren Kirche*

1 • Introduction

IN THE PREFACE TO Acts, the author, addressing Theophilus, describes the contents of the Third Gospel (τὸν . . . πρῶτον λόγον) as being about what "Jesus *did* and *taught* from the beginning" (Acts 1:1; emphasis added).[1] In Acts 4, when Peter and John are called before the council of Jewish elders and admonished to cease their preaching in the name of Jesus, they answer: "[W]e cannot keep from speaking about what we have *seen* and *heard*" (Acts 4:20; emphasis added). Thus, one notes that in Luke-Acts (cf., e.g., Luke 7:22) there is an emphasis on what has been said as well as what has been done in various contexts.[2] In this study, I will explore this twofold emphasis on what is said and done concerning the testimony of God, specifically what God has said and done in testifying to the innocence and piety of his son and the followers of the son, as well as the lack of piety on the part of those who oppose Jesus and the apostles.

PURPOSE OF THE ANALYSIS

The present study will seek to address the idea of authoritative testimony in the combined work of Luke-Acts. Specifically, I will argue that ancient audiences would have understood particular elements in the narrative of Luke-Acts to be instances of the *topos* of divine testimony, considered by ancient rhetoricians to be the most authoritative form of testimony when seeking to persuade an audience. According to the ancient rhetoricians, the gods testified through their speech (mainly by way of oracles) and their deeds; their deeds included the heavens themselves, the flight and songs of birds, sounds and/or visible emanations from the heavens (such as fire), portents on the earth, dreams and visions, and through the entrails

---

1. English citations from the Bible are from the NRSV, unless otherwise noted.

2. Danker notes, "Of the four evangelists, Luke makes most frequent use of the word-deed theme" (see Danker, *Benefactor*, 340).

The *Topos* of Divine Testimony in Luke/Acts

of sacrificial animals.³ This study will examine instances of the elements listed above found in Jewish, Greco-Roman, and early, non-canonical Christian narratives roughly contemporaneous with Luke-Acts, seeking to identify how divine testimony functions in them. I will then turn to the narrative of Luke-Acts and demonstrate that ancient audiences would have understood the *topos* of divine testimony to function in the same way as in the extra-biblical literature listed above.

History of Research

This study will combine three areas of NT scholarship that have, for the most part, in the past been considered in isolation from each other.⁴ These three areas include: (i) rhetorical *topoi* and how they relate to the study of the NT; (ii) the use of scripture citations and references in Luke-Acts; and (iii) the study of the miraculous aspects within the NT documents, with special emphasis on the gospels and Acts. In the following, I will briefly examine the previous research in these three areas, concluding with a discussion of the unique contribution this study will make to Luke-Acts scholarship.

Toposforschung

The history of scholarship regarding the application of the *topos* to the NT will be treated in some detail in the second chapter of this study. At this point, it is sufficient to provide a summary of those findings. Previously, the application of the concept of *topos* to NT studies was generally restricted to the consideration of a *topos* as a stock theme or motif, which the NT writers exploited within their writings in order to persuade their auditors. An example of this would be the *topos* of friendship in Paul's letter to the Galatians.⁵ Lately, this view of a *topos* has begun to shift, with scholars recognizing that even the ancient rhetoricians allowed for a somewhat wider semantic range as to the definition of a *topos*. In this study, I will argue that this range be broadened even more, allowing for a definition of *topos* (based on the ancient rhetorical handbooks) to include a *topos* as a

---

3. These are described by Cicero as sources of divine testimony; see *Top.* 20.76–77.

4. Exceptions, of course, do exist. These will be noted in the following summary of the history of research.

5. See, e.g., Betz, *Galatians*, 32, 221, in which he maintains that Paul, especially in Gal 4, builds his argument around a "string of friendship *topoi*."

Introduction

source of proofs, brought as evidence when arguing a case. In particular, this study will consider the *topos* of divine testimony, the most authoritative witness one could bring to bear in the law courts and public assembly, and especially how ancient audiences would have understood this use of the *topos* in ancient speeches, Hellenistic histories and biographies, and finally Luke-Acts.

OT Citations and References

Previous scholarship on the use of scripture in Luke-Acts has emphasized the idea of promise and fulfillment, which, according to S. Porter, as recently as 2006, should be considered the scholarly consensus.[6] Most scholars trace the concept of proof from prophecy theology found in Luke-Acts to P. Schubert,[7] who acknowledges that his study builds upon the work of H. Cadbury.[8] Schubert, in analyzing Luke 24 as a conclusion to the Third Gospel, argues that the glue which holds together the three main scenes in chapter 24 is the idea of proof from prophecy. Having come to this conclusion, he then examines Luke 1–9 and concludes that proof from prophecy theology is the "central theological idea throughout the two-volume work."[9]

The idea that Luke promoted a proof from prophecy theology has continued to hold sway in studies of Luke's use of scripture. Within the last twenty years, D. Bock has been a proponent of a slightly modified version of this concept.[10] Rather than proof from prophecy, Bock prefers the term "proclamation from prophecy and pattern," because, he argues, Luke does not cite Hebrew scripture as an apologetic tool. Rather than defending Jesus' messiahship through the use of scripture, Luke employs scripture citations and allusions as a way of proclaiming who Jesus is. According to Bock, in most of the Third Gospel, Jesus is portrayed as the Messiah-servant, the one who fulfills specific scriptures as well as the patterns found in the Hebrew scriptures that describe God's saving activity. At the transfiguration, the portrayal of Jesus as Lord is introduced; in Luke

---

6. Porter, "Scripture Justifies Mission," 104–26.

7. Schubert, "The Structure and Significance of Luke 24," 165–86.

8. See Schubert, "The Structure and Significance of Luke 24," 173–74n20, in which he cites Cadbury, *The Making of Luke-Acts*, 302–5.

9. Schubert, "The Structure and Significance of Luke 24," 176.

10. Bock, *Proclamation*.

The *Topos* of Divine Testimony in Luke/Acts

20 it is once again established, and from this point in the gospel (and into Acts) Jesus' lordship is seen in tension with his Messiah-servant image.[11]

Given this christology in Luke-Acts, Bock then speculates as to what Luke's purposes might have been for creating this image of Jesus. His conclusion is that Luke is attempting to erase any doubts that may exist in his auditors' minds concerning the way in which Jesus' death is part of the βουλή τοῦ θεοῦ. Also, Bock argues that Luke is attempting to reassure his audience that the mission to the Gentiles is also a part of God's overall plan for the salvation of all human beings.

Not all scholars, however, have been convinced that proof from prophecy is the focus of Luke-Acts. C. Talbert, in a 1984 essay,[12] traces the development of the proof from prophecy concept,[13] and then proceeds to offer his critique, which he states in three main points.[14] First, following M. Rese,[15] Talbert points out that not all scripture citations in Luke-Acts are used in a proof from prophecy schema,[16] and not all fulfilled prophecy in Luke-Acts has its basis in the Hebrew scriptures. Second, Talbert questions whether one can make the logical leap from proof from prophecy theology to authorial intent.[17] Talbert's third and last point is that it is not valid to extrapolate the purpose of an entire, two-volume work from a single theme found in that writing.

Given this critique, Talbert then moves to his analysis of the theme of prophecy-fulfillment as found in Luke-Acts. Here, Talbert seeks to answer the question of how an ancient Mediterranean auditor would have heard

---

11. Bock argues that Jesus is characterized as "more than a messiah" from this point on in the narrative; see *Proclamation*, 264.

12. Talbert, "Promise and Fulfillment," 91–103.

13. Talbert begins his survey with Schubert, and then reviews the work of Schubert's fellow Yale scholars N. Dahl, L. Johnson, and R. Karris.

14. It should be noted that Talbert agrees that proof from prophecy theology is a part of Luke-Acts. His argument is that proof from prophecy theology should not be considered the central theme around which Luke-Acts has been composed.

15. Rese, *Alttestamentliche Motive*.

16. Other uses of the OT include: a hermeneutical application in which the OT is used to show that current events are much like those narrated in the OT; a typological use through which the OT can assist in the understanding of current events; and finally an ethical use through which characters in Luke-Acts are portrayed as fulfilling the ethical demands of the OT. See Talbert, "Promise and Fulfillment," 93–94.

17. Talbert notes that not all instances of proof from prophecy are in support of Luke's conception of salvation history. He lists three other applications, including divine protection, encouragement of believers, and paraenesis; see "Promise and Fulfillment," 95–96.

and understood this theme. His answer is that Mediterranean auditors would have been quite comfortable with the idea of prophecy and fulfillment. Parallels between Luke-Acts and the first-century Greco-Roman milieu include: divine necessity as the controlling aspect of history; the course of history being seen in fulfilled oracles (whether those oracles were rightly understood or not); and the mention of fulfilled oracles to legitimate heroes and to give credibility to other utterances by those heroes.[18]

Recently, scholars have begun to pursue other avenues with regard to the use of scripture quotations in Luke-Acts. In a 1997 essay,[19] C. Stanley argues that a rhetorical approach to the use of scripture quotations within NT documents is necessary to balance the overabundance of studies which emphasize the interpretive traditions the author employed in selecting and commenting on the verses which are quoted. Stanley goes on to say that a profitable trajectory of research would explore how quotations of scripture serve the rhetorical, argumentative strategy employed by the author. As evidence, he engages three modern linguistic studies on the use of quotations and concludes that quotations offer an author a powerful, persuasive tool. But, according to Stanley, any study of an author's rhetorical strategy using quotations must be balanced by examining the implied reader's understanding of those same quotations.

A second study moves in this same direction. D. Stamps[20] suggests that one should consider the Hellenistic context of scripture quotations in NT documents. He argues that this would subsequently lead to the analysis of the quotation of scripture through the lens of ancient rhetoric. He recognizes that the use of authoritative traditions is found in Jewish and Greco-Roman writings from the first century and later. He also cites guidelines from ancient rhetorical handbooks that advise orators on the proper use of quotations and maxims. Finally, in his conclusion, Stamps proposes that NT authors cited the Hebrew scriptures in order to convince their Hellenistic auditors of the ancient foundation of this new religion.

Finally, R. Morgenthaler has conducted an exhaustive rhetorical-critical study of Luke-Acts.[21] In this study, Morgenthaler includes a short section in which he discusses the disciples as witnesses. Morgenthaler argues that Luke portrays the disciples in his gospel, and Peter and Paul

---

18. Talbert, "Promise and Fulfillment," 96–101. For Bock's response to Talbert's critique, see Bock, "Proclamation," 280–82.

19. Stanley, "Rhetoric," 44–58.

20. Stamps, "Use of the Old Testament," 9–37.

21. Morgenthaler, *Lukas und Quintilian*, esp. 364–85.

in Acts, as witnesses; thus, Luke-Acts is the documentation of a trial[22] in which God reveals his justice. As part of this trial motif, Morgenthaler mentions the idea of scripture quotations as instances of divine testimony as proposed by Quintilian, drawing an analogy between the quotation of scripture in Luke-Acts and oracles as mentioned in Quintilian's *Inst*. A major aspect of the present study will explore and build upon Morgenthaler's suggestion.

The Miraculous[23]

Within the last forty years several surveys of past scholarly research into the gospel miracle accounts have been published.[24] A cursory review of these essays shows that there has been a multiplicity of approaches used in analyzing the miracle accounts recorded in the synoptic gospels and Acts, especially during the twentieth century and continuing into the present day. Also, according to some scholars, there has been a shift in scholarly attitude towards the miracle stories, especially in light of recent historical Jesus research. The purpose of this section is to provide a brief overview of the various analytical methodologies applied to the study of miracle accounts in general and to Luke-Acts in particular. The results of these methodologies, especially as they impact the study of Luke-Acts, will also be highlighted.

---

22. In this regard see also Neagoe, *The Trial of the Gospel*.

23. I am intentionally avoiding the term "supernatural," as this carries with it a post-Enlightenment assumption that the world is governed by natural laws; this is clearly an anachronism when one considers the worldview of a first-century audience. Hume defined a miracle as "a transgression of a law of nature by a particular volition of the Deity, or by the interposition of some invisible agent" (*Enquiries Concerning Human Understanding*, 115 n. 1). This is the definition used by Swinburne, *Concept of Miracle*, 11 ("a violation of a law of nature by a god"). Swinburne makes a similar point to the one above concerning the supernatural nature of miracles; he argues that through the inclusion of the phrase "by a god" in the definition of miracle one must consider miracles as "in accordance with the divinely ordained natural order as a whole" (*Concept of Miracle*, 9). More recently, D. Basinger and R. Basinger argue for two definitions of miracle: (i) "a permanently inexplicable event directly caused by God"; and (ii) "an awe-producing naturally explicable event directly caused by God" (*Philosophy and Miracle*, 23).

24. See, e.g., Kertelge, "Die Wunder Jesu," 71–105; Polhill, "Perspectives on the Miracle Stories," 389–99; Weder, "Wunder Jesu," 25–49; Maier, "Wunderexegese," 49–87; Engelbrecht, "Trends in Miracle Research," 139–61; Twelftree, "The History of Miracles," 191–208; Kollmann, "Images of Hope."

G. Maier begins his history of miracle research in the eighteenth century; he argues that due to the influences of Spinoza and Schleiermacher, miracle accounts were no longer viewed as descriptions of objective events.[25] Throughout the rest of the nineteenth century, rationalism was the controlling factor in the study of the synoptic miracle stories, especially in Germany. Scholars such as D. F. Strauß, F. C. Baur, and A. von Harnack either discounted the miracles completely or sought rational explanations for what was being described in the gospels.[26] Therefore, by the end of the nineteenth century, there was a widespread consensus concerning the impossibility of miracles. Only those miracles in the gospels that could be explained through natural causes should be accepted as historical. This led to a division of miracle accounts between those which were possible (healings) and those which were not (nature miracles).[27]

Early in the twentieth century, scholars belonging to the History of Religions school began to make substantial contributions to the study of the miracle accounts. Works by scholars such as O. Weinreich, P. Fiebig, R. Reitzenstein, and L. Bieler served to demonstrate that the synoptic miracle stories did not emerge out of a literary vacuum; rather, parallel miracle accounts existed in the milieux of both rabbinic Judaism[28] and the greater Greco-Roman world.[29] One may argue that the cumulative output of the History of Religions school served to continue and even deepen the skepticism concerning the historicity of the synoptic miracle accounts, thus minimizing the significance of these narratives within their contexts, by

---

25. Spinoza argued that reports of miracles actually act as obstacles to faith because they claim the breaking of natural laws established by God. Similarly, Schleiermacher maintained that the universe and its inner workings were creative acts of God; if a miracle occurs which contradicts this natural order found in the universe, it would be a contradiction in the nature of God himself. See Maier, "Wunderexegese," 52–53.

26. Harnack, for example, maintained that the stories which related healing miracles represented accounts of actual events; he went on to say, however, that the healing itself could be explained through natural means. He rejected any miracles which, in his opinion, seemed to break natural laws. See Harnack, *What is Christianity?* 23–30.

27. See Maier, "Wunderexegese," 55. It should be noted that Maier attempts through his essay to argue that since the nineteenth-century scholarly attitudes toward the synoptic miracle reports have slowly changed from that which is described here to a general acceptance of the historicity of many miracle stories.

28. See, e.g., two works by Fiebig: *Jüdische Wundergeschichten*; idem, *Rabbinische Wundergeschichten*.

29. Examples include: Weinreich, *Antike Heilungswunder*; Fiebig, *Antike Wundergeschichten*; Reitzenstein, *Hellenistische Wundererzählungen*; and Bieler, *Theios aner*.

The *Topos* of Divine Testimony in Luke/Acts

claiming that the New Testament evangelists were simply borrowing existing stories from other religions.[30] For this study, however, the significant contribution made by this group of scholars was to show that the idea of miracles and miracle workers was a commonplace in both first-century Judaism as well as the Greco-Roman milieu in which the Third Gospel and Acts were composed. It is thus possible to use these parallel miracle accounts to reconstruct the authorial audience for which Luke-Acts was written, providing insights into how these stories would have been received and understood by the original audience. We will return to this topic shortly.[31]

---

30. Fiebig denies the historicity of the miracle accounts, and therefore minimizes the significance of these elements of the gospels. But for him this is not a problem, because, as Fiebig states, "das für uns heutzutage Wertvollste in den Evangelien liegt nicht in den Wundergeschichten, sondern in den Worten Jesu" (*Jüdische Wundergeschichten*, 97–98).

31. One idea proposed by the History of Religions school that continued to influence the study of synoptic miracles is that of the Hellenistic θεῖος ἀνήρ. The idea of the θεῖος ἀνήρ, or "divine man," was first introduced by Reitzenstein (*Hellenistischen Mysterienreligionen*, 26–27), and given full expression by Bieler (*Theios aner*) approximately two decades later. Reitzenstein argues that the origin of the *theios anēr* can be found in the spread of the cults of deities in the ancient world. Wandering religious figures, prophets for their respective gods, were responsible for the proliferation of these ancient cults in remote areas away from the normal trade routes. These figures were able to foresee the future and know people's thoughts, heal the sick, and even restore life to the dead. Bieler's contribution was to survey various first, second, and third-century Greco-Roman works, as well as the canonical gospels and the apocryphal Acts (ibid., 7–8), and from these sources deduce a standardized portrait of the Hellenistic divine man. According to Bieler, such a figure in the ancient sources was characterized by an extraordinary situation surrounding his birth, often involving some type of communication or relationship between the parents and the gods. Also, the divine man was normally an outstanding student who amazed his teachers, eventually becoming a virtuous adult who was able to see into the future and perform miraculous works involving nature, demons, and the healing of those afflicted with illnesses. Finally, amazing events normally surround the death of the figure—signs and portents appear; the body of the figure vanishes, or the figure appears after his death (ibid., 44–48).

Within the last forty years, the concept of the *theios anēr* as a point of entry for discussing the gospel miracle accounts has continued to be attractive to scholars; summaries of the development of the concept of the Hellenistic divine man and its application to gospel research can be found in the following: M. Smith, "Prolegomena," 174–99; Tiede, *Charismatic Figure*; and Holladay, Theios Aner *in Hellenistic-Judaism*, 15–45. Holladay's summary concentrates on the process of transmission of the concept of a Hellenistic divine man through Hellenistic-Judaism (in which it was combined with the OT idea of a "man of God") to the Christian authors of the NT. For critiques and nuanced perspectives, see Tiede, *Charismatic Figure*; Holladay, Theios

Introduction

In addition to the contribution of the History of Religions school, a second major emphasis on NT miracle research has come from the form critics. M. Dibelius[32] classified the synoptic miracle stories into two categories: paradigms and *Novellen*. According to Dibelius, paradigms were those miracle stories which were circulated by the early church for preaching (i.e., didactic) purposes. They were terse bits of independent traditions which were infused with religious, missionary language. Normally, the climax of paradigms consisted of words of Jesus. Tales, on the other hand, were circulated as religious propaganda. Through tales, which generally describe epiphanies, Jesus is presented as superior to other deities. Thus, the miraculous element of the story is enhanced through the relation of many details which are not found in paradigms.

Bultmann continued to apply form criticism to the miracle stories,[33] emphasizing that the synoptic miracle traditions emerged in the same atmosphere as Palestinian Jewish and Greco-Roman miracle stories. As evidence, from both of these milieux Bultmann lists numerous parallels to the gospel accounts of exorcisms, healings, accounts of people being raised from the dead, and nature miracles. According to Bultmann, this is not to say that these parallels were sources for the gospel miracle stories; rather, the parallels demonstrate the same type of development of the traditions. Bultmann argues that the miracle accounts in the gospels followed the same developmental path as those found in Jewish and Greco-Roman literature; miracle motifs and folktales became oral traditions, which were then incorporated into the gospels themselves.

For Bultmann, the significance of the miracle accounts is not found in their historicity (or lack thereof). Rather, for Bultmann, the importance

---

Aner *in Hellenistic-Judaism*; Betz, "Jesus as Divine Man," 114–33; Achtemeier, "Gospel Miracle Tradition," 174–97; Talbert, "Concept of Immortals," 419–36. In this last essay, Talbert opines that the idea of a *theios anēr* is "an auxiliary concern because of its importance in current discussion in NT study" ("Concept of Immortals," 419 n. 1, citing Achtemeier, "Gospel Miracle Traditions"). Rather than focus on the author's intention, as Achtemeier and Betz do, Talbert emphasizes what the ancient audience would have understood, arguing that there were originally two concepts of divine men, namely the immortals and that of the *theios anēr*. These two eventually merged, the point of contact between them being the virtuous life that characterized both types of figures. While some early Christians argued that Jesus was unique, others embraced the idea of a virtuous immortal, and used it in their portrayals of Jesus. For a more recent critique of *theios anēr* Christology, see Pilgaard, "Hellenistic *Theios Aner*," 101–22.

32. The following discussion is from his *From Tradition to Gospel*, 37–103.

33. See Bultmann, *History of the Synoptic Tradition*, 218–44.

is in the meaning of the stories. He thus draws a distinction between the exposition of the miracle story and the miracle itself. The miracle stories are narrated in order to draw attention to the miracle worker, and therefore, elements of the miracle itself are highlighted. For example, circumstances surrounding the miracle are mentioned, and/or the problem to be overcome is emphasized.[34] This is an important contribution by Bultmann and the form critics, as noted by other scholars.[35]

Form critical analysis of gospel miracle narratives certainly did not end with Bultmann. This type of study is seen recently in the work of G. Theissen, H. D. Betz, J. Polhill, and G. Sterling. Theissen's work[36] employs a threefold methodology; first, Theissen utilizes a synchronic approach which attempts to create a comprehensive list of motifs which appear in miracles stories. Next, Theissen considers the miracle texts diachronically, seeking to identify how the various motifs identified through the synchronic analysis have been applied, emphasized, and modified in the gospel traditions. Third, Theissen analyzes the miracle traditions with an eye toward their functionality,[37] in effect determining the *Sitz im Leben* of the miracle traditions.

Theissen, as part of the diachronic analysis, also addresses how each evangelist employed and modified the various motifs identified through his synchronic analysis. In his remarks on the Third Gospel, Theissen notes that Luke emphasizes the episodic nature of the miracle accounts he includes through the repeated use of the καὶ ἐγένετο introductory formula. From this, Theissen concludes that Luke understood that the materials he included are paradigmatic of a greater theme. This greater theme, which the miracle reports in Luke support, is that Jesus, who is anointed with the divine δύναμις through the giving of the Holy Spirit, is sent by God to usher in this particular stage of salvation history. Thus Luke, whose account is biographical in nature due to the inclusion of the birth narratives, composes a "salvation history gospel life."[38]

---

34. He states, "It is characteristic of the *miracle itself* that the actual miraculous event is almost never described, . . . only the accompanying circumstances" (Bultmann, *History of the Synoptic Tradition*, 221; emphasis in original).

35. See, e.g., Engelbrecht, "Trends in Miracle Research," 141.

36. Theissen, *The Miracle Stories*. This volume is a translation of his *Urchristliche Wundergeschichten*.

37. Functionality in three different areas is considered: the social function, the religio-historical function, and the existential function.

38. Theissen, *The Miracle Stories*, 223.

Introduction

In Theissen's work one sees the same emphasis on the meaning and function of the miracle stories as in the earlier form critics. Through his analysis of the various motifs and how, over time, these motifs were applied in the construction of the miracle accounts, Theissen attempts to determine how these early miracle traditions were understood by the authors and used to compose the gospels.[39]

Several studies have been completed in recent years that focus exclusively on miracle accounts in the Third Gospel and/or Acts. Most of these studies employ redaction criticism; there are others, however, that make use of other methodologies or have a different point of emphasis. It is to a review of these studies that I now turn.

M. Miller has produced a redactional study of the miracle accounts in Luke and Acts.[40] Miller's stated purpose is rather broad: "to discover as much as possible about miracles in Luke-Acts—how they function and what they mean—to come as close as possible to Luke's understanding of them, and to draw implications from this for Luke's purposes."[41] Miller's work is as wide-ranging as his purpose; he considers parallels from rabbinic sources, Greco-Roman sources, the LXX, and Mark's gospel. He concludes that the LXX constitutes the backdrop to Luke's miracle accounts, and that his modifications to his sources prove that he has a theological agenda which causes the gospel to be more than a narration of historical

---

39. Other scholars have subsequently attempted to build on Theissen's analysis. See, e.g., Polhill, "Perspectives on the Miracle Stories"; Betz, "Early Christian Miracle Story," 69–81; and most recently, Sterling, "Jesus as Exorcist," 467–93. Polhill takes issue with the concept of *theios anēr* as developed within the History of Religions School and argues for the significance of the gospel miracle accounts, suggesting two avenues. First, scholars should consider the eschatological context of the miracle stories; in doing so, the focus of the investigation becomes the uniqueness of the reports, rather than their similarities to other ancient miracle stories. This uniqueness is seen in the account as a whole, not in the details. Second, Polhill proposes further investigation using Theissen's structuralist approach. He argues that "the very *structure* of the miracle narratives conveys the eschatological message" contained in them ("Perspectives on the Miracle Stories," 395; emphasis in original).

Betz is also sympathetic to Theissen's project; he, however, argues for a stronger emphasis on the artistic contribution of the author through the myriad combinations and foci that result from the author's use of those motifs identified by Theissen. In this way the distinctively Christian elements can be isolated and the Christian interpretation of the miracle accounts deduced.

Sterling performs a form-critical analysis of the triple tradition that relates the exorcism performed by Jesus following the transfiguration, ultimately arguing that this account is based on an actual event in the life of Jesus.

40. M. Miller, "The Character of Miracles in Luke-Acts."

41. Ibid., iii.

events. Miller argues that this theological emphasis is one of promise and fulfillment.

In considering the technique of how miracles are performed in Luke-Acts, Miller concludes that Luke has emphasized the miracle worker as an agent of God's power. In this Luke is closer to the OT than the Hellenistic milieu; the focus of miracles in Luke-Acts is the relationship between God and the recipient of the miracle, not the miracle worker himself. Here, Miller favorably compares miracle workers in Luke-Acts with OT prophets; God works through them to proclaim his presence among the people. Therefore, in analyzing the results of the miracles in Luke-Acts, Miller is led to the conclusion that miracles "are a fulfillment of the eschatological hope which had long been nourished in Israel."[42] The miracles thus demonstrate the reality of the kingdom of God, a reality that was foreseen by the OT prophets.

Miller concludes his study by arguing that miracles in Luke-Acts serve as acts of proclamation of God's presence on earth, and his involvement in the affairs of human beings. As this activity was predicted by the OT prophets, it can be considered a fulfillment of the eschatological hope of the nation of Israel. From this conclusion, Miller then modifies Conzelmann's concept of salvation history. Rather than Conzelmann's Israel/Christ/church stages of redemptive history,[43] Miller argues for a period of God's presence in Israel, a time of God's absence, and finally God's return to be among his people.

A second redactional study that focuses on miracles in the Third Gospel is from P. Achtemeier.[44] In his article, in which he seeks to ascertain the specific Lukan emphases in the miracle accounts recorded in the Third Gospel, Achtemeier proposes that the miracles of Jesus in Luke (as compared with Mark) perform three functions: (i) miracles serve as a balance to the teachings of Jesus; (ii) miracles focus on Jesus and are used to validate Jesus and his ministry; (iii) miracles evoke faith and can contribute to one's becoming a disciple of Jesus.[45] In addition to these three functions, Achtemeier argues against J. Hull's position that Luke's approach to miracles and his characterization of Jesus is thoroughly influenced by his

---

42. Ibid., 198.

43. Conzelmann, *Theology of St. Luke*, 16–17.

44. Achtemeier, "Lucan Perspective on the Miracles," 547–62.

45. See also Tannehill, *Luke*, 86, who arrives at this conclusion through a literary analysis of the Third Gospel. Tannehill argues that the faith that is evoked through a miracle is ultimately faith in God, not the miracle worker. This theological perspective, according to Tannehill, is found throughout Luke-Acts.

Introduction

view of Hellenistic magic.[46] In his conclusions, Achtemeier notes that in Luke, more than Mark and Matthew, miracle stories can be the catalyst for faith in Jesus, for a calling to be a disciple of Jesus, and to legitimate Jesus. Achtemeier also highlights the significant influence that Hellenism has had on Luke's perspective on the miracles, while simultaneously avoiding portraying miracles as magical practices.[47]

U. Busse's 1979 monograph[48] is a third example of a redactional study of the miracles in the Third Gospel. In it, Busse disagrees with Conzelmann's thesis that Luke is writing in light of the delayed parousia; he also rejects the idea of Jesus as a *theios anēr*.[49] After a meticulous exegesis of the miracle accounts in Luke's gospel, Busse argues that there are three main purposes for the miracle stories in the Third Gospel. First, and most importantly, through Jesus' miracles one perceives the present salvation of God. Second, the miracles that Jesus performs are signs of his messianic character; i.e., he is God's agent of salvation. Lastly, miracle stories are used as testimony of God's salvation and are used as an ethical teaching tool for the disciples.

Busse then makes some overarching comments on the christological, soteriological, and eschatological use of miracle accounts in Luke. Christologically, Busse argues that the miracles are not proof of Jesus' messiahship;[50] rather, the miracle stories serve to characterize Jesus as the one who is God's agent, fulfilling God's promises within the greater context of salvation history. Jesus is portrayed as sovereign Lord, but the tension between Jesus' Macht and Ohnmacht ultimately points to God. Thus, the miracles must be interpreted as pointing to God; Jesus is only God's instrument of salvation.

---

46. Hull, *Hellenistic Magic*, 87–115.

47. Here Achtemeier specifically refutes Miller's argument (see above) that through the miracle accounts Luke characterizes Jesus as an OT prophet ("Lucan Perspective on the *Miracles*," 561n26). Achtemeier maintains that although there is evidence that Luke portrays Jesus as a prophet, the miracle stories in the Third Gospel have not been modified to promote this characterization (see ibid., 560–62).

48. Busse, *Die Wunder des Propheten Jesu*. This volume is a condensed version of his dissertation, written at Westfälischen Wilhelms-Universität, under the supervision of J. Gnilka.

49. Here Busse relies on the work of Tiede, *Charismatic Figure*.

50. At this point he disagrees with Conzelmann (*Theology of St. Luke*, 190–93). Busse states that because Jesus' miracles are misunderstood by the disciples, they cannot serve as proofs. Rather, it is only after the resurrection that the disciples gain understanding.

Soteriologically, Busse compares the miracle accounts to stones in a mosaic, due to their episodic nature.[51] The individual stones show God's salvation of the poor, the deliverance of the oppressed from demonic possession, and the healing of the sick. The picture the mosaic depicts is thus the fulfillment of God's promise of salvation to the world. Therefore, the miracles are part and parcel of the proclamation of the present kingdom of God on earth. Eschatologically, the miracles thus serve to demonstrate Luke's idea of a realized eschatology.

Finally, Busse's exegesis leads him to make some suggestions concerning Luke's *Sitz im Leben* and the occasion for the writing of the Third Gospel. Rather than the delay of the parousia (see above), Luke is writing "Erbauungsliteratur"[52] to a community that is suffering under some type of duress. Luke thus writes to encourage his community, emphasizing that they are now in that age foretold by the OT prophets, and realized through God's agent, Jesus.

A more recent redaction-critical study of the miracles in Luke-Acts is found in a 1999 volume by G. Twelftree.[53] Twelftree devotes two chapters of this work to a redactional and narrative analysis of the miracle stories in Luke-Acts.[54] His results for the most part follow those of Busse; in the area of the meaning of Lukan miracles, however, Twelftree argues that in Luke the miracles of Jesus are not just illustrative of the message of the gospel. Rather, Jesus' miracles are constitutive of the gospel. Also in disagreement with Busse,[55] Twelftree maintains that Jesus' miracles are indeed evidence that Jesus is the Messiah; in this regard, Jesus' miracles and words are equal. Overall, miracles in Luke-Acts are more significant than in Matthew and Mark, and serve as a basis for belief and discipleship. Ultimately, this belief is directed towards God.

---

51. Here (*Die Wunder*, 450), Busse refers to Luke's favorite introductory formula, καὶ ἐγένετο, as noted by Theissen and others.

52. Busse, *Die Wunder*, 484.

53. G. Twelftree, *Jesus the Miracle Worker*.

54. A second study utilizing a similar methodology is Green, "Jesus and a Daughter of Abraham," 643–54. In this article, Green notes the dearth of redaction-critical and "literary-theological" studies of miracles in Luke-Acts. He considers the healing of the bent woman from these perspectives (with priority given to the literary-theological perspective) and concludes that the healing of the bent woman reinforces Luke's emphases on the balance of teaching and deeds and the elevated status of "outsiders" in the kingdom of God. Also, Green argues that the healing is ultimately an expression of mercy with eschatological overtones, as the woman is delivered from Satan's captivity.

55. I should note that Twelftree is not in direct conversation with Busse; Busse's volume does not even appear in Twelftree's otherwise extensive bibliography.

Introduction

Other studies, while technically not using a redaction-critical methodology, focus on the special emphases of Luke's narration of miracles in the Third Gospel and in Acts. An example of this is a study by H. Kee.[56] Kee argues that Luke has employed two first-century literary conventions in order to persuade his auditors. These include elements of Hellenistic historiography[57] and romances. According to Kee, the genre of romance came to be used in cult propaganda documents; these were literary works which would allow the auditors to relive the mythic foundation of the cult.[58] In Luke's story of Jesus and the church, Israel is the foundation, much as the myth of Isis served as the foundation of the Isis cult.

For Kee, the central component of Luke's story is the theme of the kingdom of God. Miracles assist Luke in elucidating this theme in that healings and exorcisms are demonstrations of the fulfillment of prophecy. Also, dreams and other wonders function as God's confirmation of each new phase of the expansion of the kingdom. Thus, while making the narrative interesting to read, miracles also validate that the expansion of Christianity into all parts of the Roman Empire is indeed God's desire and the fulfillment of prophecy.

G. W. H. Lampe has considered the topic of miracles in Acts,[59] and argues that the wondrous deeds performed by the apostles in Acts (and Jesus in the Third Gospel) should be viewed against an OT background. Jesus, according to Lampe, is portrayed as a prophetic figure, one who acts as God's spokesperson and agent, who comes to announce the beginning of a new age. The same Spirit that empowered Jesus' miraculous deeds then empowers his disciples after his ascension. Through this and other parallels between Luke's gospel and Acts, Lampe argues that the apostles in Acts should also be seen as prophetic figures. The deeds performed by Jesus and the apostles are in fulfillment of OT prophecy and function in both Luke and Acts as signs and evidence of the proclaimed in-breaking of the kingdom.

While the studies surveyed above have the advantage of focusing specifically on the theme of the miraculous in Luke-Acts, the methodologies

---

56. Kee, *Miracle*, 190–220.

57. Ibid., 190–92; Kee specifically lists three: the prologue, speeches, and historical facts and chronological references.

58. Ibid., 194. Kee states that these works were composed "to foster devotion to the god, and to do so by describing the experiences of the main characters in ways that mirror or even reenact the experiences of the god, as told in the mythical stories of the divine struggles and triumph."

59. Lampe, "Miracles," 164–78.

employed tend to focus on the emphases of the author. While offering valuable insights, they, with some exceptions, tend to neglect the greater Greco-Roman milieu in which Luke-Acts was composed and heard. Also, these studies generally focus on the author's theology, rather than the persuasive aspects of the narrative in which these elements of the miraculous are found. Recently, studies have appeared which help fill this lacuna in scholarship. It is to examples of these studies that I now turn my attention.

M. M. Adams has recently produced a narrative study of miracle accounts in Luke-Acts.[60] Adams builds upon Achtemeier's aforementioned redactional study of the miracles in the third gospel, arguing that miracles are constitutive of a repeated pattern in Luke-Acts. This pattern consists of a call/commission from God, which leads to a ministry characterized by signs and preaching. The results of this ministry are reactions which are often negative, from which persecution ensues. Ultimately, the messenger is vindicated through some type of miracle. The pattern can be seen in the descriptions of Jesus, Peter, Stephen, and Paul, and is also paradigmatic for the church as a whole in Acts.

In a second example of a narrative-critical approach to miracles in Luke-Acts, C. Talbert, in his commentary on the Third Gospel,[61] includes a section in which he makes summary comments concerning Luke's view of miracles (as found in the Third Gospel and Acts) and in the Lukan milieu generally.[62] Talbert argues that Luke's attitude toward the miraculous mirrors the Greco-Roman and Jewish environment in which he composed his writings. In each case, Talbert finds that there was a mixed attitude toward the miraculous. On the positive side, Luke considers miracles as a potential catalyst for faith, as legitimating acts of persons or the proclaimed word, and as proof of one's virtuous character and innocence. On the negative side, for Luke miracles were not sufficient evidence to bring about one's conversion. Miracles must be supported by words,[63] and are differentiated from magic by the miracle-worker's character. Also, Luke considers conversion as having priority over being healed in a physical sense.

60. Adams, "The Role of Miracles," 235–73.
61. Talbert, *Reading Luke*.
62. Ibid., 271–76.
63. This point is also made by O'Reilly, *Word and Sign*, who argues that Jesus is the prophet like Moses, and his disciples after him carry out his prophetic ministry. O'Reilly comes to these conclusions through a primarily redactional study of word and sign in Acts, arguing that in Luke's theology, word and sign are both constitutive elements of the proclamation of salvation. Sign, however, is subordinate to word. The connection of word and miracle is also made by Tannehill, *Luke*, 77–99.

Introduction

Lastly, employing a narrative-critical approach to miracles in Acts, M. Myllykoski[64] has argued of late that miracle accounts form the backbone of the narrative in Acts 1–12. He claims that each account of the miraculous in Acts 1–12 falls into one of four categories: (i) a witness to the foundational miracle, Jesus' resurrection and ascension; (ii) a precursor to conflict; (iii) legitimation of the next stage of salvation history; or (iv) the formation of character and the growth of faith of Luke's community. Myllykoski concludes that Luke wrote to a community under duress in order to encourage his listeners with a highly idealized portrayal of the *Urgemeinde* from which they have come.

R. Strelan[65] analyzes miraculous phenomena in Acts from the ancient auditors' perspective. Strelan uses a social-scientific methodology which greatly depends on Jewish and Greco-Roman parallel texts in order to understand first-century auditors' attitudes towards these phenomena in Acts. Strelan argues that these accounts would have been understood as legitimation of the mission to the Gentiles, an apologetic for the continuing work of God, missionary propaganda, and entertainment. Finally, Strelan concludes that although the heroes in Acts are characterized as OT prophets (such as Moses and Elijah), Hellenistic readers would also have understood these acts also by interpreting them through their own cultural grid.

Finally, one study of Luke-Acts does combine the analysis of aspects of the miraculous along with the concept of proof-from-prophecy (i.e., the function of scripture citations). J. Squire's recent monograph[66] includes three chapters which investigate the role of signs, epiphanies and visions, and fulfillment of prophecy in Jewish and Greco-Roman ancient historiography and Luke-Acts. According to Squires, these three emphases[67] combine to explicate the role of the plan of God in Luke-Acts.[68] Squires concludes that this focus serves an apologetic purpose to encourage

---

64. Myllykoski, "Being There," 146–79.

65. Strelan, *Strange Acts*.

66. Squires, *Plan of God*; see esp. 78–154 (chs. 4, 5, and 6).

67. Squires also includes God's direction of events through history and the concept of necessity (δεῖ). On the use of δεῖ in Luke-Acts, see also Cosgrove, "The Divine ΔΕΙ," 168–90.

68. On the role of scripture and the fulfillment of the plan of God, see also Moessner, "The 'script' of the Scripture," 218–50. Moessner surveys Luke's use of scripture in the major defense speeches in Acts, arguing that scripture is used to emphasize the fulfillment of three major aspects of God's plan: the apostles' preaching that Christ has been raised from the dead; the crucifixion of Jesus; and Jesus' resurrection.

Christian auditors to be witnesses of and to remain strong in their faith, as well as to confirm the faith of the auditors.

With this previous scholarship as a foundation, the present study advances the discussion by combining different areas of Toposforschung and Luke-Acts scholarship, thus asking a new question. First, this investigation will argue for an understanding of *topos* as a source of proofs, used in forensic and deliberative situations in the ancient world. Specifically, I will focus on the *topos* of divine testimony, an external proof through which the rhetor cites the utterances and deeds of the gods in order to persuade the audience of the innocence or guilt of a client and/or the opposition. Thus, the study will analyze citations of Jewish scripture, as well as certain elements of the miraculous, from a rhetorical, audience-oriented perspective, seeking an answer to the question of how divine testimony through words (both spoken and written) and deeds functions within the complete narrative of Luke-Acts. Specific emphasis will be placed on how these particular elements in the narrative would have been understood by Luke's ancient audience, an audience which lived in a culture in which persuasion through rhetoric was a commonplace.

Methodology

The overall methodology that will be employed by this study can best be described using S. Chatman's communication model[69] of author → text → reader. All three of the elements in Chatman's model are significant for the methodology used in the study. Each will be described in turn, beginning with the text.

When analyzing specific passages from Luke-Acts, this study will perform a "close reading" of the text. Agreeing with Kelber,[70] this study will take seriously the fact that Luke and Acts are the result of the composition of an author; Luke-Acts has a specific plot and characters, which are developed throughout the narrative. Events that are narrated assume the significance of what has gone before as well as what will follow. Therefore, the analysis of each incident must be accomplished with regard to the whole, considering the entire context of Luke-Acts in each case. In some cases, it may be necessary to compare the Lukan passage with its parallels in Mark and/or Matthew in order to discern the specific focus in Luke.

---

69. Chatman, *Story and Discourse*.

70. Kelber, "Redaction Criticism," 14. I was directed to this through C. Talbert's citation of same; see *Reading Luke*, 4.

Introduction

The present study will be primarily one of rhetorical criticism, which reflects suppositions concerning the author of the text as well as the audience of the text. Concerning the documents in the NT, G. Kennedy asks, "How legitimate is it to approach the New Testament in terms of Greek ideas of rhetoric?"[71] Kennedy argues from a historical perspective that one is indeed justified when analyzing the NT through a rhetorical lens due to the significance of rhetoric in Greco-Roman education in the first century.[72] Rhetoric formed the core of the secondary education system in the Roman Empire. In addition, rhetorical principles were employed in almost every aspect of public life in the culture in which the evangelists and Paul grew up and lived; therefore, it is safe to assume that they were at least familiar with the rudiments of rhetoric, even if they did not formally study it. To attempt to be persuasive means that they would have had to communicate in a manner that the people around them understood.[73] Therefore, an author, who had received at least a basic education and who desired to persuade a first-century audience, would be influenced to some degree by the principles of rhetoric taught and practiced within the culture.

Other scholars, by examining the text of Luke and especially Acts, argue that the author of Luke-Acts had received some level of rhetorical training. For example, Kurz notes that Luke's use of enthymemes as described by Aristotle, the prologues which conform to Greek literary conventions, the emphasis on the trial scenes and their associated forensic rhetoric, as well as the use of inartificial proofs, including witnesses, contracts, and oracles, all serve as evidence that Luke had received an education in rhetoric.[74] P. Satterthwaite finds rhetorical influences in Luke's selection of material, the arrangement of the material (on both a macro and micro level), and the greater amount of narrative emphasis placed on important theological themes. These areas, along with the general style of the narrative and the use of speeches, cause Satterthwaite to conclude that

---

71. Kennedy, *Rhetorical Criticism*, 8.

72. Ibid., 3–12. See also Kurz, "Hellenistic Rhetoric," 171–95; Kurz cites Malherbe (*Social Aspects*, 45) in claiming that the lowest level of education that an NT writer who quotes from Greek literary works would have had would be "the upper levels of secondary education" (Kurz, "Hellenistic Rhetoric," 192). Cf. Satterthwaite, "Acts," 340–43.

73. Kennedy, *Rhetorical Criticism*, 8–10.

74. See Kurz, "Hellenistic Rhetoric," 172–84, for Luke's use of enthymemes, and ibid., 185–91, for other evidence of Luke's knowledge of rhetoric. As will become evident, the present study agrees wholeheartedly with Kurz's point concerning witnesses and inartificial proofs.

Luke was attempting to persuade his auditors using the rhetorical conventions of his time.[75] R. Burridge suggests that it is not out of the realm of possibility that Luke had some type of rhetorical training. He bases this assumption on Luke's stylistic treatment of Markan material, the speeches in Acts, and "his command of different Greek styles."[76]

Finally, M. Parsons, in his recent commentary on Acts, in which he analyzes the text from a rhetorical perspective,[77] reminds his readers that Acts was originally written to be heard. The text would therefore have been read by a lector, one who was most likely skilled to some degree in rhetorical practice. The significant point that Parsons makes is that while Acts (and Luke's Gospel) is a written document, because it was composed to be rehearsed in front of a group of auditors, it most likely shares characteristics with speeches, written in accordance with the guidelines as described in the rhetorical handbooks. Thus, one of Parsons's emphases in his analysis is on the *Progymnasmata*, or preliminary exercises.[78] The *Progymnasmata* comprised a

> curriculum . . . featuring a series of set exercises of increasing difficulty, [which] was the source of facility in written and oral expression for many persons and training for speech in public life . . . Not only the secular literature of the Greeks and Romans, but the writings of early Christians beginning with the gospels and continuing through the patristic age, and of some Jewish writers as well, were molded by the habits of thinking and writing learned in schools.[79]

According to Kennedy, the *Progymnasmata* were a part of the first-century education process for both written and oral communication. Given that Luke is writing in Greek, he clearly had some level of education which would have included the preliminary exercises. One is therefore justified in analyzing Luke-Acts with an eye toward elements of rhetoric, as described in the preliminary exercises and the rhetorical handbooks.

Performing a rhetorical analysis also has implications for the reader/auditor in Chatman's model. The auditors on which this study will concentrate are those who make up the authorial audience as described

---

75. Satterthwaite, "Acts."
76. "The Gospels and Acts," 507–32; the quotation is from ibid., 530.
77. Parsons, *Acts*.
78. Parsons, *Acts*, 9–11.
79. Kennedy, introduction to *Progymnasmata*, ix.

Introduction

by P. Rabinowitz.[80] The authorial audience is that group of auditors for which the text is composed; i.e., the author, in writing the text, makes assumptions as to the ability of the audience to understand. The authorial audience is that ideal audience which understands everything the author presents. To reconstruct the authorial audience, this study will draw from the thought of W. Iser[81] and H. R. Jauss.[82] Iser argues that readers ultimately construct the meaning of a text, using the text as a set of instructions. To construct meaning from the text, a reader relies on her "repertoire," which consists of other texts with which the reader is familiar, as well as the social and cultural ethos in which the reader lives. Jauss argues similarly, stating that the reading of a text triggers memories contained in a "horizon of expectations" which has been built up through the reading of other texts. Thus, this study will attempt to understand the text as Luke's first-century readers understood it by reconstructing their repertoire/horizon of expectations through the analysis of writings which were roughly contemporaneous to Luke's audience. As rhetoric was the primary form of persuasion used in the legal and political spheres of first-century Greco-Roman culture, an analysis of rhetorical principles as found in the Greco-Roman rhetorical handbooks and the Progymnasmata will be a necessary component of this reconstruction, especially in their discussions of the concept of *topos/locus*.

In sum, the methodology of this study will be that of rhetorical criticism, combined with a close reading of the text in order to discern the persuasive structures within the narrative as well as a vehicle to understand how the text would have been received by first-century auditors. In addition, contemporaneous Jewish and Greco-Roman writings will be analyzed in order to reconstruct the auditors' horizon of expectations.

Framework of the Argument

The main argument of this study will unfold in five chapters. The first of these chapters will provide an understanding of the *topos* of divine testimony as described in the ancient rhetorical handbooks as well as the Progymnasmata. The chapter will investigate the ancient rhetoricians' descriptions of the *topos*, in order to attempt to define this concept from the ancients' perspective. The discussion will become increasingly specific,

80. Rabinowitz, "Truth in Fiction," 121–42.
81. Iser, *The Act of Reading*.
82. Jauss, *Aesthetic of Reception*.

with the goal of arriving at the most effective type of inartificial proof, that of divine testimony. Once this is accomplished, ancient Greco-Roman speeches and philosophical treatises will be surveyed, with an eye toward the function of divine testimony through word and deed in actual arguments. The goal of this chapter is to demonstrate the high value of the *topos* of authoritative testimony, including the sources thereof, in the ancient world, and to argue that divine testimony was the strongest source of this type of proof.

The third chapter will examine how an ancient audience would have understood divine testimony through utterances by examining passages in Jewish and Greco-Roman histories and biographies, as well as early, non-canonical Christian writings roughly contemporary with Luke-Acts. In these sources, direct speech by the gods, divine speech through an inspired intermediary, and the use of oracles will be analyzed; from this analysis the function within the narratives of this type of divine testimony will be explicated. The expected result of this analysis is that divine speech is often used as testimony, either in favor of or against a person or an event. These results will then be used as a baseline and compared to the accounts of divine speech in Luke-Acts, which are examined in chapter four. As in chapter three, direct speech by God, speech through inspired intermediaries (those "filled with the Spirit"), and written utterances by God will be examined. A significant facet of the argument in this chapter is the equation, from an ancient audience's perspective, of the use of oracles in Hellenistic narratives and references to Hebrew scriptures in Luke-Acts. The chapter will ultimately demonstrate that an ancient audience would have heard the *topos* of divine testimony through utterances in Luke-Acts in the same way as in extra-biblical narratives of the same period.

The next two chapters parallel the previous two; here, however, the focus will be on the *topos* of divine testimony through deeds, rather than speech. The structure of the investigations will follow Cicero's description of what constitutes divine testimony through deeds (*Top*. 20.76–77). This description will also control which specific accounts in Luke-Acts constitute divine testimony through deeds. Therefore, not all instances of the miraculous will be considered; only those elements within the narrative that fall under Cicero's categories will be examined. The goal of these chapters is, as in chapters two and three, to demonstrate that the *topos* of divine testimony through deeds would have been understood by an ancient audience to function in ways similar to those seen in Hellenistic narratives and biographies.

2 • The *topos* of Divine Testimony and its Application in Ancient Speeches and Treatises

THE GOAL OF THIS chapter is to define how the term *topos*[1] should be understood in the rest of this work, and to explore the specific *topos* of divine testimony.[2] Examples of the *topos* of divine testimony from ancient speeches and treatises will then be provided. The chapter will finally conclude with an assessment of the persuasiveness of this particular *topos* in the first-century Mediterranean milieu in which Luke-Acts was composed and heard. Defining what I mean by *topos* is necessary for two reasons. First, in the ancient rhetorical handbooks, the term *topos* (or *locus*) was used differently by various authors and, indeed, in some cases by the same author. Thus, as will be demonstrated, the term as used by the ancient rhetoricians (and philosophers) enjoyed a somewhat wide semantic range.[3] Second, the term in modern NT scholarship has continued on this same trajectory; in general, biblical scholars' application of a *topos* to the study of NT passages tends to focus on E. Curtius's definition of a *topos* as a universal theme or cliché, applicable to any type of literature.[4]

1. *Locus* in Latin. When referencing those ancients who wrote in Greek, the word *topos* will be used; when discussing the Latin rhetoricians, *locus* will be used. Ultimately, the two terms reference the same general concept.

2. A summary of how the term *topos* has been particularly understood in NT scholarship will introduce this analysis.

3. For short summaries of the concept of *topos*, see, e.g., Cope, *Introduction to Aristotle's Rhetoric*, 124–33; J. Martin, *Antike Rhetorik*, 107–19.

4. Curtius, in his influential work, *European Literature and the Latin Middle Ages*, 79–105, argues that the ancient rhetoricians considered the topics a "stockroom" of universally applicable concepts, to be employed in the composition of speeches and

23

In this study, however, rather than a stock theme, I will consider the *topos* as a source of proofs, used in composing a speech for the purposes of defending or prosecuting one accused of some crime. In the following analysis, through a survey of the appropriate rhetorical treatises as well as examples of the *topos* of divine testimony found in forensic speeches and other works, it will be demonstrated that this is certainly a possible understanding of *topos*.

In the section that follows, I will first summarize the definition and application of the concept of *topos* in NT scholarship during the previous approximately sixty years. It is to this history of research that I now turn.[5]

The Concept of *topos* in Contemporary NT Scholarship

The definition of *topos* and its use in the NT originally emerged out of form criticism and neglected the ancient rhetoricians' definitions of *topos*. In 1953, D. Bradley offered this definition of *topos*: "the treatment in independent form of the topic of a proper thought or action, or of a virtue or a vice, etc."[6] Terence Mullins found Bradley's definition lacking and offered his own: "The Topos is a form with three essential elements: *injunction*, *reason*, and *discussion*. Two optional elements, *analogous situation* and *refutation*, might be used. Its purpose was to urge a type of behavior or attitude and there was no limit to the range of behavior discussed" (emphasis in original).[7] Mullins (as did Bradley before him) simply applied a form critical analysis to ancient texts and the New Testament to formulate

---

other forms of literature. For example, he cites the use of the *topos* of "affected modesty" (ibid., 83–85), and maintains that as early as Cicero this *topos* was used to ingratiate the orator to the judge overseeing the case. This *topos*, however, is also found in other literature, including both early Christian and non-Christian.

5. Many of the articles and essays reviewed here are also engaged by Thom, "Defining the topos," 555–73; Thom makes many of the same points as I in this review of previous scholarship.

6. Bradley, "The *Topos*," 238–46. The connection of *topos* and form criticism is clear in Bradley's work. He states, "For one such form ... I have employed as a descriptive name the Greek word *topos*" ("The *Topos*," 240).

7. Mullins, "Topos," 541–47, esp. 547. Mullins basically takes Bradley's definition and compares to it several ancient writings, including Greco-Roman, Jewish, and early Christian. Specifically, Mullins agrees with Bradley's definition of the function of a *topos* (as seen in the NT), but disagrees with his treatment of the form of the *topos*.

his definition, and did not rely on evidence from the ancient rhetorical handbooks.[8]

J. Brunt, however, reversed this trend, using the rhetorical handbooks as evidence to correct the definitions of *topos* offered by both Bradley and Mullins.[9] Brunt argued that it had become a common misconception to view a *topos* as a "stereotyped, recurring motif."[10] Instead, Brunt offers a definition quite similar to what we will see in the ancient rhetorical handbooks, especially those of Cicero and Quintilian: "*topoi* are stereotyped arguments that are applied to specific cases."[11]

During this same time, others are also seeking independently to define and apply the *topos* to the study of the NT. For example, W. Wuellner[12] reviews modern research on the *topos* as part of literary criticism, while recognizing that modern Toposforschung is "rooted" in the ancient rhetorical handbooks. Wuellner begins with Curtius's definition of *topos*, noting that Curtius recognized that both the structure and content of the argument being made could be understood under the umbrella of *topos*. Thus, Wuellner rightly admits that the *topos* is a "komplexes Phänomen." Wuellner, however, makes a contribution to the application of the *topos* to NT studies by recognizing that the author's choice of *topos/topoi* is cultur-

---

8. More recently, see also von Lips, "Die Haustafel," 261–80. Von Lips argues that rather than a Gattung, the familiar Haustafel passages in the NT should be considered a *topos*; in this he sympathetically cites Bradley's work. A. Malherbe also argues for this particular view of the *topos*. He maintains that a *topos* is a "stock treatment of subjects of interest to the moralist," and his analysis concentrates on the *topos* of friendship as found in Seneca, Plutarch, Musonius, Epictetus, and Dio Chrysostom, as well as Paul in the NT; see Malherbe, "Hellenistic Moralists," 267–333, esp. 320–25. An example of *topoi* being applied in the analysis of the New Testament is found in H. D. Betz's commentary on Galatians (*Galatians*). In his introduction to the commentary, Betz refers to Paul's argument in 4:12–20 as a "string of friendship *topoi*" (ibid., 32). In his comments on the passage in question, Betz restates this expression; he says that Paul is making his argument using "a string of *topoi* belonging to the theme of 'friendship.'" He continues by claiming that the theme of friendship was quite well known in the ancient world, and cites several ancient documents as evidence (ibid., 221). See also L. Johnson, "James 3:13—4:10," 327–47.

9. Brunt, "More on the *Topos*," 495–500.

10. Ibid., 496. Brunt admits that the form discussed by Bradley and Mullins certainly exists in classical writings as well as the New Testament; he argues, however, that it is incorrect to call it a *topos*.

11. Ibid., 498. Brunt (ibid., 497) also explains that Aristotle connected the use of *topoi* to enthymemes, which are syllogistic in nature. However, while a syllogism is a complete argument, in an enthymeme one premise of the argument is missing. The *topoi* represent the source of the enthymemes.

12. Wuellner, "Toposforschung und Torahinterpretation," 463–83.

ally conditioned and therefore can provide insight into both the audience which is the target of the persuasive discourse, as well as the rhetorical issue being argued. The value, therefore, in Wuellner's work is seen in his emphasis on the *topos* as an argumentative element, as well as his focus on the audience.

Recently, the issue of *topos* and how it relates to NT scholarship has been revisited by J. Thom. Thom seeks to provide a definition of the term *topos* by surveying both primary sources and the voluminous secondary literature on the topic.[13] As it stands, Thom's work is the most up-to-date and comprehensive treatment of this topic.

Thom argues that *topoi* in ancient rhetoric served as "'places' in which arguments may be found, that is, the general headings under which one may search for material for one's argument. As such, it forms part of the *inventio*."[14] He goes on to note that even in Aristotle's work, the term *topos* was not specific; rather, its meaning is better viewed as a continuum, "ranging from the more formal to the more substantive."[15] According to Thom, Quintilian's statement differentiating "commonplaces" (i.e., complete, self-contained arguments) from *loci* (storehouses for arguments; cf. *Inst.* 5.10.20) indicates that he is reflecting the breadth of understanding in the ancient world concerning the *topos*.

In defining the *topos*, Thom argues first that *topos* is clearly used in a different manner by modern literary theorists than what was meant by the term in antiquity. Second, Thom recognizes that even in antiquity the term had a relatively wide semantic range, and that the meanings within this range were "culturally determined." However, the foundation of these meanings is a "notion of an ordered cognitive space."[16] In other words, while the concept of *topos* in antiquity is better viewed on the basis of a spectrum or continuum (and where one finds oneself on this continuum is somewhat dependant on culture), all the possible meanings are grounded in a common idea.

Thom does not concretely flesh out this common ground; he does, however, offer three different categories or types of *topoi*. The first he calls

---

13. Thom, "Defining the topos," 555–73. He cautions that his work should not be considered the final word on the topic; rather, his essay represents "an exploratory survey," and that "[A]t most [he] will attempt to indicate some of the lines of investigation that need to be developed further" (ibid., 557).

14. Ibid., 561.

15. Ibid. By "formal," Thom is referring to *topoi* that are used as "strategies of argumentation," while "substantive" *topoi* are those that represent topics for arguments.

16. Ibid., 566.

the "logical or rhetorical *topos*," which represents a certain method of argumentation.[17] The second is the "literary *topos*"; *topoi* of this type "consist of literary themes or motifs that are used over and over again, often only as an allusion, and not in a worked out form."[18] However, Thom maintains that because of the "non-literary nature of most NT texts," this category is "not that well-represented in the NT."[19] Finally, the third type proposed by Thom is the "moral or philosophical *topos*." This type is much like the literary *topos*; the difference is, however, that there are extended treatments of these *topoi* in Hellenistic moral writings.[20]

Through his survey of primary and secondary sources, Thom's work has extreme value in the study of ancient *topoi*. There are, however, areas of his work which can be improved. One of these areas would be a more precise reading of Theon, especially in taking into account all of Theon's preliminary exercises and not only the exercise of "commonplace."[21] As I will show, by carefully considering the contexts in which Theon uses the word τόπος and its derivatives, one notices that Theon acknowledges that a *topos* can be either a complete, structured argument or a source of arguments particular to a certain case.[22] Secondly, Thom's analysis could be augmented profitably through the inclusion of Cicero's work on *topoi*; Cicero is not mentioned in Thom's essay.

Given this understanding of the concept of *topos* in current NT scholarship and those aspects thereof found to be deficient or incomplete, I will now survey the ancient rhetoricians' ideas concerning rhetorical

---

17. Ibid. He offers the example of an argument from the lesser to the greater, found in Matt 6:30.

18. Ibid., 566–67. An example, according to Thom, is the "younger-son motif in the Parable of the Prodigal Son." This definition is also emphasized by J. McDonald, *Kerygma and Didache*, 70–72. Two examples noted by McDonald include:

Seneca, *Ep.* 34.19: "I remember one day you were handling the well-known commonplace [*Memini te illum locum aliquando tractasse*],—that we do not suddenly fall on death, but advance towards it by slight degrees; we die every day."

Seneca the Elder, *Suasoriae* 1.7.9: "He then spoke the commonplace [*Dixit deinde locum*] on the variability of Fortune. He described how nothing is stable, everything fluid, now raised, now depressed in unpredictable change."

19. Thom, "Defining the topos," 567.

20. Ibid. Thom lists Plutarch as an example of the Hellenistic moral writers (he specifically mentions the *Moralia*).

21. In examining the later development of the *topos*, Thom devotes a paragraph of his study to Theon's treatment of *topos* in the *Progymnasmata*. Thom confines his comments to the formal elementary exercise of *topos*.

22. This same distinction as seen in Cicero and Quintilian, as will be demonstrated below.

topoi. From this analysis, a definition of *topos* will emerge that will require the current definitions of *topos* in NT circles to be expanded to include a *topos* as a source of proofs which includes documents, oaths, witnesses, and testimony.

Definition of topos

Topos in Aristotle

Although the concept of a rhetorical *topos* predates Aristotle,[23] his works are a convenient starting place for an attempt to wrap one's mind around the ancient rhetoricians' conception of a *topos*. The two main works in which Aristotle discusses *topoi* are his *Topica* and *Rhetorica*.

In his work *Topica*, Aristotle asserts his purpose in the opening statement of the document: "The purpose of the present treatise is to discover a method by which we shall be able to reason from generally accepted opinions about any problem set before us and shall ourselves, when sustaining an argument, avoid saying anything contradictory" (1.1.18). He continues by providing a definition of "reasoning" (συλλογισμός):

> Reasoning is a discussion in which, certain things having been laid down, something other than these things necessarily results through them. Reasoning is *demonstration* (ἀπόδειξις) when it proceeds from premises which are true and primary or of such a kind that we have derived our original knowledge of them through premises which are primary and true. Reasoning is *dialectical* which reasons from generally accepted opinions. (1.1.25–31; emphasis in original)

---

23. Kennedy (*Classical Rhetoric*, 61) notes that the idea had already surfaced in the writings of Isocrates; he states in particular that Isocrates mentioned the *topos* of possibility/impossibility and arguments which cite authoritative sources (*Hel. enc.* 4, 38). In his encomium to Helen, Isocrates writes concerning those who would, through the use of rhetoric, attempt to prove those things which are agreed upon to be false: "Nevertheless, although these men [Georgias, Zeno, Melissus] have shown that it is easy to contrive false statements on any subject that may be proposed, they still waste time on this commonplace [περὶ τὸν τόπον τοῦτον]" (*Hel. enc.* 4). In the same treatise, Isocrates continues, commenting on the appropriateness of praising Helen: "But lest I seem through poverty of ideas to be dwelling unduly upon the same theme [περὶ τὸν αὐτὸν τόπον] and by misusing the glory of one man to be praising Helen, I wish now to review the subsequent events also" (*Hel. enc.* 38). For a somewhat tentative discussion (admittedly; cf. the title of the work) of the origins of the concept of the *topos*, see D'Angelo, "The Evolution of the Analytic *Topoi*," 50–68, esp. 54–61.

Thus, from this purpose statement it is clear that Aristotle is dealing with dialectic, rather than rhetoric. What he has to say concerning dialectical argumentation does, however, help one to understand the ancient concept of a *topos*.

In Book I of *Topica*, Aristotle explores the various ways one can argue a dialectical problem and concludes with this statement: "Such then are the means by which reasonings are carried out. The commonplaces [τόποι] for the application of which the said means are useful are our next subject" (1.18.33–35). What follows in Books II-VII is a description of various τόποι and how one is to apply each of them when formulating a dialectical argument. For example, Aristotle writes, "One commonplace [τόπος] is to look whether our opponent has assigned as an accident something which belongs in some other way" (2.2.34–36). A second example is found in his discussion of a polyvalent term which is used in a certain way. Aristotle advises that one "ought to demonstrate one of the several meanings if it is impossible to demonstrate both." He continues by adding, "This commonplace [τόπος] is convertible for both constructive and destructive purposes" (2.3.29–30). These examples are indicative of Aristotle's usage of the term τόπος throughout Books II-VII of the treatise, and demonstrate that Aristotle, in this treatise, considered a τόπος to be a method of dialectical argumentation.

In *Rhetorica*, Aristotle provides his definition of rhetoric, stating that "Rhetoric then may be defined as the faculty of discovering the possible means of persuasion in reference to any subject whatever . . . But Rhetoric, so to say, appears to be able to discover the means of persuasion in reference to any given subject" (*Rhet.* 1.2.1). In discussing the methods of actually being persuasive, Aristotle lists two. Inartificial proofs are those not "furnished by ourselves but were already in existence, such as witnesses, tortures, contracts, and the like."[24] Artificial proofs are those "that can be constructed by system and by our own efforts. Thus we have only to make use of the former [inartificial], whereas we must invent the latter [artificial]" (*Rhet.* 1.2.2). These proofs fall under three categories, those of ἦθος, πάθος, and λόγος (1.2.3–6), and can be generated, according to Aristotle, by one of two methods, either inductively (primarily through the use of examples) or logically, by employing enthymemes (1.2.8–9). Aristotle then begins his discussion of *topoi*, which he describes in this way: "I mean by dialectical and rhetorical syllogisms those which are concerned with what we call 'topics'" (1.2.21). Aristotle distinguishes between

---

24. Aristotle specifically lists five inartificial proofs: laws, witnesses, contracts, that which is revealed by someone being tortured, and oaths.

general/universal *topoi* which can be applied to argumentation within any subject matter, and specific *topoi*, which are "the propositions peculiar to each class of things" (1.2.21–22).

Later in the treatise, after a discussion of the three types of rhetoric (forensic, deliberative, and epideictic), Aristotle specifically mentions twenty-eight different *topoi* which are available to the rhetor for the construction of enthymemes. Examples of the *topoi* found in this list include those arguments which are generated from opposites, the more and the less, the definition of terms, and induction (2.23.1–29). As was seen in Aristotle's *Topica*, these *topoi* represent methods of rhetorical argumentation, rather than the content of the arguments themselves.[25]

As I have previously stated, the concept of the *topos* was already familiar to the Greeks of his day; therefore, this list represents Aristotle's attempt to systematically categorize *topoi*. Aristotle's contribution to this aspect of rhetoric was to classify and generalize the use of the various *topoi*.[26]

For the purposes of the present study, however, it is important to examine briefly Aristotle's concept of inartificial proofs,[27] specifically focusing on what he says concerning witnesses. For Aristotle, witnesses fall into two categories: ancient and recent. Ancient witnesses are the most reliable, because it is no longer possible to refute or discredit them; they have, in effect, stood the test of time. Appropriate ancient witnesses include poets, "men of repute whose judgments are known to all" (here, Aristotle provides Homer as an example), "interpreters of oracles for the future" (i.e., Themistocles's interpretation of the wooden wall), and proverbial wisdom (παροιμία, 1.15.13–19).[28] Witnesses who are contemporaries of the orator

---

25. Ryan's comment is helpful; concerning enthymemes and *topoi*, he states: "To say, then, that an enthymeme is derived from a topos does not mean that the enthymeme is constructed from the topos as from a premise... Instead, the enthymeme follows the structure of the topos... The topos is not part of the argument, but it is the argument's pattern" (Ryan, *Aristotle's Theory*, 48–49).

26. J. Martin, *Antike Rhetorik*, 107.

27. Inartificial proofs, according to Aristotle, are those which are particularly appropriate for forensic speeches (1.15.1–2).

28. For a similar, albeit much later view of quoting and/or imitating ancient sources, see Longinus, [*Subl.*] 13.2–4. In this passage, the author, concerning the μίμησις of ancient sources, argues that referring to others' works is another path to the "sublime." The author uses the analogy of the steam which came from the earth at Delphi and intoxicated the pythia; the pythia is "impregnated with the divine power and is at once inspired to utter oracles." In this same way, by the imitation of historians and poets the reader is "carried away" by use of others' work. By analogy, readers are captivated by the wisdom of the ancients ("old writers [ἀρχαίων]"). The author goes on to say that

include "all well-known persons who have given a decision on any point" (these decisions can be used in similar cases) and "those who share the risk of the trial, if they are thought to be perjurers." Witnesses such as these, however, can only help establish if something occurred or not; they are not reliable in establishing "the quality of the act" (1.15.15–17).

In sum, Aristotle views *topoi* as generally agreed-upon methods of argumentation, useful both to those engaging in dialectic and those who would construct arguments through the use of rhetoric. Some *topoi*, the use of which is not tied to a particular field of inquiry, are beneficial for all cases. Others, those which Aristotle calls specific (ἴδια), are to be used only in particular types of arguments. In the area of rhetoric, *topoi* for Aristotle constitute the sources of enthymemes and are therefore useful for logical reasoning.[29]

With Aristotle's view of *topos* as a background, I will now focus on the Latin rhetoricians' views concerning the *topos*, or *locus*, beginning with Cicero and then considering the treatments found in *Rhetorica ad Herennium* and Quintilian.[30]

Locus in Cicero

I begin with Cicero's *De inventione rhetorica*, considered to be a work written by Cicero in his younger days.[31] In the introductory section of the

---

quoting or imitation is not plagiarism; rather, it is like "taking an impression from fine characters as one does from molded figures or other works of art."

29. See Kennedy, *Rhetorical Criticism*, 20–22, who briefly summarizes Aristotle's concept of *topos*; cf. a similar discussion in Kennedy, *The Art of Persuasion*, 100–103.

30. This is certainly not to say that the concept of *topos* disappears between Aristotle and Cicero; on the contrary, many ancient rhetoricians address this subject matter. The evidence is such, however, that Reinhardt can correctly note: "In light of the scanty evidence for the post-Aristotelian development of dialectical τόποι, we may assume that Cicero's *loci* reflect a post-Aristotelian tradition of rhetorical τόποι which have been rearranged and supplemented with the help of *Top.* and other sources" (Reinhardt, *Topica*, 28–29; emphasis original). See Reinhardt, *Cicero's Topica*, 18–35, for a brief overview of the various understandings of *topos* from Aristotle to Boethius. See also Kemper, "Topik," 17–32, for a summary of the *topoi* from Aristotle to Cicero.

31. See Kennedy's discussion of the situation surrounding Cicero's writing of *Inv.* in *The Art of Rhetoric*, 106–11. Kennedy argues that Cicero and his contemporaries followed the ancient convention of not mentioning a living person to whom they were indebted; only those authorities who were deceased were cited. In *Inv.* 2.50.111, Cicero does mention Crassus, but makes no reference to Antonius anywhere in the work. According to Kennedy, both of these men would have been well respected by Cicero. Thus Kennedy argues that *Inv.* was completed after Crassus's death (91 BCE), but while Antonius was still living (he died in 87 BCE).

treatise, Cicero justifies his work in the area of rhetoric by noting that many rhetors abuse the use of rhetoric, thus actually doing harm to the state.[32] For Cicero, this negative effect on the state is motivation for the training of orators in the proper use of rhetoric. He writes:

> Therefore, in my opinion at least, men ought none the less to devote themselves to the study of eloquence although some misuse it both in private and in public affairs. And they should study it the more earnestly in order that evil men may not obtain great power to the detriment of good citizens and the common disaster of the community . . . For from eloquence the state receives many benefits, provided only it is accompanied by wisdom, the guide of all human affairs. (1.4.5)

Here in the opening of *Inv.*, one sees that Cicero at an early age considers the practice of rhetoric to be a means to an end; namely, it is to be employed in service to the state.

Regarding the *loci*, in *Inv.* Cicero does not provide a general definition of *locus* for his readers.[33] One can infer, however, what Cicero understands under the term *locus* through his discussion of the part of the speech he calls "confirmation."[34] In the introduction to this section, Cicero states:

> Now it seems desirable to give in turn the rules about *confirmation* as is demanded by the regular order of the speech. Confirmation or proof is the part of the oration which by marshalling arguments lends credit, authority, and support to our case. (1.23.33–24.36; emphasis in original)

Cicero then lists the "attributes of persons or of actions" (1.24.34). The attributes concerning the person include qualities such as the person's name, his or her nature, manner of life, and financial standing.[35] In regards to actions, Cicero lists (and explains in each case) the place at which the

---

32. "For the more shamefully an honourable and worthy profession was abused by the folly and audacity of dull-witted and unprincipled men with the direst consequences to the state, the more earnestly should the better citizens have put up a resistance to them and taken thought for the welfare of the republic" (*Inv.* 1.3.5).

33. He does define what he means by "common topics"; see below.

34. In this rhetorical treatise, Cicero argues that the following are the parts of a well-organized speech: exordium (1.14.19–18.26), narrative (1.19.27–21.30), partition (1.22.31–23.33), confirmation (1.24.34–41.77), refutation (1.42.78–51.97), and peroration (1.52.98–56.109).

35. The complete list also includes "habit, feeling, interests, purposes, achievements, accidents, speeches made" (1.24.34).

action in question took place, the time (when it occurred as well as the duration of the action), occasion for the action, etc. Cicero prefaces the list of attributes and his explanations of them through a short explanation of his understanding of these attributes and how they can possibly function within the confirmatory proofs in the speech:

> But I think that it will be not inconvenient to set forth . . . a kind of raw material for general use from which all arguments are drawn, and then later to present the way in which each kind of case should be supported by all the forms of argumentation derived from this general store. (1.24.34)

Within the list of attributes of actions, Cicero elaborates on the "performance of the act" and writes, "In connection with the performance of the act (which was the second topic [*locus secundus*] under the heading of attributes of actions)" (1.26.38). From this use of terminology one can infer that in this context, Cicero considers these attributes to be *loci*. At the end of this section, one sees the same idea being expressed; Cicero concludes by stating, "All argumentation drawn from these topics which we have mentioned [*ex eis locis quos commemoraviums sumetur*] will have to be either probable or irrefutable" (1.29.44). After an extended discussion of what constitutes probable and certain arguments, Cicero offers this summary: "Now the sources of confirmatory arguments have been revealed as the occasion offered, and explained as clearly as the nature of the subject required" (1.30.49).

Considering these passages in the context of this section of the work, it seems that Cicero considers the *loci* to be the fundamental building blocks from which persuasive arguments are composed. And his concept of *topos/locus* differs significantly from Aristotle in that for Cicero, in many cases the *loci* are not the form of the argument; rather, they comprise the actual content of the arguments and proofs that are being constructed. This idea is confirmed in Cicero's later rhetorical treatises.[36]

---

36. Grimaldi also recognizes that the *loci* in Cicero are focused on the content of the arguments rather than on the form of the argument. He goes so far as to state that Cicero misunderstood Aristotle's method; see Grimaldi, "The Aristotelian Topics," 176–93, esp. 178. Emrich, in questioning Curtius's definition of a *topos* as a cliché, argues that the term *locus* is a metaphor which helps to explain the concept as seen in the Latin rhetoricians (primarily Cicero and Quintilian). Emrich notes that in these writers, a *locus* is a place at which arguments can be found ("der Sitz des Beweises"), but can also be the argument or proof in itself. See Emrich, "Topik und Topoi," 90–120, esp. 102–20.

De oratore is considered to be one of Cicero's major works from the latter phase of his life.[37] The three books that comprise *De or.* are composed as a dialog between various prominent orators in the Roman Empire, and in it Cicero describes the ideal orator. In the opening to the treatise, Cicero, in expounding on the importance of oratory, remarks (in the voice of Crassus) that

> there is to my mind no more excellent thing than the power, by means of oratory, to get a hold on assemblies of men, win their good will, direct their inclinations wherever the speaker wishes, or divert them from whatever he wishes. In every free nation, and most of all in communities which have attained the enjoyment of peace and tranquility, this one art has always flourished above the rest and ever reigned supreme. (1.8.30)

Here one sees, as was the case in *Inv.*, that Cicero connects the practice of oratory with that of statecraft, arguing that informed, educated orators (cf. 1.8.32) are essential to the well-being of the state.

Cicero introduces the subject of *loci* in Book II of *De or.* The context is one in which the dialog partners are discussing how the orator generates arguments. Antonius emphasizes that study is essential for the orator, especially the origins of arguments. Cicero has Antonius say that "we ought to bring this stock of cases and types down to Court with us, and not wait until we have accepted a brief, before we search the commonplaces [*locos*] from which to dig our proofs" (2.34.146).[38] He then makes the point that there are three aspects necessary for the discovery of arguments: "acuteness," "theory, or art," and lastly, "painstaking" (2.35.147), the most important of which is the last. An element of "painstaking" is that "the mind should dwell upon those commonplaces [*Deinde ut in eis loci*] which I shall set forth presently" (2.35.149). Cicero then links the concept of *loci* to Aristotle's *Topica*,[39] a work in which Aristotle "set forth certain com-

---

37. Kennedy argues that it was written in 55 BCE and published in the year following its composition. He also claims that *De or.* "is one of [Cicero's] most admired works and stands beside or only slightly behind Aristotle's *Rhetoric* and Quintilian's *De institutione oratoria* as a rhetorical classic"; see Kennedy, *The Art of Rhetoric*, 205 n. 84.

38. Antonius goes on to say that "the mind must needs return to those headings and those commonplaces [*locos*] which I have often mentioned as such already, from which every device for every speech whatever is derived" (2.34.146).

39. Cicero differentiates the task of an orator from dialectic as practiced by philosophers through Antonius's statement: "For we notice the overflowing copiousness of the diction of the philosophers who, I think . . . prescribe no rules for speaking, but none the less undertake to discuss with overflowing copiousness, whatever subject is

monplaces [*quosdam locos*], among which every line of argument might be found not merely for philosophical debate, but also for contentions in the Courts" (2.36.152).

After a short digression, in which Cicero discusses the merits (and disadvantages) of philosophy, he turns his attention to a discussion of the discovery of arguments. Cicero maintains (through Antonius) that an essential facet of the orator's education would include bringing the nascent orator

> to that source where no sequestered pool is landlocked, but from it bursts forth a general flood; to that teacher who will point out to him the very homes of all proofs, so to speak, illustrating these briefly and defining them in terms. (2.39.162)

These proofs would include those that are "derived from the essential nature of the case" and those "adopted from without" (2.39.163), a dichotomy that was also emphasized in *Inv*. Cicero further defines these two ideas:

> Intrinsic arguments, when the problem concerns the character of the subject as a whole, or of part of it, or the name it is to bear or anything whatever relating to the subject; extrinsic arguments, on the other hand, when topics are assembled from without and are not inherent in the nature of the case. (2.39.163)

What follows is in a similar format to the materials in *Inv*.; Cicero lists arguments available for use in various cases, starting first with the intrinsic and finishing with the extrinsic. He then concludes the discussion:

> I [Antonius] have sketched these topics as shortly as possible. For if I wished to reveal to somebody gold that was hidden here and there in the earth, it should be enough for me to point out to him some marks and indications of its positions, with which knowledge he could do his own digging, and find what he wanted, with very little trouble and no chance of mistake: so I know these indications of proofs, which reveal to me their whereabouts when I am looking for them; all the rest is dug out by dint of careful consideration . . . with these commonplaces [*locis*] firmly established in his mind and memory, and roused into activity with every topic proposed for discussion, nothing will be able to elude the orator either in our own contentions at the Bar, or in any department whatever of speaking. (2.91.174–75)

---

laid before them" (2.35.151). The context is one of oratory vs. philosophy; therefore, it is not unreasonable to assume that when Cicero mentions Aristotle's work, one which concerns the discovery of arguments, Aristotle's *Top*. is in view.

The *Topos* of Divine Testimony in Luke/Acts

Concerning the evidence found in *De or.*, the concept of *locus* is described in much the same way as in *Inv. Loci* are described as sources of arguments which are either inherent in the case being argued or external to the case. The various *loci* are available to the orator, and must only be applied to the case being argued. Cicero purposely links the concept to Aristotle, but his descriptions of the various *loci* demonstrate that for Cicero, unlike in Aristotle, the *loci* constitute the content of the arguments, rather than their form.[40]

Cicero provides the most detailed explanation of a *locus* in his work *Topica*.[41] In the beginning of this treatise, Cicero opens a dialog with Trebatius, a jurist who has sometime in the past happened upon Aristotle's *Topica* and questioned Cicero concerning Aristotle's work. Cicero notes, "And when I had made clear to you that these books contained a system developed by Aristotle for inventing arguments so that we might come upon them by a rational system without wandering about, you begged me to teach you the subject" (*Top.* 1.2). Thus, with this introduction, Cicero sets out to explain his interpretation of Aristotle's system of *topoi*.[42]

Cicero first provides a definition for *locus*:

> A comparison may help: It is easy to find things that are hidden if the hiding place is pointed out and marked; similarly if we wish to track down some argument we ought to know the places or topics: for that is the name given by Aristotle to the "regions," as it were, from which arguments are drawn. Accordingly, we may define a topic [*definire locum*] as the region of an argument, and an argument as a course of reasoning which firmly establishes a matter about which there is some doubt. (*Top.* 2.7–8)

---

40. According to Schütrumpf ("Non-Logical Means of Persuasion," 95–110), another significant difference between Aristotle and Cicero is that Aristotle differentiates between those elements in the argument for which the orator is responsible (ἔντεχνος; earlier these were called the "artificial" means of persuasion) and those for which the orator is not directly responsible (ἄτεχνος; the "inartificial"). Those arguments that fall under the heading of ἔντεχνος include arguments from ethos, pathos, and logical arguments. In Cicero's *De or.*, however, what he considers ἄτεχνος actually falls under the heading of logical proof. Schütrumpf concludes: "In Cicero, therefore, the 'non-technical evidence' does not constitute a means of persuasion in its own right, as in Aristotle; rather it is classified as subordinate to one of the three means of persuasion which for Cicero are the *only* means of persuasion" (ibid., 105).

41. An excellent overview of the content of *Top.* can be found in Gaines, "Cicero's *Partitiones oratoriae* and *Topica*," 469–70.

42. Or perhaps he does not. Gaines argues that the phrase in question should be rendered "I began to write a *Topica* in the manner of Aristotle" (Gaines, "Cicero's *Partitiones oratoriae* and *Topica*," 469); see also Stump, *Boethius's De topicis differentiis*, 21–22.

Divine Testimony and its Application in Ancient Speeches and Treatises

From this definition one notices that Cicero links his concept of *locus* to that of Aristotle.[43] What is also clear is that Cicero considers *loci* to be sources of arguments; as in *De or.*, the *locus* itself is the place or region of a particular argument.[44]

Following this definition, Cicero states that the *loci* can be divided into two categories: "Of the topics [*locis*] under which arguments are included, some are inherent in the very nature of the subject which is under discussion, and others are brought in from without" (2.8). Again, as was seen in the previous treatises, Cicero argues that there are internal and external *loci*. Internal *loci* are particular to the subject matter which is being argued; external *loci* must be derived from sources outside of the subject itself. The next section of the treatise (2.9—4.23) provides an elaboration of the internal *loci*. Among others, these include arguments from genus and species, arguments based on similarity and difference, and arguments from consequences and effects. After all the internal *loci* have been listed and briefly described,[45] Cicero makes only a short statement concern-

---

43. Bornscheuer (*Topik*, 63) notes that Aristotle did not consider the *topos* as a source of arguments; rather, he saw *topoi* as being elements of an argument; see also McAdon, "Probabilities," 226. Cf. Aristotle, *Rhet.* 2.2.13: "Let us now speak of the elements of enthymemes (by element and topic of enthymeme I mean the same thing)." As seen in the citation from *Rhet.* 1.2.21 above, Aristotle conceived of *topoi* as being elements of syllogisms and enthymemes. Stump notes that Cicero's concept of *loci* is much different from that described in Aristotle's *Topics*. In *Top.*, Aristotle presents an organization of *topoi* useful for dialectical argumentation. Aristotle emphasizes the process of developing an argument, rather than the rote memorization of possible arguments. Stump contrasts this with Cicero, who, she argues, is developing a system for forming arguments for legal cases. Thus, for Cicero, the significance of the *loci* is found in their use within oratory and rhetoric, which make use of dialectic for the purposes of arguing legal cases. Here, one notes an emphasis on the practical nature of the *loci* in Cicero. See Stump, *Boethius's De topicis differentiis*, 18–23. Leff also points out the practical nature of *loci* in the Latin rhetoricians. He, however, compares the descriptions of *loci* in Cicero and Quintilian to the later Boethius in forming this conclusion. See Leff, "Up from Theory," 203-11. On this see also the work of Van Ophuijsen ("Where Have the Topics Gone?," 131–73), who notes that Critolaus makes a statement in which he rejects rhetoric. Van Ophuijsen maintains that "far from being directed at Aristotle's more rarefied conception of the subject, this is likely to have been an assertion of its [the peripatetic school at Lyceum] claims in the face of an unphilosophical rhetoric encouraged by the new demand for unadorned and intellectually unambitious but practically effective legal speeches created by the extension of Roman jurisdiction" (ibid., 133).

44. Kemper notes that this is a shift in emphasis from that in *Rhet. Her.* (see below) and *Inv.* In these two works, *loci* are predominantly meant to be the arguments themselves. See Kemper, "Topik," 27.

45. Cicero also provides an example for each one; each example is derived from a forensic issue.

ing external *loci*. He asserts, "Extrinsic arguments depend principally on authority. Therefore, the Greeks call such means of argumentation ἄτεχνοι, that is, not invented by the art of the orator" (4.24). He then provides an example of an extrinsic argument, namely the testimony of one with knowledge of the law.

A final piece of evidence which helps illuminate Cicero's concept of a *locus* is found in his treatise *Partitiones oratoriae*. The treatise is composed as a dialog between Cicero and his son. The younger Cicero asks the elder what the overall purpose of the orator is, to which the elder answers, "To discover how to convince the persons whom he wishes to persuade and how to arouse their emotions" (2.5). In answer to the question concerning through what method one is able to persuade, the elder Cicero states, "Arguments, which are derived from topics [*ex locis*] that are either contained in the facts of the case itself or are obtained from outside" (2.5). The younger Cicero then asks about topics [*Quos vocas locos?*], to which the elder answers, "Pigeonholes in which arguments are stored" (2.5). Later, one reads that the elder Cicero maintains the same differentiation between "internal" and "external" arguments, which are described as arguments inherent to the case itself (internal) and testimony (external).

After describing the evidence of witnesses and testimony, a topic to which we will return, the elder Cicero then lists several *loci* from which internal arguments can be drawn, a list that is similar to the *loci* described in detail in *Top*. [*Part. or.* 2.7; cf. *Top.* 2.8—4.23; 5.26—18.71]. The younger Cicero then asks if all the *loci* are to be used when arguing a case. The answer he receives is that the orator should

> examine them and seek for arguments from them all; but we shall use our judgment always to reject those of little value and also sometimes to pass over those that are of general application and not intimately related to our case. (*Part. or.* 3.8)

Here one notes that the *loci* are not only sources of arguments for Cicero; they also provide a methodology for evaluating the appropriateness of a particular set of arguments.

In summarizing Cicero's concept of *locus* as found in his rhetorical treatises, Cicero considers the *loci* to be the sources of arguments for an orator arguing a case. In particular, Cicero is focused on what was indeed the emphasis in his own career, namely arguing mostly forensic cases in service to the State. The *loci* can be subdivided into internal and external arguments, internal arguments being those that are connected to the facts of the case being argued; external arguments are those from outside the case and are mostly concerned with witnesses and testimony. These various *loci* are concerned with the contents of the arguments themselves, and are to be scrutinized by the orator in order to assist in the process of crafting the most persuasive speech possible.[46] Thus, there is an emphasis in Cicero on the practicality and utility of the *loci*, rather than the theory of argumentation as was seen in Aristotle.[47]

While this is certainly the primary sense for the term *locus* in Cicero's writings, it is, however, not the only one. For example, Cicero can use the term to imply a common theme to which one might refer while giving a speech. In *De or.* he writes,

> And indeed when, while a man is speaking—as often happens—such commonplaces [*loci*] have cropped up as demand some mention of the immortal gods, of dutifulness, harmony, or friendship, of the rights shared by citizens, by men in general, and by nations, of fair-dealing, moderation or greatness of soul, or virtue of any and every kind. (*De or.* 1.13.56)

Later in *De or.*, Crassus encourages Antonius to go beyond what seems to be the current understanding of *locus*, saying,

---

46. In comparing Cicero's idea of *locus* to Aristotle's presentation of *topoi*, Bornscheuer persuasively argues that the main difference is one of means and ends. For Aristotle, according to Bornscheuer, it was important for the orator to know the means of persuasion for every eventuality. Bornscheuer contrasts this with Cicero, who, he argues, is much more practical and therefore sees an intimate connection between the speech and the situation in which the speech is offered. Cicero ultimately makes this connection through the selection of *loci*. Bornscheuer also notes that the emphasis on the practicality of oratory in Cicero is a direct result of his involvement in Roman politics, so that his system of rhetoric is governed by political and public ends. See Bornscheuer, *Topik*, 71–90. Reinhardt somewhat similarly argues that Cicero developed his concept of *locus* as a result of the Roman legal system becoming more formalized. Around the second century BCE, trials in Rome became more structured, which led to an increased emphasis on the arguments being made, rather than the reputation of the one making the arguments. This occurred along with an increase in legal literature, which included the classification of cases. Thus, Cicero's system of *loci* served the legal system as a τέχνη which would assist orators in becoming more familiar with the legal system and equip them to argue cases more persuasively. See Reinhardt, *Topica*, 53–66.

47. Hohmann argues that in Cicero, dialectic becomes a tool which supports rhetoric. For example, in Cicero's *Top.* 6, dialectic is used to evaluate the various arguments available to the orator. For Hohmann, therefore, *Top.* is a rhetorical work (rather than dialectical), in which the emphasis falls on application of *loci* and the practicality of using them within a speech. Hohmann, "Rhetoric and Dialectic," 41–51.

> [R]ather please omit that part of your programme which none of our friends here wants, touching the commonplaces [*locis*] which supply us with what we have to say in our cases: although you discuss these things with brilliant originality, they are for all that really rather easy and widely current in maxims. Produce for us the sources of what you so often handle and always in inspired fashion. (*De or.* 2.29.127)

Here, at the very least, Cicero provides evidence that he is familiar with an understanding of a *locus* as a proverb or maxim, or perhaps (as seen above) a stock theme, exemplary model, or pattern to which orators often refer.

A second, slightly different view of *locus* is found in *Inv.* Here, Cicero describes a "common" *locus*, "common" distinguishing an argument that can be used in multiple cases. It is, therefore, an argument of a more general nature. Cicero writes,

> In every case some of the arguments are related only to the case that is being pleaded, and are so dependent on it that they cannot advantageously be separated from it and transferred to other cases, while others are of a more general nature, and adaptable to all or most cases of the same kind. These arguments which can be transferred to many cases, we call common topics [*locos communes*]. A common topic either contains an amplification of an undisputed statement . . . or of a doubtful statement against which there are also plausible lines of argument . . . A speech, however, is occasionally rendered distinguished or brilliant by introducing common topics and some topic [*locis communibus et aliquo loco*] backed up by arguments when the audience is already convinced. (*Inv.* 2.14.47–15.48)

In this passage, what Cicero infers through the phrase *locis communibus et aliquo loco* is that there are "common" *loci* (as described above) and simply *loci*; the difference between the two is that common *loci* are arguments applicable to any case, while *loci* are particular to the case being argued.[48] Also, Cicero argues that the common *loci* are to be carefully constructed and embellished (note in the quote above he calls for them to include "an

---

48. This same distinction will be found in Theon's *Progymnasmata* as well. Pernot, in his study of *topos* and commonplace, concludes that *topoi* represented a system of examining a plethora of cases with a limited number of patterns or examples, while through a commonplace a rhetor could treat a specific issue as a general question. See Pernot, "Lieu et lieu commun," 253–84.

amplification"), which provides the impression they are arguments in a more complete form than simple *loci*.⁴⁹

Locus in Ad Herennium

I will now explore the concept of *locus* as described in other Latin and Greek authors, beginning with the rhetorical treatise *Ad Herennium*. In *Rhet. Her.*, in the author's discussion of amplification, he lists ten areas from which to draw *loci* in support of summarizing statements (*epilogoi*) found in the speech. The author writes:

> Amplification is the principle of using Commonplaces [*per locum communem*] to stir the hearers. To amplify an accusation it will be most advantageous to draw commonplaces from ten formulae. (*Rhet. Her.* 2.30.47)

The greater context of this statement is the description of the summarization that a rhetor is to do periodically within the speech.⁵⁰ These summaries have a threefold purpose: summarizing the previous points, reinforcing and building on what has been stated ("Amplification"), and inciting the emotions of the audience (*Rhet. Her.* 2.30.47).

Locus in Quintilian

In Quintilian's *Institutio oratoria* one finds a similar perception of *locus*. Quintilian discusses the *locus* in the context of the part of the speech he

---

49. Leff's comments are apposite and should be cited in full (see Leff, "Commonplaces and Argumentation," 448):

> Obviously, the commonplace is an argument elaborated more carefully and fully than other types of argument. But the distinction between *loci* and *loci communes* should not be understood as a distinction between two kinds of argument, since, for Cicero, the *loci* are not arguments, but resources used in discovering materials for arguments; they provide individual pieces—the timbers and planks as it were—which enter into the construction of arguments. The *loci communes* are finished products that integrate logical argument, emotional appeal, and style into a single structure. They are "minor forms" that contribute to the general development of a discourse but can be detached and appreciated as independent units.

50. Conclusions (*epilogoi*) are found "in the Direct Opening, after the Statement of Facts, after the strongest argument, and in the Conclusion of the Speech" (*Rhet. Her.* 2.30.47).

calls the proof, and which he considers the most significant.[51] Quintilian makes the same distinction as was seen in Aristotle and Cicero, categorizing proofs as either "nontechnical" or "technical," corresponding to Aristotle's "inartificial" and "artificial" proofs.[52] The sources for the inartificial proofs include judgments rendered in previous cases, rumors, statements made by those being tortured, documents, oaths, and the testimony of witnesses. After discussing these forms of proof in some detail, Quintilian turns his attention to the "technical" proofs, those invented by the orator.

Quintilian categorizes technical proofs into "signs," arguments, or examples (*Inst.* 5.9.1). He discusses *loci* in the context of arguments. For Quintilian, *loci* are "Places where Arguments are found," and are not "what are nowadays commonly meant by *loci*, namely set pieces against luxury, adultery, and the like, but the area in which Arguments lurk and from which they have to be draw out" (*Inst.* 5.10.20–21). Three things are significant here. First, Quintilian, like Cicero, argues that the *loci* represent sources of arguments from which the orator must select in order to argue the case at hand ("so every Argument is not found everywhere, and we have therefore to be selective in our search" [*Inst.* 5.10.22]). Second, Quintilian, again in a similar fashion to Cicero, albeit more explicitly, distinguishes his definition of *locus* from (what Cicero termed) the common *loci*, which Quintilian describes as stock arguments against (or, presumably, for) certain familiar themes.[53] The third point comes from the greater context. Quintilian, in this case unlike Cicero, does not call the inartificial proofs "*loci*"; he restricts *loci* to those proofs inherent to the case which must be discovered and selected by the orator.

Topos in Theon

Theon, in the *Progymnasmata*, provides evidence of a similar distinction between two concepts of *locus*/*topos* already seen in Cicero and Quintilian. Within the *Progymnasmata* there is an exercise entitled ΠΕΡΙ ΤΟΠΟΥ. Within this exercise Theon defines what he means by τόπος:

---

51. "For neither the Prooemium nor the Narrative has any function except to prepare the judge for the Proof . . . Lastly of the five parts into which we divided the forensic speech, any one of the other four may sometimes be unnecessary for the Cause; but there is no dispute which does not need proof" (*Inst.* 5.pr.).

52. Quintilian indeed cites Aristotle at this point; cf. *Inst.* 5.1.1.

53. See Thom, "Defining the topos," 555–73, who makes a similar point as the one I am making here.

> Topos (*topos*)[54] is language amplifying something that is acknowledged to be either a fault or a brave deed. It is of two kinds: one is an attack on those who have done evil deeds, ... the other in favor of those who have done something good ... It is called a *topos* because starting from it as a "place" we easily find arguments (*epkheiroumen*) against those not admitting that they are in the wrong. For this reason some define it as a starting point for epicheiremes. (Theon, *Progymnasmata* 106 [Kennedy, ed. and trans., 42])

A commonplace is therefore a source of a formal argument directed at one who has made a particularly bad (or good) moral decision. It is 'formal' in that Theon suggests a specific structure for a commonplace (see Theon, *Progymnasmata* 107 [Kennedy, ed. and trans., 44]). In this passage one sees the structure which Theon proposes, as well as suggestions for the proofs. Although he does not specifically use the term *topos*, the language that Theon utilizes concerning the selection of proofs sounds much like the description of a *topos* that I have been considering.

In the descriptions of other preliminary exercises, however, Theon does use the term *topos* in the sense of a particular theme or motif used within an argument. For example, in his discussion of refutation and confirmation (found within the section on narrative in Kennedy's edition of the *Progymnasmata*), Theon states:

> As for refutation and proof, we said that the same topics [οἱ αὐτοὶ τόποι][55] are useful in fables, but in narratives the topics of the false and impossible [ἀπὸ τοῦ ψεύδους καὶ ἀδυνάτου τόποι][56] are also fitting. (Theon, *Progymnasmata* 93 [Kennedy, ed. and trans., 40])

Theon's use of the term *topos* is certainly different here than in the section on commonplace. Here, rather than being a complete formal argument, the *topoi* constitute the subject matter used to construct the refutation or confirmation of the narrative. This usage of the term *topos* is more akin to the predominant definition of *locus* in Cicero's writings and as seen in Quintilian.[57] Thus, to understand Theon's use of the term *topos* correctly,

---

54. As noted above, the Greek here reads Τόπος; the Greek text is from Patillion and Bolognesi, *Théon*, 106.6.

55. Patillion and Bolognesi, *Théon*, 93.6.

56. Ibid., 93.8.

57. Notice that in Kennedy's translation, he chooses the word "topics" rather than *topoi* as in the section on the preliminary exercise of commonplace. This same

the context in which Theon uses the term is extremely significant. For Theon, a *topos* can be a formal exercise in which a person is blamed (or less often, praised) for a particular moral choice. This exercise requires a fairly rigid structure, which Theon describes. He also, however, uses the term *topos* in a manner similar to Cicero; namely, a *topos* can be the source of a line of argumentation, used in support of any of a number of preliminary exercises. These *topoi* are many and varied, one of which is the testimony of others.

Topos in other Rhetorical Treatises

Theon's view, namely that a *topos* is a form of proof that provides the content of epicheiremes, is echoed in the treatise by Anonymous Seguerianus. The writer of ΤΕΧΝΗ ΤΟΥ ΠΟΛΙΤΙΚΟΥ ΛΟΓΟΥ, a document most likely written around the beginning of the third century,[58] discusses *topoi* in the section of the treatise entitled ΠΕΡΙ ΠΙΣΤΕΩΝ. The author makes the same distinction between artistic and non-artistic proofs[59] that we have seen in other ancient rhetoricians. It is in the subsection describing the artistic proofs (that is, the proofs that are composed by the orator) that the author describes the *topos*. For this author, the *topoi* represent those proofs from which one composes epicheiremes.

A second treatise written at approximately the same time as *Art of Political Speech* and entitled *Art of Rhetoric* is attributed to Apsines of Gadara.[60] In this treatise, the author also discusses the concept of *topos*. In

---

distinction is seen in Theon's exercises concerning encomion and invective (Theon, *Progymnasmata* 111 [Kennedy, ed. and trans., 51]; cf. Patillon and Bolognesi, *Théon*, 111.11), prosopopoeia (Theon, *Progymnasmata* 117–18 [Kennedy, ed. and trans., 49]; cf. Patillon and Bolognesi, *Théon*, 118.1), and thesis (Theon, *Progymnasmata* 121 [Kennedy, ed. and trans., 56]; cf. Patillon and Bolognesi, *Théon*, 121.14–15, 24).

58. Kennedy bases this estimate on the sources that appear in the document; see Dilts and Kennedy, eds., *Two Greek Rhetorical Treatises*, xiii.

59. The author lists the following as examples of non-artistic proofs (which are generally defined as originating "from material at hand"): "witnesses, decrees, contracts, oracles." These are summarized as being "such things, as many are written down" (Anonymous Seguerianus, *Art of Political Speech* 145, in Dilts and Kennedy, eds., *Two Greek Rhetorical Treatises*). The author does, however, qualify the use of these inartistic proofs through the following statement: "Overall, invention in the case of these proofs is non-artistic, but the use is artistic" (ibid., 145).

60. Kennedy notes that the treatise, in the form in which we now have it, shows evidence of having been edited by a later editor/redactor; see Dilts and Kennedy, eds., *Two Greek Rhetorical Treatises*, xvii.

the first section in which the author treats the prooemium, he lists several θεωρήματα out of which one can compose the prooemium. The way in which these are described is similar to the lists of *topoi/loci* seen in Aristotle, Cicero, and Quintilian, as the author provides various arguments that can be used within the prooemium to address a specific situation within the speech.[61] For example, the author suggests that the θεώρημα of "from what follows" is an appropriate argument when the judge has made a previous judgment on a case from which the current case is derived. Thus these themes suggest possible arguments of which the orator can take advantage in the prooemium of the speech.

Later in the work the term τόπος is explicitly used in several contexts. The refutation "by reversal is supported from the following topics [ἐκ τόπων τούτων]" (Apsines, *Art of Rhetoric* 5.1). What follows is a listing of possible proofs, both artistic and inartistic, that will assist the orator in refuting the claims of the opponent through the negation of the charges. In the chapter entitled ΠΕΡΙ ΤΗΣ ΤΩΝ ΚΕΦΑΛΑΙΩΝ ΚΑΤΑΣΚΕΨΗΣ, Apsines writes: "[N]ow let us look at the most important headings, considering from what topics they are composed [ἐκ τοίων τόπων σύγκειται] and by what kind of arguments they are confirmed, and first let us speak about final headings" (*Art of Rhetoric*, 9.1). Here, one sees that each heading[62] can be elaborated through the use of various *topoi*; in each case the *topoi* are suggested arguments one can employ to demonstrate the legality, rightness, advantage, etc. of one's case.

Finally, in the section on epilogues, *topoi* are mentioned once again. Here, the concept of *topos* has the widest range of meanings in the treatise. For example, the author claims that the epilogue itself is a *topos* ("The epilogue is a topic in three parts ['Ο ἐπίλογος τόπος τριμερής ἐστιν]" [Apsines, *Art of Rhetoric* 10.1]). The epilogue has three subdivisions: "recapitulation [ἀνάμνησις]," "pity [ἔλεος]," and "indignation [δείνωσις]" (Apsines, *Art of Rhetoric* 10.1). However, of these three, both recapitulation and pity are called *topoi*.[63] And in the section in which the author discusses pity,

---

61. Kennedy argues that θεώρημα in this section refers to "a topic from which an idea or argument can be drawn," and notes that later in the treatise the term τόπος will be employed in referring to a similar concept (Dilts and Kennedy, eds., *Two Greek Rhetorical Treatises*, 77 n. 5). For Kennedy, this is evidence that the original treatise has been edited (cf. ibid., xvii).

62. Several headings are discussed, including what is legal [περὶ νόμου], customary [περὶ ἔθου], just [περὶ δικαίου], advantageous [περὶ συμφέροντος], possible [περὶ δυνατοῦ], and honorable [περὶ ἐνδόξου].

63. "The narration and the demonstration (*apodeixis*) are grouped under the

he mentions the "common topic from judgment and actions of the past [ἀπὸ κρίσεως καὶ ἀπὸ ἔργων γεγενημένων τὸν κοινὸν τόπον τοῦτον]" (*Art of Rhetoric*, 10.16). Therefore, for this author, a *topos* is a major part of the speech (the epilogue), which is subdivided into *topoi*, and each of these *topoi* can be supported through other (common) *topoi*!

This survey of the ancient rhetoricians' views of *topos/locus* has demonstrated that this concept enjoyed a rather wide range of meaning. For Aristotle, the *topos* represented a source of logical argumentation, the *topos* serving as the structure of the argument. For Cicero and Quintilian, a *locus* was the place in which the orator would find a source of arguments from which the orator would select the ones appropriate for arguing the case at hand. But Cicero and Quintilian both differentiate between *loci* as sources of arguments and *loci communes*, which were stock, self-contained arguments useful for any case. Also, Cicero demonstrates that he is familiar with the *locus* being used as a theme or example to which the orator refers in the course of the speech.

Theon and other rhetoricians show that they are familiar with this range of meanings as well. Theon describes the preliminary exercise of *topos*, in which the student is instructed to blame, or praise, a person or thing through the use of a specified, structured argument. But he also uses the term *topos* more in line with Cicero and Quintilian's predominant use of *locus*, that of a source of possible arguments. These uses (and others) are also found in later treatises authored by Anonymous Seguerianus and Apsines. Given the rather wide semantic range for the term *topos* among the ancient rhetoricians, it is not surprising that a multiplicity of meanings for the term *topos* can be found in modern NT scholarship, as was demonstrated earlier.

Above, in my review of J. Thom's investigation of *topos*, I noted that his study did not include Cicero's concept(s) of *loci*. From the analysis of Cicero's treatment of *loci* in *Topica*, one sees that his complete concept of *locus* does not perfectly fit any single criterion within Thom's schema. Internal *loci*, those which are inherent to the subject of the argument, line

---

pragmatic, the prooemium and the epilogue under the pathetical. How then, since we have said that the epilogue belongs to the pathetical aspect, do we say that reminder, being a topic of it, is part of the pragmatic? [τὴν ἀνάμνησιν τόπον οὖσαν αὐτοῦ μέρος πραγματικῆς εἶναί φάμεν;]" (*Art of Rhetoric* 10.2). And on pity, the author writes: "Whenever we are going to arouse pity (*eleos*), we shall prepare the judges ahead of time so this will be useful for us; for one ought not to enter on this topic suddenly, but after some preparation [οὐ γὰρ ἐξαίφνης ἐπιχειρεῖν δεῖ τούτῳ τόπῳ, ἀλλὰ μετὰ παρασκευῆς]" (*Art of Rhetoric* 10.15).

Divine Testimony and its Application in Ancient Speeches and Treatises

up with Thom's first category, the strategic, or rhetorical *topoi*. However, Cicero's external *loci*, those arguments that are drawn from outside of the subject, are more difficult to categorize. They do not seem to fit any of the types that Thom suggests. The external *loci* as envisioned by Cicero are not literary themes which are rehearsed over and over (Thom's second type), nor are they moral *topoi* (the third type). One can say that the external *topoi* are strategic or rhetorical in that they are employed to persuade an audience or jury; but, given Thom's example of his first type of *topos* (arguing from the greater to the lesser), the external *loci* do not exactly fit this category either. Therefore, I propose that Thom's continuum should be extended to include Cicero's external *loci*; I will demonstrate that these external *loci* focus on witnesses and testimony.

To summarize the findings of this analysis to this point, I am arguing that the current understanding in NT scholarship of the term *topos* should be expanded to include what Cicero calls external arguments or proofs and what Quintilian labels inartificial proofs.[64] Arguments drawn from these *loci* focus on documents, oaths, witnesses, and testimony. These *loci* are more substantive than formal in nature, as they represent the content of the argument selected by the orator rather than the form of the argument. Also, especially in Cicero and Quintilian, the *loci* are used to facilitate the development of arguments in legal cases; there is a strong emphasis on the outcome of the speech, namely the goal of persuading a judge of the validity of one's case. I will now investigate a particular aspect of the external *loci*, specifically that of divine testimony.

The topos of Divine Testimony

In *Topica*, when introducing the external arguments, Cicero states, "External arguments depend principally on authority" (*Top.* 4.24). He then gives a more detailed explanation of the external *loci* later in his treatise. After a short introduction to those *loci* which "are extrinsic or brought in from without" (*Top.* 19.72),[65] he writes:

---

64. Although Quintilian does not specifically label these types of arguments as *loci*, he discusses them within a context of proofs used in a speech. Thus, his concept of inartificial proofs parallels that of Cicero, for whom the inartificial proofs are *loci*.

65. Cicero at this point adds the following comment: "[L]et us say a few words about these topics from without, although they bear no relation to your discussions of the law [*etsi ea nihil omnino ad vestras disputationes pertinent*]" (*Top.* 4.72). Cicero's comment is not meant to infer that these *loci* are unnecessary for arguing forensic cases; rather, he is implying that Trebatius, a jurist, would normally be his own authority

The *Topos* of Divine Testimony in Luke/Acts

> This form of argumentation, that is said not to be subject to the rules of art, depends on testimony. For our present purpose we define testimony as everything that is brought in from some external circumstance in order to win conviction. Now it is not every sort of person who is worth consideration as a witness. To win conviction, authority is sought; but authority is given by one's nature or by circumstances. (*Top.* 19.73)

Thus, Cicero's concept of an external *locus* is based almost exclusively on the testimony of others.[66] He warns, however, that effective testimony is produced only by those who exhibit some type of authority, either through the nature of the witness or the circumstances in which the witness finds him or herself. Cicero then continues, defining what he means by authority through nature or circumstances:

> Authority from one's nature or character depends largely on virtue; in circumstances there are many things which lend authority, such as talent, wealth, age, good luck, skill, experience, necessity, and even at times a concurrence of fortuitous events. For it is common belief that the talented, the wealthy, and those whose character has been tested by a long life, are worthy of credence. (*Top.* 19.73)

Thus, authority from character can only be attributed to those who are virtuous, while authority from circumstances is based on wealth, talent, and a character which has been proven through many experiences in life, for "people generally put faith in those who are experienced" (*Top.* 19.73).

After a short digression in which he discusses the *loci* of necessity (which is a sub-topic of experience), and "the concurrence of fortuitous

---

and would not normally require an outside authority to lend credibility to his case. See Reinhardt, *Topica*, 342.

Here I am confining the discussion to authoritative witnesses being invoked for the purpose of persuasion. There is, however, a second, very significant aspect to the concept of authority, namely the authority of the one speaking. For an interesting treatment of this topic, in which Cicero's use of authority in his speech *Pro Sulla* is analyzed, see Goodwin, "Cicero's Authority," 38–60. Goodwin likens Cicero's use of authority in this speech to an honor-shame transaction, in which the auditors are "blackmailed" into accepting Cicero's authority (and therefore his position) rather than insult his dignity by disagreeing with him.

66. The statement "everything that is brought in from some external circumstance in order to win conviction [*Testimonium autem nunc dicimus omne quo dab aliqua re externa sumitur ad faciendam fidem*]" (*Top.* 4.73) certainly allows for other forms of evidence than simply testimony of witnesses. Cicero, however, chooses to focus his treatment on witnesses, both human and divine.

events," Cicero turns his attention back to the testimony of one who possesses authority due to a virtuous character. He states,

> The testimony which produces conviction through virtue is of two kinds; one sort gets its efficacy by nature, the other acquires it by hard work. That is to say, the surpassing virtue of the gods is the result of their nature, but the virtue of men is the result of hard work. The testimony of the gods is covered thoroughly enough by the following: first, utterances, for oracles get their name from the fact that they contain an utterance (*oratio*) of the gods; secondly, things in which are embodied certain works of the gods. First, the heavens themselves and all their order and beauty; secondly, the flight of birds through the air and their songs; thirdly, sounds[67] and flashes of fire from the heavens,[68]

---

67. Cf. Pliny the Elder, *Nat.* 2.58.148: "We are told that during the wars with the Cimbri a noise of clanging armour and the sounding of a trumpet were heard from the sky, and that the same thing has happened frequently both before then and later."

68. Seneca writes: "Hear what I think about those fires which the atmosphere drives across the sky." In the same context he continues, "Also, we have more than once seen a flaming light in the shape of a huge ball which was then dissipated in mid-flight. We saw a similar prodigy about the time of the death of the deified Augustus" (*Nat.* 1.pref. 17.2–3). See also *Nat.* 1.15.5: "Among these you may also include a phenomenon which we read about frequently in history: the sky seems to be on fire." He then goes on to give an example which occurred during the reign of Tiberius Caesar. Cf. Pliny the Elder, *Nat.* 2.58.148: "It has often been seen, and is not at all surprising, that the sky itself catches fire when the clouds have been set on fire by an exceptionally large flame." Here, however, Pliny does not connect this to a specific event. He does, however, associate "a burning shield scattering sparks" which "ran across the sky at sunset from west to east" to the time of Lucius Valerius and Gaius Marius, albeit not to a particular incident during their rule (*Nat.* 2.34.100). Here one must include lightning, which is, according to the ancients, a form of fire in the heavens. See Seneca, *Nat.* 2.12.2; in his discussion of lightning (both "flashes" and "bolts") and thunder, he writes: "It is further agreed that both lightning flashes and lightning bolts are either fiery or have the appearance of fire." Later, he continues: "It is generally agreed that a lightning bolt is fire and so is a lightning flash, which is merely fire that would have become a lightning bolt if it had acquired more force" (*Nat.* 2.21.1). Seneca also argues that lightning, when rightly interpreted, foretells future events; see *Nat.* 2.32.1–51.1 for his discussion of interpreting lightning as well as other forms of augury. Especially pertinent to this study are his remarks concerning Jupiter and lightning (*Nat.* 2.41.1–46.1). Seneca first states the position of the Etruscans, namely that Jupiter sends lightning for three reasons: to warn; to do good (but this can also do damage); and for destruction. Seneca himself disagrees. He promotes his Stoic viewpoint by stating that "lightning bolts are not sent by Jupiter but all things are so arranged that even those things which are not done by him none the less do not happen without a plan, and the plan is his. For, although Jupiter does not do these things now, it is Jupiter who brought it about that they happen. He is not present at every event for every person but he gives the signal,

and portents given by many objects on earth, as well as the foreshadowing of events which is revealed by the entrails (of sacrificial animals). Many things also are revealed by visions seen in sleep. The testimony of the gods is at times adduced from these topics in order to win conviction. (*Top.* 20.76–77)

A human is virtuous through hard work; the gods, however, are virtuous simply because of who they are.[69] And the virtuous testimony of the gods is possible through several ways listed above, examples of which I will provide in this chapter and explore throughout chapters three through six of the present study.

Other ancient authors also demonstrate that the concept of divine testimony was not limited to Cicero.[70] The author of *Rhet. Her.* is familiar with this form of proof. In the section in which he describes the *epilogoi* within the speech (noted above), ten sources of *loci* are listed for use within the *epilogos*. The first listed is the *locus* of authority, and includes a form of divine testimony:

The first commonplace [Primus locus] is taken from authority, when we call to mind of what great concern the matter under discussion has been to the immortal gods, or to our ancestors,

---

the force, the cause, to all" (*Nat.* 2.46.1). For Pliny the Elder's discussion of this topic, see *Nat.* 2.52.137–54.141.

69. Cicero states this despite the claims of Euhemerus, who, appealing to intellectual elites, had argued (early in the third century BCE) that most of those recognized as gods had originally been mortal human beings, who were then deified after their deaths. See the discussion in Seznec, *Survival of the Pagan Gods*, 11–13.

70. *Topica* is not the only work of Cicero in which he mentions divine testimony. In *Part. or.* 2.6, the following dialog between the elder Cicero and his son appears after the elder Cicero states that what brings conviction in a speech are "[A]rguments, which are derived from topics that are either contained in the facts of the case itself or are obtained from outside" (*Part. or.* 2.5):

"Son: How then do you distinguish between the two kinds of arguments you speak of?

Father: Arguments thought of without using a system I term arguments from outside, for instance the evidence of witnesses. . . .

[At this point there is a question and answer concerning internal arguments.]

Son: What kinds of evidence are there?

Father: Divine and human. Divine evidence is for instance oracles, auspices, prophecies, the answers of priests and augurs and diviners; human evidence is what is viewed in the light of authority and inclination and things said either freely or under compulsion—the evidence that includes written documents, pledges, promises, statements made on oath or under examination" (*Part. or.* 2.6).

Divine Testimony and its Application in Ancient Speeches and Treatises

or kings, states, barbarous nations, sages, the Senate; and again, especially how sanction has been provided in these matters by laws. (*Rhet. Her.* 2.30.48)[71]

Quintilian also mentions divine testimony as a source of proofs, and seems to follow the author or *Rhet. Her.* closely. He does so after his introduction to *loci* (*Inst.* 5.10.20; cf. the discussion above) and in the context of arguments drawn from outside the subject matter. The general category in which divine testimony is found is that of authority (*Inst.* 5.11.36). Specifically, proofs from authority are "opinions which can be attributed to nations, peoples, wise men, distinguished citizens, or famous poets" (*Inst.* 5.11.36–37). After discussing these categories, and also including proverbial wisdom, Quintilian then states:

> Under this head, and indeed as the first item, some put the Authority of the Gods, which is derived from oracles . . . This is a rare thing, but can be of use . . . When these belong to the Cause, they are called "divine testimonies"; when they are adduced from other sources, they are Arguments. (*Inst.* 5.11.42)[72]

Thus Quintilian, while his description is not nearly as comprehensive as Cicero's, does demonstrate that he was aware of this form of proof.

Finally, the author of *Art of Political Speech* is also aware of this method of proof. In the section on proofs (περί πιστεύων) and within the context of discussing the most typical *topoi*, the author concludes his list of *topoi* with the following: "Judgment will be taken from that of gods, heroes, prose writers, philosophers, poets [Κρίσις δὲ ληφθήσεται ἀπὸ θεῶν, ἀπὸ ἡρώων, ἀπὸ συγγραφέων, ἀπὸ φιλοσόφων, ἀπὸ ποιητῶν]" (Anonymous Seguerianus, *Art of Political Speech* 181 [Dilts and Kennedy]). This is similar to Quintilian's statement above, indicating perhaps that Quintilian is one of the author's sources, or that they are both drawing from a common tradition.[73]

---

71. Cf. the discussion above concerning Aristotle and the use of authority as an inartificial proof.

72. Quintilian then gives several examples of Cicero's use of divine testimony in treatises and speeches, some of which will be examined below.

73. In his section on θέσις, Theon also references the *topos* of authority as a way of providing proofs for one's thesis; he does not, however, mention the gods. He writes: "A more advanced student should include in each of the topics just mentioned the evidence of famous men, poets and statesmen and philosophers . . . and one should not make mention of these things randomly or by chance, but amplifying the examples, first from what has been done by an individual, private man, then by those in authority or a king" (Theon, *Progymnasmata* 122 [Kennedy]).

Therefore, Cicero and other authors of ancient rhetorical handbooks emphasize a particular *topos/locus*, one that is "inartificial" or "external" to the case being argued, and is based on the testimony of one in authority. The authority of the witness is based on many factors, including the witness's age, social standing, wealth, experience, and virtue. According to Cicero, because the gods are virtuous by their very nature (while human beings have to work to achieve virtue), they are the ultimate authorities which one can call as witnesses. The gods, therefore, can be tapped as a source of "divine testimony" [*divina testimonia*]. This testimony comes in many forms, including through oracles, sounds and visible emanations from the sky, dreams and visions, and the entrails of sacrificial animals. Many examples of these forms of testimony can be found in ancient speeches and treatises; it is to these examples that I now turn.

Application of the *topos* of Divine Testimony in Speeches and Treatises

Oracles as Divine Testimony

In his discussion of proof through divine testimony, Quintilian provides the example of the oracle at Delphi stating that Socrates was the wisest of all human beings (see *Inst.* 5.12.42). The specific statement to which Quintilian refers is found in Plato's *Apology* (20e-21a) in the context of Socrates's defense before his Athenian accusers.[74] Cicero also refers to this statement in various contexts. For example, in *De amicita*, Cicero argues against the non-traditional view that "soul and body perish at the same time, and that all things are destroyed by death" (4.13). In doing so, he cites Socrates's view that human souls had their origins in God; he prefaces this remark by stating that Socrates was judged to be the wisest of all human beings by the oracle of Apollo (4.13).[75] Another oft-quoted oracle

---

74. "And, men of Athens, do not interrupt me with noise, even if I seem to you to be boasting; for the word which I speak is not mine, but the speaker to whom I shall refer it is a person of weight [ἀξιόχρεων]. For of my wisdom—if it is wisdom at all—and of its nature, I will offer you the god of Delphi as a witness . . . Well once [Chaerephon] went to Delphi and made so bold as to ask the oracle this question; . . . he asked if there were anyone wiser than I. Now the Pythia replied that there was no one wiser." Note here that Plato connects the oracle itself with divine speech, a theme to which I will return.

75. Cicero also references this oracle in *Amic.* 2.7, 10; *Sen.* 21.78; and *Acad.* 1.4.16. See also Valerius Maximus, who also references this oracle in his *Memorable Doings and Sayings* (3.4.ext. 1). In this particular section, Valerius discusses those who despite

which serves as proof in speeches and treatises is the famous inscription at Delphi, γνῶθι σεαυτόν. Seneca, in addressing Marcia's grief over the loss of her son, argues that all humans are mortal, and should therefore become accustomed to the idea that all will one day pass away. He then cites the Delphic inscription, stating that this "clearly, is the meaning of that famous utterance attributed to the Pythian oracle" (*Marc.* 11.2–3).[76]

There are many examples of the use of other, less famous oracles in speeches and treatises. In Lycurgus's speech against Leocrates, in which Lycurgus accuses Leocrates of deserting Athens in a time of need,[77] Lycurgus cites examples from the past of brave Athenians in order to contrast them with Leocrates's behavior. One such example is that of Codrus, who was obedient to an oracle received by the Peloponnesians, who were marching on Athens. The oracle, as told to the Peloponnesians, stated that they would be successful in their attack on Athens as long as the king of Athens was spared. When Codrus was informed of the oracle, he disguised himself as a simple peasant and went outside the city walls, where he was killed by the Peloponnesians, thus sacrificing himself in order to save the city. Lycurgus, therefore, casts aspersions on his opponent by comparing him to this virtuous Athenian who, in obedience to an oracle, did not leave the city and even sacrificed himself in order to save the city (Lycurgus, *Against Leocrates* 83–89).

A second example is found in Dio Chrysostom's oration concerning his exile in Athens. Chrysostom justifies his banishment through the use of oracles as evidence of his innocence, both indirectly and directly. First, he cites the example of Croesus, king of the Lydians, who received an oracle from Apollo which told him to leave his kingdom. In addition, Croesus should leave without feeling shame (37.6).[78] Chrysostom uses this

---

lowly origins rose to positions of prominence. As a non-Roman example, Valerius names Socrates, using the oracle as proof of his intellectual and virtuous stature.

76. Cicero makes use of this oracle in a second argument for the immortality of the soul (*Tusc.* 1.22.52). Here, Cicero claims that a body is simply a container for the soul; one's existence is therefore defined by the soul, not the physical body. The Delphic inscription, which he attributes to Apollo, is therefore the god's command to know one's soul, not one's physical body. Cf. also Dio Chrysostom, 10.22; 67.3; Plato *Charm.* 164b-65b; [*Alc. maj.*] 1.124a-b. Aristides also references this oracle in his *In Defense of Oratory* 78–83; see the analysis of this passage below.

77. Specifically, Leocrates fled Athens and went to Megara when Philip won a victory over the Athenians at Chaeronea.

78. At this point, Dio Chrysostom quotes the oracle in full:

> "Wait till the time shall come when a mule is monarch of Media:
> Then, thou delicate Lydian, away to the pebbles of Hermus;
> Haste thee and no longer stay, nor have awe of being a coward" (37.7).

example to draw a parallel to his own situation; he, too, is in exile and feels no shame. He goes on to explain that he also received an oracle, which told him "to keep doing with all zeal the very thing wherein [he was] engaged, as being a most honourable and useful activity" (37.9). Thus, Chrysostom defends his exile by citing the example of another who was in exile in obedience to an oracle, and, in addition, directly citing an oracle that he himself received and to which he was obedient.

Aristides, in his *In Defense of Oratory*, also employs the *topos* of divine testimony by referencing oracles. In this treatise, Aristides argues against Plato's statement in *Gorgias* (463a-465c) that the practice of oratory does not require art.[79] In order to refute this claim, Aristides states, "I invoke [καλῶ δ'] Hermes, God of Oratory, Apollo, Leader of the Muses, and all the Muses, to be my guides" (*In Defense of Oratory* 19), thus summoning the gods as witnesses. He does so "because of the two following circumstances: we argue neither against the meanest of the Greeks nor in defence of the meanest of subjects [οὔτε γὰρ πρὸς τὸν φαυλότατον τῶν Ἑλλήνων οὔθ' ὑπὲρ τῶν φαυλοτάτων οἱ λόγοι]" (*In Defense of Oratory* 19). Because of the stature of his opponent, Aristides feels impelled to marshal the most significant of witnesses.

Aristides uses the witness of the gods through oracles in several ways in his defense of the practice of oratory.[80] First, he argues that Greek statesmen such as Lycurgus[81] and even Plato himself[82] consulted the oracle at Delphi in crafting legislation for the state (*In Defense of Oratory* 23-41); this is evidence of the value of the gods' testimony through oracles,[83]

---

79. "[Oratory] seems to me, Gorgias, not to be an artistic practice [εἶναι ἐπιτήδευμα τεχνικὸν μὲν οὔ], but that of a soul taking aim, courageous, and naturally clever in associating with men. Its total effect I call flattery" (Aristides, *In Defense of Oratory* 22).

80. Aristides emphasizes his use of evidence in this section; he states, "Then my argument will be made not from lack of taste, but for proof [ἔπειτ' οὐ τοῦ φορτικοῦ χάριν εἰρήσεται, ἀλλὰ τῆς ἀποδείξεως], which we claim is lacking in these [i.e., Plato's] arguments" (*In Defense of Oratory* 27-28).

81. "Men go to Delphi and inquire about constitutions. And then they legislate according to the voice which comes from the Pythian priestess, beginning with Lycurgus, who came after many others, but must be called first for the sake of argument" (*In Defense of Oratory* 38).

82. "[A]nd [Plato] says that then he must act, 'if the Pythian priestess assents,' but before that he does not dare" (*In Defense of Oratory* 41; cf. Plato, *Resp.* 540c).

83. Aristides summarizes this section with the statement, "So be it! Here is the evidence for our argument, from Delphi and Pythian Apollo [αὕτη μὲν ἐκ Δελφῶν ἡ μαρτυρία τῷ λόγῳ καὶ παρὰ Ἀπόλλωνος (τοῦ) Πυθίου]" (*In Defense of Oratory* 42).

which, he further argues, is not provided through any type of "art." Therefore, how can Plato argue that oratory is worthless because it also does not depend on art?[84] Second, he argues that Plato considers inspired prophecy and poetry to be the result of madness [μανία], but madness of divine origin,[85] which is capable of resulting in much good. Therefore, Aristides argues, if madness is an outlet for divine inspiration (and is artless) and is therefore a source of worth, then why should all forms of artless activities be censured? (see *In Defense of Oratory*, 50–57). Finally (see 78–83), Aristides introduces the Delphic oracle which proclaimed Socrates to be the wisest of all humans. He states that Socrates claimed to know nothing, yet the oracle proclaimed him to be the wisest person alive. Assuming both to be true, Aristides harmonizes the two statements by arguing that Socrates "did not know anything through an art [τὸ μὴ τέχνῃ]" (*In Defense of Oratory* 81). He then summarizes this part of the argument with the following statement:

> [A]nd through Socrates the God has borne witness [καὶ διὰ τοῦ Σωκράτους ὁ θεὸς μεμαρτύρηκεν] about both points [that Socrates was not ashamed to be "artless," and that he did not know anything through art], when he gave the oracle that Socrates was the wisest of men. Therefore he confirms with his own testimony that twofold testimony of Socrates [ὥστε διπλῆν οὖσαν τὴν τοῦ Σωκράτους μαρτυρίαν ἑτέρᾳ κυρίᾳ τῇ παρ' αὐτοῦ βεβαιοῖ]. (*In Defense of Oratory* 81)

Therefore, in Aristides one finds an extended example of the use of oracles being considered as the testimony of the gods and being used as supporting evidence in the defense of the practice of oratory.

A final example[86] is found in the lesser declamations of Quintilian, considered to be school exercises through which students practiced

---

84. This is basically an argument from the greater to the lesser, the greater being the "artless" testimony of the gods through oracles. Aristides summarizes: "Therefore, evidence and support has come . . . from all the gods [οὐκοῦν παρὰ . . . τῶν θεῶν μαρτυρία ψῆφος ἐπῆκται], that such an argument is worthless, which either seeks art or belittles whatever does not have it" (*In Defense of Oratory* 45).

85. Cicero will cite the gods as the source of madness as well; the context, however, is quite different. See comments below in connection with his speech against Clodius, *De haruspicum responso*.

86. Other examples could be cited; Demosthenes cites the law, and then quotes oracles in his case against Meidias, thus providing evidence for the illegality of Meidias's actions (striking Demosthenes) and for his impiety (see *Mid.* 47–55).

declamation. In this clearly fictitious case,[87] a priest is accused of aiding and abetting Alexander and his army by dedicating a temple. In the narrative within the declamation, one learns that Alexander's campaign was successful until he burned down a particular temple. Once he did, a plague swept through his army. In order to stop the plague, Alexander sought an oracle, which told him he must rebuild the temple that he destroyed. When Alexander requested that the priest dedicate the newly built temple, the priest agreed on the condition that Alexander would withdraw from the city. In his defense against the charges of aiding the enemy, the priest cites the oracle to Alexander; he claims that both he and Alexander were obedient to the oracle, Alexander in building the temple and he in dedicating it.

Before moving on to other forms of divine testimony found in ancient speeches and treatises, it is appropriate to mention one other aspect which relates to oracles as forms of proof. Very often in ancient writings poets and other famous figures are cited and their words given the significance of oracles. For example, the Elder Seneca writes to his sons, who are aspiring orators, and urges them not to use their contemporaries as role models. He describes the younger generation thusly: "they are lazy, their intellects asleep; no-one can stay awake to take pains over a single honest pursuit. Sleep, torpor and a perseverance in evil that is more shameful than either have seized hold of their minds" (Seneca the Elder, *Controversiae* 1. pref. 8). He then cites Marcus Cato's statement that "an orator, son Marcus, is a good man skilled in speaking" (*Controversiae* 1. pref. 9). But he prefaces this remark by stating:

> That well-known saying of Cato was really an oracle . . . for surely an oracle is the divine will given human expression; and what high priest could the gods have found more holy than Marcus Cato, not so much to teach mankind as to scold it. (*Controversiae* 1. pref. 9)

In this passage, one notices that the Elder Seneca is citing a human authority (a widespread *topos* among the ancient rhetoricians), but also seeks to add significance to that authority through the claim that the source of the speaker's words is the gods themselves. This is a common methodology that was often practiced in antiquity.[88]

---

87. The author of the declamation references an attack made by Alexander against Athens.

88. See, e.g., Cicero, who quotes a verse from Ennius's *Annales* and then states, "Our poet seems to have obtained these words, so brief and true, from an oracle"

Divine Testimony and its Application in Ancient Speeches and Treatises

Divine Testimony through Deeds and Other Means

Other forms of divine testimony (as described by Cicero in *Top.* 20.76–77) are found in ancient speeches and treatises as well. Quintilian, in mentioning divine testimony as a form of proof, cites Cicero's speech against Catiline as an example.[89] In this speech, which Cicero delivers to the people of Rome and not the Senate,[90] Cicero describes to the people how he was able to thwart Catiline's plot to take over the Republic. Cicero explains his ability to do so by attributing his success to the gods:

> If I were to say that I foiled them [Catiline and his co-conspirators], I should be taking too much credit for myself—an intolerable presumption. It was Jupiter, the mighty Jupiter, who foiled them; it was Jupiter who secured the salvation of the Capitol. . . . The immortal gods have been my guides in my purpose and determination and have led me to this vital evidence. (*Cat.* 3.22)[91]

(*Resp.* 5.1). See also Aeschines (*Ctes.* 135–36), who quotes Hesiod and then states, "If you disregard the poet's meter and examine only his thought, I think this will seem to you to be, not a poem of Hesiod, but an oracle directed against the politics of Demosthenes [ἀλλὰ χρησμὸν εἰς τὴν Δημοσθένους πολιτείαν]" (*Ctes.* 136); Lycurgus (*Against Leocrates* 92), who prefaces a quotation of poetry by stating, "For the first step taken by the gods in the case of wicked men is to unhinge their reason; and personally I value as the utterance of an oracle these lines, composed by ancient poets and handed down to posterity [καὶ μοι δοκοῦσι τῶν ἀρχαίων τινὲς ποιηταὶ ὥσπερ χρησμοὺς γράψαντες τοῖς ἐπιγινομένοις τάδε τὰ ἰαμβεῖα καταλιπεῖν]." Here, however, one must exert caution, as the various terms translated "oracle" can carry a wide range of meanings, not unlike the term *topos*.

89. See Quintilian, *Inst.* 5.12.42. The other examples that Quintilian cites in this passage are discussed below.

90. The significance of this is that this speech is therefore technically not a species of forensic rhetoric in that it is not a formal accusation of Catiline. It is, rather, Cicero's report to the people of what has taken place, and in places sounds much like a self-encomium (cf. Dio Cassius's statement: "[Cicero] was the greatest boaster alive and regarded no one as equal to himself" (*Hist. Rom.* 38.12.7; see also Plutarch, *Comp. Dem. Cic.* 2.1: "[W]hereas Cicero's immoderate boasting of himself in his speeches proves that he had an intemperate desire for fame"). Heibges argues that while this speech is deliberative in nature, the citation of the direction of the gods is nonetheless employed by Cicero in order to persuade his audience more effectively that he has taken the correct course of action; see Heibges, "Religion and Rhetoric," 833–49.

91. Cicero employs the same strategy in a forensic speech, through which he defends Sulla against the accusation that he was a part of this same conspiracy. In that speech, Cicero states: "Thwarted on this charge, Torquatus returns to the attack and makes another accusation against me. He says that I falsified the entry in the public records of what was said. Immortal gods!—for I grant you your due and cannot with

Even before action was taken, Cicero claims to have had foreknowledge from the gods of the situation. He emphatically states:

> Even so, citizens, my conduct of this whole matter may be thought to display both foresight and action that depended upon the wisdom and the will of the immortal gods. We can make this assumption . . . because so closely have the gods stood by us at this time to bring us their help and assistance that we can almost see them with our eyes. Even if I do not mention those portents, the meteors that were seen in the west at night and lit up the sky, even if I leave out the thunderbolts and the earthquakes, even if I omit the other portents which have occurred so frequently in my consulship that the immortal gods seemed to be foretelling these events which are now coming to pass. (*Cat.* 3.18)[92]

Cicero, through this passage, builds up to the ultimate evidence of the involvement of the gods.

This evidence is described in the next passage. Cicero relates to the people how, in view of many portents similar to those described in the previous passage,[93] the seers ordered that a more prominent statue of Jupiter be erected; the new statue, however, was to face east, rather than west (as was the case of the previous, smaller statue), in order that the portended plot to overthrow the Republic would become visible to the senate and the people. According to Cicero, there were many delays in actually erecting the statue, resulting in the statue being put in place that very morning,

---

honesty claim for myself the sole credit for distinguishing unaided the number, variety and speed of the dangers in that storm which burst so furiously upon the State—it was surely you who then kindled in my mind the desire to preserve my country, you who turned me from all other considerations to the single thought of delivering the Republic, you in short who amid the deep shadow of uncertainty and ignorance illumined my thoughts with the brightness of your light" (*Sull.* 40).

92. Pliny the Elder also records a lightning strike which he interprets to be an omen with respect to Catiline; see *Nat.* 2.52.137.

Cicero's statement recorded here is an excellent example of the rhetorical figure of speech known as paralipsis (*occultatio*), as described in *Rhet. Her.* 4.27.37: "Paralipsis [*occultatio*] occurs when we say that we are passing by, or do not know, or refuse to say that which precisely now we are saying."

93. "You remember, of course, that in the consulship of Cotta and Torquatus a large number of objects on the Capitol were struck by lightning, images of the gods were overthrown and statues of men of old overturned and the bronze tablets of our laws melted; even the statue of Romulus, the founder of Rome, was struck . . . On that occasion the soothsayers assembled from the whole of Etruria and said that murder and arson, the end of the rule of law, rebellion and civil war, the destruction of the whole city and of our empire were upon us, unless the immortal gods were placated by every means and used their power virtually to alter the path of destiny" (*Cat.* 3.19).

concurrent with the plot being made known and subsequently foiled (*Cat.* 3.20-21). Cicero considers this undeniable evidence of the gods' favor and intercession.[94]

Another example of thunder and/or lightning being used as divine testimony is found in a discourse by Dio Chrysostom. The context of the discourse is that Dio is chiding the Alexandrians for their frivolity and lack of seriousness. Part of the issue, he explains, is that the Alexandrians welcome orators who "declaim speeches for display, and stupid ones to boot" (32.9). Dio himself, however, feels that he is addressing them "by the will of some deity [ἀλλ' ὑπὸ δαιμονίου τινὸς γνώμης]" (32.12). He strengthens this statement by adding,

> For when divine providence is at work for men, the gods provide, not only good counselors who need no urging, but also words that are appropriate and profitable to the listener. And this statement of mine should be questioned least of all by you, since here in Alexandria the deity is most in honour, and to you especially does he display his power through almost daily oracles and dreams. (32.12)

Dio thus establishes his authority through divine testimony. First, he tells his leaders that if he is indeed speaking on the behest of the god, his words will be "appropriate and profitable" for his hearers. Second, he reminds his readers that the god who has commanded him to speak is the same one who speaks to the Alexandrians on a regular basis through oracles and dreams.

Later, in the speech, Dio is rebuking his auditors for their conduct at the chariot races in the stadium. According to Dio, the crowds' excitement and subsequent behavior is completely inappropriate. As proof of the inappropriateness of their behavior, Dio first quotes a passage from the *Iliad*, which describes a race during which the crowds stood by and watched in silence (32.79-80; cf. *Il.* 23.368-72, 448). He then reminds the auditors that Ajax "behaved in rather unseemly fashion as a spectator by abusing Idomeneus with reference to the horses of Eumelus" (32.80). Dio goes on to say that Ajax "also was guilty of impiety toward Athena at the capture of Troy and on that account was himself smitten with a

---

[94] "Who here can be so blind to the truth, so impetuous, so deranged in his mind as to deny that, more than any other city in the whole world that we see about us, Rome is governed by the will and the power of the immortal gods?" (*Cat.* 3.21) Heibges expresses some doubt as to the timing concerning the erection of the statue and the coup being averted. She intimates that this confluence of events may have been manipulated in order to bring about the desired results; see Heibges, "Religion and Rhetoric," 844.

thunderbolt [κεραυνωθείς] and thereby caused the storm and shipwreck that befell them all" (32.80). Through the citation of Homer, which is used as an example of divine testimony, Dio provides supporting evidence of the people's need to change their behavior.[95]

An example of divine testimony through dreams is found in Cicero's philosophical treatise *Laelius de Amicitia*, directly following a passage to which I have already referred. The immediate context of the reference is the death of Laelius's friend Scipio and his subsequent argument that the soul does not perish along with the body. Laelius maintains that Scipio himself was convinced of this, "making use of arguments which he had heard, he said, from Africanus the Elder through a vision in his sleep" (*Amic.* 4.14).[96] Laelius therefore uses Scipio's arguments that he received in a dream to bolster his own view that the soul lives on after the death of a human being.

A second example of dreams being used as divine testimony is found in Artistides's treatise *In Defense of Oratory*, a treatise in which, as has already been seen, one finds divine testimony through oracles used as a source of proof. In the same section referenced above, Aristides cites the dreams that Asclepius provided as a means of healing (see *In Defense*

---

95. Another speech falsely attributed to Dio Chrysostom, which includes multiple instances of the *topos* of divine testimony, is the oration to the Corinthians. The central issue with which the speech is concerned is a bronze statue of the speaker which has ostensibly been removed. The speaker begins by relating the story of Arion, a passenger on a ship sailing to Corinth, whom the ship's crew threatened to throw overboard. Arion began to sing, and dolphins, which heard the song, surrounded the ship. He jumped overboard and was carried by a dolphin to safety. The sailors were put on trial and executed; Arion erected a bronze statue in Taenarum (where the dolphin delivered him), the statue depicting himself on the dolphin. He then relates the story of Periander, "whom the Greeks were wont to call tyrant, though the gods called him king" (37.5). He then provides evidence of this by quoting an oracle (37.5). But even though Periander was held in so high regard by the gods, no statue was erected to him in Corinth. Herodotus also visited the city, but the city did not provide remuneration for him. The speaker uses these examples as evidence that the Corinthians do not value what is truly valuable; what is truly valuable, in the case of Arion and Periander, is that for which the gods show high regard and to which they testify through the miraculous deed and oracle mentioned. Not content to rest his case, the speaker continues his accusations by claiming that Daedalus himself crafted the statue (37.9), and that it was erected in a place that belongs to both Helius and Poseidon (37.12), to which the Sibyl sang praises (37.13). The speaker uses all of these varied (somewhat indirect) methods of divine testimony to bolster his case that his statue was wrongfully removed.

96. Laelius continues by saying: "If the truth really is that the souls of all good men after death make the easiest escape from what may be termed the imprisonment and fetters of the flesh, whom can we think of as having had an easier journey to the gods than Scipio?"

of Oratory 58–65). Aristides's argument is that human doctors are practitioners of an art. There are those patients, however, who receive healing through means such as the cult of Asclepius;[97] this healing through dreams is not performed in connection with art. Therefore, just as healing can come through dreams and not through art, oratory can be useful even if it is not an art, as Plato argues. Oratory can be useful in that it can also be inspired by the gods:

> Then if dreams free the companies of Asclepius from the art of medicine, and the Bacchants of Dionysus transform the gifts of the Nymphs, whenever they become inspired, why is it shameful or beyond the realm of nature to accept the idea of men inspired in oratory, and to believe that they can refer to the Gods as patrons? (*In Defense of Oratory* 75)

Many examples of divine testimony through auspices are found in the speeches of Cicero. Most of these examples center on the *lex Aelia Fufia*, a law, or laws,[98] which were enacted in order to curtail political assemblies when the auspices were unfavorable.[99] The examples cited below are

---

97. Quite possibly Aristides was one of these; cf. the discussion of the Asclepius cult at Pergamum and Aristides's involvement with it in Behr, *Aelius Aristides*, 23–90.

98. Cicero mentions this in several different contexts; see, e.g., *Vat.* 7.18; *Har. resp.* 48; *Phil.* 2.32.81–34.84.

99. A passage from Dio Cassius is helpful for understanding this practice; in *Hist. Rom.* 38.13.3–6, Dio explains that, although he does not know the exact origins of the practice, at some time the Romans began searching the heavens for omens in conjunction with significant political decisions. According to Dio, if one consulted the heavens and saw some type of ominous portent, the assembly was by law not allowed to consider any legislation on that day. He adds that this practice was certainly abused by some in order to prevent legislation they opposed to be enacted. Gardner has an excellent explanation of the *lex Aelia Fufia* and the subsequent repeal of this law by Clodius. See Gardner, "The *Lex Aelia Fufia* in the Late Republic," in Cicero, *Volume XIII*, 309–22. See also works cited by Gardner, including Greenridge, "Repeal," 158–61; W. McDonald, "Clodius," 164–79; and Weinstock, "Clodius," 215–22. More recent studies, which have appeared since Gardner's summary, include: Mitchell, "*Leges Clodiae*," 172–76; Linderski, "Römischer Staat und Götterzeichen," 444–57; and Tatum, "Cicero's Opposition," 187–94. All of these essays grapple with the question of exactly what aspect of the *Lex Aelia Fufia* did Clodius's law repeal.

Cicero attributes great significance to this practice. In *De legibus*, he sheds light on this tradition when he states: "But the highest and most important authority in the State is that of the *augurs*, to whom is accorded a great influence" (*Leg.* 2.12.31). He then continues by asking a series of rhetorical questions: "What is of graver import than the abandonment of any business already begun, if a single augur says, 'On another day?' What power is more impressive than that of forcing the consuls to resign their offices? What right is more sacred than that of giving or refusing permission to

relatively tangential, but they do involve the testimony of the gods through signs and portents in the sky and illustrate how an orator could use (and perhaps abuse) this practice to discredit his opponent, albeit somewhat indirectly.

One example of Cicero's use of this concept can be found in his speech against M. Antonius in the Philippic orations. Specifically, Cicero accuses Antonius of violating the *lex Aelia Fufia* by allowing decisions to be made in opposition to the auspices. He writes:

> Our augur [Antonius] is too bashful to interpret the auspices without his colleagues. And yet those auspices need no interpretation; for who does not know that, when Jupiter is thundering, no transaction can legally be carried out? (*Phil.* 5.7)[100]

Here, Jupiter's thundering is considered by Cicero as an ill omen, through which Jupiter displays his displeasure with the proceedings. According to Cicero, it is common knowledge that the gods testify in this fashion and that such a testimony should not be ignored.

A second example comes from Cicero's speech against Vatinius. Cicero begins this particular line of questioning with the statement, "And, since all important things have their beginning with the Immortal Gods [*Et quoniam omnium rerum magnarum ab dis immortalibus princiia ducuntur*]" (*Vat.* 5.13). Next, he accuses Vatinius of being a Pythagorean, therefore demonstrating "contempt for the auspices under which this city has been founded, upon which the whole State and its authority depend" (*Vat.* 6.14). The accusation that Cicero brings against him in this regard is couched in terms of rhetorical questions and explanatory comments[101] preceded by a strong string of invectives.[102] Specifically, Cicero's charge

---

hold an assembly of the people or of the plebeians, or that of abrogating laws illegally passed?" (*Leg.* 2.12.31).

100. It is possible, however, that here Cicero is invoking Jupiter somewhat ironically.

101. "Do you know of any tribune of the commons since the foundation of Rome who transacted business with the commons, when it was well known that an announcement had been made that the heavens had been watched? I should like you to answer this. During your tribunate of the commons, the Aelian and Fufian Laws still existed in the State, those laws which often checked and crippled revolutionary tribunes, those laws which on one except yourself has ever ventured to resist . . . I ask you, did you ever hesitate, contrary to those laws, to transact business with the commons and summon a Meeting? Have you ever heard that any of the most seditious tribunes of the commons was so audacious as to summon a Meeting in defiance of the Aelian or the Fufian Law?" (*Vat.* 7.17–18).

102. "What audacity was yours, what violence! What your nine colleagues held

against Vatinius is that he disregarded the laws governing the use of augury, indirectly accusing Vatinius of being impious towards the gods and their testimony, and thereby discrediting him.[103]

Another example of divine testimony comes from Cicero's defense of Milo. In the speech, Cicero does not argue that Milo is not responsible for the death of Clodius. Rather, his defense is that because Clodius was actually conspiring to kill Milo, the death of Clodius at the hands of Milo's slaves was justified (see, e.g., Cicero, *Mil.* 11). Also, Cicero portrays Clodius as one who desired to rule over Rome as a dictator, claiming rights to the property of the Roman citizens (*Mil.* 77–78).[104] Therefore, Cicero presents Clodius's death as a benefit to Rome for which Milo should be praised, not punished. In fact, Cicero argues that it is actually by the gods' favor that this act has occurred:

> But for this blessing [the death of Clodius], gentlemen, the fortune of the Roman people, your own happy star, and the immortal gods claim your gratitude. Nor indeed can any man think otherwise, unless there be any who thinks that there is no such thing as divine power and control, who is not stirred by the greatness of our empire or by yonder sun or the march of the constellated heaven or by nature's round of ordered change or (last and greatest) by the wisdom of our ancestors, who themselves paid strict observance to worship and rites and auspices, and have handed them on to us their descendants . . . Wherefore it is this very power, which has often shed upon this city wealth and blessing beyond all thought, that now has uprooted and abolished this scourge, having first roused such a mood in him that he dared to prove with violence and challenge with the sword the bravest of men, and so was vanquished by one over whom, had he won the victory, he stood fair to enjoy impunity and licence for all time. (*Mil.* 83–84)[105]

---

should be regarded with awe, you alone, one sprung from the mud, the lowest of the land in every way, regarded as contemptible, trivial, ridiculous!" (*Vat.* 7.17). Craig studies Cicero's use of and the audience's reception of invective in his speech *Pro Milone* in "Audience Expectations," 187–213.

103. A similar accusation is found in Cicero's speech against Clodius. Here, Cicero argues that Clodius's tribunate is actually invalid, in that it was established while the augurs were searching for omens in the skies. See *Dom.* 14.39–41.

104. Concerning Clodius, Cicero states, "It is impossible to express in words or even to form a conception of all the guilt, all the capacity for destruction, that were in him" (*Mil.* 78).

105. A. R. Dyck argues that Cicero is attempting to "situate the event [Clodius's murder] rather in a larger cosmic context." See Dyck, "Narrative Obfuscation," 219–41, esp. 233.

Cicero argues that it was the gods, whose favor for Rome is as evident as the order of universe, who incited Clodius to attempt to murder Milo, which in turn resulted in Milo's slaves killing Clodius.[106] Thus the gods testify, in a sense, against Clodius by provoking him to attempt a crime for which he was (justly) murdered.

Cicero also employs the *locus* of divine testimony in a more general fashion. An example cited by Quintilian (*Inst.* 5.12.42) is Cicero's defense of Ligarius, in which Cicero references the judgment of the gods. Quintus Tubero has accused Ligarius of consorting with the enemy; it seems, however, that in actuality Ligarius's offense amounted to something of a more personal nature rather than a crime (cf. *Lig.* 2–17). In remarks addressed to Caesar, who is judge over the case being argued, Cicero draws an analogy between Caesar and Ligarius (who was serving in Africa) during the onset of the civil war. Cicero reminds Caesar that in the beginning Caesar "held that that movement was a secession, not a war, not an outburst of hatred between foes, but of dissension between citizens, a dissension in which either party had the welfare of the state at heart, but in which each . . . swerved from the interest of the general body" (*Lig.* 19). Cicero continues:

> Between the two causes it was at the time difficult to decide, for the reason that on either side there was something to approve; to-day that cause must be adjudged the better, whereto the gods added their assistance. (*Lig.* 19)

Thus, Cicero argues that only in retrospect is it possible to see which cause was the "right" cause, and only because the gods have given their testimony. In the greater argument of Ligarius's innocence, Cicero is maintaining that because it was difficult to ascertain which side was the "enemy," Ligarius is guilty perhaps of bad judgment, but certainly not a crime.

The final example of divine testimony cited by Quintilian is Cicero's speech against Clodius now known as *De haruspicum responso*. This speech includes a plethora of examples of divine testimony, beginning with Cicero's explanation of the event that triggered the speech. An odd sound was heard and interpreted by the seers as being from the gods and

---

106. Later in the speech, Cicero will state: "Then it was that the immortal gods, as I remarked a while ago, instilled into [Clodius's] reckless and desperate brain the thought of laying a plot against my client" (*Mil.* 88). Here, Dyck's comments are appropriate: "Milo, on trial *de vi*, is reduced to a tool of the divine *vis*, which holds in check the *vis* of Clodius by infatuating him and leading him to his destruction" ("Narrative Obfuscation," 235).

that "sacred and hallowed sites were being turned to secular purposes" (*Har. resp.* 9). Cicero claims that Clodius is behind this interpretation, and that specifically what is in view is Cicero's own home, built for him by the State (*Har. resp.* 9–10; 16). Cicero, in rebuttal, interprets the ominous noise differently:

> I am glad to have been given an opportunity . . . of speaking on the general theme of this prodigy, which I am inclined to believe is the most solemn that has been announced to this order for many years past; for you will find that this prodigy [*toto prodigio*] and the response occasioned thereby are nothing but a warning to us, uttered almost by the voice of Jupiter Best and Greatest, concerning Clodius' mad wickedness and the terrible dangers that threaten us. (*Har. resp.* 10)

Cicero understands the noise which was heard to be a warning from the gods, and attributes this warning to various misdeeds of his opponent Clodius. Thus the noise itself, according to Cicero, is a divine testimony, and Cicero uses divine testimony to further implicate Clodius.[107]

A few further examples of Cicero's use of divine testimony will suffice to provide a sense of its application in this speech. In arguing that the prodigy is evidence of the gods' anger over Clodius's desecration of the Megalesian games,[108] Cicero calls out to the gods: "Ye immortal gods! How could ye speak with us more clearly, if ye were with us and moving in our midst? Ye have signified and ye openly declare that the games have been desecrated" (*Har. resp.* 25). A second example is found in Cicero's charge that the prodigy is a warning that the gods are angry over the neglect of sacrificial rites. He quotes the soothsayers' report in this regard: "Ancient and secret sacrifices have been performed with laxity, and have been desecrated" (*Har. resp.* 37). His comment on this is in the form of a rhetorical question which links this statement to testimony from the gods

---

107. In stating that he will first dispense with Clodius's case against his home, but then further accuse Clodius, Cicero says: "I shall even be delighted, to comply with the portents of the immortal gods [*portentis deorum immortalium*] and the obligations which they impose" (*Har. resp.* 11).

108. Cicero accuses Clodius of inviting a rabble of slaves to the games: "So these games, the sanctity whereof is so deep that it has been summoned from distant lands and planted in this city . . . were performed by slaves, viewed by slaves, and were indeed converted under Clodius' aedileship into a Megalesia of slaves" (*Har. resp.* 24). This last part of this statement (*hos ludos servi fecerunt, servi spectatverunt, tota deniue hoc aedile servorum Megalesia fuerunt*) is an example of *conduplicatio* (i.e., reduplication), a figure of speech described in *Rhet. Her.* 4.28.38: "Reduplication is the repetition of one or more words for the purpose of Amplification or Appeal to Pity."

themselves: "Is it the soothsayers who utter these words, or the gods of our ancestors and of our households?" (*Har. resp.* 37). He then goes on to associate Clodius with this matter. In this same section, Cicero claims that Clodius is deranged, and that this is so due to the punishment of the gods.[109]

Finally, in the conclusion of this speech, Cicero calls for Clodius to be punished, reiterating his position that the noise was a warning from the gods (*Har. resp.* 61). He reinforces this by asking another rhetorical question: "And if other manifestations, less impressive, perhaps, though more widely bruited, have not failed to move us, shall not the feelings of all of us be stirred *by the actual voice of the immortal gods*? (*Har. resp.* 62; emphasis mine). Cicero then makes reference to an earthquake, which occurred in a nearby town at approximately the same time. This, too, he deems a "portent," which is "as a voice, nay, an eloquent appeal, of the immortal gods that this must be viewed, when the world with its seas and lands shudders with a weird motion, and by a sound beyond experience and beyond belief conveys to us tidings of the future" (*Har. resp.* 62–63).[110]

A final example from Cicero comes from *De legibus*, his treatise on the law. Here Cicero is arguing for the divine origin of Rome's laws. In an argument quite similar to the one already seen above in his defense of Milo, Cicero argues that the people must understand that "the gods are the lords and rulers of all things, and that what is done, is done by their will and authority; that they are likewise great benefactors of man" (*Leg.* 2.7.15). He goes on to say that the observation of nature should motivate humanity to thank the gods for their goodness and that nature gives evidence of a greater reason which governs it (*Leg.* 2.7.16). Finally, this same reason is the basis for Rome's legal system. Cicero concludes this section by stating:

---

109. Cicero vehemently states (note the use of *conduplicatio*, which serves to heighten the punishment by the gods): "It was by mortals [*Homines*] that you were defended in this loathsome business, from mortals [*homines*] that your deep guilt and degradation drew praise, mortals [*homines*] who gave you a verdict of acquittal though you all but avowed your sin, mortals [*hominibus*] who expressed no resentment at the affront which your adultery had inflicted upon them, mortals [*homines*] who put into your hands weapons to be used either against me, or later against our invincible fellow-citizen; mortals [*hominum*], I grant you freely, have done you benefits that could not be exceeded. But what punishment could be visited upon a man by the immortal gods severer than madness and infatuation?" (*Har. resp.* 38–39).

110. For earthquakes considered as portents, see Pliny the Elder, *Nat.* 2.181.191–192, 86.200. After noting several earthquakes, he writes: "Nor yet is the disaster a simple one, nor does the danger consist only in the earthquake itself, but equally or more in the fact that it is a portent; the city of Rome was never shaken without this being a premonition of something about to happen" (*Nat.* 2.86.200).

Divine Testimony and its Application in Ancient Speeches and Treatises

> Who will deny that such beliefs are useful when he remembers how often oaths are used to confirm agreements, how important to our well-being is the sanctity of treaties, how many persons are deterred from crime by the fear of divine punishment, and how sacred an association of citizens becomes when the immortal gods are made members of it, either as judges or as witnesses [*quamque sancta sit societas civium inter ipsos diis immortalibus interpositis tum iudicibus, tum testibus*]. (*Leg.* 2.7.15)

Thus Cicero associates the goodness of Rome's laws with the gods who are active participants in the legal system through their testimony and judgment.

The examples above demonstrate that the *topos* of divine testimony was used abundantly as proof or evidence in ancient speeches and philosophical treatises. The examples also show the breadth of situations in which ancient rhetors were able to apply the *topos* in forensic and deliberative cases involving law, politics, and even in philosophical works. The method of the present study, as explained in chapter one, is to consider how the *topos* of divine testimony would have been heard and understood by an ancient audience, especially in the case of Luke-Acts. Therefore, it is appropriate at this time to consider, albeit briefly, the question of the persuasiveness of this particular *topos* in the ancient world. It is to this question I now turn.

The Persuasiveness of the topos of Divine Testimony

First, it is important to remember that the primary goal of ancient rhetoric was to persuade one's audience of the validity of one's case.[111] For example, Cicero in *De inventione* says, "The function of eloquence seems to be to speak in a manner suited to persuade an audience, the end is to persuade by speech [*finis persuadere dictione*]" (*Inv.* 1.5.6).[112] Similarly, in

---

111. See Litfin, *St. Paul's Theology of Proclamation*, 91–108, 109–36. In these two chapters, Litfin analyzes the importance of persuasion as described by Cicero and Quintilian (ibid., 91–108), and by other ancient rhetoricians (109–36). He also helpfully includes a discussion of the role of the audience and the need for rhetoricians to adapt their speeches to the intended audience in order to be persuasive. I am indebted to Litfin for the primary references in this section.

112. In comparing the emphases of philosophy and rhetoric as seen in the writings of Cicero and Quintilian, C. Neumeister (*Grundsätze der Forensischen Rhetorik*, 23–24) argues that for the rhetor, "Zweckmäßigkeit" was paramount, as opposed to a determination of the "Wahrheit" in the case of the philosophers.

The *Topos* of Divine Testimony in Luke/Acts

De oratore, he maintains that "the duty of an orator is to speak in a style fitted to convince" (*De or.* 1.31.138). Quintilian also expresses this idea; in considering the different definitions of rhetoric, among the diversity of opinions he finds this one area of agreement: "They almost all believe that the function of oratory lies in persuading or in speaking in a way adapted to persuade." He then concludes, "So the commonest definition is that 'rhetoric is the power of persuading'" (*Inst.* 2.15.3, 5). Given this emphasis on the results of rhetoric,[113] namely to persuade an audience and to adapt one's presentation to the audience in order to do so,[114] one can argue that simply the fact that the *topos* of divine testimony appears in these speeches and treatises noted above is evidence of their persuasiveness in the context in which they were written and/or spoken.[115] If the rhetorician indeed desired to persuade the audience, then these arguments must have been considered to be convincing.

The emphasis on the orator's consideration of the audience is even more significant when one considers other ancient writings in which authors describe their individual attitudes towards the gods and divination. One example is from Cicero himself. In the first half of *De divinatione*, Cicero, through the character Quintus, Cicero's younger brother, espouses the contemporary Stoic worldview concerning divination and augury,[116] one in which these aspects of religion were acceptable and beneficial to the people.[117] The second half of the treatise is spoken through the character

---

113. The practical nature of this aspect of rhetoric is reinforced by Cicero's statement in *De inventione* (which directly precedes Cicero's concept of the function of rhetoric given above): "Therefore we will classify oratorical ability as a part of political science" (*Inv.* 1.5.6). This is a linkage which has already been noted.

114. See Litfin, *Paul's Theology of Proclamation*, 92–97, 104–6. In these sections, Litfin discusses the views of Cicero and Quintilian regarding adapting a speech to the audience. For example, Litfin cites Quintilian, *Inst.* 12.10.56, in which Quintilian states: "The judge's attitude to what he hears is also very important— . . . his face is often itself the speaker's guide. You must therefore press points you see are to his liking, and retreat smartly from those which are not well received." Cf. Cicero's thoughts on adapting the style of the speech to the audience in *De or.* 3.55.210–12. Here, I am extrapolating from Cicero's admonition to modify the *style* of the speech to correspond to the audience to include the choice of *content* in a speech as well.

115. See Brunt, *Roman Imperial Themes*, 297: "The frequency of [Cicero's] public appeals to religion is surely proof that belief was still widespread."

116. Beard, "Cicero and Divination," 33–46, esp. 33.

117. At the beginning of the treatise, Cicero has Quintus state: "My own opinion is that, if the kinds of divination which we have inherited from our forefathers and now practice are trustworthy, then there are gods and, conversely, if there are gods then there are men who have the power of divination" (*Div.* 1.5.9).

of Marcus Cicero himself, and consists of a complete refutation of what Quintus has put forward as a defense of divination and augury.[118] The negative attitude toward divination and augury described by Marcus Cicero in this treatise has caused scholars to question where Cicero himself actually stood on this issue.[119] For my purposes in this study, however, I would argue that the question of the "historical" Cicero's opinion of divination is insignificant, and it is insignificant for two reasons.

First, I have already discussed the significance for the rhetorician of persuasion and adapting one's case to the audience. Thus, the important question for the rhetor is not, "What do I believe?" Rather, the more significant question is, "What proofs and evidence will convince my audience?"[120] Thus, Cicero can write,

> Now nothing in oratory, Catulus, is more important than to win for the orator the favour of his hearer, and to have the latter

---

118. Beard emphasizes the polemical tone of the second half of the treatise when she states that Cicero "ridicules" his brother's positions. Beard attributes Marcus's position on divination to his rationalism; see Beard, "Cicero and Divination," 33.

119. Beard argues that the scholarly consensus is that *Div.* is Cicero's attempt to describe his skepticism toward popular religion ("Cicero and Divination," 34). Representatives of this opinion include Brunt, who argues, "It may be doubted if Cicero himself had firm religious convictions"; see Brunt, *Roman Imperial Themes*, 295. See also Linderski, "Cicero and Roman Divination," 458–84. Linderski recognizes that what Cicero states concerning the gods and divination in *De legibus* is almost completely antithetical to the second half of *Div.*, and therefore seeks to resolve this conflict in Cicero's thought. He does so by noting that augury and divination were ultimately tools of statecraft in the Republic, and were manipulated in the midst of power struggles. Cicero, according to Linderski, was a supporter of these tools until he was on the losing end of some of the internal conflicts during which the manipulation occurred (see some of the examples above which include references to the *lex Aelia Fufia* and *lex Clodia*). Therefore, Cicero comes out against divination, but not religion per se. Against this view are both Beard ("Cicero and Divination") and Heibges, "Cicero, a Hypocrite," 304–12. Heibges maintains that Cicero reveals his true attitude toward religion in his speeches and treatises, in which he promotes a Stoic view of the world, which included a strong emphasis on natural theology. Beard, in "Cicero and Divination," argues that the structure of *Div.* precludes one from inferring Cicero's opinion on divination. Rather, because both the "for" and "against" positions are explained, Cicero leaves the final judgment up to the reader.

120. Dyck, commenting on Cicero's speech in behalf of Milo, states: "Questions of religious belief and its foundations are seldom broached before the bar . . . As a 'philosophic orator,' however, [Cicero] was prepared to touch on such matters insofar as his case might benefit" (Dyck, "Narrative Obfuscation," 233). For a short discussion of the importance of ethos and pathos as found in Aristotle, Cicero, and Quintilian, see Remer, *Humanism*, 20–21. The primary citations found in this section (and others as well) are also found in Remer.

so affected as to be swayed by something resembling a mental impulse or emotion, rather than by judgement or deliberation. For men decide far more problems by hate, or love, or lust, or rage, or sorrow, or joy, or hope, or fear, or illusion, or some other inward emotion, than by reality, or authority, or any legal standard, or judicial precedent, or statute [*quam veritate aut praescripto aut iuris norma aliqua aut iudicii formula aut legibus*]. (*De or.* 2.42.178)

For the present discussion, it is important to note that Cicero places a higher value on convincing his audience by emotional appeal than "reality" (*veritas*).[121] Quintilian makes a similar statement; in the context of the appeal to emotions within a speech, he says, "But where force has to be brought to bear on the judges' feelings and their minds distracted from the truth, there the orator's true work begins" (*Inst.* 6.2.5). Therefore, given this emphasis on conviction at all costs, Cicero's personal views concerning augury and divination are not significant.[122] What is significant is the judge's (or audience's) opinion of the evidence, and it is this second point noted above that I now address.

In the first chapter of this study I explained in the section describing the proposed methodology that I would focus on the implied audience

---

121. Cf. Cicero, *Off.* 2.14.51: "It is always the business of the judge in a trial to find out the truth; it is sometimes the business of the advocate to maintain what is plausible, even if it be not strictly true." Interestingly, authority here is also listed, which on a surface level would seem to be detrimental to the argument being made in this study. Two points are therefore in order: (i) The fact that Cicero finds emotional appeal more significant for convincing an audience than an appeal to authority does not preclude the orator from using both in the same speech. Indeed, in the examples above, we have seen both at work simultaneously, especially in the use of the figure of speech of repetition. (ii) The word translated "authority" here is *praescripto*; the context here and Cicero's use of this term in other contexts (cf., e.g., *Inv.* 2.45.132) suggests he is referring to the regulations of the state.

122. Burriss, "Cicero," 524–32, argues: "Despite his religious disbelief, Cicero always speaks of religion with the deepest respect; and he praises the wisdom of the old Romans in making it possible for the same men to have charge of religious as well as state matters." Burriss also admits that "Cicero might defend religion on the grounds of political expediency." For an opposing view, see Goar, 108–11. In concluding his analysis of Cicero's *De legibus* and *De divinatione*, Goar states, "It appears, then, that the attitude toward Roman religion which Cicero assumed in the orations was more or less sincere, though more dogmatically asserted than in *De Legibus, De Divinatione* and the other essays" (110). He continues, "Because he was socially and politically conservative, as well as being a moralist and a teacher, Cicero seems to have embraced Stoic-Platonic religious views as a necessary political, moral and intellectual position, rather than as emotional belief" (111). This is certainly not to say, however, that an appeal to divine testimony is an appeal to a fabrication on the part of the rhetor.

Divine Testimony and its Application in Ancient Speeches and Treatises

of Luke-Acts and other extra-biblical works of the same period. Thus the methodology of this study and Cicero's (and Quintilian's, as well as others') focus on the audience reception of the proofs and evidence presented in speeches line up in conjunction. And the evidence from antiquity, from Cicero himself and from numerous others,[123] clearly points to the fact that in the ancient world, it was accepted that the gods were intimately involved in the affairs of humanity, which included their pronouncing judgment on human beings as well as guiding their affairs. From the first half of *De divinatione*, it is readily apparent that there was a worldview in Cicero's time that included human-divine communications, a worldview which Cicero seems to desire to counter in the second half of the treatise.[124] Because this attitude toward and acceptance of the divine existed, it is no surprise that an orator would exploit it in order to win conviction.

A second example is found in the Plutarch's *De superstitione*, in which he satirizes dreams[125] and ridicules the idea of a soul being tormented after death. As will be demonstrated in the chapter five, however, dreams are extremely important in Plutarch's *Lives*, especially when the subject of the *bios* is near death. Also, in *De superstitione*, Plutarch attacks eclipses as portents,[126] but in the *Lives*, eclipses are seen as both scientific/natural phenomena as well as omens for the subject of the *Life*.[127] I have shown that

---

123. There are excellent recent studies of this phenomenon; two of note which are particularly relevant to this study include: Klauck, *The Religious Context of Early Christianity*, 153–249. In this chapter, Klauck discusses issues pertinent to the New Testament, including healings, forms of prophecy and divination (particularly oracles and dreams), magic, and astrology; see also Strelan, *Strange Acts*. For an overview of the ancient attitude towards the supernatural, see 18–32. Strelan's main argument is that the "strange acts" of which one reads in the book of Acts would not have been considered "strange" at all to first-century auditors, but would have been part and parcel of the cultural milieu in the first century.

124. Dyck, in his study of Cicero's speech in behalf of Milo, specifically regarding Cicero's placing of his argument in a context in which the goodness and providence of the gods is emphasized, notes that in Cicero's *De natura deorum*, even Cotta, the skeptical character in the dialogue, is amenable to traditional religious practices. Dyck then states that this "is a further sign that this traditional religion still enjoyed well nigh universal respect." Dyck then cites *Har. resp.* 9.18, in which Cicero argues, "In the first place, speaking for myself, I look for authority and guidance in religious observance to our ancestors." See Dyck, "Narrative Obfuscation," 234.

125. Plutarch, *Superst.* 165f–166a; see also the story of Midas, *Superst.* 168f–169a.

126. Plutarch, *Superst.* 169a–b.

127. These points are made by F. Brenk in his comprehensive analysis of Plutarch's religious views; see Brenk, "An Imperial Heritage." The phenomena of dreams, eclipses, and other forms of divine testimony will be the subject of chapter five.

The *Topos* of Divine Testimony in Luke/Acts

in the writings of Cicero, even though he was possibly not personally convinced of the validity of augury and divination, he was not reserved in his use of divine testimony as proofs. In chapter five, I will demonstrate the same point for Plutarch: although in *Superst.* Plutarch expresses reluctance in completely believing that natural phenomena represented portents, he, too, is quite willing to cite them as proofs in his writings.

Before moving into the analysis of the use of the *topos* of divine testimony in ancient narratives, including Luke-Acts, it is important to return to the work of W. Wuellner.[128] Wuellner argues that the choice of *topoi* by ancient authors from which they built their arguments was a culturally-conditioned process and was determined by the rhetorical situations they faced.[129] Therefore, given first-century culture, a culture which is dominated by the concept of gods who are intimately involved in the lives of human beings and who communicate their pleasure and displeasure through various methods, it is easy to understand why a speaker or author in the first century would select the *topos* of divine testimony as evidence of what that person is trying to prove.

In sum, in this chapter I first addressed how the term *topos* is currently being applied to NT studies. The conclusions from this study were that the term *topos*, when applied to NT studies, is somewhat polyvalent. It can refer to a line of argumentation, literary themes, or moral *topoi* that receive extensive treatment in philosophical treatises, categories that overlap to some degree. I then surveyed the ancient rhetoricians in order to ascertain their definitions of *topos/locus*. I have shown that one possible definition for *topos* is a source of proofs from which an orator can draw in order to bring evidence in a forensic or deliberative speech. In the Latin rhetoricians, and particularly in Cicero, there is a strong emphasis on legal applications of *topoi* and the use of rhetoric in service to the State. My argument here is that this particular definition is underrepresented in NT studies involving rhetoric and *topoi*.

I then moved to a particular *topos* described in many rhetorical writings, the external *topos* of divine testimony, which receives its fullest explanation in Cicero's *Topica*. Through many examples I demonstrated that the testimony of the gods, which occurs through various means, was widely applied in ancient speeches and treatises when arguing a case or seeking to persuade an audience. Specifically, orators often applied this form of testimony in order to praise one's client, or, conversely, to denigrate an

---

128. Wuellner, "Toposforschung."
129. Ibid., 467, 468.

Divine Testimony and its Application in Ancient Speeches and Treatises

opponent. Likewise, the testimony of the gods was used to demonstrate the gods' support or lack thereof for a potential course of action. Finally, I argued that ancient audiences would have perceived this particular form of evidence as extremely persuasive.

Given this position, the next task is to examine Luke-Acts and other similar extra-biblical works in order to investigate if and how the *topos* of divine testimony is applied in these more narrative genres. In the next four chapters of this study, I will attempt to demonstrate that the *topos* of divine testimony was used rhetorically by ancient authors of narratives, including histories and biographies, in order to praise and denigrate characters, and to convince readers of the validity or inconsistency of a particular course of action.

3 • The *topos* of Divine Testimony through Utterances in Hellenistic Narratives

Given that a possible definition of *topos* from the ancient rhetorical handbooks is a source of evidence or proof, and having demonstrated that the *topos* of divine testimony was applied in ancient speeches in order to defend a client or prosecute an opponent, I am now prepared to begin the analysis of ancient narratives, in order to ascertain how the *topos* of divine testimony functions in those works. The overall goal of this study is to examine how ancient audiences would have heard and understood the instances of divine testimony found in Luke-Acts. Before analyzing Luke-Acts, however, it will be necessary first to survey (roughly) contemporary extra-biblical sources in order to compile a database of comparative material.[1] This material will assist in defining the "repertoire" or "horizon of expectations" of the auditors of Luke-Acts discussed in the introduction to this study. The survey of extra-biblical sources and the comparison of the results to the analysis of the material in Luke-Acts will demonstrate that not only does divine testimony appear in the same forms as described by Cicero,[2] it occurs within similar contexts and functions in the same way within these narratives. Much like its use in ancient speeches, divine

---

1. It must be stated up front that the comparison being made is not to the instance of divine testimony itself; i.e., the goal of the investigation is not to find extra-biblical "parallels" to Luke-Acts (although these will be pointed out when they are discovered). The comparison, rather, is to the function(s) of the *topos* of divine testimony as found in Hellenistic narratives and Luke-Acts.

2. With one exception: divine testimony through the examination of the entrails of sacrificial animals does not occur in Luke-Acts.

testimony was used in narratives to legitimate or denigrate characters portrayed in those narratives.

Ancient Narratives, Persuasion, and the Use of Rhetoric

It is appropriate, however, before beginning that analysis, to examine briefly the question of whether one should expect to find this *topos* in what are narratives, rather than speeches or treatises. In short, because ancient narratives of diverse genres were written to be persuasive, one should indeed expect to find elements of argumentation.

An example of a historical work written for persuasive purposes is Diodorus Siculus's *Bibliotheca historica*. In the preface to this work, Diodorus writes:

> For it is an excellent thing to be able to use the ignorant mistakes of others as warning examples for the correction of error, and, when we confront the varied vicissitudes of life, instead of having to investigate what is being done now, to be able to imitate the successes which have been achieved in the past . . . For this reason one may hold that the acquisition of a knowledge of history is of the greatest utility for every conceivable circumstance of life. (*Hist.* 1.1.4)

Another example is Livy's *Historiae*; in the preface to that work, Livy explains that one of the emphases of his composition is "what life and morals were like" during the period covered by his history (*Hist.* 1.pr.9). He continues by expressing his desire that the reader should consider "how, with the gradual relaxation of discipline, morals first gave way, as it were, then sank lower and lower, and finally began the downward plunge which has brought us to the present time" (*Hist.* 1.pr.9). Livy then presents the reader with the main benefit of historical writings:

> What chiefly makes the study of history wholesome and profitable is this, that you behold the lessons of every kind of experience set forth as on a conspicuous monument; from these you may choose for yourself and for your own state what to imitate, from these mark for avoidance what is shameful in the conception and shameful in the result. (*Hist.* 1.pr.10)

Here one clearly sees that for Diodorus and Livy, the study of history has an ethical purpose in that the reader of history is presented with examples, both positive (which are to be imitated) and negative (which are to be shunned).[3]

Plutarch envisions a similar purpose for his *Lives*. His goal for the *Lives* is best seen in the introduction to two of these works. In the opening lines of *Timoleon*, Plutarch writes:

> I began the writing of my "Lives" for the sake of others, but I find that I am continuing the work and delighting in it now for my own sake also, using history as a mirror and endeavoring in a manner to fashion and adorn my life in conformity with the virtues therein depicted. (*Tim.* 1.1)

A similar thought is found in the introduction to the *Life* of Pericles:

> A color is suited to the eye if its freshness, and its pleasantness as well, stimulates and nourishes the vision; and so our intellectual vision must be applied to such objects as, by their very charm, invite it onward to its own proper good.
>
> Such objects are to be found in virtuous deeds; these implant in those who search them out a great and zealous eagerness which leads to imitation. (*Per.* 1.3–4)

Plutarch was interested to show the "virtuous deeds" of his heroes in order that he and others might become familiar with them and eventually imitate them. To do so, he had to use "history as a mirror"; it was necessary for him to use historical accounts of these men and select those events which occurred in their lives that best showed their true character. Also, Plutarch had to shape his narratives in order to elicit a decision from his readers to imitate the character of those they read about in their own lives.[4]

Concerning the "character" of Plutarch's characters in the *Lives*, A. Wardman's comment is instructive; he writes:

> But character, for Plutarch, is not merely man as he is recorded in his actions. It is a shorthand for registering ideas about virtue

---

3. Cf. Dionysius of Halicarnassus, *Ant. rom.* 1.1.2; in the preface to his work, he states that historians "ought . . . to make choice of noble and lofty subjects and such as will be of great utility to their readers." Dionysius continues by arguing that the history of Rome is worthy of consideration because it is "a subject noble, lofty and useful to many" (*Ant. rom.* 1.2.1). See also the preface to Polybius's history, in which he states: "But all historians . . . have impressed on us that the soundest education and training for a life of active politics is the study of History, and that the surest and indeed the only method of learning how to bear bravely the vicissitudes of fortune, is to recall the calamities of others" (Polybius, *Hist.* 1.1.2).

4. Stadter, "Rhetoric," 251–69.

and for discussing what virtue is. By Plutarch's time it was common practice for philosophers to explain what they meant or recommended by virtue, by referring to well-known instances of virtuous action. *Authority and precedent* had replaced that argumentative enquiry into first principles which makes the Platonic dialogues of lasting interest (emphasis added).[5]

For the purposes of this study, Wardman's statement is illuminating, given what Cicero has to say about testimony, witnesses, and virtue in *Topica* (cf. *Top*. 19.73 and the discussion of this passage in chapter two). Cicero, in *Topica*, argued that the best witnesses were those who are authoritative; authority, in turn, depends on one's virtue. The gods, by nature, are virtuous and thus constitute the highest authority one can call as a witness. Therefore, this study will argue that through Plutarch's (and other ancient authors') writings, ancient audiences would have understood divine testimony to function as a method of authoritatively witnessing to the virtuous character of a person in a narrative.[6]

These compositions of differing genres (historiographical—Diodorus and Livy; ancient biography, or βίος—Plutarch) exhibit similar purposes, that of encouraging readers to consider carefully the characters portrayed and the events described as exemplars of how one should (and should not) live. On the one hand, R. Burridge describes βίος as an ancient genre "nestling between history, encomium and moral philosophy, with overlaps and relationships in all directions."[7] βίος is historic in that it deals with events that occurred in the heroes' lives which took place in the past;[8] it is encomiastic in that the heroes' virtuous deeds are praised.[9] Finally, it

---

5. Wardman, *Plutarch's Lives*, 36.

6. The converse is of course also true; the lack of virtue of a character can also be emphasized through divine testimony. As will be shown, this is certainly not the only function of the *topos* of divine testimony.

7. Burridge, *What are the Gospels?* 68.

8. Russell notes, however, in discussing Plutarch's *Lives*, that "chronology and development in time are of secondary concern even though the overall arrangement . . . is chronologically straightforward." This is due to the fact that Plutarch's main concern is not the historic aspect of the life, rather to answer the question (as Russell states), "What sort of man was he?" (Russell, *Plutarch*, 102).

9. Wardman, commenting on Plutarch, is cautious at this point: "The eulogy or encomium is not to be regarded as a distant forbear of Plutarchian biography" (Wardman, *Plutarch's Lives*, 10). He offers four major differences between the *Lives* and a "typical encomium, if we can allow ourselves to conceive of such a thing." These are: (i) An encomiast uses all events in the subject's life as praise, including "passive events" (i.e., good luck), whereas Plutarch generally does not consider luck a category to be praised;

is similar to moral philosophy in that the reader is called on to judge (and eventually imitate) the virtues displayed by the heroes.[10]

On the other hand, T. Penner argues convincingly that ancient historians[11] in the first century were writing what he calls "epideictic history."[12] As evidence, Penner cites Cicero, who argued that history, like rhetoric, was to be persuasive in nature and linked the writing of history to epideictic rhetoric.[13] In summarizing the motivation for the writing of history in the ancient world, Penner lists the following four factors: (i) there was a utilitarian motivation to the writing of history—i.e., history was intended to benefit the auditor through instruction (*paideia*); (ii) history was written in order to overcome the perceived weaknesses of others' histories; (iii) there was an overarching emphasis on morality and virtue in ancient historiography; and lastly, (iv) ancient historians were motivated to write coherent, plausible narratives which described the events and also contained the elements of persuasion necessary to accomplish their purposes.[14]

(ii) the encomiast credits the good fortune of the hero's country to the hero more than Plutarch ("the worth of political life is not to be measured by the degree of imperialist power"); (iii) the encomiast assumes, more than Plutarch, that the audience is familiar with the subject; (iv) there is a mutual dependence between the encomiast and the hero that is not found in Plutarch. The encomiast has the difficult task of describing the greatness of the subject, but the greatness of the subject is dependent on the work of the encomiast. Plutarch considers, however, that his heroes' actions speak for themselves; he himself adds nothing to them. See Wardman, *Plutarch's Lives*, 14–15.

10. Talbert states, "Plutarch's main purpose in writing these Lives was clearly a moral one. He wanted to provide for the imitation of noble examples"; Talbert, *What is a Gospel?*, 96.

11. To some degree I am creating a false dichotomy between the genres of βίος and historiography in the ancient world. While they are certainly different genres, I have already noted above the element of history found in a βίος. Penner rightly argues that in the first century what one finds is a conflation of various genres, including biography, historiography, and that of novel. Thus, he can state, similar to Burridge (see above), that "the line between history, encomium, and biography was becoming difficult to establish firmly"; Penner, *In Praise*, 135. On this point, see Cape, "Persuasive History," 212–28. Cape argues that the emphasis in rhetoric at the time of Cicero was on accomplishing a particular goal (see previous chapter in which I have made this same point), which included bringing change and emotionally affecting audiences. Therefore, because history and oratory shared many of the same ends, Cape concludes that it is not surprising they would use some of the same means.

12. Penner, *In Praise*, 114.

13. Penner, *In Praise*, 125–26; Penner specifically mentions Cicero, *De or.* 2.36; *Leg.* 1.2.5; and Quintilian, *Inst.* 12.11.4.

14. Penner, *In Praise*, 174–79. See also Rothschild, *Luke-Acts*. Rothschild maintains that beginning in the fifth century BCE, due to the need and desire to champion their account of history, ancient historians used various contemporary means to

Divine Testimony through Utterances in Hellenistic Narratives

It is at this point of narrative that I wish now to bring Luke-Acts into the discussion. It is tempting to equate Luke-Acts with the genre of βίος or ancient historiography and therefore argue that it, too, is persuasive literature, as the other exemplars of its genre. There continues to be, however, a great deal of debate concerning the genre of Luke-Acts, particularly that of Acts.[15] Thus it is best to draw comparisons between Luke-Acts and other ancient writings at the level of narrative. I have argued above that works such as ancient βίοι and historiography are narratives written with persuasive intentions. I will now attempt to demonstrate that the author of Luke-Acts also intended to write a persuasive narrative.

In the preface to the Third Gospel, Luke writes:

> Ἐπειδήπερ πολλοὶ ἐπεχείρησαν ἀνατάξασθαι διήγησιν περὶ τῶν πεπληροφορημένων ἐν ἡμῖν πραγμάτων, καθὼς παρέδοσαν ἡμῖν οἱ ἀπ' ἀρχῆς αὐτόπται καὶ ὑπηρέται γενόμενοι τοῦ λόγου, ἔδοξε κἀμοὶ παρηκολουθηκότι ἄνωθεν πᾶσιν ἀκριβῶς καθεξῆς σοι γράψαι, κράτιστε Θεόφιλε, ἵνα ἐπιγνῷς περὶ ὧν κατηχήθης λόγων τὴν ἀσφάλειαν. (Luke 1:1-4)

Here one recognizes that Luke is writing a διήγησις in order that his auditors, particularly Theophilus, might have assurance of what they have been taught. M. Parsons has considered Luke-Acts in conjunction with the preliminary exercises as described by Theon;[16] Parsons concludes that the progymnasmata assist the reader in understanding many of Luke's literary conventions.[17] In his discussion of Theon's preliminary exercise of narrative,[18] Parsons notes that Theon emphasizes the quality of

---

"authenticate" their accounts. These methods drew from "epic, tragic, and scientific approaches." Rothschild compares the historians and their readers/auditors to lawyers attempting to convince the judge and jury of the validity of their cases. Therefore, this literature was by nature persuasive; Rothschild, *Luke-Acts*, 95. Cf. also Marincola, *Authority and Tradition*.

15. It is accepted by many that the Third Gospel is comparable to a βίος; see, e.g., Talbert, *What is a Gospel?*; Burridge, *What are the Gospels?* On the genre of Acts, see Phillips, "The Genre of Acts," 365-96. Phillips surveys recent scholarship on the question of the genre of Acts and concludes that a consensus seems to be forming around the idea that Acts is a combination of features found in various ancient writings, including that of βίοι, historiography, novels, and scientific treatises.

16. Parsons, *Luke*, 15-39.

17. Parsons does not argue that there is a direct dependence between Luke-Acts and Theon's *Progymnasmata*. Rather, the preliminary exercises as described by Theon offer a view of basic rhetorical practices in the first century, rhetorical practices that would have been common currency among authors and auditors in the ancient world.

18. Parsons, *Luke*, 22-25.

The *Topos* of Divine Testimony in Luke/Acts

"plausibility/ persuasiveness" in a narrative, and that Luke exhibits this quality, especially when compared to one of his sources, the Gospel of Mark.[19] E. Güttgemanns also argues that the fact that Luke is writing a διήγησις is evidence that Luke-Acts is a persuasive work.[20] In this essay, Güttgemanns cites both Quintilian (*Inst.* 4.2.31) and Cicero (*Part. or.* 9.31) in maintaining that because Luke-Acts is a narrative, it must contain argumentative elements, including proofs.[21] Significantly, for the purposes of the present study, Güttgemanns argues that: (i) there is a connection between narration as described in the rhetorical handbooks and proofs; (ii) rhetoric is a narrative art through which a speaker/author elucidates a specific issue; (iii) in rhetoric, persuasion is primary; (iv) within rhetoric proofs and arguments are communicated.[22] Güttgemanns also notes that the narrative which follows Luke's preface serves as a confirmation of what Theophilus has already been taught.

Other scholars, from their studies of the preface to the Third Gospel, note that Luke sets out to construct a narrative, which is persuasive by nature. For example, V. Robbins[23] examines Luke 1:1–4 as well as Acts 1:1 in connection with ancient didactic βίοι, finding affinities between Luke's writings and these βίοι. He then compares the prefaces to Luke-Acts to the latter section of Acts (Acts 15–28) and finds intertextual evidence between the prefaces and the letters and defense speeches in Acts. Thus, Robbins

---

19. Specifically, Parsons cites the calling of the disciples as an example of the more plausible/persuasive nature of Luke's narrative (ibid., 24–25). While Mark simply states that Jesus appears and calls Andrew and Simon, who dutifully follow, Luke prefaces his account with multiple miracle stories. These miracle accounts make the end result, i.e. the disciples' decision to follow Jesus, more persuasive. Parsons, in examining Luke 1:1–4 for rhetorical influences (ibid., 40–50), concludes that Luke is attempting to improve upon his sources (i.e., Mark) by compiling a more plausible and well-ordered narrative, one that, for example, begins with the birth account of Jesus. Parsons cites other scholars who argue that Luke is critiquing his sources; see ibid., 50nn31–32. In addition to those cited by Parsons, see K. Yamada, "The Preface," 161–64. Yamada is mainly arguing that Luke's preface indicates he is writing history, not a scientific treatise as claimed by L. Alexander (see, e.g., "Luke's Preface," 48–74; idem, *The Preface*); see also Robbins, "Prefaces," 94–108, and idem, "The Claims of the Prologues," 63–83.

20. Güttgemanns, "In welchem Sinne," 9–26. In this essay, Güttgemanns specifically analyzes what he calls "technical terms" within the Lukan prologue which point to the rhetorical nature of Luke-Acts.

21. Ibid., 14–20. Specifically, Güttgemanns lists ten assertions which follow from his analysis of Luke-Acts as a narrative as described by Quintilian and Cicero.

22. Here Güttgemanns cites Cicero, *Inv.* 1.24.34, a passage I have already referenced, in which Cicero introduces the sources of proofs.

23. Robbins, "Prefaces."

concludes that Luke-Acts is a type of didactic βίος, written in defense of Christianity, and therefore contains persuasive elements.

Some scholars highlight the fact that, in the prologue to Luke's Gospel, it is stated that Luke's purpose is to confirm what Theophilus has already been taught and is thus persuasive. For example, R. Dillon examines Luke 1:1–4 in view of the greater narrative in which it is found.[24] Dillon's purpose is fourfold, namely to examine: (i) the context in which Luke-Acts was written; (ii) the subject matter addressed; (iii) the procedure the author utilized; and (iv) the purpose of the writings. For the purposes of the present study and the current argument, (iii) and (iv) are most significant.[25] According to Dillon, the procedure the author used was to narrate the traditions used as sources not in chronological order, but rather in an order that was appropriate for relating sacred history.[26] Finally, the purpose of the work was to relate both the words and deeds of Jesus and his followers in an attempt to convict and bring certainty, not simply to pass along historical knowledge.[27]

Therefore, given the emphasis on persuasion found in ancient narratives of diverse genres, it is appropriate that one scrutinizes these writings through a rhetorical lens, with the goal of identifying how ancient auditors would have understood the proofs and arguments found within them.[28] It is to this task that I now turn. In the following analysis, I will attempt to identify the *topos* of divine testimony through utterances in works roughly contemporary with Luke-Acts, seeking in each case to determine its rhetorical function within the narratives. This information will then be used

---

24. Dillon, "Previewing Luke's Project," 205–27.

25. Concerning the context, Dillon claims that Luke-Acts constitutes a narrative/kerygma combination written to a group two generations removed from Jesus himself. Regarding the subject matter, Dillon emphasizes that Luke is not only relating events, but how those events have been "brought to full measure" in the lives of those to whom the writings are addressed. Dillon, "Previewing Luke's Project," 206–17.

26. Ibid., 217–23. Others have since made similar arguments, all of which revolve around the fact that Luke's narrative is in order in a rhetorical, persuasive sense, but not necessarily in strict chronological order. Acts 10–11 is often cited as an example. See, e.g., Parsons, *Luke*, 44–47; Tannehill, *Gospel According to Luke*, 9–12.

27. Dillon, "Previewing Luke's Project," 223–27. See also Tannehill, *Gospel According to Luke*, 9–12.

28. For overviews of the rhetorical nature of Luke and/or Acts, see, e.g., Kennedy, *Rhetorical Criticism*, 107–8 (Third Gospel in general), 114–40 (speeches in Acts); Satterthwaite, "Acts Against the Background of Classical Rhetoric," 337–79; Burridge, "Gospels and Acts," 507–32.

The *Topos* of Divine Testimony in Luke/Acts

in analyzing Luke-Acts, ultimately to determine how ancient auditors of this work would have understood this *topos*.

This investigation of extra-biblical sources is not meant to be exhaustive. To attempt to determine all the instances of divine testimony in narrative sources written around the time of Luke-Acts would be beyond the scope of this study. Therefore, several works, including histories, annals, and biographies, written from the third century BCE through the second century CE, will be surveyed. I will include writings from Greco-Roman, Jewish, and early Christian sources. From these documents, enough examples will be elucidated to sketch the aforementioned "horizon of expectations" of Luke's original audience.

In the analysis of these works concerning the use of the *topos* of divine testimony through utterances, it is important to keep in mind one of the significant, overarching purposes of the works, namely that of providing examples of people and situations so that auditors might learn from them and, in some cases, imitate them.[29] Because a *topos* is applied as a form of proof, one should expect that the application of this particular *topos* in most cases will somehow serve the overall purpose of the project in which it is found. Therefore, the overarching rhetorical function of this *topos* is the gods' testimony concerning individuals, groups, and events that occur within the narratives. Through these deeds the gods express their judgments and attitudes toward the characters and their actions. Thus, the *topos* serves as a form of characterization, both for individuals and groups.[30]

---

29. Clearly the converse is also possible, i.e., the avoidance of those who are less than virtuous.

30. Pritcher, in discussing the portrayal of characters in ancient historical works, argues that one method of characterization in these works occurs when a character is implicitly compared to another character within the narrative. Pitcher terms this "structural characterization"; see Pitcher, "Characterization," 1:112–15. As I will show, this often occurs within the context of divine testimony, in that the gods will show approval of a character through their testimony, and simultaneously demonstrate disdain for another, often an opponent of the "approved" character. Russell makes note of this in discussing the syncrises within Plutarch's lives; he states, "The character of a hero may be clarified by a succession of comparisons with others." Russell argues that Plutarch uses the technique of syncrisis throughout the *Lives*; syncrises are not limited to the formal comparisons that accompany many of the paired *Lives* ("Thus what we may call 'syncritical' technique is used throughout to throw the main character into relief and display both his virtues and his limitations"). See Russell, "On Reading," 89–90. On characterization through religious themes, see also Levene, *Religion in Livy*, 34, who suggests that Livy possibly introduces religious elements into his *Historiae* "to characterize individuals." The comment of Swain concerning divine intervention in

Divine Testimony through Utterances in Hellenistic Narratives

The analysis of the *topos* of divine testimony through utterances (as Cicero expressed: "The testimony of the gods is covered thoroughly enough by the following: first, utterances, for oracles get their name from the fact that they contain an utterance [*oratio*] of the gods; secondly, things in which are embodied certain works of the gods" [*Top.* 20.76-77]) as found in Hellenistic narratives will proceed in three phases. First, I will provide examples of the testimony of the gods through direct, divine speech from Hellenistic biographies, histories, and other narratives. Next, I will consider instances of divine speech through an intermediary ("inspired" speech) from these same sources. Finally, I will investigate divine testimony through oracles. In each case the divine testimony will be examined for its function within the narrative context in which it is located. In the following chapter, I will then analyze Luke-Acts and provide examples from these same three categories. Through these two chapters my goal is to demonstrate that an ancient audience, given the extra-biblical evidence of divine testimony through utterances, would have understood the instances of divine speech in Luke-Acts to function in a similar manner,[31] and that the *topos* is used rhetorically to sanction characters and the movements of which they are a part in the narrative.

As stated above, this analysis will be divided into three parts: divine testimony through direct speech; divine testimony through an intermediary; and divine testimony through oracles. It is to these examples that I now turn, beginning with instances of divine testimony through direct speech.

DIVINE TESTIMONY THROUGH DIRECT SPEECH

In this category I have chosen to include voices that characters hear for which there is no discernible source.[32] In general, divine voices are sources

---

Plutarch is also worthy of quotation: "We should not forget that the involvement of suprahuman power in men's lives often functions as a moral or ethical register—how does a hero get on in a particular circumstance?" Swain goes on to aver that Plutarch did not see humans as robots, completely subject to the divine will. "Rather, what men have to offer in terms of virtue or benefits is made use of by the divine to carry out its wishes." See Swain, "Plutarch," 275–76.

31. I will especially argue that ancient auditors would have understood the function, on a narrative level, of oracles in Hellenistic narratives similarly to the role of the Jewish scriptures in Luke-Acts.

32. Hanson, "Dreams and Visions," 1395–427, includes a category which he terms an "auditory dream-vision" (1411–12). This category, however, is one in which the

The *Topos* of Divine Testimony in Luke/Acts

of warning and guidance, but, as will be demonstrated, are not limited to these functions. Examples from Hellenistic histories,[33] as well as Jewish and early Christian literature, will suffice to illustrate this method of the *topos* of divine testimony.

First, Dionysius of Halicarnassus describes a scene in a battle between the Tyrrhenians and the Romans in which a voice plays a prominent role (*Ant. rom.* 5.16.1–3).[34] According to Dionysius, both armies had suffered greatly in previous combat. But, Dionysius mentions that "there was greater dejection and despair of their cause on the side of the Romans because of the death of their leader;[35] and the thought occurred to many of them that it would be better for them to quit their camp before break of day" (*Ant. rom.* 5.16.2). The Romans are thus characterized as already beaten and ready to quit the fight. It is at this point that the gods testify in order to encourage the Roman soldiers:

> While they were considering these things and discussing them among themselves, about the time of the first watch a voice was heard from the grove near which they were encamped, calling aloud to both armies in such a manner as to be heard by all of them; it may have been the voice of the hero to whom the precinct was consecrated, or it may have been that of Faunus, as he is called . . . The voice of the divinity exhorted the Romans to be of good courage, as having gained the victory, and declared that the enemy's dead exceeded theirs by one man. (*Ant. rom.* 5.16.2–3)

At their lowest point, a god[36] speaks clearly to the Roman soldiers, encouraging them with the news that their losses were not as bad as the enemy's, and the prophecy that they will win the battle. The *topos* functions here as

---

voice that is heard is perceived through some type of dream or vision. Hanson uses Acts 18:9 as an example: Εἶπεν δὲ ὁ κύριος ἐν νυκτὶ δι' ὁράματος τῷ Παύλῳ. Therefore, what I am discussing here would not fit this category; what I am considering are voices that are not associated with any kind of visual experience, whether waking or sleeping.

33. Bevan, *Sibyls and Seers*, 99–101, argues that while divine communication through an audible voice is common in OT literature, it "is hardly known amongst the Greeks." In Roman literature, according to Bevan, it is much more prevalent. Aune (*Prophecy*, 431 n. 146) disagrees, but fails to provide any evidence for his position.

34. A similar account is also found in Livy, *Hist.* 2.7.2.

35. This is a reference to Brutus, who had been killed in a fight with Arruns, a son of Tarquinius, who had challenged Brutus to man-to-man combat; cf. *Ant. rom.* 5.15.1–4.

36. Which god is not clear, even to Dionysius. Livy states that it was Silvanus (*Hist.* 2.7.2).

Divine Testimony through Utterances in Hellenistic Narratives

divine revelation, but also as evidence that the gods were on the side of the Romans, rather than their enemies.

Another example of the testimony of the gods through voices comes from Livy.[37] Livy relates that Marcus Caedicius, who was a plebeian, was in the Nova Via at night when he heard a voice "more distinct than a man's, which bade him tell the magistrates that the Gauls were approaching" (*Hist.* 5.32.6).[38] Unfortunately, when this was reported, the magistrates failed to heed the warning, and the Gauls eventually sacked Rome. At this point in the narrative, the voice serves as a simple warning, and therefore a prophecy of impending peril. But this does not comprise the entire function of the divine testimony in the greater narrative context.

The warning received by Marcus Caedicius is referenced by Camillus after the defeat of the Gauls,[39] in the context of addressing the senate. Livy describes Camillus as having "scrupulous attention to religion" (*Hist.* 5.49.8); in demonstration of this aspect of his character, Camillus orders that a temple be built "for propitiating the voice which was heard in the night to foretell disaster before the Gallic War, and was disregarded" (*Hist.* 5.50.5). Therefore, this instance of divine testimony is invoked in a later, deliberative setting. Camillus uses the previously received testimony of the gods, a warning issued by a voice, to convince the senate of the need to build a temple.[40]

A third example of this use of the *topos* comes from Plutarch's *Life of Lycurgus*. The context for the passage is somewhat unusual; it is found within a lengthy description of the form of παιδεία instituted by Lycurgus.

---

37. Cf. Cicero, *Div.* 1.45.101.

38. On the surface, there is no divine origin to the voice. The context, however, requires it. Livy adds the following parenthetical comment concerning the Nova Via: "where the chapel now stands above the temple of Vesta" (5.32.6). From this statement, and a later reference in the narrative (that a temple was erected to propitiate this voice which was ignored; cf. 5.50.5 and comments below), one can rightly understand the voice to have had divine origins. Cicero also understands the voice in this way. In *Div.* 1.45.101, he writes: "Not long before the capture of the city by the Gauls, a voice, issuing from Vesta's sacred grove, which slopes from the foot of the Palatine Hill to the New Road, was heard to say, 'the walls and gates must be repaired; unless this is done the city will be taken.'"

39. Livy attributes the defeat of the Gauls to the gods and human beings: "But neither gods nor men would suffer the Romans to live ransomed" (*Hist.* 5.49.1). "Ransomed" refers to the payment of gold demanded by the Gauls from the Romans.

40. Linderski, "Roman Religion," 55, states: "And Camillus, assailing in a grand speech the plan to move the capital to Veii, after Rome was destroyed by the Gauls, adduces solely religious arguments, above all this: *Urben auspicatio inauguratoque conditam habemus* (5.52.2)."

The *Topos* of Divine Testimony in Luke/Acts

The section in question begins in *Lyc.* 14,[41] and continues through *Lyc.* 25.5. In *Lyc.* 23, however, Plutarch provides various historians' opinions on Lycurgus's reputation as a soldier.[42] Within this short section, Plutarch states:

> And yet there are some who say, as Hermippus reminds us, that at the outset Lycurgus had nothing whatever to do with Iphitus and his enterprise, but happened to come that way by chance, and be a spectator at the games; that he heard behind him, however, what seemed to be a human voice, chiding him and expressing amazement that he did not urge his fellow-citizens to take part in the great festival; and since, on turning round, he did not see the speaker anywhere, he concluded that the voice was from heaven, and therefore betook himself to Iphitus, and assisted him in giving the festival a more notable arrangement and a more enduring basis. (*Lyc.* 23.2)

Within the immediate context of this passage, Plutarch notes two dissenting opinions concerning Lycurgus. Hippias the Sophist maintains that Lycurgus was "very well versed in war and took part in many campaigns" (23.1); this statement is supported by data from Philostephanus. However, Demetrius the Phalerean argues that "he engaged in no warlike undertakings, and established his constitution in a time of peace" (23.1).

Plutarch continues by stating that "indeed, the design of the Olympic truce would seem to bespeak a man of gentleness, and predisposed to peace" (23.2), thus apparently agreeing with the opinion of Demetrius the Phalerean. Plutarch then goes on to explain the voice from heaven, which encouraged Lycurgus to ally himself with Iphitus in promoting the Olympic festival.[43] Because the Olympiad was essentially a sacred festival,[44]

---

41. *Lyc.* 14.1: "Τῆς δὲ παιδείας, . . ."

42. Thus, it seems to function as a "narrative aside." On the use of narrative asides in Luke-Acts, see Sheeley, *Narrative Asides*. Sheeley lists three figures of speech noted by Quintilian that address various ways in which speeches are interrupted (*Narrative Asides*, 31–32). Of those listed (*parenthesis*, *apostrophē*, and *parekbasis*), this digression in Plutarch's narrative is best seen as an example of *parekbasis*. Quintilian states that a *parekbasis* is implemented in a speech to "allow excurses of various kinds at all points in the Cause: for instance, Encomia of persons or places, descriptions of areas, exposition of historical or legendary events" (*Inst.* 4.3.12). He continues: "A *parekbasis*, in my view, is the treatment of a theme relevant to the purposes of the Cause that branches out from the basic structure" (*Inst.* 4.3.14).

43. On Lycurgus's role in establishing the Olympiad and the various traditions surrounding it, see Chrimes, *Ancient Sparta*, 319–47.

44. See Littlewood, "Olympic Games," 514–15. The first day of the Olympiad seems

Divine Testimony through Utterances in Hellenistic Narratives

Plutarch's narration of the divine voice functions as divine guidance to Lycurgus, simultaneously providing divine sanction on Lycurgus's participation in and promotion of the festival. This short encomium of Lycurgus, based upon an instance of divine testimony through utterances, therefore serves as evidence of the statement that Plutarch makes in the syncrisis of Lycurgus and Numa: "For their points of likeness are obvious from their careers: their wise moderation, their *piety* [εὐσέβεια], their talent for governing and educating, and their both deriving their laws from a divine source" (*Comp. Lyc. Num.* 1.1; emphasis added).

Another example of a divine voice is found in Josephus's list of portents, which he associates with the fall of Jerusalem. Josephus describes seven portents, the last of which is a voice which emanates from the temple during the celebration of the feast of Pentecost:[45] "[T]he priests . . . reported that they were conscious, first of a commotion and a din, and after that of a voice as of a host [φωνῆς ἀθρόας], 'We are departing hence'" (*B.J.* 6.299–300).[46] That the voice is of divine origin is not explicitly stated, but the context demands that one understand that it is. First, the voice is heard within a cluster of omens and portents, the divine origin of which cannot be disputed. Second, the voice comes from the inner parts of the temple while the priests are on duty, thus supplying a context of prayer and worship with which the divine testimony is associated.[47] Finally, the voice is described as ἀθρόας, thus adding significance to it.

The voice serves to reinforce other portents which are occurring at the same time. In this context, the voice serves as a warning to the people to leave the temple. Others, however, who do not understand the significance of the portents, dupe the people into believing that staying is their best alternative.

Divine voices are also found in non-canonical, early Christian narratives. Two examples will illustrate the use of this *topos* in this literature.

---

to have been set aside for prayer and acts of sacrifice, as were the third and sixth days as well.

45. The first six include a star in the shape of a sword, a bright light which illuminates the altar in the temple, a cow which gives birth to a lamb, a massive gate which moves without being pushed, and an apparition of chariots in the air. See *B.J.* 6.288-99; I will treat these aspects of the divine testimony through deeds later in chapter five.

46. Tacitus also records this voice, but gives it a slightly more explicit divine origin: "Of a sudden the doors of the shrine opened and a superhuman voice cried [*et audita maior humana vox*]: 'The gods are departing'" (*Hist.* 5.13).

47. Through this analysis it will be demonstrated that divine testimony of all types occurs quite often within this context.

The *Topos* of Divine Testimony in Luke/Acts

The first instance of a divine voice is found in *Martyrdom of Polycarp*. Significantly, it occurs just after Polycarp has been described as being in prayer,[48] and as Polycarp goes before the proconsul to be examined; thus, Polycarp begins his trial.[49] As he does, the text reads: "But as he entered the stadium a voice came to Polycarp from heaven [φωνὴ ἐξ οὐρανοῦ ἐγένετο]: 'Be strong Polycarp, and be a man [ἴσχθε, Πολύκαρπε, καὶ ἀνδρίζου]'" (*Mart. Pol.* 9.1). There is no doubt concerning the source of the voice; it is clearly stated that it is from heaven.[50] It is also clear how the divine testimony functions in the narrative. Polycarp, who has demonstrated his piety through his two hours of prayer, enters into his trial and receives encouragement through the divine voice to be brave. The overarching function of the *topos*, however, especially given the context of the trial, is to pronounce Polycarp innocent, even before the trial begins.

A second example of divine testimony through direct speech in early Christian, non-canonical writings is found in the Gospel of Peter. In the account of Jesus' resurrection, a heavenly voice is heard twice.

> But when the morning of the Sabbath dawned, a crowd from Jerusalem and the region round about came that they might see the sealed sepulcher. But in the night in which the Lord's day dawned, . . . there was a great voice in heaven [μεγάλη φωνὴ ἐγένετο ἐν τῷ οὐρανῷ]. And they saw the heavens opened, and two men descend from there in a great brightness and approach the tomb . . . And while [the soldiers] were telling what they had seen, again they saw three men coming out from the tomb, and two of them supporting one, and a cross following them, and the head of the two reaching to heaven, but that of the one who was led by them overpassing the heavens. And they heard a voice out of the heavens [καὶ φωνῆς ἤκουον ἐκ τῶν οὐρανῶν] saying: "Have

---

48. "And [Polycarp] asked [his captors] for an hour to pray without being disturbed. When they gave their permission, he stood and prayed, being so filled with God's grace that for two hours he could not be silent" (*Mart. Pol.* 8.2–3). The description of his prayer is also noteworthy: "Then he finished his prayer, having remembered everyone he had ever met, both small and great, reputable and disreputable, as well as the entire universal church throughout the world" (*Mart. Pol.* 9.1).

49. On the proconsul's ability to conduct trials and assess penalties, see Sherman-White, *Roman Society*, 1–23.

50. Schoedel (*Polycarp*, 64) maintains that the voice is an element of the *imitatio Christi* that is found throughout this document. Schoedel cites John 12:28 as a parallel from the NT.

Divine Testimony through Utterances in Hellenistic Narratives

you preached to those who sleep?" And a response was heard from the cross: "Yes." (*Gos. Pet.* 9.34–10.42)[51]

The divine origin of the voice is explicitly stated in both cases. The voice primarily serves to explain the event of the resurrection, an extraordinary occurrence. But to understand fully the function of this testimony, one must consider the greater narrative context in which the voice occurs.

Prior to the resurrection scene in which the auditor experiences the divine voice(s), the "Jews and the elders and the priests" make a statement following Jesus' death; the text states: "they began to lament and to say: 'Woe on our sins! Judgment has come close and the end of Jerusalem'" (*Gos. Pet.* 9.34–10.42). Here one understands that those who earlier called for Jesus' death now regret what they have done. After the passage in question, the text states that "when those who were with the centurion[52] saw this, they hurried by night to Pilate . . . and reported everything they had seen. They were greatly distressed and said: 'In truth he was the Son of God'" (*Gos. Pet.* 11.45). Therefore, given this context, in which those who witnessed this resurrection event and thus recognized the true identity and innocence of Jesus, the divine testimony through the voice of God serves to reinforce this conclusion. It also functions as a legitimation of those who explain to Pilate that "in truth he was the Son of God" (11.45).[53]

In sum, divine voices in these narratives serve to encourage the hearers, issue a warning through prophecy, give guidance to the one who hears the voice, and to explain an extraordinary event in the narrative. Also, I have shown that a voice from the gods was used in a deliberative setting in an attempt to convince a group of people of a course of action (in this case, the building of a temple). In all cases, the voices also function as the gods' (or God's) testimony toward a person or group of people, sanctioning their actions within the narrative, or, in the case of Polycarp, to declare him innocent of any wrongdoing. Thus, as in ancient speeches, divine testimony through the gods' speech is used to cast characters in both a positive and negative light.

---

51. All English translations of *The Gospel of Peter* are from Kraus and Nicklas, *Das Petrusevangelium und die Petrusapokalypse*.

52. This group includes "the elders [τοὺς πρεσβυτέρους]"; cf. 10.38.

53. See Omerzu, "Die Pilatusgestalt," 340. Concerning the voice in 10.41 (as well as 10.35), Omerzu states: "Die Rede wird jeweils als Wahrnehmung der Wachen dargestellt." He continues: "Die Zuverlässigkeit des Zeugnisses wird dadurch bekräftigt, dass die Soldaten als gehorsame und gewissenhafte Befehlsempfänger gezeichnet werden."

The *Topos* of Divine Testimony in Luke/Acts

Divine Testimony through the Speech of an Inspired Intermediary

In this section I will consider examples of figures in narratives who are speaking the words of a deity, normally being described as inspired in some way.[54] Most of the examples from Hellenistic sources involve the Pythia; there are, however, as I will demonstrate, other examples of human beings with no prophetic vocation who speak for the gods. This analysis will make clear that this type of divine testimony functions similarly to the direct speech of the gods, discussed in the previous section.

The first example is from Diodorus Siculus's history of Rome, and involves a response by the Pythia which settles a dispute between warring peoples. Diodorus explains that Tachos, a general leading Spartan and Egyptian forces against the Persians, founded the city of Leucê. Soon after Tachos's death, the citizens of Clazomenae and Cymae went to war over the rightful possession of this city. Some time later, "someone suggested that the god be asked [ἐρωτῆσαι θεόν] which one of the two cities should be master of Leucê" (*Hist.* 15.18.2). Diodorus then adds,

> The Pythia decided [ἔκρινεν Πυθία] that it should be the one which should first offer sacrifice in Leucê, and that each side should start from his own city at the rising of the sun on a day upon which both should agree. (*Hist.* 15.18.2)

From this narrative, it is clear that Diodorus equates the speech of the Pythia with that of the god.[55] The response of the Pythia serves as divine

---

54. There has been a great deal written concerning inspired speech in the ancient world and in the NT; much of this scholarship is devoted to exploring the link between oracular, inspired speech and glossolalia in the NT. For a current overview, focusing on the phenomenon of glossolalia in Corinth, see Forbes, *Prophecy and Inspired Speech*, 1–43. For a summary and explanation of the various prophets and seers associated with ancient oracular sites, see Aune, *Prophecy in Early Christianity*, 35–48. In this helpful section, Aune discusses the role of "technical diviners" (mantics for hire), the Sibyl and Bakis, θεομάντεις, χρησμοδόται, χρησμολόγοι (those who compiled and maintained oracular records), and ἐγγαστρίμυθοι (inspired prophets who spoke under spirit-possession), among others. Concerning prophecy through μανία, see Dodds, *The Greeks and the Irrational*, 64–101; in this chapter, Dodds discusses three types of "madness": "prophetic madness," focusing on Apollo; "ritual madness" in association with Dionysius; and "poetic madness," poetry written through the inspiration of the Muses.

55. This is certainly a case of suppliants seeking an oracle to decide a dispute between two parties; no oracle, per se, is mentioned. Divine testimony through oracles proper will be treated below. Here, no mention is made of the Pythia's inspiration; it was well-known, however, in the ancient world that the Pythia spoke for, and under

Divine Testimony through Utterances in Hellenistic Narratives

guidance for these two parties, and thus settles the dispute between the two groups. Through the divine guidance, the origins of the city are grounded in a divine decision. Interestingly, ultimately the Clazomenians win the contest by founding a new city nearer to Leucê than the Cymaeans.[56] Also through the divine testimony, the Cymaeans are portrayed as those willing to align themselves with the wishes of the god, which are made known through the Pythia.

While there are many examples of the Pythia speaking the words of Apollo, there are also instances in which a human being is inspired to speak divine words. I will consider several of these below. The first is also from Diodorus Siculus, and involves a statement made by Agesilaus, the Spartan king and military leader. The context involves the Spartan march against Thebes in the fourth century BCE. Agesilaus engaged the Thebans and a force of Athenian mercenaries near Thebes; his opponents, however, occupied the higher ground outside the city. When Agesilaus attacked, he first encountered the Athenian troops, who held their position as ordered. Seeing this, "Agesilaüs . . . judged it inadvisable to force a way against the higher ground and compel his opponents to show their valor in a hand-to-hand contest, and, having learned by trial that they would dare, if forced, to dispute the victory, he challenged them in the plain" (*Hist.* 15.32.6). The Thebans, however, refuse to leave their positions on the crest; therefore, Agesilaus leads his troops "to plunder the countryside unhampered, and so took a great quantity of spoil" (*Hist.* 15.32.6).

The Spartan officers subsequently question Agesilaus's decision not to press the attack. Diodorus explains that

---

the inspiration of, the god. For example, Plutarch writes, "[T]he god of this place [i.e., Delphi] employs the prophetic priestess [τῇ Πυθίᾳ] for men's ears just as the sun employs the moon for men's eyes. For he makes known and reveals his own thoughts, but he makes them known through the associated medium of a mortal body and a soul that is unable to keep quiet, or, as it yields itself to the One that moves it, to remain of itself unmoved and tranquil, but, as though tossed amid billows and enmeshed in the stirrings and emotions within itself, it makes itself more and more restless" (*Pyth. orac.* 404e). See also Plato, *Phaedr.* 244b: "For the prophetess [προφῆτις] at Delphi and the priestesses [ἱέρειαι] at Dodona when they have been mad have conferred many splendid benefits upon Greece both in private and in public affairs, but few or none when they have been in their right minds; and if we should speak of the Sibyl and all the others who by prophetic inspiration have foretold [μαντικῇ χρώμενοι ἐνθέῳ] many things to many persons and thereby made them fortunate afterwards, anyone can see that we should speak a long time."

56. Diodorus states that "ὁι δὲ Κλαζονένιοι, διάστημα πλέον ἀπέχοντες, τεχνάζονται τι τοιοῦτο πρὸς τὴν νίκην" (*Hist.* 15.18.3).

> as it was, the Lacedaemonians had won the victory without the risk; for when the countryside was being sacked, the Boeotians had not dared to rally to its defense; but if, when the enemy themselves had conceded the victory, he had forced them to endure the risks of battle, perhaps through the uncertainty of fortune the Lacedaemonians might even have come to grief in the contest. (*Hist.* 15.33.1)

Diodorus continues:

> Now at the time [Agesilaus] was thought in this reply of his to have estimated the possible outcome fairly well, but later in the light of events he was believed to have uttered no mere human saying but a divinely inspired oracle [οὐκ ἀνθρωπίνην ἀπόφασιν, ἀλλὰ θεῖόν τινα χρησμὸν εἰρηκέναι]. (*Hist.* 15.33.2)

The later events of which Diodorus writes involve the defeat of the Spartans at Leuctra and also at Mantineia, ending Spartan supremacy.[57]

Therefore, the inspired words spoken by Agesilaus demonstrate that his actions as military commander were indeed divinely led. While the words were initially understood to be wise, it was not until later events unfolded that they were seen to be prophetic. The divine testimony through Agesilaus serves to sanction his actions as military leader, and to highlight the disaster that later befalls the Spartans when they ignore the leadership of the gods.

A second example of a human being who is not associated with an oracular site, but nevertheless speaks inspired words, is found in Plutarch's *Life* of Themistocles. Here one learns that Themistocles is running from the Greeks who desire to capture him (*Them.* 26.1); he comes to Aegae, where he seeks safety at the house of his friend, Nicogenes. The auditor learns that "after the dinner, which followed a certain sacrifice [εἶτα μετὰ τὸ δεῖπον ἐκ θυσίας τινος]," Nicogenes's children's tutor (Olibus) became "rapt and inspired [ἔμφρων γενόμενος καὶ θεοφόρητος[58]]" and recited a verse:

---

57. "For the Lacedaemonians, having taken the field against the Thebans with a mighty army and having compelled them to fight for their freedom, met with a great disaster. They were defeated, namely, at Leuctra first, where they lost many of their citizen soldiers and their king Cleombrotus fell; and later, when they fought at Mantineia, they were utterly routed and hopelessly lost their supremacy" (*Hist.* 15.33.3). Diodorus's account of the Theban victory at Leuctra is found in *Hist.* 15.51.1–56.4. Significantly, the Spartans attack despite oracles which predicted their defeat; see Diodorus Siculus, *Hist.* 15.54.2. Cf. Plutarch, *Pel.* 20.4, an account I will address below.

58. On θεοφόρητος, cf. Dionysius of Halicarnassus, *Ant. rom.* 14.9.3, where he describes those fighting to protect their homeland: "Nature herself lends a certain

"Night shall speak, and night instruct thee, night shall give thee victory" (*Them.* 26.2). Olibus thus utters a divinely inspired prophecy which is fulfilled in the following narrative.

That night, Themistocles does indeed have a dream,[59] in which the gods testify that he would eventually find a safe haven in Persia. When Themistocles has an audience with the Persian king, he cites this dream (as well as an oracle; see below) as evidence of the divine providence that brought him to seek asylum in Persia, which the king provides for him. Therefore, the inspired speech of Olibus functions within this complex of divine testimonies as the gods' approval of the life and fate of Themistocles.

A third example of an inspired prophet is found in Josephus's account of the fall of Jerusalem. In this passage, Josephus elaborates on several portents that he associates with the Romans' sack of Jerusalem.[60] After discussing these portents, Josephus states: "But a further portent was even more alarming [τὸ δὲ τούτων φοβερώτερον]" (*B.J.* 6.300). This portent that Josephus describes occurs four years prior to the actual fall of Jerusalem during the Feast of Tabernacles. Josephus explains this event thusly:

> [O]ne Jesus, son of Ananias, a rude peasant, who, standing in the temple, suddenly began to cry out, "A voice from the east, a voice from the west, a voice from the four winds; a voice against Jerusalem and the sanctuary, a voice against the bridegroom and the bride, a voice against all the people." (*B.J.* 6.301–302)

That this man is an inspired prophet is proven through the context of the passage. First, his words are related within the narration of multiple divine testimonies concerning the fall of Jerusalem. Thus, Jesus's speech is to be understood as a further testimony of God. Second, the man speaks κατὰ τὸ ἱερόν, giving his words a divine origin. Third, and most significantly, Josephus explicitly states that the man is speaking under some type of inspiration: "Thereupon, the magistrates, supposing, as was indeed the case, that the man was under some supernatural impulse [νομίσαντες δ'

---

courage in the face of danger and gives them a spirit of ecstasy like that of men possessed by a god [πνεῦμα ἐνθουσιῶδες ὥσπερ τοῖς θεοφορήτος]." See also Dionysius of Halicarnassus, *Thuc.* 34.18, a passage in which Dionysius chides those who "have admired Thucydides immoderately, crediting him with nothing less than divine inspiration [ὡς μηδὲν τῶν θεοφορήτων διαφέρειν]."

59. This incident will also be discussed in chapter five, under the category of the *topos* of divine testimony through dreams.

60. See the treatment of this passage in chapter five under the category "Divine Testimony through Objects and Events in the Heavens." Also, see above concerning the voice that emanates from the temple during this same time.

οἱ ἄρχοντες, ὅπερ ἦν, δαιμονιώτερον τὸ κίνημα], brought him before the Roman governor" (*B.J.* 6.303).

The man refuses to cease prophesying, and is ultimately vindicated by the fall of Jerusalem.[61] Josephus himself provides the summary statement through which his auditors are to understand this divine testimony through inspired speech (along with the instances of divine testimony preceding it): "Reflecting on these things one will find that God has a care for men, and by all kinds of premonitory signs shows His people the way of salvation, while they owe their destruction to folly and calamities of their own choosing" (*B.J.* 6.310). Through the divine testimony, God is characterized as desiring to save his people, while the people are simultaneously portrayed as being foolish for disregarding God's words through the inspired prophet.

To summarize, divine testimony through the speech of intermediaries serves primarily as prophecy and to provide divine guidance and affirmation in particular situations. Fulfilled prophecies are ways in which the one issuing the prophecy is further legitimated within the greater narrative. The revelation of the will of the gods through divine testimony also allows the character who receives that revelation to align him or herself with the divine will, thus portraying that character as in concord with the desires of the gods.[62] Having discussed divine testimony through the direct speech of the gods and speech through an intermediary, I will now turn my attention to divine testimony through oracles.

Divine Testimony through Oracles

In the past there has been very little scholarship concerning the rhetorical use of oracles in Hellenistic histories and biographies.[63] Concerning

---

61. "So for seven years and five months he continued his wail, his voice never flagging nor his strength exhausted, until in the siege, having seen his presage verified [ἔργα κληδόνος], he found his rest" (*B.J.* 6.308).

62. Clearly, the converse is also true.

63. Rothschild laments this in her study; although she is specifically seeking studies which engage the topic of prophecy-fulfillment in ancient historiography, her statement is also true on a more general level. See Rothschild, *Luke-Acts*, 150. She lists Crahay, *La Littérature Oraculaire chez Hérodote*, and Momigliano, "Prophecy and Historiography," 101–8 (Rothschild, *Luke-Acts*, 150n33). As Rothschild mentions, Momigliano's study is concerned with the Sibylline oracles and their function within Jewish and Christian writings. Rothschild's own survey is confined to examples from Homer and ancient Greek histories (specifically, she analyzes passages from Herodotus

the historical analysis and evaluation of oracles, the converse is true.[64] My strategy here will be to survey references to oracles in Hellenistic histories and biographies with an eye toward their use as divine testimonies. As in the analyses above, I will seek to ascertain the rhetorical function of the account of the oracle within the narrative. Ultimately, this analysis will demonstrate that oracles, as with other forms of the *topos* of divine testimony, serve many functions, but the over-arching purpose is one of legitimation or disapproval of a character or characters within the narrative.

The analysis will consider instances of oracles in Hellenistic histories and biographies, categorized by how these references to oracles function within the narrative. It is to the analysis of these examples I now turn.

---

and Thucydides). In examining prophecy-fulfillment in Hellenistic historiographical works, she considers one example from Dionysius of Halicarnassus (*Ant. rom.* 1.23) and one from Josephus (*Ant.* 2.212ff). Her conclusion is that prophecy-fulfillment serves to provide divine substantiation for "implausible events" within the narratives. More specifically, the legitimation provided by the prophecy-fulfillment schema was "a means of appealing to more critical audiences through strategies of authentication" (*Luke-Acts*, 158). Squires, in his monograph (*Plan of God*, 121–51), includes a chapter (ibid., 121–51) in which he discusses the significance of fulfilled prophecies in Hellenistic literature and how prophecy-fulfillment emphasizes the βουλὴ τοῦ θεοῦ in Luke-Acts. C. Talbert has made an important contribution to the narrative function of oracles and their fulfillment in the ancient world; see his "Promise and Fulfillment," 91–103 (Rothschild recognizes this as well and engages Talbert in her survey of the history of scholarship concerning prophecy-fulfillment in Luke-Acts; see Rothschild, *Luke-Acts*, 146–48). Specifically concerning oracles, Talbert lists two ways in which oracles functioned in ancient narratives: the course of history was seen in fulfilled oracles (whether those oracles were rightly understood or not); and the mention of fulfilled oracles served to legitimate heroes and to give credibility to other utterances by those heroes. I will have more to say concerning this essay in the section below which deals with the citation of scripture in Luke-Acts.

64. On this subject the literature is vast and to survey it would exceed the scope of the present study. Representative works include: Parke and Wormell, *The Delphic Oracle* (this is a two-volume work: vol. 1 describes the history and inner workings of Delphi; vol. 2 is a compendium of oracular responses); Hoyle, *Delphi*; Parke, *Greek Oracles*; Bouché-Leclercq, *Histoire de la Divination*, 3:1–270; Fontenrose, *The Delphic Oracle*; Parker, "Greek States," 76–108; Bowden, *Classical Athens*.

Aune (*Prophecy in Early Christianity*, 23–79) provides a great deal of helpful background information concerning ancient oracular sites and those who administered them. Especially beneficial is his categorization of the various types of oracular questions and responses; see ibid., 52–77.

The *Topos* of Divine Testimony in Luke/Acts

Oracles as Fulfilled Prophecies

This category includes oracles that have been received at some time in the past,[65] and which are fulfilled by contemporary events. Often, as the events transpire, an oracle is recalled which is seen as being fulfilled. In this way, the oracle gives meaning to the event, but the reverse is also true; thus, event and oracle mutually interpret one another. Also in this category are those oracles which are fulfilled despite a character's misunderstanding of them. A third type of oracle as fulfilled prophecy includes particularly enigmatic oracles which require correct interpretation on the part of those who receive them. Finally, oracles are often received around the time of the birth of a character or sometime later and serve as prophecies of the future prominence of the figure to whom the oracle refers. I will now provide examples of oracles that function in each of these ways.[66]

The first example is found in Dionysius's *Antiquitates romanae*, specifically in his account of Aeneas's arrival in Italy. Dionysius states that Aeneas's landing in Italy was "due both to the oracles which reached their fulfillment in those parts and to the divine power which revealed its will in many ways" (*Ant. rom.*1.55.1). The revelation of divine power occurs through "springs of the sweetest water," which "were seen rising out of the earth spontaneously" (*Ant. rom.* 1.55.1), at a time when Aeneas's men were suffering from thirst and there was no water to be found.[67] After Aeneas makes a sacrifice to the gods out of gratitude for the water, the men then decide to eat, first dropping parsley[68] on the ground on which they place their food. When the food was eaten, the men then ate what had been thrown on the ground, at which point one of them remarks, "Look you, at last we have eaten even the table" (*Ant. rom.* 1.55.3). The narrator then

---

65. Oftentimes the reception of the oracle is not narrated. A character will find him- or herself in a situation, and the narrator will state that the character recalls an earlier oracle which is now, given the events of the narrative, being fulfilled.

66. I must admit that these categories are somewhat loose, and there is some overlap between them. For example, the right interpretation of an oracle is inherent to recognizing that an earlier oracle is being fulfilled by contemporary events.

67. The divine nature of the springs is emphasized through the spontaneous (αὐτόματοι) appearance of the water, especially when there was none visible. Also, Dionysius goes on to say that there was so much water that "all the army drank and the place was flooded as the stream ran down to the sea from the springs" (*Ant. rom.*1.55.1). Thus, the remembrance of the oracle has been placed in a context in which divine actions are already a part of the narrative.

68. Or wheat cakes, as Dionysius notes (*Ant. rom.* 1.55.2).

states, "they all cried out with joy that the first part of the oracle [τὰ πρῶτα τοῦ μαντεύματος] had now been fulfilled" (*Ant. rom.* 1.55.3).[69]

When they realize that the oracle had been partially fulfilled, "Aeneas brought the images of the gods out of the ship to the place appointed by him," and "others prepared pedestals and altars for them" (*Ant. rom.* 1.55.5). Following this celebration, Aeneas prepares a sacrifice to the gods. Therefore, the divine testimony through an oracle takes place within the context of religious celebration, and represents a previously received oracle being fulfilled through the meal. The divine testimony itself functions as the gods' sanction of Aeneas and his band settling in Italy. But it further serves to emphasize Aeneas's piety, which is displayed throughout the account through his attention to religious rites and the remembrance of the oracle itself.

A second example of an earlier oracle being remembered in a current situation takes place in Quintus Curtius's *History of Alexander*. In the narrative context, Alexander is attempting to push into Persia, but has suffered defeat by attempting to attack through a narrow pass (5.3.1–23). Seeking counsel, Alexander orders that prisoners be brought to him. Among these prisoners is a man who spoke both Greek and Persian; this prisoner advises Alexander to take a heretofore unknown route through the woods, in which their movements would be sheltered from the enemy (5.4.4). When Alexander asks him how he knows of this route, the prisoner tells him that earlier, he was a shepherd in that area and had been captured twice, once by the Persians in Lycia, and now by Alexander's army. Quintus Curtius then states: "The king was reminded of the prediction given by an oracle; for when he consulted it, the reply was made that a citizen of Lycia would be his guide on the road leading into Persia" (*History of Alexander* 5.4.11).

Significantly, Alexander orders the prisoner to lead him to this path, "uttering a prayer that it might result favorably" (*History of Alexander* 5.4.12). Through the prayer, Alexander is portrayed as recognizing the intervention of the gods through the prisoner and the fulfilled oracle.[70] Ulti-

---

69. Dionysius then states that "a certain oracle had been delivered to them . . . to sail westward till they came to a place where they should eat their tables" (*Ant. rom.* 1.55.4). The second part of the oracle was that "they should follow a four-footed beast as their guide, and wherever the animal grew wearied, there they should build a city" (*Ant. rom.* 1.55.4).

70. Also part of the characterization in this section is Alexander's solemn response to the prisoner's continued warning that the path was difficult to follow. "Then said the king: 'Take my word for it that none of those who follow will refuse to go where you will lead the way'" (*History of Alexander* 5.4.13). Through the statement Alexander is portrayed as having great authority, which has been substantiated through the divine

mately, Alexander's piety is rewarded through a complete victory over the Persians.[71] Therefore, the divine testimony through the oracle sanctions Alexander's campaign into Persia, and serves to depict him as following the will of the gods.

A third example of an oracle which was received sometime in the past and is fulfilled by a current event is narrated by Plutarch in the *Life of Pyrrhus*. Near the end of the *Life*, Pyrrhus leads his army in an intense battle for the city of Argos, in which Pyrrhus's army is faring none too well. During the battle,

> among the numerous votive-offerings in the market-place [Pyrrhus] caught sight of a wolf and bull in bronze, . . . and he was dumbfounded for he called to mind an ancient oracle regarding himself which declared that it was fated for him to die when he saw a wolf fighting with a bull. (*Pyrrh.* 32.4)

Pyrrhus rightly understands his situation as fulfillment of the oracle; shortly thereafter he is killed.[72]

To understand the role of the divine testimony in Pyrrhus's death one must consider the context of the entire βίος. Generally, from the beginning of the βίος, Pyrrhus is the object of Plutarch's praise.[73] As Pyrrhus's life

---

testimony of the fulfilled oracle.

71. Quintus Curtius describes the aftermath of the battle thusly: "The king fortified a camp on the same spot where he had routed the enemy" (*History of Alexander* 5.5.1).

72. The way in which he is killed is also significant for understanding the divine testimony in this passage. When he realizes that the battle is a lost cause, Pyrrhus attempts to fight his way through the enemy. First, however, he "took off the coronal [τὴν στεφάνην], with which his helmet was distinguished, and gave it to one of his companions" (*Pyrrh.* 34.1). This is a sign of cowardice on the part of Pyrrhus. He is subsequently wounded, staying on his horse. He engages the soldier who wounded him; the mother of that solider, however, happens to be watching the action from a window above. When she recognizes her son in hand-to-hand combat with Pyrrhus, "lifting up a tile [κεραμίδα] with both her hands," she "threw it at Pyrrhus. It fell upon his head below his helmet and crushed the vertebrae at the base of his neck, so that his sight was blurred and his hands dropped the reins" (*Pyrrh.* 34.2). Pyrrhus is then accosted by a second soldier, who attempts to cut off his head. But the soldier, being somewhat distraught, was not able to make a clean cut: "[H]is blow did not fall true, but along the mouth and chin, so that it was only slowly and with difficulty that he severed the head" (*Pyrrh.* 34.3). The account of Pyrrhus's death is narrated in great (grisly) detail, with much ekphrastic language. Through the description of the account, the auditor understands that Pyrrhus's death is anything but glorious: it is at the hands of an older woman, who is not even a combatant; and rather than quick and decisive, it is slow, certainly painful, and carried out in a clumsy manner.

73. Several examples will suffice: His father, Alcetas, is described as "a man who

Divine Testimony through Utterances in Hellenistic Narratives

unfolds, however, the picture becomes less clear. After narrating Pyrrhus's military defeats in Italy and Sicily, Plutarch states:

> [A]nd men believed that in military experience, personal prowess, and daring, he was by far the first of the kings of his time, but that what he won by his exploits he lost by indulging in vain hopes, since through passionate desire for what he had not he always failed to establish securely what he had. (*Pyrrh*. 26.1)

This passage acts as a "hinge" in the *Life* of Pyrrhus. From this point, the focus of Pyrrhus's biography is his unchecked ambition.[74] Thus his ignominious death, attested through the divine testimony of a fulfilled oracle, serves as the gods' condemnation of this aspect of Pyrrhus's personality.[75]

The fulfillment of oracles can also occur even when the oracle is misunderstood.[76] Two examples will be sufficient to illustrate this phenomenon. The first is from Diodorous Siculus's *Bibliotheca historica*. Philip, king of Macedonia, decides to attack the Persians. While sending a squadron of troops under the leadership of Attalus and Parmenion into Asia, he,

---

won high repute at the time of the Lamian war and acquired the highest authority among the confederates after Leosthenes" (*Pyrrh*. 1.4); as an infant, Pyrrhus is saved from a flood by a man named Achilles (2.6); Pyrrhus has the power to heal, and does so even if a suppliant was not able to pay (3.4); the big toe on his right foot "had a divine virtue" (3.5); even after defeating the Macedonians, they praised and admired him (8.1); "[Pyrrhus] was also kind towards his familiar friends, and mild in temper, but eager and impetuous in returning favors" (*Pyrrh*. 8.4).

74. See, e.g., 30.1; "Pyrrhus, too, was more than ever possessed by a fierce ambition to become master of [Argos]"; here, the context is important. Just prior to this statement the auditor learns that Pyrrhus has had a dream of throwing thunderbolts at the Spartans (29.1). He understands this to be a positive omen, but is warned that "the Deity might be indicating in advance to Pyrrhus also that the city was not to be entered by him" (30.2). Pyrrhus is subsequently defeated by the Spartans.

75. This interpretation is further strengthened by an "internal syncrisis" between Pyrrhus and his enemy, Antigonus. For example, in the buildup to the attack on Argos, the Argives ask to be left alone. Antigonus agrees, and even gives his son as a hostage as a sign of his goodwill. Pyrrhus also agrees, but does not leave anything as a pledge. The narrator interprets: "but since he gave no pledge, he remained under suspicion" (*Pyrrh*. 31.2). Also, Antigonus is distraught at the death of Pyrrhus, and even chastises his son for bringing him Pyrrhus's severed head (see *Pyrrh*. 31.4). On the concept of "internal syncrisis" in Plutarch, see Russell, "On Reading Plutarch's *Lives*," 89–90. See also Beck, "Interne 'synkrisis,'" 467–89. Beck discusses internal syncrisis in Plutarch's *Lives* in general, and analyzes the *Lives* of Marcellus and Fabius in particular.

76. On the fulfillment of oracles despite their being misunderstood in the ancient world, see Talbert, "Promise and Fulfillment," 98–99, who cites Herodotus's famous account of Croesus and his misunderstanding of the Delphic oracle he received when he inquired as to whether he should attack the Persians.

"wanting to enter upon the war with the gods' approval, asked the Pythia whether he would conquer the king of the Persians" (*Hist.* 16.91.2). The oracle provided by the god through the Pythia is quoted:

> Wreathed is the bull. All is done. There is also the one who will smite him. (*Hist.* 16.91.2)

Philip interprets the oracle as being in his favor,[77] thinking that "the Persian would be slaughtered like a sacrificial victim" (*Hist.* 16.91.3). The auditor learns, however, through the narrator's comments that the oracle actually prophesied that Philip, "in the midst of a festival and holy sacrifices, like the bull, would be stabbed to death while decked with a garland" (*Hist.* 16.91.3). Thus, with this misunderstanding, Philip proceeds with his plans for the invasion of Persia.

Before doing so, Philip plans a lavish festival and sacrifices in conjunction with his daughter's marriage to Alexander, king of Epirus. Many important statesmen pay homage to Philip, and the herald from Athens even stated that if anyone attempted to assassinate Philip and sought refuge in Athens, the assassin would be handed over for justice. The narrator then comments: "The casual phrase seemed like an omen sent by Providence to let Philip know that a plot was coming" (*Hist.* 16.92.2). Philip receives a second "clue" concerning the reality of the situation: he requests a noted actor, Neoptolemus, to sing a song appropriate to the upcoming assault on Persia. His words,[78] however, are also ominous and speak to Philip's vanity and ambition; they, too, are also completely misunderstood by Philip.[79]

On the morning of the next day, a procession is planned before the start of the games. In the procession would be statues of the twelve Olympic gods,[80] "and along with these was conducted a thirteenth statue,

---

77. Although, as the narrator states, "Philip found this response ambiguous" (*Hist.* 16.91.3).

78. "Your thoughts reach higher than the air; You dream of wide fields' cultivation. The homes you plan surpass the homes that men have known, but you do err, guiding your life afar. But one there is who'll catch the swift, who goes a way obscured in gloom, and sudden, unseen, overtakes and robs us of our distant hopes—death, mortals' source of many woes" (*Hist.* 16.92.3).

79. "Philip was enchanted with the message and was completely occupied with the thought of the overthrow of the Persian king, for he remembered the Pythian oracle [πυθόχρηστον χρησμὸν] which bore the same meaning as the words quoted by the tragic actor" (*Hist.* 16.92.4). Note the irony here, in that the verses do mean the same thing as the oracle; Philip has managed to misinterpret both equally, due to being "completely occupied with the thoughts of the overthrow of the Persian king."

80. Diodorus uses particularly memorable language (even ekphrastic to some

suitable for a god, that of Philip himself, so that the king exhibited himself enthroned [σύνθρονον ἑαυτὸν ἀποδεικνύντος] among the twelve gods." During the procession, Philip is stabbed by an assassin (Pausanias) and killed.[81] Significantly, Diodorus writes: "[B]ut as the praises and congratulations of all rang in his ears, suddenly and without warning the plot against the king was revealed as death struck" (*Hist.* 16.93.2).

Therefore, the oracle is indeed fulfilled, despite Philip's complete lack of understanding of its meaning. Philip's spiritual ignorance, however, plays an important role in his characterization in this passage. Diodorus portrays Philip as vain and conceited, to the point of equating himself with the gods. Therefore, his death, as rightly predicted by the oracle (and verses sung by Neoptolemus), is the gods' condemnation of his attitude. The divine testimony through the misunderstood oracle serves as the gods' disapproval of Philip.

A second example of a misunderstood oracle being fulfilled concerns Hannibal in Plutarch's *Life* of Titus Flamininus. Hannibal knows of an oracle concerning his death which predicts he will die and be covered by "Libyssan soil."[82] Thus, according to his understanding, he is safe as long as he is not in Libya. Unbeknownst to Hannibal, however, the oracle is referring to a nearby village by the name of Libyssa. Titus comes after Hannibal, and when he does, Hannibal chooses to kill himself before Titus can do so. Hannibal's death, therefore, fulfills the oracle.

The fulfillment of the oracle through Hannibal's suicide is part of a greater portrayal of Titus by Plutarch as being self-seeking and taking advantage of a much weaker opponent. After the death of Hannibal, a notorious enemy of Rome, Plutarch notes that

> many of [the members of the senate] thought the conduct of Titus odious, officious and cruel; for he had killed Hannibal

---

degree) to emphasize the grandeur of the statues "wrought with great artistry and adorned with a dazzling show of wealth to strike awe in the beholder" (*Hist.* 16.92.5).

81. Diodorus provides an extended explanation of why Pausanias killed Philip (see 16.93.3–94.4). The reasons involved Pausanias's jealousy of another (also by the name of Pausanias), who was admired by the king, as well as the abuse of Pausanias the assassin at the hands of Attalus, the king's advisor, followed by Philip's lack of punishment of Attalus.

82. "There was an ancient oracle, as it would appear, concerning Hannibal's death, and it ran as follows:—'Libyssan earth shall cover the form of Hannibal.' Hannibal thought this referred to Libya and a burial at Carthage, and believed that he would end his days there; but there is a sandy tract in Bithynia on the sea-shore, and on its border a large village called Libyssa" (*Flam.* 20.3–4).

when he was like a bird permitted to fly and without a tail, and there had been no necessity for his doing this, but he did it to win fame, that his name might be associated with the death of Hannibal. (*Flam.* 21.1)

This is in harmony with the characterization of Titus in this passage. Previous to the account of Hannibal's death, Titus is described as seeking to kill Hannibal to satisfy his desire for fame and glory, which previously had an outlet in military service and service to the state.[83] Thus, his pursuit of Hannibal "made him odious to most people" (20.2).[84] The divine testimony through the oracle therefore portrays Hannibal's death as a "good death," in line with the gods' will, while simultaneously portraying Titus negatively, as the one who preys upon a weakened foe.[85]

Above I have provided examples of divine testimony through oracles that are fulfilled despite being misunderstood. The converse of this situation is also true; when the gods testify through oracles that are difficult to understand, if a character is able to understand the oracle in spite of its enigmatic qualities, that character is portrayed in a positive light and the gods testify therefore to his or her ability to understand the divine will. An example of this function of oracles is found in Dionysius of Halicarnassus.[86] In this account, within the legendary history of the origins of Rome, King Tarquinius kills Marcus Junius,[87] leaving a son by the name of Brutus. Brutus feigns madness and stupidity in order to keep Tarquinius

---

83. "Now, the native ambition of Titus [φύσει Τίτου φιλότιμον], as long as it had sufficient material to gratify it in the wars which I have mentioned, met with praise, ... but after he had ceased to hold office and was well on in years, he met the rather with censure, because, although the portion of life which still remained to him did not admit of great activity, he was unable to restrain his passion for glory and youthful ardor" (*Flam.* 20.1).

84. This reading of Titus is strengthened by the last chapter of the *Life*, in which there is an "internal syncrisis" between Titus and Scipio Africanus. In contrast to Titus, Scipio treated Hannibal with respect, even after defeating him in battle (see *Flam.* 21.1–2). Plutarch summarizes the section thusly: "Such conduct on the part of Scipio most people admired, and they blamed Titus for having laid violent hands on one whom another had slain" (*Flam.* 21.4).

85. Another piece of evidence, albeit external to this *Life*, is found in the syncrisis between Pelopidas and Marcellus. There, Plutarch writes that he cannot praise either Pelopidas or Marcellus for their death; he does, however, "admire Hannibal because, in battles so numerous that one would weary of counting them, he was not even wounded" (*Comp. Pel. Marc.* 3.1).

86. A similar account is found in Livy, *Hist.* 1.56.6–13.

87. Who, Dionysius relates, was descended from one of Aeneas's original group of colonists.

from killing him. As entertainment for his own two sons, Tarquinius allows Brutus to live with him.

At some time a plague strikes Tarquinius's kingdom, and he sends his two sons, Arruns and Titus, to Delphi to inquire of the god what they must do to propitiate the gods and therefore remove the plague. Brutus accompanies them on their journey. When they make a sacrifice to the gods, the sons of Tarquinius laugh at Brutus, because his offering consists of a wooden staff. Unbeknownst to the brothers, Brutus has hollowed out the staff and filled it with gold, thus pleasing the god. After receiving a response to their inquiry concerning the plague, the brothers ask the oracle which of them will be the next ruler of Rome: "and the god answered, 'the one who should first kiss his mother'" (*Ant. rom.* 4.69.3). Dionysius then states:

> The youths, therefore, not knowing the meaning of the oracle, agreed together to kiss their mother at the same time, desiring to possess the kingship jointly; but Brutus, understanding what the god meant [συνεὶς ὅ βούλεται δηλοῦν ὁ θεός], as soon as he landed in Italy, stooped to the earth and kissed it, looking upon that as the common mother of all mankind. (*Ant. rom.* 4.69.4)

Thus, Brutus is portrayed as clearly understanding the will of the gods, while the sons of the king do not.

Following this passage the oracle is fulfilled.[88] Tarquinius is deposed and Brutus is named one of the consuls of the new republic. The divine testimony of the oracle received by Arruns, Titus, and Brutus therefore functions as the gods' prophecy that Brutus would be ruler over the Republic of Rome. It also serves, however, to portray Brutus positively in comparison to the negative portrayal of Arruns and Titus.[89] Brutus, the "dullard," is ironically the only one who brings a proper sacrifice to the god and can understand what the god is saying through the oracle.

---

88. An important event narrated previous to this one plays a significant role in the following narrative. Lucretia, wife of Collatinus (a relative of the Tarquinius family), is raped by Tarquinius's eldest son Sextus. After explaining to her father what happened, Lucretia commits suicide (see *Ant. rom.* 4.64.1–67.2). This serves as the trigger point for the overthrow of the Tarquinius family as tyrants over Rome and the institution of the republic.

89. And, I would argue, the entire family of Tarquinius. Almost simultaneously, while Arruns and Titus are mocking Brutus for his meager sacrifice and then misunderstanding the god's pronouncement, Sextus is raping a woman, which leads to her suicide. Thus, the negative portrayal of the brothers through the oracle extends to the entire family.

The *Topos* of Divine Testimony in Luke/Acts

A final function of fulfilled oracles is seen in Suetonius's *Life* of Vespasian. Prior to narrating Vespasian's rise to power, Suetonius provides a long list of portents throughout Vespasian's life that pointed to his future greatness. Suetonius prefaces this account by stating:

> While Otho and Vitellius were fighting for the throne after the death of Nero and Galba, [Vespasian] began to cherish the hope of imperial dignity, which he had long since conceived because of the following portents. (*Vesp.* 8.5.1)

These portents include: at Vespasian's birth, his greatness is portended by a shoot from a sacred oak tree (*Vesp.* 8.5.2); while Aedile he is covered in mud as punishment for not keeping the streets clean—this was seen as an omen that he would later protect Rome when it was being oppressed by some enemy (*Vesp.* 8.5.3); one time while Vespasian is eating, a dog brings him a human hand, and another time while at the table an ox, which broke free of its yoke, came in where he was eating and bowed its neck to him (*Vesp.* 8.5.4); Vespasian dreamed that he would receive good fortune when Nero had a tooth removed, and the next day a doctor showed him the tooth he had just extracted from Nero (*Vesp.* 8.5.5); Vespasian also "consulted the oracle of the god of Carmel in Judaea"; when he did, "the lots were highly encouraging, promising that whatever he planned or wished, however great it might be, would come to pass" (*Vesp.* 8.5.6).[90] Therefore, the divine testimony through an oracle[91] participates in this complex of omens and portents, all pointing to the same eventuality: Vespasian as emperor of Rome.

Thus the (eventually) fulfilled oracle serves as the gods' sanction of Vespasian as emperor. This is reinforced by the ensuing narrative which describes Vespasian's term as emperor. Shortly after he decides to vie for the throne, he meets a blind, lame man, who tells him that Serapis has told him in a dream that Vespasian would heal him, which he does (*Vesp.* 8.7.2–3). The rest of the *Life* consists of a long encomium of Vespasian, which is introduced thusly: "during the whole period of his rule he considered nothing more essential than first to strengthen the State, which was

---

90. This prophecy by the oracle is substantiated by divine speech through an intermediary. In this case, it is "one of [Vespasian's] high-born prisoners, Josephus by name"; Suetonius continues, "as he was being put in chains, [Josephus] declared most confidently that he would soon be released by the same man, who would then, however, be emperor" (*Vesp.* 8.5.6).

91. The oracle is neither quoted nor paraphrased; it is simply stated that he received one.

Divine Testimony through Utterances in Hellenistic Narratives

tottering and almost overthrown, and then to embellish it as well" (*Vesp.* 8.8.1).[92] The gods' testimony of Vespasian's becoming emperor, therefore, should be heard as part of the author's praise of Vespasian.

In sum, oracles are often found in ancient narratives as prophecies which are fulfilled in the course of the narrative. This includes oracles which were received at some time in the past and fulfilled through current events (with the event and oracle mutually interpreting each other), oracles that are fulfilled despite being misunderstood, oracles that are fulfilled through the actions of wise characters able to interpret them, and oracles that characters receive early in life which point to a future, memorable career for that character. In all these cases, I have demonstrated that the fulfilled oracles function as the divine sanction or disapproval of a character or group of characters. In the case of previously received oracles which are fulfilled by current events, the context must determine if the oracle is the gods' testimony for or against the character receiving the oracle.

Oracles as Commands and Warnings

Oracles do not only function as fulfilled prophecies. Oracles also serve as commands and warnings from the gods to characters in the narrative. Thus, the characters who receive these oracles demonstrate piousness through their reactions to this divine guidance through commands and warnings. Several examples will illustrate this use of the *topos*.

Diodorus Siculus narrates an account involving a war between the Sybarites and the Crotoniates in which the Sybarites are defeated. The Sybarites, being displaced from their original settlement, must find another. The Sybarites appeal to the Athenians and Lacedaemonians for support in founding a new colony. Significantly, the Lacedaemonians "paid no attention to them, but the Athenians promised to join in the enterprise" (*Hist.* 12.10.4). After asking others to join the enterprise, those assisting the Sybarites "received an oracular response from Apollo that they should found a city in the place where there would be 'Water to drink in due measure, but bread to eat without measure'" (*Hist.* 12.10.5).

---

92. The only negative comment in the entire section is that "the only thing for which he can fairly be censured was his love of money" (*Vesp.* 8.16.1). All of section 8.16 explores the evidence for this statement. The encomium, however, resumes again in 8.17.1.

The settlers then establish a new colony near a spring called Thuria.[93] All is well for a short while, until the original Sybarites attempt to place only their own people in positions of authority (*Hist.* 12.11.1). This continues until the other citizens begin to resist the Sybarites, and other Greek colonists take up residence in the new settlement. Once these Greeks join the colony, the colony makes peace with the Crotantiates and a democratic government is formed (*Hist.* 12.11.2–3). Charondas is selected as their leader, and he is lauded for his abilities as lawgiver (*Hist.* 12.11.3–4).[94]

Therefore, the Athenians are positively portrayed in this passage, while the Spartans are not. The Spartans ignore the Sybarites call for help, while the Athenians come to their aid. The positive portrayal of the Athenians also includes their obedience to the oracle;[95] this positive characterization is reinforced by the "second wave" of Greeks who help the struggling colony by making peace with the Crotantiates and implementing a democratic government.

A second example is from Livy's *Historiae* in the context of Rome's on-going struggle against Hannibal. Both armies are beset by sickness; thus, there is a temporary lull in the fighting. Also, Livy explains that during the year there were "frequent showers of stones" (*Hist.* 29.10.5), and for this reason the Sibylline books were consulted. Livy states that

> an oracle was found that, if ever a foreign foe should invade the land of Italy, he could be driven out of Italy and defeated if the Idaean Mother should be brought from Pessinus to Rome. (*Hist.* 29.10.5)

This oracle from the Sibylline books was confirmed by a group which went to Delphi and received an oracle which stated that "a much greater victory was in prospect for the Roman people than that from spoils of which they were bringing gifts" (*Hist.* 29.10.6).[96] The Romans take these

---

93. Therefore, the settlement itself is called "Thurium" (*Hist.* 12.10.6).

94. Diodorus includes an extended section in which he details many of Charondas's laws; see 12.12.1–19.3.

95. The founding of colonies "κατά τινα χρησμόν" is certainly a prevalent theme in antiquity.

96. Thus, actually two independent divine testimonies are received, which serve as mutual reinforcement of one another, emphasizing the divine intervention in the situation. The inevitable outcome is also highlighted by "Publius Scipio's state of mind, virtually forecasting the end of the war" (29.10.7).

testimonies seriously, and begin to discuss the logistics of fulfilling the Sibylline oracle.[97]

The Romans determine to send a request to King Attalus of Pergamum for assistance (*Hist.* 29.11.1–2); they send a delegation there, which makes a stop in Delphi. The god tells them "that they should gain what they sought with the help of King Attalus," and "after conveying the goddess to Rome they were then to make sure that the best man at Rome should hospitably welcome her" (*Hist.* 29.11.6). Thus, the two previous oracles are confirmed by a third, and a new command is given. The goddess is indeed conveyed to Rome (*Hist.* 29.11.6–8), and the senate carefully deliberates who should be named the "best man" to meet her, finally deciding on Publius Scipio (*Hist.* 29.14.8).

Eventually, Hannibal is defeated by the Romans, thus fulfilling the oracles and rewarding the Romans for their obedience. Significantly, in this passage, the oracles give commands which require not only obedience on the parts of the recipients, but also thoughtful action in selecting the "best man" to receive the goddess. In both of these ways, the Romans, and especially Publius Scipio, are positively portrayed by the divine testimony through the various oracles received.

An oracle that serves as a warning but goes unheeded is found in Plutarch's *Life* of Pelopidas. In this account, Plutarch tells his auditors that the Spartans have allied themselves with all the other Greek states and are now on the march against Thebes. When the Spartans invade Boeotia, the Boeotians are filled with fear. As Pelopidas goes out to lead the Theban army, his wife pleads with him "not to lose his life," which Pelopidas disregards.[98] Prior to the battle, Pelopidas has a dream, in which he sees the daughters of Scedasus "weeping at their tombs, as they invoked curses upon the Spartans." He also sees Scedasus himself, "bidding him sacrifice to his daughters a virgin with auburn hair" (*Pel.* 21.1). This dream has been previously explained to some degree. In a short excursus, Plutarch tells his auditors that the tombs of Scedasus's daughters, who had been "ravished by Spartan strangers" at some time in the past, are near Leuctra.[99]

---

97. "And so, that they might the sooner be in possession of the victory which foreshadowed itself in oracles, forecasts and responses, they planned and discussed what should be the method of transporting the goddess to Rome" (29.10.8).

98. Pelopidas's reply: "This advice, my wife, should be given to private men; but men in authority should be told not to lose the lives of others" (*Pel.* 20.2). Given the characterization of Pelopidas in this section of the βίος, this is certainly meant to be understood as a wise reply to his wife's entreaty.

99. Pausanias explains that Scedasus's daughters committed suicide following the

Plutarch goes on to say that Scedasus made an issue of this with the Spartans, but because he could not get a hearing, he, too, killed himself where his daughters were buried. Ever since that time,

> prophecies and oracles kept warning the Spartans to be on watchful guard against the Leuctrian wrath. Most of them, however, did not fully understand the matter, but were in doubt about the place, since in Laconia there is a town near the sea which is called Leuctra, and near Megalopolis in Arcadia there is a place of the same name. (*Pel.* 20.4)

Through this excursus and Pelopidas's dream, the auditor learns that the Spartans have been warned through divine testimony to avoid the "Leuctrian wrath," and that a battle on the Leuctrian plain looms ominously.[100]

Eventually, the Spartans are defeated, and Plutarch praises Pelopidas for his role in their defeat:

> [A]nd since Pelopidas engaged [the Spartans] with incredible speed and boldness, their courage and skill were so confounded that there was a flight and slaughter of the Spartans such as had never before been seen. Therefore, although Epaminondas was boeotarch, Pelopidas, who was not boeotarch, and commanded only a small portion of the whole force, won as much glory for the success of that victory as he did. (*Pel.* 23.4)

The divine testimony through the oracle to the Spartans is crucial for understanding the passage. Pelopidas is positively portrayed through the reception of the dream and its correct interpretation (i.e., avoiding a human sacrifice). The Spartans, on the other hand, are characterized negatively in that they are unable or unwilling to understand the oracles concerning

---

atrocities: "Scedasus, who lived near Leuctra, had two daughters, Molpia and Hippo. These in the bloom of their youth were wickedly outraged by two Lacedaemonians, Phrurarchidas and Parthenius. The maidens, unable to bear the shame of their violation, immediately hanged themselves" (Pausanias, *Descr.* 9.13.5).

100. Before the battle, however, the issue of the sacrifice is taken up by Pelopidas and his colleagues. Some argue that they should take the dream (itself a form of divine testimony) seriously and perform a human sacrifice (arguing, interestingly, that Leonidas had "in obedience to the oracle [τῷ χρησμῷ τρόπον], sacrificed himself [*Pel.* 21.2]); others argue against such a sacrifice. The issue is settled when "a filly broke away from the herd of horses and sped through the camp, and when she came to the very place of their conference, stood still. The rest only admired the color of her glossy mane, which was fiery red . . . ; but Theocritus the seer, after taking thought, cried out to Pelopidas: 'Thy sacrificial victim is come, good man; so let us not wait for any other virgin, but do thou accept and use the one which Heaven offers thee'" (*Pel.* 22.1–2).

Divine Testimony through Utterances in Hellenistic Narratives

the "Leuctrian wrath" that they are about to face. Both Pelopidas and the Spartans are faced with interpretive situations; one is successful, and the other is not.[101]

A final example of oracles as commands or warnings is found in Plutarch's *Life* of Demosthenes. In this instance, as the example above, oracles as warnings are disregarded, to the detriment of Demosthenes. Plutarch narrates events from Demosthenes's life which demonstrate to the auditor that Demosthenes is a great orator and statesman.[102] Faced, however, with the threat from Philip, Plutarch sounds a different note:

> But it would seem that some divinely ordered fortune in the revolution of affairs, which was putting an end at this time to the freedom of the Greeks, opposed their efforts, and showed forth many signs of what was to come. (*Dem.* 19.1)

Included among these signs were

> dire prophecies which the Pythian priestess made known, and an ancient oracle which was recited from the Sibylline books.[103]
> (*Dem.* 19.1)

Plutarch then reveals that Demosthenes does not take these prophecies seriously. He writes that

---

101. See Russell, "On Reading," 87–88. Russell argues that Plutarch, because he is writing biographies, takes advantage of his freedom to interpret history in order to portray the virtues and vices of his characters. Russell states that Plutarch does this in two ways: (i) the motivations of the hero; and (ii) "the attribution of public or communal action to the hero's own initiative." Here, Russell highlights Plutarch's account of Pelopidas at Leuctra as an example of this phenomenon.

102. E.g., Demosthenes encourages the Greeks to invade Euboea, which they successfully accomplish (*Dem.* 17.1); he convinces the Greeks to intercede for Byzantium and Perinthus (*Dem.* 17.2); he is also successful in persuading the Greeks to unify against Philip (*Dem.* 17.3); finally, Philip's conquest of Phocia is proof for Demosthenes that the Greeks must go to Thebes and seek an alliance. He is successful in this, and Philip immediately asks for peace (*Dem.* 18.3). Plutarch summarizes this section by stating that Demosthenes "was beloved by both peoples and exercised supreme power, not illegally nor unworthily, . . . but rather with perfect propriety" (*Dem.* 18.3).

103. Plutarch quotes the oracle: "From the battle on Thermodon may I be far removed, to behold it like an eagle in clouds and upper air. Tears are for the conquered there, and for the conqueror, death" (*Dem.* 19.1). Plutarch notes some confusion regarding the reference to Thermodon; it is either the name of a river or a god (*Dem.* 19.2). Either way, Thermodon is mentioned in a second oracle: "For the battle on Thermodon wait thou, all-black bird; there thou shalt have in abundance the flesh of men" (*Dem.* 19.3).

> [Demosthenes] is said to have had complete confidence in the Greek forces, and to have been lifted into a state of glowing excitement by the strength and ardor of so many men eager to engage the enemy, so that he would not suffer his countrymen to give heed to oracles or listen to prophecies; nay, he even suspected the Pythian priestess of being in sympathy with Philip. (*Dem.* 20.1)

Here one learns that not only is Demosthenes personally not giving credence to the oracles, he is influencing his fellow Greeks to disregard them as well.

This negative view of Demosthenes is substantiated by Philip's defeat of the Greeks at Chaeroneia (*Dem.* 20.3; cf. *Dem.* 21.1).[104] It is also corroborated by Plutarch's description of Demosthenes's conduct during the battle:

> Up to this point, then, he was a brave man; but in the battle he displayed no conduct that was honorable or consonant with his words, but forsook his post, cast away his arms, and ran away most disgracefully. (*Dem.* 20.2)

Demosthenes, therefore, while being portrayed as a skilled orator and servant of Greece, is negatively portrayed in this section through his lack of regard for the testimony of the gods through oracles.

In this section I have shown that oracles can serve as commands and warnings. As the testimony of the gods, oracles as commands and warnings allow characters the freedom to demonstrate their obedience to the command-oracle or give heed to the gods' warning through the oracle. Of course, the converse is also true. Through oracles as commands and warnings, characters have the opportunity to demonstrate their disregard for the divine.

Manipulation of Oracles

Characters often engage in the manipulation of oracles for their own benefit and are therefore negatively characterized in the narrative as disregarding the significance of the divine testimony through the oracles. Two examples will illustrate this use of oracles as divine testimony.

---

104. Brenk, *In Mist Apparelled*, 252, comments that "the warning against engaging at Chaironea is fully vindicated by the outcome of the battle."

Diodorus Siculus describes a time in the history of Sparta and Athens in which the Spartans were no longer the dominant naval power in the region (*Hist.* 11.50.1). In order to gain back naval superiority, the Spartan Gerousia proposed a war with the Athenians. This was met by and large with approval, as the majority of Spartans could see the material benefits that would accompany a defeat of Athens (*Hist.* 11.50.2–4). In order to argue their point,

> [t]hey kept calling to mind also the ancient oracle [ἀνεμιμνῄσκοντο δὲ καὶ τῆς ἀρχαίας μαντείας] in which the god commanded them to beware lest their leadership should be a "lame" one, and the oracle, they insisted, meant nothing other than the present; for "lame" indeed their rule would be if, having two leaderships, they should lose one of them.[105] (*Hist.* 11.50.4)

Those who are part of the faction desiring war with Athens thus take advantage of the ambiguity of the oracle in order to advance their position. The agreement of the majority makes war seem likely.[106]

Diodorus, however, then tells of one Hetoemaridas, "a member of the Gerousia . . . who was a direct descendant of Heracles and enjoyed favor among the citizens by reason of his character" (*Hist.* 11.50.6). Hetoemaridas is able to convince the Gerousia that war with Athens was indeed not a good idea, and war is therefore avoided. Clearly, through his family lineage and good reputation with the people, Hetoemaridas is portrayed by Diodorus in a favorable light. Those who manipulate the enigmatic quality of the oracle, along with those who concur with their opinion, are therefore implicitly compared with Hetoemaridas, acting as negative foils to his good character.

A second example of manipulation of the same oracle is found in Plutarch's *Life* of Agesilaus. Early in this *Life*, the auditor learns that Agesilaus is lame ("As for his deformity, the beauty of his person in its youthful prime covered this from sight, while the ease and gaiety with which he bore such a misfortune, being first to jest and joke about himself, went far

---

105. "Two leaderships" here indicates dominance of land and sea. See translator's footnote at this point in the LCL text. This is also an example of oracles and prophecies being used in an attempt to persuade others to make a certain decision. I will discuss this use of oracles as divine testimony below. It is, in addition to these functions, a command/warning from the gods.

106. Diodorus notes: "Since practically all the citizens had been eager for this course of action and the Gerousia was in session to consider these matters, no one entertained the hope that any man would have the temerity to suggest any other course" (*Hist.* 11.50.5).

towards rectifying it" [*Ages.* 2.2]). After Agis's death, Lysander promotes Agesilaus as the next king, and his proposal meets with general approval. Plutarch then states that

> there was a diviner [χρησμολόγος] in Sparta, named Diopeithes, who was well supplied with ancient prophecies [μαντειῶν τε παλαιῶν], and was thought to be eminently wise in religious matters. This man declared it contrary to the will of Heaven that a lame man should be king of Sparta, and cited at the trial of the case [ἐν τῇ δίκῃ] the following oracle.[107] (*Ages.* 3.3-4)

It is significant that this takes place in the context of a trial; Plutarch thus describes the oracle, as a testimony of the gods, being used as evidence.

Lysander answers Diopeithes, however, by arguing that the oracle was referring instead to the rightful heir to the throne being of illegitimate birth, thus making him unsuitable for kingship.[108] He then attempts to support his assertion through a reference to divine testimony.[109] Agesilaus is ultimately named king (cf. *Ages.* 4.1); he is, however, criticized for his participation in this scheme. In the syncrisis between Agesilaus and Pompey, Plutarch writes:

> Agesilaus, on the contrary, appeared to get his kingdom by *sinning against both gods and men*, since he brought Leotychides under condemnation for bastardy, although his brother had recognized him as his legitimate son, *and made light of the oracle concerning his lameness.* (*Comp. Ages. Pomp.* 1.2; emphasis added)

Through his involvement in the manipulation of the oracle, Agesilaus is condemned by Plutarch.

In sum, in the examples above, oracles are manipulated or knowingly misinterpreted by characters in order to justify those characters' personal or public agendas. In this way characters demonstrate their lack of regard

---

107. The oracle states: "Bethink thee now, O Sparta, though thou art very glorious, lest from thee, sound of foot, there spring a maimed royalty; for long will unexpected toils oppress thee, and onward-rolling billows of man-destroying war" (*Ages.* 3.4).

108. The child in question, by the name of Leotychides, is allegedly the offspring of Timaea (Agis's wife) and Alcibiades, who, the auditor learns, came to Sparta after being exiled from Sicily; see Plutarch, *Ages.* 3.1–2.

109. "And Agesilaus declared that Poseidon also had borne witness to the bastardy of Leotychides [τὸν Ποσειδῶ καταμαρτυρεῖν τοῦ Λεωτυχίδου τὴν νοθείαν], for he had cast Agis forth from his bedchamber by an earthquake, and after this more than ten months elapsed before Leotychides was born" (*Ages.* 3.5). This passage will be analyzed in chapter 5, in the section on divine testimony through signs and portents in creation.

for the gods, and are thus negatively portrayed in the narratives. Those who oppose such characters, however, are seen in a positive light.

Oracles as Means of Persuasion

I have shown that oracles function primarily as the fulfillment of prophecies, but they also serve as commands and warnings from the gods. In addition, oracles can be manipulated by characters for their own purposes. A fourth way in which divine testimony through oracles functions is in the context of characters attempting to influence others. This usage of oracles is normally found in the context of deliberative, political situations. Two examples will be sufficient to illustrate this use of the *topos* of divine testimony through utterances.

The first example comes from Tacitus's *Annals*, and involves a dispute between a delegation from Byzantium and the Roman senate. The Byzantians are seeking to lessen the amount of tribute they are being called on to pay. In doing so, they "reviewed their entire history" (*Ann.* 12.62). This history included earlier situations in which the Byzantians had assisted the Romans.[110] One way in which they had supported the Romans was by allowing them to pass through their land, which was "conveniently placed for the transit of generals and armies by land or sea, and equally so for the conveyance of supplies" (*Ann.* 12.62).

Tacitus adds that the reason the Byzantians occupied the territory that had been so valuable to the Romans was in response to an oracle.[111] Namely, when they consulted the oracle concerning where they should found their settlement, it stated that they were to "seek a home opposite the country of the blind" (*Ann.* 12.63). Tacitus goes on to explain that the Chaldeans were actually the first in this area, but they were too "blind" to recognize the fruitfulness of the land on the (now) Byzantine side. Therefore, the Byzantians were able to allow the Romans passage through this area because they were led to this land by the gods, through their testimony through an oracle. Thus, the Byzantians are able to convince

---

110. See *Ann.* 12.62; these included: a treaty between the two parties against the Macedonians; sending troops to fight alongside the Romans against Antiochus, Perseus, and Aristonicus; assistance in the war against Antonius; and aid provided to Sulla, Lucullus, and Pompey.

111. Thus, it must be admitted that, in this case, it is not a character in the narrative who uses an oracle to influence a proceeding. In the context of this narrative, however, Tacitus uses the oracle as divine proof that the Byzantians were strategically placed.

the Romans to lessen the amount of tribute over the next five years (*Ann.* 12.63).

A second example of oracles used to influence the decisions of others is found in Plutarch's *Life* of Agis. The greater context for this incident is Epitadeus's law, making it legal for a man to give his estate to anyone, thus concentrating the wealth of the state in the hands of a few.[112] Agis, however, desires to reverse this state of affairs and return to the traditional Spartan egalitarianism.

To do so, Agis has Lysander elected as ephor, and Lysander formally introduces the legislation in the senate, which causes a dispute among the senators (*Ag. Cleom.* 8.1–9.1). In order to persuade those who are not convinced that this was the correct course of action,[113] Lysander, Mandrocleidas, and Agesilaus[114]

> begged [those opposed to the legislation] . . . to call to mind the earlier oracles [τῶν τε προτέρων χρησμῶν μνημονεῦσαι] which bade them beware of the love of riches as a fatal thing for Sparta, as well as the oracles which had lately been brought to them from Pasiphae[115] [τῶν ἔναγχος ἐκ Πασιφάας κεκομισμένων αὐτοῖς]. (*Ag. Cleom.* 9.1)

Oracles, both those received recently and in the distant past, are referenced in the assembly in order to try to persuade the senate to pass the proposed legislation. In addition, Agis pledged "very large contributions to the constitutions which he was trying to establish" (*Ag. Cleom.* 9.3).[116]

---

112. "Epitadeus . . . introduced a law permitting a man during his lifetime to give his estate and allotment to any one he wished, or in his will and testament so to leave it" (*Ag. Cleom.* 5.2). Plutarch then adds: "This man, then, satisfied a private grudge of his own in introducing the law [Epitadeus had a falling out with his son and apparently enacted the law in order to prevent his son from inheriting his estate]; but his fellow citizens welcomed the law out of greed, made it valid, and so destroyed the most excellent of institutions" (*Ag. Cleom.* 5.3).

113. Those not convinced include, ironically, Agis's own mother and his sister, who, "owing to the multitude of her retainers, friends, and debtors, had great influence in the state and took a large part in public affairs" (*Ag. Cleom.* 6.4).

114. Plutarch had earlier informed his auditors that these were influential men who sided with Agis; see *Ag. Cleom.* 6.2.

115. Plutarch, in a short excursus, explains that there was a temple to Pasiphae nearby (in Thalamae) and that "her oracle there was held in honor" (*Ag. Cleom.* 9.2).

116. Plutarch's comment is significant: "The people, accordingly, were filled with amazement at the magnanimity of the young man, and were delighted, feeling that after a lapse of nearly two hundred years a king had appeared who was worthy of Sparta" (*Ag. Cleom.* 10.1).

Divine Testimony through Utterances in Hellenistic Narratives

A faction headed by Leonidas, however, opposes the legislation, and it is ultimately defeated by a single vote (*Ag. Cleom.* 11.1).[117] Oracles are invoked in order to persuade the senate of the correct course of action. Ultimately, the divine testimony through oracles functions as a divine sanction of the proposed changes by Agis, and likewise, the disapproval of those opposing him. Further evidence for this is found in the syncrisis of Agis and Cleomenes and the Gracchi.[118] There, Plutarch writes that "the policies of the Gracchi were opposed by the greatest Romans, whereas those which Agis instituted and Cleomenes consummated were based upon the fairest and most imposing precedents, namely, the ancient rhetras or unwritten laws concerning simplicity of life and equality of property, for which Lycurgus was voucher to them, and the Pythian Apollo to Lycurgus" (*Comp. Ag. Cleom. cum Ti. Gracch.* 2.3).

In these examples, oracles are used by characters (or the narrator) to justify positions in deliberative settings. Thus the oracles serve directly as testimonies of the gods and assist the character in influencing a group of people to make a certain decision. The oracles simply add weight to the case being made.

Oracles used as Evidence in a Trial

Similar to the above, oracles can be used in forensic situations in which a character is attempting to defend him or herself against charges or a group of people is trying to justify a particular action. Thus the oracle becomes part one's defense. Two examples will illustrate this use of the *topos*.

Oracles function in this way in Quintus Curtius's *History of Alexander*, within the context of Philotas's defense speech. Philotas has been accused of colluding against Alexander, and is called to make his defense before Alexander's generals and the assembly.[119] In his speech, Philotas provides many proofs of his innocence, including: he has already been exonerated by Alexander (6.10.11–12); the plot was revealed to him by an insignificant boy, and he therefore didn't feel the need to relay this information to

---

117. Plutarch notes that the "common people" backed Agis; the rich, however, were on the side of Leonidas (*Ag. Cleom.* 11.1).

118. This is an unusual syncrisis in which two pairs of *Lives* are compared.

119. Alexander, however, is not present. After demanding that Philotas be allowed to defend himself, and asking Philotas whether he would speak in Macedonian or Greek, Alexander leaves the assembly (*History of Alexander* 6.9.31–36).

Alexander (6.10.15);[120] he could have killed the one who revealed it to him (6.10.19-20); he had a chance to kill Alexander and did not (6.10.20-21); his decision to speak in Greek rather than Macedonian shows he has no aspirations to rule Macedonia (6.10.23); against the charge that he was friends with one of the conspirators, Amyntas, Philotas states that he was, only because Amyntas was Alexander's cousin (6.10.24).

Finally, Philotas answers the charge that he "also wrote that [he] pitied those who had to live under a man who believed himself the son of Jupiter"[121] (*History of Alexander* 6.10.26). Against this charge Philotas claims that what he wrote was written "to the king, but not about the king" (*History of Alexander* 6.10.27).[122] Philotas then states, "But since the truth of the oracle is sure, let the god bear witness in my case [*sit dues causae meae testis*]." He continues, "He who has recognized our king as son will not suffer those who have plotted against his stock to be concealed. If you believe tortures to be more trustworthy than oracles, I do not refuse even that testimony for bringing the truth to light" (*History of Alexander* 6.10.28-29).

Thus, Philotas invokes the oracle received by Alexander as evidence of his innocence. He believes that Jupiter has indeed declared Alexander to be his son, and that the same god who did so through an oracle will testify to his (Philotas's) own innocence. Philotas is therefore portrayed in a positive light, falsely accused of the crime of conspiracy.[123]

A second example of an oracle being used in defense of one's actions is found in Plutarch's *Life* of Solon. The context involves a war between Athens and Megara over the island of Salamis. Plutarch provides two accounts of how the island came to be a possession of Athens.[124] The second

---

120. Philotas adds that the didn't even hear it from someone involved in the plot; he heard it from the brother (Cebalinus) of one of the conspirators.

121. Philotas is, of course, referring to the oracle Alexander received at Siwah in Egypt, declaring him to be the son of a god.

122. Philotas means that it would be better if Alexander considered the oracle a personal message from the god, and not publicly flaunt it. Besides, according to Philotas, Alexander had urged him to be frank and to say what was on his mind.

123. Here agreeing with Rutz, "Curtius Rufus," 2329-57, albeit for different reasons. Rutz writes: "Die gesamte Darstellung des Philotas tendiert also dahin, die *claritas iuvenis* (Curt. 7, 1, 2) hervorzuheben und zu diesem Zweck alles Negative zu unterdrücken, das Positive aber soweit wie möglich zu steigern" (2350).

124. The first, "the popular" account [τὰ μὲν οὖν δημώδη τῶν λεγομένων], is that Solon deceived the Megarians by having soldiers on Salamis dress up as women and act as if they were celebrating a festival. The Megarians, thinking they were meeting a group of women, were easily routed (*Sol.* 8.4-6).

Divine Testimony through Utterances in Hellenistic Narratives

report is "that Solon first received this oracle from the god at Delphi [αὐτῷ τὸν ἐν Δελφοῖς θεὸν χρῆσαι]" (*Sol.* 9.1).[125] After receiving the oracle and sacrificing to Periphemus and Cychreus, Solon, along with five hundred Athenians, captured the island (*Sol.* 9.2–3).[126]

In order to adjudicate the dispute over Salamis and thus end the war, the Athenians and Megarians call on the Spartans to act as judges to decide the fate of Salamis. The Athenians bring their evidence to the trial,[127] the final piece of which is described thusly:

> However, they say that Solon was further supported by sundry Pythian oracles [τῷ μέντοι Σόλωνι Πυθικούς τινας βοηθῆσαι λέγουσι χρησμούς], in which the god spoke of Salamis as Ionian. (*Sol.* 10.4)

Solon and the Athenians are supported in their claim of sovereignty over Salamis by the testimony of the gods through oracles.[128] The oracles also function as divine sanction on Solon and his leadership of Athens; this is supported by the statement following this section:

> These events, then, made Solon famous and powerful. But he was even more admired and celebrated among the Greeks for what he said in behalf of the temple at Delphi, namely, that the Greeks must come to its relief, and not suffer the people of Cirrha to outrage the oracle, but aid the Delphians in maintaining the honor of the god. (*Sol.* 11.1)

---

125. The oracle is then quoted as follows: "The tutelary heroes of the land where once they lived, with sacred rites propitiate, whom the Asopian plain now hides in its bosom; there they lie buried with their faces toward the setting sun" (*Sol.* 9.1).

126. Plutarch seems to prefer this record of the events (see *Sol.* 9.4); following the narration of this account, he provides confirmatory evidence in the form of ceremonies in which the approach of Solon's ship is enacted (*Sol.* 9.4).

127. One report was that a passage from Homer was read, in which it was insinuated that Salamis was under Athenian rule; another report, however, was that Solon stated that Philaeus and Eurysaces, sons of Ajax, who eventually were citizens of Athens, handed over the island to Athens. Also, Solon supposedly argued that the dead on Salamis were buried "in Athenian fashion," not as the Megarians do (*Sol.* 10.1–3). This, however, was disputed by the Megarians (*Sol.* 10.3).

128. Powell, "Religion," 15–31, in analyzing various accounts of the Greek invasion of Sicily, states that "arguments from divination, like those from any important secular premise, will tend to be most influential when arguments from other premises are weakest" (ibid., 20). This seems to be the case here in Plutarch's *Life* of Solon. Solon provides several arguments, but what tips the balance in the case is the argument from divine testimony through oracles.

The *Topos* of Divine Testimony in Luke/Acts

Thus Solon demonstrates through his actions that to which the gods have testified through oracles; Solon is a pious man, whom the gods favor.

The use of oracles as evidence in a trial setting is very similar to the previous function. The examples analyzed here demonstrate that oracles are used by characters to defend themselves or their actions in forensic settings. Again, the oracles are used by the characters as the direct testimony of the gods concerning their situations.

Oracles which Explain Other Divine Testimony

Finally, oracles can be used to explain other signs and portents for which the gods are responsible. An example from Livy's *Historiae* will illustrate this use of oracles. In Livy's account of the Romans' conquest of Veii, Livy relates that many portents occurred while the Romans were at war with the Etruscans.[129] The strangest portent, however, was that the level of the Alban Lake, near Veii, rose, despite a lack of rain (*Hist.* 5.15.2).[130] A group is sent to Delphi to solicit a response from the god as to the meaning of this phenomenon. Meanwhile, a Roman soldier outside the city of Veii overhears a man of that city explaining "in a prophetic strain [*in modum cecinit*]" that "until the water should be drawn off from the Alban Lake the Romans never could take Veii" (*Hist.* 5.15.4). It is ascertained that this man is a soothsayer; therefore, he is subsequently captured and brought before the Roman senate, where he repeats his prophecy (*Hist.* 5.15.6–10).[131] The senate, however, does not take the man's statement seriously,[132] and decides to wait for the party to return from Delphi.

When the envoys do return from Delphi, they bring a response from the god which fully substantiates the soothsayer's statement (*Hist.* 5.16.8). The attitude of the Romans towards the old soothsayer from Veii

---

129. These portents could not be rightly interpreted since the Romans were at war with the Etruscans, the consummate soothsayers of the time.

130. Livy states that the lake rose "without any rains or other cause to make it less a miracle" (*Hist.* 5.15.2), thus indicating that the gods were responsible for this portent.

131. Before the senate, the man tells the assembly that "what he had then uttered under divine inspiration [*quae tum ceinerit divino spiritu instinctus*], he could not now unsay and recall; and perhaps in concealing what the immortal gods wished to be published guilt was incurred no less than by disclosing what should be hid" (*Hist.* 5.15.10). He then goes so far as to tell the senators how to lower the level of the lake.

132. Specifically, and significantly, the senate made "slight account of his authority, as not sufficiently trustworthy in so grave a matter" (*Hist.* 5.15.12).

completely changes.[133] Eventually, after drawing the water off the lake and offering the proper sacrifices to the gods, Veii is utterly defeated (*Hist.* 5.21.5, 17).

The oracle, therefore, serves to explain the divine testimony through the rising of the lake without any inflow of water and simultaneously to substantiate the prophecy of the soothsayer from Veii. Ultimately, the oracle sanctions the Romans' conquest of Veii.[134] But the oracle also serves to legitimate the soothsayer from Veii. Prior to the oracle, his prophecy was ignored, due to his lack of status. The oracle, however, demonstrates the gods' approval of the soothsayer, and his reputation as a witness therefore increases.

In sum, the oracles presented in this part of the study serve as the gods' testimony concerning the characters who receive them in various ways. I have shown that oracles can function as: fulfilled prophecies (including previously received oracles fulfilled by present events, oracles being fulfilled despite the misunderstanding of same, oracles requiring correct interpretation and subsequent action in order to be fulfilled, and prophecies concerning the future career of the subject of the narrative); commands and warnings; words from the gods that are manipulated by human characters; a means of persuasion in deliberative settings; evidence in trial settings; and as a means to explain a previous sign received from the gods. In all these cases, I have shown that the overarching function of oracles is one of the gods' testimony, both in favor of and against characters in the narratives.

SUMMARY OF RESULTS OF ANALYSIS OF DIVINE TESTIMONY THROUGH UTTERANCES IN HELLENISTIC NARRATIVES

These findings for the use of oracles as divine testimony are in concert with what I have shown to be the function of divine testimony through the direct speech of the gods and through the speech of inspired intermediaries. In the case of oracles, as is true of direct divine speech and divine speech through an intermediary, the divine testimony through the

---

133. "The captive soothsayer began from that moment to be held in great repute, and the military tribunes . . . set out to employ him about the expiation of the Alban prodigy and the due appeasement of the gods" (*Hist.* 5.17.1).

134. "The Veientes, unconscious that they were already given up by their own soothsayers, and by foreign oracles, that some of the gods had already been invited to share in their despoiling" (*Hist.* 5.21.5).

The *Topos* of Divine Testimony in Luke/Acts

utterance of the gods often occurs at a significant point in the narrative. It is at these noteworthy events that a character is portrayed as being either pious or impious, and divine testimony plays an important role in that portrayal. Also, I have shown that in many cases, divine testimony is found in conjunction with some type of religious expression, including prayer, sacrifices, or a festival. Finally, divine testimony through utterances of all types occurs frequently along with other types of divine testimony, reinforcing the portrayal at that point.

Through the examples of divine testimony by direct speech and intermediaries, one can see that divine testimony served as encouragement and affirmation of characters, as commands and warnings to characters, as the explanation of a divine act, and as prophecies which are fulfilled later in the narrative, thus acting as the gods' sanction of that character. Given the data from the analysis of divine testimony through oracles, it is clear that divine testimony through oracles functions in similar and complementary ways. While some functions seen in the examination of oracles had already been noted (e.g., commands/warnings, fulfilled prophecies, and persuasion), the analysis of divine testimony through oracles also provided other functions (i.e., evidence at a trial). I have shown, however, that the overarching function of divine testimony through utterances is the same as that seen in chapter two: the portrayal of a character as either in harmony with the will of the gods (and therefore pious), or the character is depicted as being not in alignment with the gods' will (and therefore impious). As participants in ancient trials were legitimated or denigrated through divine testimony, so also characters in ancient narratives are portrayed as either pious or impious through the application of the *topos*.

In the next chapter, I will turn my attention to the *topos* of divine testimony through utterances in Luke-Acts, and will demonstrate through the analysis there that ancient auditors would have understood the function(s) of this form of the *topos* in Luke-Acts in very similar ways as in the examples above.

4 • The *topos* of Divine Testimony through Utterances in Luke-Acts

IN THE PREVIOUS CHAPTER, by means of an analysis of a variety of Hellenistic narratives composed at approximately the same time as Luke-Acts, I determined that the *topos* of divine testimony through utterances functioned in various ways, all of which served to emphasize the piety or impiety of characters in the narratives. This is the same conclusion drawn from the analysis of the use of this *topos* in ancient speeches and philosophical treatises (see chapter two). Given these results as a backdrop, I am now prepared to examine Luke-Acts. The analysis of the instances of the *topos* of divine testimony through utterances in Luke-Acts will proceed along the same lines as the analysis of the extra-biblical material in the previous chapter. I will break the analysis into the same three categories as employed above: divine testimony through direct speech;[1] divine testimony through the inspired speech of a human intermediary; and finally, divine testimony through reference to and the citation of Jewish scripture.[2] The mode of operation will remain consistent—each passage in which the *topos* occurs will be considered in its narrative context in order to ascertain its function within the greater narrative context in which it is found.

---

1. This category will be further subdivided into speech by God or the Holy Spirit, and speech through angels.
2. Here, however, I will first demonstrate, through a short excursus, that it is appropriate to equate the use of scripture in Luke-Acts with the reference to oracles in Hellenistic writings.

The *Topos* of Divine Testimony in Luke/Acts

Divine Testimony through Direct Speech

In this category of the *topos* of divine testimony through utterances, I will consider examples in which God speaks, the Holy Spirit speaks (directly, not through an intermediary), or an angel speaks. Examples are found in both Luke and Acts.

Luke 9:28–36

The first example I will examine[3] is Luke's account of the transfiguration of Jesus in Luke 9.[4] Earlier in the narrative, Herod, upon hearing of the deeds of Jesus,[5] asks the question, τίς δέ ἐστιν οὗτος περὶ οὗ ἀκούω τοιαῦτα (Luke 9:9)?[6] The transfiguration of Jesus thus figures prominently in answering this question.[7] In 9:28, Jesus παραλαβὼν Πέτρον καὶ Ἰωάννην καὶ Ἰάκωβον ἀνέβη εἰς τὸ ὄρος προσεύξασθαι, thus supplying the context of prayer and worship so often associated with instances of divine testimony.[8] While in prayer on the mountain, Jesus is transformed both physically (τὸ εἶδος τοῦ προσώπου αὐτοῦ ἕτερον) and in his attire (ὁ ἱματισμὸς αὐτοῦ λευκὸς ἐξαστράπτων; 9:29).[9] Moses and Elijah also appear (9:30), and Peter begins

---

3. Clearly, the first example of direct speech by God in the Gospel of Luke is found in 3:21–22, at the baptism of Jesus. I will, however, consider this in chapter six in conjunction with the investigation of divine testimony through deeds, specifically the flight of birds.

4. Lee argues that the Transfiguration constitutes the core of NT theology; see Lee, "On the Holy Mountain," 143–59.

5. The narrative here is not specific; it simply states, Ἤκουσεν δὲ Ἡρῴδης ὁ τετραάρχης τὰ γινόμενα πάντα (Luke 9:7). Given the context, it is safe to assume that Luke is referring to the miraculous deeds of Jesus which have occurred since his inaugural sermon in Nazareth (4:16–30).

6. Talbert, *Reading Luke*, 107, notes that Jesus also asks the same question in 9:20. Brawley (*Centering on God*, 50), connects Herod's question to Jesus' deeds, of which he has heard.

7. According to Ellis (*Christ and the Future*, 62–69), the transfiguration is one of five answers provided through the narrative in chapter nine. In this chapter, Jesus is portrayed as: (i) the provider of the necessities of life (Luke 9:16); (ii) the Messiah (9:20); (iii) God's only son who is the mediator of God's salvation (9:35); (iv) a teacher, through whose works God gives evidence of his glory (9:43); and (v) the Son of man who must suffer (9:22, 29ff, 44).

8. Talbert, *Reading Luke*, 107–108, calls this a "prayer scene."

9. The language here is standard for describing visions of divine beings; see, e.g., Ezek 1:7 (οἱ πόδες αὐτῶν καὶ σπινθῆρες ὡς ἐξαστράπτων χαλκός, describing the feet of the winged creatures in Ezekiel's vision); Dan 10:6 (τὸ πρόσωπον αὐτοῦ ὡσεὶ ὅρασις

Divine Testimony through Utterances in Luke-Acts

to speak of building shelters and staying on the mountain (9:33). At this point a cloud covers "them,"[10] and a voice from the cloud states: Οὗτός ἐστιν ὁ υἱός μου ὁ ἐκλελεγμένος, αὐτοῦ ἀκούετε (9:35).[11]

The voice reminds the auditor of the voice at Jesus' baptism. Here, as in that situation, the divine testimony is clearly one of affirmation of Jesus.[12] But equally as obvious, the voice issues a command to Peter and John: αὐτοῦ ἀκούετε. The nature of the command is best understood through what precedes and follows this account; Jesus has just explained to his disciples that he must suffer and be killed as part of his mission (see 9:21-22). Thus the divine affirmation, in context, specifically sanctions the words

---

ἀστραπῆς, describing a heavenly being in a vision); cf. *T. Ab.* 7.3-4 ("And while I (Isaac) was thus watching and exulting at these things, I saw heaven opened, and I saw a light-bearing man coming down out of heaven, flashing more than seven suns"); and ibid., 16.6 ("When Death heard these things he left the presence of the Most High and donned a most radiant robe and made his appearance sunlike and become more comely and beautiful than the sons of men, assuming the form of an archangel, his cheeks flashing with fire"); see also Philo, *Mos.* 1.66. Humans who are being portrayed in a divine way are described in a similar fashion; see, e.g., Plutarch, *Rom.* 28.1-2; Philo, *Mos.* 2.68.

D. Luther ("The Mystery," 92-102) describes Jesus' transfiguration as the "prolepsis of the new creation" (ibid., 102). Foster notes that "polymorphism" was a standard means of describing Jesus for both docetists and pre-Nicean theologians. For docetists, Jesus' ability (seen in Luke 9 and 24) demonstrated that for him, the material realm was less significant. For non-docetists, Jesus' transformation, especially after his resurrection, demonstrated his victory over death. See Foster, "Polymorphic Christology," 66-99. For other studies of the transfiguration and its contribution to christology, see: idem, "Exegetical Notes," 188-89; Williams, "The Transfiguration," 13-25 (here, Williams argues that the transfiguration is the revelation of Jesus as Son of God); idem, "The Transfiguration (Part 2)," 17-27, in which Williams furthers his earlier discussion by arguing that the Transfiguration reveals a new epoch in salvation history. For the possible Jewish background of the Transfiguration account, see Basser, "The Jewish Roots," 30-35; Basser reads the synoptic accounts of Jesus' transfiguration through the lens of rabbinic literature, in which he finds a midrash on Ps 43. Here, the liberation of Egypt through Moses is compared to the liberation that will come through the Messiah. In this same passage, Elijah is named as the messenger who will announce the arrival of the Messiah.

10. Green, *Luke*, 383-84, argues that the cloud serves as the "divine presence," and covers Peter and John. According to Green, previously in the account the emphasis was on visual elements (see ibid., 377); now, with the covering of the cloud, the emphasis shifts to the disciples' sense of hearing, rather than sight.

11. Schneider, *Lukas: Kapitel 1-10*, 214, claims that the divine voice is the "peak" of revelation, a particularly appropriate comment given the setting of the divine voice.

12. Fitzmyer, *Luke I-IX*, 792, aptly states that the voice in 3:21-22 introduces Jesus' earthly ministry just as the voice here introduces Jesus' journey to Jerusalem.

which Jesus has spoken to the disciples.[13] In the narrative that follows, it becomes apparent that the disciples have a difficult time understanding this fact.[14] Thus, while the main function of the divine testimony is the divine approval of Jesus, secondarily the divine testimony alerts the auditor to the fact that the disciples may not completely understand exactly who Jesus is.[15]

Acts 13:1–3

A second example of direct, divine speech occurs in Acts 13. Acts 13:1–3 is a commissioning story,[16] in which Saul and Barnabas are "set apart" (ἀφορίζω; 13:2) by the congregation[17] in Antioch. Luke describes the context as λειτουργούντων δὲ αὐτῶν τῷ κυρίῳ καὶ νηστευόντων (13:2a), thus providing a setting of worship and fasting that prepares the auditor for an instance of divine testimony. The congregation is told directly by the

---

13. Green's comments are appropriate: "In short, in the transfiguration scene Jesus and his words, even when they are unconventional or seem bizarre, receive divine sanction" (Green, *Luke*, 377). T. Martin states, "When the implied author brings God into the Gospel's conversation, it is to expose the reader to the most authoritative voice possible" ("What Makes Glory Glorious?," 13).

14. J. Miller, *Convinced*, 157–58, in his treatment of this passage (Miller considers this a dream-vision), emphasizes the disciples' lack of understanding in the immediate context of the transfiguration. See also Moessner, "Luke 9:1–50," 575–605, who argues that the narrative immediately following also demonstrates the disciples' lack of understanding (actually, more correctly, their disobedience). For example, Moessner notes that in 9:33–47, the disciples are unable to exorcise a demon, which is due to their disobedience with regard to the divine voice.

15. The auditor already has a hint that this is the case through Peter's words on the mountain and the fact that the divine voice interrupts his speech. Also, the narrator explicitly describes Peter, while he is speaking, as μὴ εἰδὼς ὃ λέγει (9:33). In addition to these points, Green (*Luke*, 383) argues for two additional elements in the narrative which point in this direction: first, the disciples are described as being "sleepy" (ὁ δὲ Πέτρος καὶ οἱ σὺν αὐτῷ ἦσαν βεβαρημένοι ὕπνῳ; 9:32), which Green interprets as being indicative of their spiritual condition (on this, see also Tannehill, *Luke*, 224); also, Peter addresses Jesus as Ἐπιστάτα (9:33), as opposed to Κύριε.

16. For the form of commissioning stories, see Hubbard, "Commissioning Stories," 103–26. Oddly, in this essay, Hubbard does not refer to Acts 13:1–3. He rectifies this, however, in his later essay on the same subject; see Hubbard, "The Role of Commissioning Accounts," 197. Talbert, *Reading Acts*, 116, provides the details concerning the form of this particular commissioning account: introduction, 13:1–2a; "confrontation," 13:2b; commissioning proper, 13:2c; conclusion, 13:3.

17. Parsons, *Acts*, 184, argues that the αὐτῶν in the genitive absolute of 13:2 refers to the entire congregation, not just those listed in 13:1.

Divine Testimony through Utterances in Luke-Acts

Holy Spirit[18] to commission Saul and Barnabas for a specific task: εἶπεν τὸ πνεῦμα τὸ ἅγιον, Ἀφορίσατε δή μοι τὸν Βαρναβᾶν καὶ Σαῦλον εἰς τὸ ἔργον ὃ προσκέκλημαι αὐτούς (13:2b), which it does (13:3).[19] The commissioning itself is accomplished through the laying on of hands (see 13:3).[20]

The *topos* in this case, as seen in the previous example, serves as a divine command to the church in Antioch. The congregation, as well as Saul and Barnabas, are portrayed as obedient to the command through their immediate submission to the divine directive.[21] The importance of this command is seen in its relation to the overall narrative of Luke-Acts. As I will show, God testifies at the beginning of Jesus' earthly ministry through the giving of the Holy Spirit (in the form of a dove) and divine speech. In Acts 2, divine testimony also accompanies the beginning of the apostles' ministry (on this, see below). Here, Saul and Barnabas's first missionary efforts are also commenced through the testimony of the Holy Spirit in the form of a command.[22]

In Luke-Acts, there are multiple examples of direct, divine speech, the source of which is angelic beings. I will consider angelic speech through visions in chapter six; in the following, I will consider those points in the narrative in which angels speak to human characters in situations in which it is not explicitly stated that a character is experiencing a dream-vision.[23]

---

18. As noted by Parsons, *Acts*, 184, this is the only time that the Holy Spirit directly addresses a group of people in Acts. Some scholars argue that the Holy Spirit is speaking through a prophet within the congregation (cf. 13:1); see, e.g., Talbert, *Reading Acts*, 116; Tannehill, *Acts*, 160. Best, "Acts XIII. 1–3," 344–48, notes that this is the first time in Acts that the church intentionally sends out missionaries for the singular task of evangelism; Best sees a parallel to the dedication of the Levites in Num 8 in the OT.

19. The commissioning itself follows more fasting and prayer (τότε νηστεύσαντες καὶ προσευξάμενοι; 13:3). J. Miller, *Convinced*, 221, argues that the fasting and prayer that occur after the Holy Spirit speaks is evidence that the congregation continues to consider whether to commission Saul and Barnabas. He comes to this conclusion by comparing this passage to the immediate obedience of Philip (in Acts 8) and Peter (in Acts 10) to the Spirit's directives. This seems, however, to be highly speculative.

20. L. Johnson, *Acts*, 221, and Parsons, *Acts*, 185, both note that the laying on of hands should be considered as a conferral of authority to Saul and Barnabas. This is certainly true, the ultimate authority being derived from the Holy Spirit's commission.

21. *Contra* J. Miller, *Convinced*, 221 (see n. 19 above).

22. See Parsons, *Acts*, 184, who also recognizes the work of the Holy Spirit in all three of these cases. Cf. Tannehill, *Acts*, 160. L. Johnson, *Acts*, 221, remarks that 13:4 emphasizes the divine nature of the commissioning; there the text states: Αὐτοὶ μὲν οὖν ἐκπεμφθέντες ὑπὸ τοῦ ἁγίου πνεύματος κατῆλθον εἰς Σελεύκειαν.

23. Here, clearly one could disagree (as some do; see discussion below) with my decision to treat these within the category of divine speech rather than dream-visions.

The *Topos* of Divine Testimony in Luke/Acts

Luke 2:8–20

Here, the ἄγγελος κυρίου appears[24] to the shepherds outside of Bethlehem in order to announce to them the birth of Jesus, which was prophesied to Mary in 1:32–33. Thus, the announcement[25] serves as the fulfillment element of the prophecy-fulfillment schema so prevalent throughout Luke-Acts,[26] and would have been understood as an affirmation of Jesus' birth. It also serves to interpret the birth of Jesus and its meaning for "all people" (2:10).[27] The angel's proclamation to the shepherds[28] has an additional function as well. The angel tells the shepherds that τοῦτο ὑμῖν τὸ σημεῖον, εὑρήσετε βρέφος ἐσπαργανωμένον καὶ κείμενον ἐν φάτνῃ (2:12), which is a prophetic statement, almost immediately fulfilled in 2:16–17.[29]

After the angelic visitation, the shepherds immediately go to Bethlehem to verify what they were told through the divine speech. In this way they are characterized as giving great significance to what the angels have said. They also tell others, who are "amazed"[30] at what the shepherds

---

At the end of the day, however, both divine speech and dream-visions are elements of the *topos* of divine testimony; the decision to include angelic speech in one category or the other does not affect the overall argument being made here.

24. J. Miller, *Convinced*, 147, treats this as a dream-vision, noting that the visual element in this account is emphasized as compared to the angel's interactions with Zechariah and Mary. Fitzmyer, *Luke I–IX*, 409, points out that the verb ἐφίστημι is typically used in ancient Greek literature to describe a vision. Green, *Luke*, 131, tentatively associates this angel with Gabriel, since Gabriel has already made two appearances in the narrative up to this point.

25. Green, *Luke*, 132, notes that the structure of this announcement (9a, angel; 9b, fear; announcement proper, 10–11; promise of a sign, 12) is similar to the earlier two given to Zechariah and Mary. Green goes on to say that it differs in that it is given to "outsiders" (the shepherds are not part of the family, and they are outside the social circle of Zechariah/Elizabeth and Mary), and it is given after the fact, rather than before.

26. See Talbert, *Reading Luke*, 33; cf. L. Johnson, *Luke*, 52.

27. L. Johnson, *Luke*, 52, states: "[T]he angelic presence gives a divine legitimation not only to the events but to the interpretation of them in the narrative itself." Regarding the interpretation by the angels, Coleridge makes a similar point, arguing that the angelic speech serves to interpret the events of the narrative for the Luke's auditors; see Coleridge, *The Birth of the Lukan Narrative*, 143.

28. The proclamation of the angel of the Lord is accompanied by the praise of the heavenly host in 2:13–14. For an analysis of the different versions of the Gloria, (Greek, Latin, Syriac, and Coptic, as well as the author's reconstruction of same in Hebrew) see Olsson, "Gloria," 89–94; cf. idem, "Canticle," 147–66.

29. Talbert, *Reading Luke*, 33. The sign serves as evidence of the truth of the angel's pronouncement; see L. Johnson, *Luke*, 50.

30. Luke 2:18: καὶ πάντες οἱ ἀκούσαντες ἐθαύμασαν περὶ τῶν λαληθέντων ὑπὸ τῶν ποιμένων πρὸς αὐτούς.

Divine Testimony through Utterances in Luke-Acts

have to say (2:17–18). Therefore, the divine testimony of the angels serves to sanction the shepherds[31] and their witness. The divine testimony also serves as divine sanction of the birth of Jesus, as it is part of the greater complex of divine testimony surrounding the birth, childhood, and pre-ministry stage of Luke's account of Jesus.[32]

Luke 24:1–12 / Acts 1:1–14

Divine testimony through the speech of angels also occurs in Luke's account of Jesus' resurrection in Luke 24:1–12 and Jesus' ascension in Acts 1:1–14. These two passages both involve two angels,[33] whose speech serves to interpret what is occurring in the narrative, and also, in the case of Acts 1, to prophesy.[34] In Luke 24, the angels remind the women who discover the empty tomb of what Jesus had said earlier, thus interpreting for them

---

31. This is all the more striking when one considers the low social standing of shepherds in first-century Palestine. Talbert, *Reading Luke*, 35, terms them "outcasts" within their cultural environment. Green, *Luke*, 130–31, states that shepherds in general were at the "bottom of the scale of power and privilege." While he does not specifically address shepherds in first-century Palestine, G. Lenski (*Power and Privilege*, 66–78) in a sociological study does draw attention to the marginal status of the peasant class throughout history and across various socio-cultural contexts.

32. This is especially true when one considers the implicit comparison to Augustus, who is mentioned in 2:1 in the political background to the event of Jesus' birth. On this comparison, see Fitzmyer, *Luke I–IX*, 393–94; Brown, "Meaning," 532–33; Green, *Luke*, 134–35. Green points out that Augustus was known as "Savior" and "Lord," as well as a benefactor of the people. The use of σωτήρ and κύριος in 2:11, as well as the angel's statement (in 2:10), εὐαγγελίζομαι ὑμῖν χαρὰν μεγάλην ἥτις ἔσται παντὶ τῷ λαῷ, of which Jesus is the subject, leads Green to state: "Together [these connections to Augustus in the text] underscore the exalted status Jesus has in God's purpose and with the community of God's people" (ibid., 135).

33. In Luke 24:4, the men are described as being ἐν ἐσθῆτι ἀστραπτούσῃ, which is similar to the description of Jesus at the transfiguration (ὁ ἱματισμὸς αὐτοῦ λευκὸς ἐξαστράπτων; Luke 9:29). The two men in Acts 1:10 are described as being ἐν ἐσθήσεσι λευκαῖς. Therefore, with Dillon (*Eye-Witnesses to Ministers*, 22), I understand these two figures in both Luke 24 and Acts 1 to be divine beings. See also L. Johnson, *Luke*, 387, who argues that the participial form of the verb ἀστράπτω used in 24:4 gives the narrative a supernatural aspect. He also tentatively associates the two men in Luke 24 with those in Acts 1.

34. The two passages parallel each other: the angels are introduced similarly (Luke 24:4/Acts 1:10); the men's clothing is consistent (Luke 24:4/Acts 1:10); the women and disciples are both rebuked through a question (Luke 24:5/Acts 1:11); the women are reminded of the words of Jesus, while the disciples are told to look forward to Jesus' return (Luke 24:6–7/Acts 1:11). See Tannehill, *Acts*, 19.

The *Topos* of Divine Testimony in Luke/Acts

what has happened through Jesus' earlier prophecies.[35] The women then report what they heard from the angels to the disciples, who consider the women's testimony "λῆρος" (Luke 24:11). At this point, Peter views the empty tomb for himself (Luke 24:12).[36]

The angels' words in Luke 24 thus serve primarily as divine testimony to the reality of Jesus' resurrection to Luke's auditors. They also function as divine legitimation of the women as witnesses to Jesus' resurrection. Simultaneously, given the disciples' reaction of unbelief concerning what the women tell them, the disciples are portrayed negatively in that they do not believe the testimony of the angels, related to them through the women who were in the tomb. Thus there is an implicit syncrisis between the women and the disciples, the women being validated by divine testimony, and the disciples being chastised through their disbelief.

In Acts 1:1–14, two angelic figures interpret Jesus' ascension for the disciples gathered in Jerusalem. Their words, recorded in 1:11,[37] constitute a rebuke and a promise. First, the angel asks a question: Ἄνδρες Γαλιλαῖοι, τί ἑστήκατε βλέποντες εἰς τὸν οὐρανόν; (1:11a). Second, the angel then utters a prophetic statement: οὗτος ὁ Ἰησοῦς ὁ ἀναλημφθεὶς ἀφ' ὑμῶν εἰς τὸν οὐρανὸν οὕτως ἐλεύσεται ὃν τρόπον ἐθεάσασθε αὐτὸν πορευόμενον εἰς τὸν οὐρανόν (1:11b). Therefore, as in Luke 24, the *topos* of divine testimony serves to interpret the extraordinary event of Jesus' ascension, as well as a prophecy concerning Jesus' return. The divine testimony through

---

35. Talbert, *Reading Luke*, 256, states that the angels' words "interpret the empirical data" presented by the empty tomb. L. Johnson, *Luke*, 387, recognizes the "backward" view of the passage; he also argues that the angel's question in 24:5 (Τί ζητεῖτε τὸν ζῶντα μετὰ τῶν νεκρῶν) is a rebuke in the form of a reminder. Mainville ("De Jésus à l'Église," 192–211) argues that the women's recognition of the empty tomb and the angels' words form a narrative "bridge" from Jesus of Nazareth to the living, resurrected Christ (see esp. ibid., 195). This is the first of many "bridges" that Mainville identifies in Luke 24.

36. Talbert, "The Place of the Resurrection," 24, maintains that Peter's viewing of the empty tomb in 24:12 constitutes a second witness, significant in a Jewish context. I would slightly amend this statement to say that, from the auditor's perspective, Peter is actually the third witness, after the angels themselves and the women.

Some significant manuscripts omit Luke 24:12. Metzger, however, argues that v. 12 is in harmony with the statement in 24:24, and should therefore be included. See Metzger, *A Textual Commentary*, 157–58.

37. Pervo (*Acts*, 41) argues that Acts 1:7–11 is structured chiastically, with Jesus' ascension (v. 9) in the center. Significantly, the B and B′ elements of the chiasm are rebukes, one by Jesus in v. 8 (an implied rebuke), and the speech of the angelic beings in vv. 10b–11. Thus, through this structure, the significance of the words of the angels is emphasized through their chiastic association with the words of Jesus.

Divine Testimony through Utterances in Luke-Acts

the angels' words testifies to the divine nature of Jesus' resurrection, and serves as a divine call on the disciples to prepare themselves to serve as witnesses.[38]

Acts 8:26, 29

In Acts 8:26, 29, Philip is led to the Ethiopian eunuch through direct commands given to him by an "angel of the Lord" (8:26) and the Spirit (8:29).[39] The command attributed to the angel directs Philip to go down to the road connecting Jerusalem and Gaza. Once on the road, Philip encounters the Ethiopian eunuch in his chariot, traveling back from Jerusalem to Ethiopia. The Spirit tells Philip to go up to the chariot.[40] Thus, through divine testimony in the form of commands,[41] Philip has a divinely-ordained encounter with the Ethiopian eunuch, the result of which is the eunuch's conversion and baptism (8:36–40).[42]

---

38. See Tannehill, *Acts*, 19, who considers this passage a divine "call to action." Parsons, *Acts*, 28, recognizes the twofold nature of the angels' words, noting that there is both rebuke and promise in them. He concludes, however, commenting on Jesus' last words to the disciples and the angels' speech, by stating: "Despite the reproaches, both dialogues end with promises to the disciples, thus inviting a favorable judgment of the disciples by the audience."

39. The account of Philip and the Ethiopian eunuch is found in 8:26–40. Pervo (*Acts*, 219–23) maintains that this account lines up thematically with the Emmaus story in Luke 24:13–35, calling the parallels between the two accounts "striking." Squires argues that Acts 8:4—12:25 is a pivotal narrative in Acts, in which the auditor is prepared for the inclusion of the Gentiles into the Jewish-Christian community. See Squires, "The Function," 608–17.

40. Talbert, *Reading Acts*, 74, argues that 8:26–30b unfolds in two panels which parallel each other. In vv. 26–28, the angel tells Philip to go (v. 26); he goes (v. 27a); and he sees (vv. 27b–28). In vv. 29–30b: the Spirit tells Philip to go (v. 29); he runs to the chariot (v. 30a); once at the chariot he hears (v. 30b).

41. L. Johnson, *Acts*, 155, terms it "divine guidance." Van Unnik, "Der Befehl an Philippus," 1:328–39, considering only the angel's command to Philip in 8:1–3, sees the significance in the command in that it makes no logical sense. Philip, in 8:1–25, has already been portrayed as a successful evangelist; the command, as van Unnik understands it, would be to send Philip to a road in the wilderness in the middle of the day, a place and time at which one would not expect to meet others. Thus, the command introduces a new, radical movement in the spread of the gospel. One should note, however, that much of van Unnik's thesis rests on translating κατὰ μεσημβρίαν in a temporal sense, i.e., "at noon." For a convincing argument against this translation and for a directional sense of μεσημβρίαν, see Culy and Parsons, *Acts*, 162.

42. According to Talbert, *Reading Acts*, 74, and Parsons, *Acts*, 111–12, there are three scenes in this narrative (vv. 26–30b—the divine guidance which unites Philip

The *Topos* of Divine Testimony in Luke/Acts

Clearly, the *topos* of divine testimony through utterances functions here as divine commands, to which Philip is obedient. Thus, Philip is portrayed as a compliant witness to Jesus, and the gospel's reach extends even to Ethiopia. Through divine testimony, Philip is sanctioned as a witness to the gospel,[43] and the conversion of the Ethiopian eunuch is given divine approval.[44]

Acts 5, 12

The last two examples of the *topos* of divine testimony through direct speech of the gods come from Acts 5 and Acts 12, narratives in which angels free disciples from prison. In Acts 5, the apostles are described as performing many signs and wonders (σημεῖα καὶ τέρατα πολλὰ);[45] Peter especially is described as performing acts of healing and exorcisms (5:12–16). Two results are described: (i) the tremendous growth of the nascent Christian community (5:14); and (ii) the jealousy (or zeal)[46] of the high priest and other Jewish leaders (ἐπλήσθησαν ζήλου; 5:17).[47] Therefore, the disciples are arrested and imprisoned (Acts 5:18).

---

and the eunuch; vv. 30c–35—Philip's interaction with the eunuch; vv. 36–40—the results of the encounter). I have not dealt with the second scene, but will do so in my discussion of divine testimony through the use of scripture. At this point, it is sufficient to say that the divine guidance through the angel's and Spirit's commands sets up Philip's interaction with the eunuch, which is the focal point of the account; see the chiastic structure of which 8:35 is the center in Parsons, *Acts*, 118.

43. Tannehill, *Acts*, 108, states, "As one who is divinely directed, Philip acts with authority."

44. L. Johnson, *Acts*, 158, emphasizes the high political status of the Ethiopian eunuch, and thus sees legitimation for the spread of the gospel through his conversion. He writes, "It is no small part of apologetic literature to emphasize how one's special claims have met with approval from respectable people." While agreeing with Johnson to some degree, I would argue that the greater apologetic point is made through the divine testimony of the angel/Spirit in the passage.

45. On the importance of σημεῖα in Acts and their interrelatedness to the spoken word, see O'Reilly, *Word and Sign*. In this monograph, O'Reilly argues that whenever the expression "σημεῖα καὶ τέρατα" (or something similar) is used, it is in close conjunction with the proclaimed word. Thus, signs authenticate the proclaimed word of the apostles, and together they function to legitimate the gospel. For a similar argument, see Weiß, "Zeichen und Wunder," 73–94.

46. Talbert argues that the Jewish religious leaders described here are exhibiting zeal for the purity of the Jewish religion; see Talbert, *Reading Acts*, 52–53.

47. The text at this point specifically states: ὁ ἀρχιερεὺς καὶ πάντες οἱ σὺν αὐτῷ, ἡ οὖσα αἵρεσις τῶν Σαδδουκαίων.

Divine Testimony through Utterances in Luke-Acts

At this point, Luke explains that an angel of the Lord frees the apostles from their cell(s) (5:19)[48] and gives them the following command: Πορεύεσθε καὶ σταθέντες λαλεῖτε ἐν τῷ λαῷ πάντα τὰ ῥήματα τῆς ζωῆς ταύτης (5:20). After receiving this command, the apostles respond obediently: ἀκούσαντες δὲ εἰσῆλθον ὑπὸ τὸν ὄρθρον εἰς τὸ ἱερὸν καὶ ἐδίδασκον (5:21a). The divine testimony through the words of the angel again functions as a command, to which the apostles readily submit.[49] Significantly, the divine testimony of the angel's words[50] (and actions) serves to assert God's pronouncement of the apostles' innocence,[51] while simultaneously casting aspersions on those who would wrongly try to imprison them.[52]

In Acts 12, Peter is imprisoned by Herod, who, according to Luke, does so in order to curry favor with the Jews (12:3). Peter, described as being restrained with two chains and sleeping between two soldiers (with more guards at the door of the prison; 12:6) is freed by an angel.[53] The angel gives him a series of commands: Ἀνάστα ἐν τάχει (12:7); Ζῶσαι καὶ ὑπόδησαι τὰ σανδάλιά σου (12:8a); Περιβαλοῦ τὸ ἱμάτιόν σου καὶ ἀκολούθει μοι (12:8c).[54] In each case, Luke narrates a result of the command: καὶ

---

48. Parsons (*Acts*, 77) correctly recognizes the irony of the apostles being freed by an angel, when their imprisonment was due in part to the Sadducees (cf. Acts 23:8).

49. Pervo (*Acts*, 143) emphasizes that Peter has been liberated in order to continue to proclaim the gospel; thus the scene serves as an example of being empowered for mission through resurrection (he notes the use of the word ζωή in 5:20).

50. Weaver, *Plots of Epiphany*, 104–114, argues that the angel's words have three emphases. First, the words have an "inceptive force," which indicates a new, divinely directed movement in the spread of the gospel; hence, the words are a form of commissioning. Second, the command has a "locative" aspect; the apostles are specifically told to proclaim the gospel in the temple. Here, Weaver states that "the angel sanctions the Christian leaders and their proclamation within the Jerusalem temple." Third, the command to speak πάντα τὰ ῥήματα τῆς ζωῆς ταύτης is a call to preach the resurrection of Jesus. Thus, Weaver connects the act of being freed from prison to resurrection from the dead; on this, see below in the discussion of Acts 12.

51. Haenchen, *Apostelgeschichte*, 209, notes that this is a "Gerichtsszene."

52. Talbert recognizes that prison escapes represented a specific Gattung in antiquity. He goes on to note that the purpose of this Gattung often was to demonstrate that a god's purposes could not be obstructed by human beings; see Talbert, *Reading Acts*, 53.

53. Luke describes the angel's arrival with the statement: καὶ φῶς ἔλαμψεν ἐν τῷ οἰκήματι (12:7). Brenk, "Greek Epiphanies," 354–63, recognizes the importance of light in epiphanies (cited by Weaver, *Plots of Epiphany*, 165). Brenk, however, emphasizes the sanctifying aspect of lightning in Greek epiphanies and relates it to Paul's commissioning in Acts 9.

54. Scholars have recognized the Exodus imagery in this passage; see, e.g., Strobel, "Passa-Symbolik," 210–15; Garrett, "Exodus from Bondage," 656–80. Garrett, in her

ἐξέπεσαν αὐτοῦ αἱ ἁλύσεις ἐκ τῶν χειρῶν (12:7); ἐποίησεν δὲ οὕτως (12:8b); καὶ ἐξελθὼν ἠκολούθει (12:9).[55] Through these results, especially in 12:7 and 12:8b, Peter is portrayed as obedient to the commands of the angel.[56]

Again, the divine testimony through the angel's commands and actions serve as a divine declaration of Peter's innocence in the face of Herod's accusations.[57] Also, as seen in Acts 5, the divine testimony here demonstrates God's disapproval of Herod's attempt to hinder the spread of the gospel through the imprisonment of Peter.[58] This interpretation is strengthened by the narrative at the end of chapter twelve, in which a vain Herod meets his demise through an angel of the Lord (see 12:20–23). Thus, human beings from the religious establishment and the political arena attempt to obstruct the movement of the gospel; in both cases, the apostles are declared to be innocent through divine testimony, and their accusers are pronounced guilty.

In summary of the function of the *topos* of divine testimony through direct speech in Luke-Acts, in the majority of cases, the *topos* functions as

---

essay, also compares Peter's liberation from prison to the resurrection, in that at their core both acts are a defeat of Satan. For Peter's liberation as a resurrection from death in general, see Horton, *Death and Resurrection*, 40–45. On imprisonment as a metaphor for death, see Wansink, *Chained in Christ*, 74–78. For a completely different view, see Morton, "Acts 12:1–19," 67–69, who reads this account as an example of ancient comedy, going so far as to call it "slapstick." Morton correctly recognizes the build-up of tension in the narrative through 12:1–5, but dubiously sees the resolution of that tension in a series of comedic scenes. Pervo offers yet a third possibility; he argues that this narrative represents "a symbolic portrayal of Peter's 'passion,' 'resurrection,' and vindication that, through initiatory language, makes it a paradigm of Christian experience" (Pervo, *Acts*, 302).

55. Parsons (*Acts*, 174–75) reads this somewhat differently. He argues that the commands of the angel demonstrate the angel's authority, which is certainly correct, but that Peter is portrayed as passive in the narrative (See also Weaver, *Plots*, 162–66; Weaver describes Peter as an "automaton"). From an authority standpoint, Parsons is correct. The angel is in complete control.

56. Prayer also plays a significant role in the narrative. After Peter is liberated from the prison, Luke explains that he goes to Mary's house, where the community is gathered and at prayer (12:12).

57. Wall, "Successors," 628–43, understands the report of Peter's liberation from prison as a hinge between the account of his ministry and that of Paul. Through his liberation, Peter is legitimated and therefore empowered to assign his successor in Jerusalem (i.e., James; cf. 12:17).

58. Haenchen, *Apostelgeschichte*, 331, recognizes the implicit syncrisis between Peter and Herod: "Blickt man auf diese beiden eigentlichen Schwerpunkte, die Rettung des Petrus und den Tod des Herodes, dann treten diese beiden Personen als Gegenspieler in der lukanischen Komposition hervor."

Divine Testimony through Utterances in Luke-Acts

a command to the recipient of the divine speech and therefore as a revelation of divine guidance. But it can also serve as a prophecy which is later fulfilled in the narrative, thus affirming the event in question (see the example from Luke 2), or as a reminder of earlier prophecies which current events now fulfill (the angels at Jesus' tomb in Luke 24) and explain the occurrence. Finally, direct divine speech in Luke-Acts also functions as the interpretation of an extraordinary occurrence, as the angel's speech to the apostles in Acts 1. These are functions which I have demonstrated are also found in the examples of the *topos* of divine testimony through utterances in Hellenistic histories and biographies, and therefore would have been readily understood by the ancient auditors of Luke-Acts.

DIVINE TESTIMONY THROUGH THE SPEECH OF AN INSPIRED INTERMEDIARY

In this section I will analyze those instances in Luke-Acts in which a human being is described as speaking πλησθεὶς πνεύματος ἁγίου (Acts 4:8). There are examples of this type of the *topos* of divine testimony throughout Luke-Acts; several will be considered here.

Luke 1:67–79; 2:25–35

Here, I will examine two instances of inspired speech from the birth narratives of John the Baptist and Jesus which involve prophetic, inspired speech through Zechariah and Simeon.[59] One should note that Luke describes Zechariah in terms which emphasize his piety and obedience.[60] In the passage under consideration here, Zechariah demonstrates his obedience to the angelic command to name his son John.[61] Forthwith, he regains his ability to speak, which Luke describes thusly: Καὶ Ζαχαρίας ὁ πατὴρ αὐτοῦ

---

59. Green, *Luke*, 142–43, recognizes that within the greater context of the birth narrative, Zechariah and Simeon are parallel figures, providing inspired prophecy concerning John and Jesus respectively.

60. He is, however, made to be mute as punishment for doubting the angel's words. In chapter six, I will discuss the character of Zechariah in the context of his vision of the angel Gabriel while serving as priest in the temple.

61. Carter attempts to answer the question, "Why Zechariah?" His answer (see Carter, "Zechariah," 239–47) is that Zechariah is righteous and a worshipper of God, demonstrated in this passage through his obedience in naming his son John and praising God with his first words in the Benedictus.

ἐπλήσθη πνεύματος ἁγίου καὶ ἐπροφήτευσεν λέγων (Luke 1:67). What follows indeed contains a prophetic statement,[62] but is preceded by an extended praise of God, grounded in his past actions on behalf of Israel.[63]

The divine testimony through the inspired prophecy of Zechariah[64] serves within the extended comparison of the births and early lives of John and Jesus to demonstrate the divine approval of Jesus' messenger, John. John will be called προφήτης ὑψίστου (1:76a), and will precede Jesus, announcing to the people his coming and the promise of forgiveness of sins (1:76b–77).[65] The comparison to Jesus is reinforced by Simeon's prophecy in the temple, proclaimed when Mary and Joseph bring Jesus to be presented in the temple, which is the next example of divine testimony to be analyzed.

Simeon is described by Luke in terms similar to those used in his description of Zechariah; Simeon is δίκαιος καὶ εὐλαβής (2:25), and πνεῦμα ἦν ἅγιον ἐπ' αὐτόν (2:25).[66] In addition, the auditor learns that: ἦν αὐτῷ

---

62. It is significant to recognize, along with Dillon ("Benedictus," 457–80), that Zechariah's speech is written in a poetic form, signaling the departure from pure narration. This is also the case in the speech by Olibus in Plutarch's *Life* of Themistocles (26.2; discussed in chapter 3).

63. The break at 1:76, in which Zechariah's speech changes from third-person (speaking of what God has done) to second-person (directly addressing the child, John) is noted by many scholars. See, e.g., Klein, *Lukasevangelium*, 121. L. Johnson, *Luke*, 47, thus describes this speech as a "hinge," through which Gabriel's words to Zechariah are fulfilled, and a new prophecy concerning John is proclaimed. In this way Zechariah's speech serves also to recapitulate what the angel originally told Zechariah. The second part of the speech (1:76–79) describes how John will fulfill his role. See Talbert, *Reading Luke*, 30. Talbert (*Reading Luke*, 30) and Tannehill (*Luke*, 33) also recognize that the prophetic portion of Zechariah's speech is fulfilled in Luke 3:16 and 7:26–27. Attempts to assign a chiastic structure to this passage, based on the multiple uses of key words, are ultimately unconvincing. See, e.g., Auffret, "Lc 1.68–79," 248–58; Klein, *Lukasevangelium*, 120.

Gathercole, "Heavenly ἀνατολή," 471–88, argues that ἀνατολή in this context should be understood as describing a preexistent, Davidic messiah.

64. Green, *Luke*, 115, recognizes the significance of Zechariah being filled with the Spirit. He compares Zechariah to the OT prophets, who are described as being anointed with the Spirit in order that the audience understands that they are spokespersons for God. He states, "Because he is 'filled with the Spirit,' Zechariah's words command attention and engender faith in his message."

65. Shuler, "Rhetorical Character," 183, argues that John's role as a prophet is emphasized through: the mention of God's act of "visiting" (ἐπεσκέψατο; 1:68); reference to OT prophets (1:70); "prophetic references" to enemies (1:71, 74); and the "goal" of service to God (1:75).

66. Green, *Luke*, 142–43, adds that both men are in the temple. He also includes

κεχρηματισμένον ὑπὸ τοῦ πνεύματος τοῦ ἁγίου μὴ ἰδεῖν θάνατον πρὶν [ἢν] ἂν ἴδῃ τὸν Χριστὸν κυρίου (2:26).[67] Finally, when Mary, Joseph, and Jesus are in the temple, Simeon enters ἐν τῷ πνεύματι (2:26). Thus, Simeon is portrayed as being addressed and led by the Spirit, and is therefore an inspired, reliable character.[68]

The divine testimony through Simeon's inspired speech is prophetic, foreseeing the ministry of Jesus both to Gentiles and Israel (2:32). But when Simeon turns his attention to Mary, his prophecy takes on an ominous tone, anticipating the division of the people, as well as suffering for Mary.[69] Therefore, as Zechariah prophesied concerning the future career of his son John as one who would go before Jesus, preparing the people for God's salvation (1:76–77), here Simeon prophesies concerning the future career of Jesus as the agent of God's σωτήριον (2:30).[70] Both careers are therefore sanctioned through divine testimony, provided through inspired characters, sustaining the comparison between John and Jesus that is found throughout the accounts of their births.

Anna, the prophetess, as a parallel figure to Simeon (and thus, implicitly, to Zechariah). See also Klein, *Lukasevangelium*, 143; Tannehill, *Luke*, 38–39.

67. L. Johnson, *Luke*, 55, rightly recognizes that the verb χρηματίζω is often used in Hellenistic literature to describe the receiving of oracles.

68. Green, *Luke*, 144, cogently states: "The focal point of the characterization of Simeon in this narrative is his believability." Cf. L. Johnson, *Luke*, 56, who describes Simeon as "a reliable prophetic spokesperson." Figueras argues that the figures of Simeon and Anna are portrayed to represent Moses and Elijah (respectively), and therefore the witness of the law and the prophets to Jesus' birth; see Figueras, "Syméon et Anne," 84–99. For an analysis of a visual portrayal of this scene from the fourteenth century, see Hornik and Parsons, *"Presentation in the Temple,"* 31–46. Hornik and Parsons argue that Ambrogio, while being the first artist to represent the infant Jesus as a child in his painting, simultaneously emphasizes the salvific significance of Jesus found in the literary account.

69. Brown, "Presentation of Jesus," 2–11, argues that the background for the sword image in 2:35 is Ezek 14:17. He also sees a parallel in *Sib. Or.* 3.316: "[F]or a sword will pass through your midst and a scattering and death and famine will lay hold of you." L. Johnson, *Luke*, 57, calls Simeon's statement to Mary a "symbolic representation." For the purposes of this study, this is significant; Olibus also delivers an inspired, prophetic message (Plutarch, *Them.* 26.2; see chapter 3), which is somewhat obscure and expressed in symbolic terms.

70. Berger ("Das Canticum Simeonis," 27–39) emphasizes that Simeon is an "Augenzeuge des Heils." I agree fully, and would add my own emphasis that Simeon, as an inspired witness, is therefore an agent of divine testimony, providing divine testimony through prophecy.

The *Topos* of Divine Testimony in Luke/Acts

Acts 4:5–12

In Acts 4:8, Luke specifically describes Peter as πλησθεὶς πνεύματος ἁγίου before addressing the religious leaders (see 4:5–6). His speech in this narrative consists of an explanation of the healing of the lame man outside the temple (narrated in Acts 3:1–11) in the context of a trial before the Jewish council.[71] Talbert is certainly correct when he argues that "valid testimony to Christ requires two witnesses."[72] He goes on to say that, in this case, the two witnesses are the Holy Spirit (manifest through the healing of the lame man) and the apostles. I would slightly nuance Talbert's position by stating that through divine speech, Peter is actually providing a *divine* testimony through his words concerning the healing of the lame man and its explanation. Peter, being filled with the Spirit, is God's spokesperson in this trial scene. God therefore testifies through both deed (the healing) and word (the inspired speech of Peter).

Thus, Peter's inspired speech serves as an explanation of a σημεῖον (cf. 4:16, 22) as part of his own defense.[73] The result of his speech is the council's remark recorded in 4:13: Θεωροῦντες δὲ τὴν τοῦ Πέτρου παρρησίαν καὶ Ἰωάννου, καὶ καταλαβόμενοι ὅτι ἄνθρωποι ἀγράμματοί εἰσιν καὶ ἰδιῶται, ἐθαύμαζον ἐπεγίνωσκόν τε αὐτοὺς ὅτι σὺν τῷ Ἰησοῦ ἦσαν.[74] Being filled with the Spirit, Peter and John are characterized as possessing παρρησία,[75]

---

71. So Talbert, *Reading Acts*, 41. See also Witherington, *Acts of the Apostles*, 193, who argues that this speech is "judicial in character."

72. Talbert, *Reading Acts*, 37.

73. The explanation for the healing is that it was performed ἐν τῷ ὀνόματι Ἰησοῦ Χριστοῦ τοῦ Ναζωραίου, whom ὁ θεὸς ἤγειρεν ἐκ νεκρῶν (4:10). Thus, the resurrection of Jesus and the healing are linked through Peter's inspired speech. See, e.g., Tannehill, *Acts*, 61–62.

74. On the understanding of ἀγράμματοί καὶ ἰδιῶται by the ancient audience of Luke-Acts, see T. Kraus, "'Uneducated,'" 434–49. Through a study of the use of these terms in the non-literary papyri, Kraus concludes that the terms should not be understood in a pejorative sense in this context.

75. For a survey of παρρησία in the NT, see Marrow, "Parrhēsia," 431–46. Marrow links Peter and John's boldness to their testimony, stating that Peter and John "displayed just such *parrhēsia* (Acts 4:31) simply because they knew that they could not but speak 'of what we have seen and heard'" (ibid., 442). He goes on to argue that the apostles' *parrhēsia* was not a goal to be obtained through discipline and work, but rather was "a divine gift to be prayed for" (443).

It is interesting to consider the links between the idea of παρρησία in the ancient world and Cicero's concept of a virtuous witness. In his book, *Paul and the Popular Philosophers*, 45–47, Malherbe, in his discussion of the ideal philosopher, argues that Dio Chrysostom sees the philosopher's "boldness" as a result of his "purifying his own

although they were ἀγράμματοί and ἰδιῶται. Through the *topos* of divine testimony, Peter and John are characterized as possessing a particular "boldness" as witnesses for Christ.[76]

Acts 13:9–12

The greater context of Acts 13:9–12 is the mission to which Saul and Barnabas were called by the Holy Spirit in 13:1–3 (see above in the section on direct speech). 13:9–12 narrates an example of inspired speech by Paul, in which he utters inspired words in a "power encounter"[77] with Bar-Jesus (Elymas),[78] the associate of Sergius Paulus, the proconsul of Cyprus.[79] Bar-Jesus attempts to obstruct the witness of Paul and Barnabas to the proconsul (13:7–8), which causes Paul, πλησθεὶς πνεύματος ἁγίου (13:9), to prophesy:[80] καὶ νῦν ἰδοὺ χεὶρ κυρίου ἐπὶ σέ, καὶ ἔσῃ τυφλὸς μὴ βλέπων

---

mind." Malherbe goes on to say that it is the philosopher's "knowledge of his own purity and that he is a friend and servant of the gods that allows him to speak with *parrēsia*." Thus, speaking with "boldness" is "speaking with purity of mind." Cicero, in his discussion of divine testimony (see chapter 2), argues that what constitutes a reliable witness is one who is virtuous; the gods, therefore, are the most reliable witnesses because they are virtuous by nature (see *Top.* 19.73). Therefore, when the disciples are described as having παρρησία, their role as divine witnesses is emphasized to an ancient auditor familiar with these concepts.

76. This is analogous to the situation of the old man of Veii, described by Livy, *Hist.* 5.15, and discussed in the previous chapter. There, I argued that the man's change of status in the Romans' eyes was due to his demonstrated ability to discern the meaning of the prophecy concerning the lowering of the Alban Lake (which was substantiated by a Delphic oracle). Here, Peter and John, as divinely inspired witnesses, are able to explain the healing of the lame man and thus are seen as having παρρησία, when in reality they are simply common men. Through their divine testimony, they undergo a status change in the opinion of the Jewish council.

77. Talbert, *Reading Acts*, 118.

78. Concerning the identity of Elymas, see Kilgallen, "Acts 13:4–12," 223–37; Kilgallen argues that Elymas is a non-believing Jew, who represents opposition to the gospel as seen by Jesus, Peter, and Stephen. See also Strelan, "Bar Jesus," 65–81; Strelan claims that Paul exposed Bar Jesus as a false prophet within a Christian community, one who was leading members of that community astray through his teaching.

79. For the route through Cyprus Paul and Barnabas possibly took, see Gill, "Paul's Travels," 219–28. Through the study of inscriptional evidence, Campbell cautiously suggests that Paul and Barnabas's journey through Cyprus took place approximately 37 CE, at the end of Tiberius's reign as emperor. See Campbell, "Possible Inscriptional Attestation," 1–29.

80. Talbert rightly sees this account as being "in the form of a prophetic response to a resistor of God" (Talbert, *Reading Acts*, 118).

The *Topos* of Divine Testimony in Luke/Acts

τὸν ἥλιον ἄχρι καιροῦ (13:11a). The prophecy is immediately fulfilled: παραχρῆμα τε ἔπεσεν ἐπ' αὐτὸν ἀχλὺς καὶ σκότος, καὶ περιάγων ἐζήτει χειραγωγούς (13:11a).

Paul, therefore, through the *topos* of divine testimony through inspired speech, prophesies[81] that Bar-Jesus will be temporarily blinded. The reliability of Paul as God's spokesperson is reinforced by the immediate fulfillment of the prophecy, thus providing divine sanction for Paul's (and Barnabas's) mission to Cyprus in particular and the mission in general to which they were called by the Holy Spirit.[82] Paul's prophetic speech also serves as divine disapproval of Bar-Jesus, and ultimately Satan, as Bar-Jesus is addressed by Paul as υἱὲ διαβόλου and ἐχθρὲ πάσης δικαιοσύνης.[83]

Acts 21:4, 10–12

In these passages, part of the narrative describing Paul's journey to Jerusalem,[84] characters, who are described as speaking to Paul διὰ τοῦ πνεύματος (21:4), as well as speaking for the Holy Spirit (τάδε λέγει τὸ πνεῦμα τὸ ἅγιον; 21:11), warn Paul not to continue on his journey to Jerusalem. In 21:4, the speakers are the disciples in Tyre, who encourage Paul not to go to Jerusalem; the reason for this warning[85] is not stated.

---

81. Pervo (*Acts*, 326) calls Paul's words "an oracle of judgment."

82. Parsons, *Acts*, 190, deserves to be quoted in full: "Paul has demonstrated his authority over the forces of Satan and thus proven himself worthy of the mission set before him." On this, see also Garrett, *Demise of the Devil*, 79–87. L. Johnson, *Acts*, 226, argues that through this narrative, Paul is being portrayed as a prophet as Jesus and Peter before him. See also Tannehill, *Acts*, 161. Schreiber notes the connection in the theology of Luke between the proclaimed word and the doing of miracles, as portrayed in the character of Paul; Schreiber, "Signifikanz der Pauluswunder," 119–34.

83. On the positive and negative portrayals of the main characters in this narrative, see Parsons, *Acts*, 187–90. Parsons describes Paul as an "agent of God," while Bar-Jesus is an "agent of Satan." He also draws further comparisons between these two: in Acts 9, Saul was blinded and led by the hand, as is Bar-Jesus here (cf. L. Johnson, *Acts*, 224); Bar-Jesus is accused of attempting to make the "straight" "crooked," while Saul is found in a house on a street called "Straight"; Saul is blinded for a time, as is (apparently; see 13:11) Bar-Jesus. As Parsons notes, however, the auditor never learns about the restoration of Bar-Jesus's sight.

84. According to Talbert, *Reading Acts*, 175, the narrative account in Acts 20:1–21:26 is the outworking of Paul's decision to go to Jerusalem, and from there to continue on to Rome: ἔθετο ὁ Παῦλος ἐν τῷ πνεύματι διελθὼν τὴν Μακεδονίαν καὶ Ἀχαΐαν πορεύεσθαι εἰς Ἱεροσόλυμα, εἰπὼν ὅτι Μετὰ τὸ γενέσθαι με ἐκεῖ δεῖ με καὶ Ῥώμην ἰδεῖν (Acts 19:21).

85. L. Johnson, *Acts*, 369, translates the verb in τῷ Παύλῳ ἔλεγον διὰ τοῦ πνεύματος

Despite the prophetic warning from these disciples, Paul continues on his way to Jerusalem (21:5-6). In 21:10-12, the speaker is Agabus the prophet (cf. Acts 11:27-28). His statement is a symbolic prophecy,[86] which also serves as a warning to Paul that his journey to Jerusalem will result in his imprisonment by "the Gentiles" (21:12).

In both of these cases, the divine testimony through the inspired speakers serves as a prophetic warning to Paul, the second example being more explicit than the first. Both are examples of direct testimony from the Spirit to Paul, recorded in 20:23: τὸ πνεῦμα τὸ ἅγιον κατὰ πόλιν διαμαρτύρεταί μοι λέγον ὅτι δεσμὰ καὶ θλίψεις με μένουσιν.[87] These prophecies are fulfilled by the ensuing narrative, in which Paul is indeed held captive, eventually coming under house-arrest in Rome. The warnings, announced to Paul through divine testimony through inspired speech, serve to emphasize Paul's resolve to go to Rome, despite the inevitability of his capture and imprisonment.[88] Paul is therefore portrayed as resolute in his Spirit-led decision, first announced by the narrator (and Paul) in 19:21. Here, clearly the divine testimony serves to emphasize Paul's obedience to the leading of the Spirit (cf. 20:23).[89]

---

as "warned," based on the context of the speech. See also Parsons, *Acts*, 296, who sees two parallel warnings in 21:1-6 and 21:7-16.

86. The prophecy consists of a symbolic action, accompanied by Agabus's words which serve to clarify the symbolism, as most commentators recognize; see, e.g., Talbert, *Reading Acts*, 184; Parsons, *Acts*, 297.

87. See Haenchen, *Apostelgeschichte*, 535: "Der mit Kap. 21 einsetzende Reisebericht erlaubt es Lukas, die allgemeine und blasse Andeutung von 20:23 in sich steigernden Szenen dem Leser konkret vor Augen zu führen." See also L. Johnson, *Acts*, 371.

88. Tannehill, *Acts*, 264, recognizes that at this point in the narrative, Paul must make a choice, and that both options are presented in relation to the Spirit. On the one hand, the disciples and Agabus, through the Spirit, warn Paul that if he chooses to continue his journey, it will result in imprisonment. Paul, through the Spirit, has resolved to "see Rome." As Tannehill points out, the Spirit does not settle the issue for Paul. Rather, the two Spirit-inspired alternatives serve to increase the tension in the narrative. See also Patsch, "Prophetie," 228-32, who argues that Agabus's actions are typical of an OT "Zeichenhandlung," an important aspect of which is the inescapable outcome of the prophecy. He correctly recognizes, however, that this is not a magical incantation; rather, it is a warning from God to which Paul must respond.

89. Haenchen (*Apostelgeschichte*, 523n6), commenting on 20:23, emphasizes the divine initiative in this passage (and the ensuing narrative). This is certainly correct, in that Paul "must" (δεῖ in 19:23) arrive in Rome. The narrative in chapter 21, however, is structured in a way that allows the auditor to see Paul as obedient to his divine calling, even in the face of prophetic warnings that it is dangerous to continue.

The *Topos* of Divine Testimony in Luke/Acts

In sum, the *topos* of divine speech through inspired characters functions in Luke-Acts in several ways. Inspired characters are sources of divine prophecy, as in the cases of Zechariah, Simeon, and Paul. Also, inspired speech is used in a character's defense in a trial setting, as demonstrated by the example of Peter in Acts 4, in which he explains the σημεῖον of the healing of the lame man. Finally, inspired speech can serve as warnings, as seen in the examples of the disciples in Tyre and Agabus. To ancient auditors of Luke-Acts, these would certainly have been familiar functions of the *topos* of divine testimony through utterances, as all of these functions were seen in the examples from Hellenistic literature above. I will now turn my attention to the analysis of divine testimony through reference to Hebrew scripture in Luke-Acts.

Divine Testimony through Reference to Scripture

Jewish Scripture in Luke-Acts and References to Oracles in Hellenistic Narratives

Before exploring the function of references to scripture in Luke-Acts as instances of the *topos* of divine testimony through utterances, it is necessary first to argue that an ancient auditor would have understood scripture references in the same way as references to oracles in contemporary Hellenistic literature. This has already been argued to some degree by Talbert.[90] In his essay, Talbert provides two reasons for an ancient auditor's understanding of the schema of prophecy-fulfillment in Luke-Acts as it appears in Hellenistic writings. First, in Hellenistic literature, significant historical events are often substantiated by fulfilled oracles, even when those oracles are misunderstood.[91] Likewise, in Luke-Acts, Jewish scripture is often cited as being fulfilled through occurrences in the narrative (in some cases, despite being misunderstood).[92] Second, as I have demonstrated earlier, fulfilled oracles also serve to provide the gods' sanction of characters and thus legitimate other actions and words of those characters. As Talbert

---

90. See Talbert, "Promise and Fulfillment," 96–101, in which Talbert argues that Luke's schema of prophecy-fulfillment would have been readily understood in an ancient Mediterranean milieu.

91. I have provided examples of this phenomenon in chapter 3.

92. As previously mentioned, Talbert recognizes that this can occur even when characters have not understood the meaning of the passage of scripture in question; see Talbert, "Promise and Fulfillment," 99.

argues, and I will show below, the citation of scripture functions in this way in Luke-Acts as well. Talbert's analysis of the understanding of oracles and the citation of scripture is, however, limited to the area of prophecy and fulfillment (which is the focus of his essay as a whole). In the present study, I am thus building on Talbert's work and attempting to demonstrate that oracles and the Jewish scriptures would have been understood as functioning in other ways as well, as seen in the analysis of oracles in Hellenistic histories and biographies in the previous chapter.

Thus there are other, more formal aspects in which an ancient auditor would have similarly understood the reference to oracles in Hellenistic writings and Jewish scripture in Luke-Acts. First, the way in which oracles and scripture are referenced is comparable. As seen in chapter three, oracles in Hellenistic histories and biographies are often quoted in full after some type of introductory statement.[93] Other times, the content of the oracle being referenced is simply summarized.[94] Finally, it can simply be mentioned that an oracle had been received without quoting it or summarizing its contents.[95] Likewise, the characters in Luke-Acts quote Greek versions of the Jewish scriptures directly, summarize passages of scripture (as Stephen does in his speech in Acts 7), or simply refer to scriptures in general, as in Luke 24:27, when the narrator states that the Lukan Jesus, beginning with the Law and prophets, διερμήνευσεν αὐτοῖς ἐν πάσαις ταῖς γραφαῖς τὰ περὶ ἑαυτοῦ. Thus, in this purely formal aspect, ancient auditors would have heard the use of oracles and scripture in a similar way in these works.

A second way in which oracles and scripture in Luke-Acts would have been understood in a comparable manner is that an ancient audience would have considered both to be divine communication.[96] In Hellenistic writings, this equation is made both explicitly and implicitly.[97] An auditor

93. See, e.g., the example previously discussed from Diodorus Siculus, *Hist.* 16.91.

94. E.g., Quintus Curtius, *History of Alexander* 5.4, discussed previously.

95. See earlier discussion of Dionysius of Halicarnassus, *Ant. rom.* 1.55.3.

96. It is significant to note that Josephus refers to divine communication using the Greek word χρησμός, and in many cases the divine communication in question is through scripture. For example, in his description of the Zealots' disdain for prophecy, Josephus claims that the Zealots "scoffed at the oracles of the prophets as imposters' fables [τοὺς τῶν προφητῶν χρησμοὺς ὥσπερ ἀγυρτικὰς λογοποιίας ἐχλεύαζον]" (*B.J.* 4.386). Later, in the same work he attributes the cause of the Jewish revolt to "an ambiguous oracle [χρησμὸς ἀμφίβολος], . . . found in their sacred scriptures [ἐν τοῖς ἱεροῖς εὑρημένος γράμμασιν]" (*B.J.* 6.312).

97. For example, in the introduction to Plutarch's *Life* of Demosthenes, Plutarch quotes the famous Delphic oracle, "Know thyself"; he then comments that if it were

The *Topos* of Divine Testimony in Luke/Acts

encounters this same pattern in Luke-Acts as well. Frequently, in introducing citations of scripture, Luke employs stereotyped formulae which involve some form of the verb γράφω.[98] This provides a clue to the reader that scripture is about to be quoted. In many cases, however, Luke makes explicit that a citation of a passage from the Jewish scriptures should be understood as divine speech through an expansion of the introductory formula or some other means.[99] Also in Luke-Acts, the auditor hears other, less direct methods of equating the scripture with divine speech. For example, in Acts 1:16, Peter states that ἔδει πληρωθῆναι τὴν γραφὴν ἣν προεῖπεν τὸ πνεῦμα τὸ ἅγιον διὰ στόματος Δαυὶδ περὶ Ἰούδα.[100]

Not all references to oracles in Hellenistic literature, however, are explicitly or implicitly attributed to divine speech. This is also the case with scripture references in Luke-Acts. But in both the Hellenistic writings and Luke-Acts, enough of the references to oracles and to the Hebrew scriptures are attributed to divine speech, both directly and indirectly, so that an ancient auditor would consider *all* such references as divine speech. Statements made which equate scripture with God's speech throughout the two-volume work of Luke-Acts have the cumulative effect of allowing

---

easy to fulfill the command of this oracle, "it would not be held to be a divine injunction [οὐκ ἂν ἐδόκει πρόσταγμα θεῖον εἶναι]" (*Dem.* 3.2). An example, also from Plutarch, in which an oracle is implicitly attributed to divine speech, is in the life of Theseus. Here, Aegeus is told through an oracle to abstain from sexual relations until he returns to Athens. In the narrative, one reads that Aegeus recites the oracle to Pittheus; at this point Plutarch states that Aegeus "communicated to Pittheus the words of the god [τὴν τοῦ θεοῦ φωνὴν]" (*Thes.* 3.3).

98. On the various introductory formulae used for OT citations in Luke-Acts, see Fitzmyer, "Use of the Old Testament," 524–38.

99. For example, in Luke 2:23, Exod 13:12 is quoted following the phrase καθὼς γέγραπται ἐν νόμῳ κυρίου, thus attributing the quotation to "the law of the Lord." In Acts 2:17, the Lukan Peter quotes the prophet Joel and inserts the phrase λέγει ὁ θεός into the text from Joel 3 which he recites. In Paul's speech in Acts 13, Paul quotes Isa 55:3 and Ps 16:10, prefacing his quotation of Isa 55:3 in Acts 13:34 with the statement, οὕτως εἴρηκεν, the subject of εἴρηκεν being God (cf. 13:32). A third example is found in Acts 28:25, in which the Lukan Paul states, Καλῶς τὸ πνεῦμα τὸ ἅγιον ἐλάλησεν διὰ Ἡσαΐου τοῦ προφήτου πρὸς τοὺς πατέρας ὑμῶν, then completing the thought with a citation of Isa 6:9–10.

100. Thus an intermediary speaks divine words, a phenomenon common to Hellenistic writings as already noted; often the Pythia is the inspired intermediary who delivers the words of the god to the suppliant. For other examples from Acts, see 4:24–26 (Ps 2:1–2. is quoted; in this case, the Lord speaks *by* the Holy Spirit *through* David). See also Peter's general statement relating certain sayings of the prophets to divine speech in Acts 3:21; Peter speaks of the universal restoration ὧν ἐλάλησεν ὁ θεὸς διὰ στόματος τῶν ἁγίων ἀπ' αἰῶνος αὐτοῦ προφητῶν (cf. 3:18).

Divine Testimony through Utterances in Luke-Acts

the auditor to understand the use of Jewish scripture to be divine communication, either coming directly from God or through an intermediary, such as one of the prophets. Therefore, through various means, an ancient auditor would have clearly understood references to oracles and scripture as a reference to divine speech.

Equating the citation of scripture with oracles is emphasized through consideration of the works of Philo. Philo, like Josephus (see above), often cites a passage from the Jewish scriptures and, in doing so, refers to it as a χρησμός.[101] For example, Philo describes Jeremiah as one who speaks for God by stating: "out of his manifold inspiration [Jeremiah] gave forth an oracle spoken in the person of God [ἅτε τὰ πολλὰ ἐνθουσιῶν χρησμόν τινα ἐξεῖπεν ἐκ προσώπου τοῦ θεοῦ]" (*Cher.* 49). This serves as an introduction for Philo's citation of Jer 3:4. Significantly, Philo also cites scripture (referring to the scripture as a χρησμός) as a witness, frequently doing so in order to bring evidence of what he is arguing. In *Conf.* 94, the scriptures are said to testify that true freedom is serving God: "What then is the liberty which is really sure and stable? . . . It is the service of the only wise Being, as the oracles testify [καθάπερ μαρτυροῦσιν οἱ χρησμοί], in which it is said, 'Send forth the people that they may serve me.'"[102] And as proof of God's sovereignty, Philo writes, "To this sovereignty of the Absolutely Existent the oracle is a true witness in these words [ὁ χρησμὸς ἀληθὴς μάρτυς λέγων ὧδε]" (*Cher.* 108); what follows is a citation of Lev 25:23.[103] Thus, in the works of Philo, one notes the confluence of the concepts of scripture as divine communication, the use of the word χρησμός (or its derivatives) in referencing scripture, and the idea of scripture as a "witness."

I will now turn my attention to the analysis of passages in Luke-Acts in which the Jewish scriptures are quoted or referenced. I will limit my analysis to those cases in which, through some type of introductory statement, it would be clear to an auditor unfamiliar with the Jewish scriptures

---

101. For Philo, in general, God communicates to humanity through oracles (*Opfi.* 8; *Leg.* 3.142, 215). Philo also uses the term χρησμός when scripture is quoted; for example, in arguing that God cannot be described in anthropomorphic terms, Philo grounds the premise for his argument in Num 23:19 (οὐχ ὡς ἄνθρωπος ὁ θεός), which is "a moral most pertinent in the oracles of revelation [ἐν τοῖς ἱεροφαντηθεῖσι χρησμοῖς]" (*Deus* 62; see also *Sobr.* 17; *Ebr.* 60, 82; *Plant.* 63; *Leg.* 3.245; *Cher.* 51; *Sacr.* 57; *Det.* 46, 74, 86, 126; *Post.* 169).

102. Here, Philo cites Exod 8:1.

103. Other examples of Philo's claim that the OT testifies include: *Conf.* 94; *Mut.* 90; *Abr.* 262, 270; *Migr.* 115; *Leg.* 3.129; *Det.* 166; *Cher.* 124.

The *Topos* of Divine Testimony in Luke/Acts

that an external source is being quoted.[104] Also, in order to limit the scope of the study, not every reference to scripture in Luke-Acts will be discussed. Enough examples, however, will be analyzed in order to gain a full understanding of how these references would have been understood by ancient auditors as divine testimony. The examples will be discussed in canonical order.

Luke 2:21–24

The context for this passage is the presentation of Jesus in the temple (see above on Simeon's inspired speech). Luke sets the stage with this statement: ὅτε ἐπλήσθησαν αἱ ἡμέραι τοῦ καθαρισμοῦ αὐτῶν κατὰ τὸν νόμον Μωϋσέως, ἀνήγαγον αὐτὸν εἰς Ἱεροσόλυμα παραστῆσαι τῷ κυρίῳ (2:22).[105] The specific law concerning Jesus' presentation is then referenced: καθὼς γέγραπται ἐν νόμῳ κυρίου ὅτι Πᾶν ἄρσεν διανοῖγον μήτραν ἅγιον τῷ κυρίῳ κληθήσεται (2:23; cf. Exod 13:2).[106] Following this, Luke explains that Mary and Joseph offered the requisite sacrifice concerning Mary's uncleanness, citing Lev 12:8:[107] κατὰ τὸ εἰρημένον ἐν τῷ νόμῳ κυρίου, ζεῦγος τρυγόνων ἢ δύο νοσσοὺς περστερῶν (2:24b).

In this case, the divine testimony through scripture is explicitly attributed to God; the reference to Exod 13:2 is prefaced with καθὼς γέγραπται ἐν νόμῳ κυρίου. Leviticus 12:8 is introduced in a similar manner: κατὰ τὸ

---

104. For example, as mentioned by many scholars (see, e.g., Green, *Luke*, 186), there is an allusion to Ps 2:7 in the direct speech by God in Luke 3:21–22. I will not discuss this passage in the following analysis, as it is not clearly marked as a reference to or citation of Jewish scripture. For a complete listing of references to the OT in Luke-Acts, both citations and allusions, see Morgenthaler, *Lukas und Quintilian*, 193–229.

105. It is odd that Luke writes of αἱ ἡμέραι τοῦ καθαρισμοῦ αὐτῶν, when according to the law only Mary was considered ritually unclean. Green uses the term "difficulties" to describe Luke's use of αὐτῶν and waiting until the eighth day to name Jesus; see Green, *Luke*, 140. For possible explanations for αὐτῶν, see Bock, *Proclamation*, 83–84. Brown, "Presentation of Jesus," 3–4, sees these, along with the fact that Luke thought it necessary to have Jesus presented in Jerusalem, as "minor confusions." He also lists the association of the offering of two pigeons with the presentation as erroneous; this "confusion" is mitigated, however, by viewing the passage as a chiasm (see below).

106. This is clearly not an exact quotation. Klein, *Lukasevangelium*, 144, therefore uses this as evidence to make the leap that Luke's gospel was written in a Hellenistic environment because: (i) this is not a verbal citation; and (ii) Luke is misapplying the law to the narrative situation.

107. The passage (2:22–23) is structured as a chiasm: A—purification (22a); B—presentation of Jesus (22b); A'—law concerning presentation (23); B'—law concerning purification. See Talbert, *Reading Luke*, 38.

εἰρημένον ἐν τῷ νόμῳ κυρίου. The function of the divine testimony is clear to the auditor; the law is cited here as commands which are to be obeyed. Mary and Joseph are therefore portrayed through the divine testimony as obedient to the law.[108] This indirectly serves to characterize Jesus in a positive way by demonstrating that his parents were pious Jews.[109]

Luke 3:4-6

In this passage, Luke has John the Baptist quote Isa 40:3-5 as part of his prophetic ministry of announcing the arrival of Jesus (cf. 1:16-17, 76-77).[110] In the narrative context in which it is found,[111] John quotes this passage from Isaiah as a prophecy, which is now being fulfilled through his ministry.[112] Thus, the divine testimony through the citation of Jewish scripture functions as a previously received prophecy which is fulfilled by current events. According to Luke, John is the one to whom the prophet was alluding.[113] John's ministry is given divine sanction by way of the divine testimony through the citation of scripture, which is in harmony with the divine testimony concerning John seen throughout this section.[114] As already noted, the divine approval of John's ministry through divine testi-

---

108. This is, according to commentators, the point of this account; see, e.g., Green, *Luke*, 140; Talbert, *Reading Luke*, 37.

109. On the significance of the piety of Jesus' parents, see Tannehill, *Luke*, 56. Concerning the parents of the subject of an encomium, see Theon, who, on the preliminary exercise of encomium, writes: "You should elaborate it with the following headings. ... then you will state the person's origin, which you will divide into nation, homeland, ancestors, and parents" (*Progymnasmata* 22R).

110. For a thorough treatment of the details concerning this citation, see Rusam, *Das Alte Testament*, 151-63.

111. Tannehill, *Luke*, 48, recognizes that the quotation of Isa 40 is preceded by a description of John's activity. Thus, according to Tannehill, the auditor's understanding of the quote is guided by the previous comments by the narrator. For a comparison of the portrayals of John in Josephus and Luke, see Park, "Eine Untersuchung," 59-83.

112. Schürmann's quote is appropriate: "Hier erfüllt sich alles so, wie es Is (40,3ff.) vorherverkündet hat" (Schürmann, *Lukasevangelium*, 154). Green, however, argues that the emphasis is not on the fulfillment of prophecy; rather, Luke, through the scripture citation, is attempting to locate John and his role within the scope of salvation history; see Green, *Luke*, 171.

113. Bock, *Proclamation*, 99: "John is the foretold herald who *initiates the pattern* of what will be, in this case, God's decisive act of salvation" (emphasis in original).

114. E.g., John's birth is announced through angelic proclamation, and at his birth Zechariah, through inspired speech, prophesies concerning John's future ministry.

mony ultimately serves to cast Jesus in an even more positive light, as John is the one who will go before and "prepare the way of the Lord."[115]

Luke 4:1–13

This narrative is Luke's account of Satan's temptation of Jesus in the wilderness.[116] It contains several references to the Jewish scriptures, three by Jesus, and one by Satan.[117] The context of Jesus' baptism and the divine voice of affirmation associated with it (Luke 3:21–22) are prominently in the background of this account;[118] through the temptation narrative the question is implicitly asked: does Jesus truly know what it means to be the son of God?[119] Satan tempts Jesus three times,[120] and each time Jesus

---

115. On this, see Chakoian, "Luke 3:1–16," 400–404. Chakoian sees the significance of John in three ways: it is through John that Jesus is connected to salvation history; John, as a prophet, goes before the one who is a greater prophet than he; and John serves as a prototype of the Christian evangelist. This third point is also made by Talbert, *Reading Luke*, 31. For a somewhat similar argument, see also Rusam, *Das Alte Testament*, 161–63; Rusam argues that the connections between the portrayal of John (including his citation of scripture) and the later proclamation of the Christian missionaries in Acts serves as an implicit legitimation of the Christian mission.

116. J. Miller, *Convinced*, 150–53, treats this passage as a dream-vision, as does Schiavo, "Temptation," 141–64. Schiavo argues, therefore, that in Q Jesus was portrayed as an eschatological warrior who would defeat Satan in battle.

117. Jesus references: Deut 8:3 in Luke 4:4; Deut 6:13 in 4:8; and Deut 6:16 in 4:12. Satan references Ps 90:11–12 LXX in 4:10–11. Each reference to scripture is prefaced with some type of introductory formula which includes a form of γράφω (or λέγω; see 4:12).

118. This point is made by Downing, "Psalms," 131–37; see also the genealogy in 3:23–38, which ends with the words [υἱός] τοῦ θεοῦ. Cf. Talbert, *Reading Luke*, 47, and Green, *Luke*, 191.

119. See Talbert, *Reading Luke*, 47–48, who answers this question by referring to the genealogy that precedes this passage and therefore arguing that Jesus is the new Adam, who refuses temptation, rather than gives in to it. See also Green, *Luke*, 192–94; Green maintains that being the Son of God entails faithful obedience on the part of the son, which Jesus demonstrates through this account. See also Riesner, "Versuchung und Verklärung," 201.

Taylor ("Temptation," 27–49) argues that the Sitz im Leben of the temptation accounts is the persecution of early Christians by Agrippa I. Thus, Satan here represents Agrippa I, and Jesus' withstanding of the temptation (persecution) was meant to be read in an exemplary fashion. On the exemplary nature of Jesus' responses to Satan's temptations, see Kilgallen, "Jesus Tempted," 228–33.

120. In the second temptation (4:5–8), Satan tempts Jesus with world dominion. D. Rudman ("Authority," 77–86) compares 4:6 with Dan 1–6, arguing that in certain

counters with a citation of scripture, refusing to yield to the temptation. Thus, Jesus is portrayed positively as the son of God, being obedient to his father's commandments, which are given through the law. The answer to the question is therefore answered with a positive response: Jesus does understand what it means to be the son of God.[121]

The divine testimony through the scriptures functions on a second level as well. Satan also quotes scripture, but does so in way that skews the meaning of the text. In the third temptation, Satan dares Jesus to throw himself down from the top of the temple,[122] citing Ps 90:11–12 LXX to imply that God will not let Jesus be harmed.[123] Satan manipulates the meaning of this passage in order to imply that God's favor is available regardless of the situation.[124] Jesus, however, in his response, demonstrates that one must carefully apply God's promises as found in scripture. Therefore, through the interchange associated with the third temptation, Jesus proves himself to be the one who can correctly interpret the scriptures, while Satan does so unreliably, actually attempting to manipulate the citation for his own purposes. In this way, through the use of divine testimony, Jesus is positively portrayed as the obedient son who can correctly interpret the

---

Jewish (and, later, Christian) circles, the world was considered to be ruled by chaos. That Satan is ruler of the world and can offer dominion to Jesus reflects this line of thinking.

121. For the christological implications of this passage and its relation to the rest of Luke, see Schlosser, "Les Tentations," 403–25.

122. For an analysis (a word study including several extra-biblical sources) of the somewhat enigmatic phrase ἐπὶ τὸ πτερύγιον τοῦ ἱεροῦ in Luke 4:9, see Blumenthal, "'Zinne des Tempels,'" 274–83.

123. Green, *Luke*, 194, argues that Satan thus misinterprets "Son of God" to mean something in conflict with a faithful, obedient son, who does that which the father desires. See also Tannehill, *Luke*, 59; Labahn, "Der Gottessohn," 413–14. Labahn argues that the issue is not God's protection of his son; on this Satan is correct. Rather, "es geht um die illegitime Beanspruchung von Gottes Schutz, die als Versuchung gedeutet wird." Cf. E. Koskenniemi, who also argues that Satan does understand the citation. Koskenniemi, in comparing this account with other temptation accounts in Jewish literature, notes the inversion of roles in the passage in that here, Satan is the one who quotes scripture; in the Jewish literature, the one being tempted normally quotes the Psalms as a defense. Satan, by citing Ps 90, is attempting to lead Jesus to doubt that he is God's son; throwing himself from the temple and allowing God to save him will prove that he is who he believes he is. See Koskenniemi, "Roles Inverted," 261–68.

124. Kimball states that Satan "twists" Ps 90 LXX to suit his own purposes; see Kimball, *Jesus' Exposition*, 93.

law;¹²⁵ simultaneously, Satan is discredited through his manipulation of scripture.¹²⁶

Luke 4:16–30

The passage 4:16–30, in which a citation of the Jewish scripture is found, is highly significant in Luke's gospel, in that it constitutes the first description of an event from Jesus' earthly ministry.¹²⁷ The setting for this passage is a synagogue service in Nazareth, a context of worship. In this passage, Jesus speaks in the synagogue, reading from the book of Isaiah.¹²⁸ After the reading, the narrator states (concerning Jesus): καὶ πτύξας τὸ βιβλίον ἀποδοὺς τῷ ὑπερέτῃ ἐκάθισεν· καὶ πάντων οἱ ὀφθαλμοὶ ἐν τῇ συναγωγῇ ἦσαν ἀτενίζοντες αὐτῷ (4:20), thus heightening the tension in the narrative. Jesus then states, Σήμερον πεπλήρωται ἡ γραφὴ αὕτη ἐν τοῖς ὠσὶν ὑμῶν (4:21). Thus, in its immediate narrative context, this instance of divine testimony through the citation of scripture functions as a prophecy which was formerly received and is now fulfilled through events which are currently unfolding.¹²⁹ Jesus' mission, the narration of which begins

---

125. Rusam (*Das Alte Testament*, 165-69) correctly notes that this is the first time in Luke-Acts that a character (and not the narrator) has cited scripture. He continues by arguing that because of the heavenly voice in Luke 3:21–22, Jesus is to be seen as one who can reliably cite scripture.

126. Talbert (*Reading Luke*, 48) states, "[Jesus] knew the appropriate, as opposed to the satanic, use of Scripture, rejecting the devil's interpretation in vv. 10–11 of Psalm 91:11–12." Talbert goes on to argue that Jesus' correct understanding of scripture is a direct result of his being anointed with the Spirit (cf. 4:1–2).

127. See, e.g., Green, *Luke*, 207, who describes this passage as having "central importance" for Luke's gospel. See also Drouot, "Le discourse inaugural," 35–44, who argues that through the passage the reader is introduced to Jesus in his prophetic role. For the connections of this passage to the temptation narrative, see Genuyt, "L'annonce rejetée/entravée," 43–54.

128. The specific passages which Jesus reads are from a Greek version of Isaiah 61:1–2 and 58:6. Combrink ("Structure and Significance," 27–47) has performed an extensive study of the organization of this passage. He finds that the passage is structured as a chiasm, the center of which is the quotation from Isaiah. For an exhaustive analysis of this citation, see Rusam, *Das Alte Testament*, 171–201.

129. Rese, *Alttestamentliche Motive*, 220, categorizes this usage of the OT in Luke-Acts as "Erfüllung und Weissagung." Kimball explains Jesus' reference to Isaiah as "prophetic" and "typological." It is prophetic in that Jesus considers himself the fulfillment of the reference to Isaiah; it is typological, according to Kimball, in that Jesus casts himself in the mold of the servant-messiah described in Isa 61; Kimball, *Jesus' Exposition*, 118. See also Porter, "Scripture," 117. Porter claims that this passage

Divine Testimony through Utterances in Luke-Acts

at this point, thus receives divine sanction through its fulfillment of the passages from Isaiah which Jesus read.[130] Jesus himself is also portrayed in a positive light through his citation of the passages from Isaiah; in doing so, he demonstrates that he has aligned himself with God's purposes as described in the Jewish scriptures.[131]

Luke 7:27

This citation of Greek versions of Mal 3:1 and Exod 23:20[132] is spoken by the Lukan Jesus to the crowd after he gives John's messengers an answer to John's question regarding Jesus' identity (7:18–23). After John's messengers

---

represents a "clear instance of the prophetic fulfillment of the Old Testament."

130. Scholars recognize, however, given the greater context of the narrative of Luke's gospel, that the citation also looks forward, describing Jesus' ministry of healing, exorcisms, and preaching. Hence it is called a "programmatic prophecy." See, e.g., Talbert, *Reading Luke*, 18–19; L. Johnson, *Luke*, 81; Kimball, *Jesus' Exposition*, 97; Rusam, *Das Alte Testament*, 203–7; and Porter, "Scripture," 117, who writes that "this passage used the Old Testament to outline Jesus' mission and, hence, to describe the purposes of the Gospel itself." See also Pathrapankal, "The *Nazareth Manifesto*," 291–308, who claims that this sermon and the crowd's subsequent reaction "constitute the underlying theme of the entire earthly ministry of Jesus in the theology of Luke" ("The *Nazareth Manifesto*, 302); Matthey ("Luke 4:16–30," 3–11) states that this passage is composed as a "policy document" for Jesus' ministry; Hertig, "Jubilee Mission," 168–79, who argues for the "holistic" nature of Jesus' mission, introduced here. According to Hertig, Jesus' mission has four holistic aspects: (i) it was not only proclaimed, but performed as well; (ii) it involved both the spiritual and material realms; (iii) it was universal in scope, and targeted toward a particular group of people; and (iv) it was both present and future; Prior, "Liberation Theology," 79–99, claims that through this passage, and especially the references to scripture, Luke has presented many of the major themes of Luke-Acts, including the Holy Spirit, prophecy-fulfillment through Jesus, good news for the poor, the in-breaking of God's kingdom, and the universal nature of the good news of salvation. For a more complete treatment of the connections between 4:16–30 and the rest of Luke-Acts, see Neirynck, "Luke 4,16–30," 358–95. Neirynck builds his case by comparing this sermon by Jesus to those of Peter and Paul in Acts. Finally, see Baawobr, "Opening," 29–53. Baawobr performs a narrative analysis of this passage and compares it to the *bagr* initiation ceremony performed by the Dagara people of Ghana, examining the connections between the programmatic openings of these two works and the greater narratives in which they are found.

131. See Tannehill, *Luke*, 67, who argues this point, stating that the "interrelated passages from Isaiah function as a group in expressing for the narrator of Luke-Acts the divine promise which is being realized through Jesus and his witnesses."

132. See, e.g., L. Johnson, *Luke*, 123, who expresses the lack of certainty of most scholars concerning this citation with his statement: "The passage appears to be a mixed citation from LXX Exod 23:20 and Mal 3:1."

The *Topos* of Divine Testimony in Luke/Acts

leave, Jesus begins to speak about John, explaining to the crowd that John is περισσότερον προφήτου (7:26). He then goes on to explain what he means[133] through the citation of the passage(s) noted above: οὗτός ἐστιν περὶ οὗ γέγραπται, Ἰδοὺ ἀποστέλλω τὸν ἄγγελόν μου πρὸ προσώπου σου, ὃς κατασκευάσει τὴν ὁδόν σου ἔμπροσθέν σου (7:27). The introductory formula, περὶ οὗ γέγραπται, informs the auditor that Jesus is citing scripture at this point.

The function of the divine testimony through scripture is that John represents the fulfillment of prophecy. It is significant in that this is now the fourth instance of divine testimony, in various forms, all of which serve to provide divine sanction of John and his ministry.[134] In 1:17, John's ministry is foretold by Gabriel in a dream; in 1:76, Zechariah repeats John's purpose through inspired speech, and in 3:4–6 John cites Isaiah in describing his ministry as the fulfillment of prophecy (see above on these verses). Here, Jesus himself quotes scripture to affirm once again John's ministry.[135] Thus, the auditor must recognize the significance of John and his message through these four instances of divine testimony.[136]

But this does not exhaust the importance of this example of divine testimony. Jesus goes on to say that μείζων ἐν γεννητοῖς γυναικῶν Ἰωάννου οὐδείς ἐστιν· ὁ δὲ μικρότερος ἐν τῇ βασιλείᾳ τοῦ θεοῦ μείζων αὐτοῦ ἐστιν (7:28).[137] Therefore, not only is John significant in God's greater economy; the common people, represented by the crowds, are also important in the kingdom being inaugurated by Jesus, and announced by John.[138] Also, Luke adds the parenthetical comment in 7:30 that οἱ δὲ φαρισαῖοι καὶ οἱ

---

133. Klein, *Lukasevangelium*, 283.

134. L. Johnson, *Luke*, 124, maintains that the audience is prepared for this statement through similar proclamations in 1:17, 76; 3:4–6, 15–16.

135. Green, *Luke*, 298–99, calls attention to the fact that Luke has changed the personal pronouns in the citation from "me" to "you" (Luke 7:27: Ἰδοὺ ἀποστέλλω τὸν ἄγγελόν μου πρὸ προσώπου σου; Mal 3:1 LXX: ἰδοὺ ἐγὼ ἐξαποστέλλω τὸν ἄγγελόν μου καὶ ἐπιβλέψεται ὁδὸν πρὸ προσώπου μου), and opines that this demonstrates the importance of John's ministry for the people.

136. Rusam, *Das Alte Testament*, 163–64, makes a similar point, but does not connect Jesus' citation of scripture to divine testimony.

137. For an excellent discussion of the interpretive issues and a brief survey of recent scholarship concerning this verse, see Viviano, "The Least," 41–54. Viviano concludes that the statement, from the compilers of Q, is a comparison of John the Baptist to Jesus, who is "the least in the kingdom of God." Viviano comes to this association through the description of Nebuchadnezzar in Dan 4:14 (4:17).

138. Green, *Luke*, 299, argues that this verse refers to the "inversion" which is characteristic of the new kingdom.

νομικοὶ τὴν βουλὴν τοῦ θεοῦ ἠθέτησαν εἰς ἑαυτούς, μὴ βαπτισθέντες ὑπ' αὐτοῦ.[139] The "Pharisees and lawyers" are thus also characterized, in this case negatively, because they have rejected John's message, which has been legitimized through Jesus' citation of scripture. Therefore, the people to whom Jesus is speaking and the religious leaders of the day are also indirectly characterized through the divine testimony.

Luke 20:27-40, 41-47

This passage, in which the Sadducees make reference to the law, is one of three accounts which explore the question of Jesus' authority.[140] Luke provides the setting for this section in 20:27: Προσελθόντες δέ τινες τῶν Σαδδουκαίων, οἱ ἀντιλέγοντες ἀνάστασιν μὴ εἶναι, ἐπηρώτησαν αὐτόν. Thus the auditor receives a veiled clue as to what is about to transpire; the Sadducees will question Jesus in an attempt to justify their views concerning the resurrection. This is exactly what happens; in asking their question of Jesus, they refer to Moses' writings concerning levirate marriage[141] and a hypothetical woman who marries seven different brothers, all of whom die (20:28-32). Ultimately, the question they pose to Jesus is ἡ γυνὴ οὖν ἐν τῇ ἀναστάσει τίνος αὐτῶν γίνεται γυνή (20:33). The question, however, is an attempt to cast doubt on Jesus' views on the resurrection, rather than a request to hear his opinion of this particular situation.[142]

Jesus' answer to their question is recorded in 20:34-38. In vv. 34-36, Jesus argues that the question is illogical.[143] According to Jesus, the Sadducees are confusing earthly life with eternal life (vv. 34-36), and therefore

139. L. Johnson, *Luke*, 124-25, in recognizing that 7:29-30 are not in the parallel account in Matthew's gospel, forcefully states that this "is one of Luke's most important interjections."

140. Talbert, *Reading Luke*, 221, understands the emphasis of Luke 19:45—20:18 to be a warning to the religious leaders in Jerusalem. Within this section, Talbert sees three attempts to undermine the authority of Jesus: 20:1-19, 20-26, and 27-33. See also Green, *Luke*, 697.

141. Levirate marriage is discussed in Deut 25:5-10. Deuteronomy 25:5 states, "When brothers reside together, and one of them dies and has no son, the wife of the deceased shall not be married outside the family to a stranger. Her husband's brother shall go in to her, taking her in marriage, and performing the duty of a husband's brother to her."

142. Kimball, *Jesus' Exposition*, 170, argues that the hypothetical situation concocted by the Sadducees is designed to make a mockery of Jesus' views on the resurrection.

143. See Talbert, *Reading Luke*, 227-28. Cf. Anderson, "Implicit Information," 13-14; Anderson argues that Jesus' response renders their question "irrelevant."

do not understand "that age" (20:35), i.e., the time of the resurrection.[144] Jesus then goes on to justify belief in the resurrection, using references to the law to do so. In vv. 37–38, Jesus recalls God's appearance to Moses in the burning bush (Exod 3), in which Moses λέγει κύριον τὸν θεὸν Ἀβραὰμ καὶ θεὸν Ἰσαὰκ καὶ θεὸν Ἰακώβ (20:37).[145] Jesus concludes his argument for the validity of the resurrection in 20:38: θεὸς δὲ οὐκ ἔστιν νεκρῶν ἀλλὰ ζώντων, πάντες γὰρ αὐτῷ ζῶσιν.[146]

In this section, the Sadducees are attempting to manipulate the meaning of the references to levirate marriage in the Jewish law in order to justify their own position concerning the resurrection. Specifically, they recall Deut 25 in their question to Jesus, who rebuffs their question by his own reference to the law. Jesus is portrayed as the one who correctly understands and can therefore apply and interpret the scripture. At the same time, the Sadducees are shown to be guilty of impiety through their attempt to twist the meaning of the divine testimony through the law. In their attempt to call Jesus' authority into question, they demonstrate that they themselves have no authority to apply the law correctly.

This interpretation is reinforced in the narrative that follows. In 20:41–47, Jesus addresses the people concerning the scribes[147] and employs divine testimony through the Psalms in order to question the scribes' view of the messiah. He does so through a rhetorical question (Πῶς λέγουσιν τὸν Χριστὸν εἶναι Δαυὶδ υἱόν)[148] and the citation of Ps 109:1 LXX: αὐτὸς γὰρ Δαυὶδ λέγει ἐν βίβλῳ ψαλμῶν, Εἶπεν κύριος τῷ κυρίῳ μου,

---

144. Fitzmyer, *Luke X–XXIV*, 1300, argues that Jesus' answer is that marriage in "this age" is for the purposes of procreation, and will therefore be unnecessary in the "age to come."

145. Against those scholars who claim that Jesus employs a rabbinic form of argumentation (cf., e.g., Caird, *St. Luke*, 224), Cohn-Sherbok argues that Jesus' line of reasoning does not match that of other rabbis who argue for the resurrection of the dead from scripture. Cohn-Sherbok, therefore, concludes that this depiction is in harmony with the overall portrayal of Jesus in the gospels; he is pictured as "not skilled in the argumentative style of the Pharisees and Sadducees." See Cohn-Sherbok, "Jesus' Defence," 72.

146. πάντες refers to Abraham, Isaac, and Jacob in v. 37.

147. Following Green, *Luke*, 723–24. The text in 20:41 is somewhat ambiguous: Εἶπεν δὲ πρὸς αὐτούς, Πῶς λέγουσιν τὸν Χριστὸν εἶναι Δαυὶδ υἱόν. The referent of αὐτούς is most likely the people; cf. 20:45. The subject of λέγουσιν is then the scribes, again referring to 20:45–47.

148. At this point, the Lukan Jesus is most likely referring to various texts to which the scribes refer which claim that the messiah will come from David's lineage. Green, *Luke*, 723, suggests 2 Sam 7:12–14 as a possibility. See also Fitzmyer, *Luke X–XXIV*, 1310–11, for a discussion of the relevant OT texts.

Κάθου ἐκ δεξιῶν μου ἕως ἂν θῶ τοὺς ἐχθρούς σου ὑποπόδιον τῶν ποδῶν σου (20:42–43). Here, Jesus again demonstrates his knowledge of the scriptures in order to demonstrate: first, that being an ancestor of David is not the most important criteria for the messiah;[149] and second, the scribes, while they may agree with Jesus on the issue of the resurrection (cf. 20:39), they, too, like the Sadducees, are not reliable interpreters of the scriptures (cf. 20:45–47). Therefore, though Jesus' authority throughout this section of Luke's gospel is questioned, through divine testimony Jesus is portrayed as the truly authoritative one.[150]

Luke 24:25–27, 44–49

In these two passages, Jesus is attempting to explain his death and subsequent resurrection to his disciples. The first passage is found within the context of Jesus' discussion with the two disciples on the road to Emmaus;[151] the second is found in the account of Jesus' appearance to the eleven in Jerusalem. In both instances, Jesus explains the events surrounding his

---

149. Luke's exact use of Ps 109:1 LXX is notoriously difficult to discern. Kimball, *Jesus' Exposition*, 182–83, surveys the three most prevalent interpretations in modern scholarship: (i) Luke cites Ps 109:1 in order to reject the notion that the messiah is in David's line; (ii) Ps 109:1 is cited in order to demonstrate that the messiah is "more than a mere son of David"; (iii) Jesus is calling himself Son of Man as seen in Dan 7:9–13. Kimball rejects (i) and (iii) above, arguing for the second interpretation. Fitzmyer, *Luke X-XXIV*, 1312–13 lists these as well. See also Green, *Luke*, 724, who calls this text an "enigma," which is ultimately not resolved. Juel, *Messianic Exegesis*, 142–44 (commenting on Mark 12:35–37), rejects the interpretation that Jesus is denying his davidic ancestry. Rather, Jesus presents two passages from the Psalter that seemed to contradict each other; the contradiction, however, is resolved when one considers them in association with Jesus' death and resurrection.

150. A similar situation is narrated in Luke 10:25–37, in which a lawyer attempts to "test" Jesus (ἐκπειράζων αὐτόν; 10:25). The "test" involves the proper interpretation of scripture, in this case Lev 19:18. The lawyer, described as θέλων δικαιῶσαι ἑαυτὸν (10:29), then questions Jesus as to whom "neighbor" refers. Jesus answers him through the parable of the Good Samaritan, thus demonstrating his superior ability to interpret the law. Jesus is thus portrayed positively, while the lawyer demonstrates his inability to understand God's testimony through the law.

151. Read-Heimerdinger and Rius-Camps compare this account as told in the Alexandrian text to the one found in Codex Bezae. They argue that the account in the Bezan text represents a more theological, Jewish re-telling (based upon its many allusions to the story of Jacob at Bethel in Genesis) and thus actually pre-dates the more factual, Alexandrian account. See Read-Heimerdinger and Rius-Camps, "Emmaous or Oulammaous," 23–42.

The *Topos* of Divine Testimony in Luke/Acts

death and resurrection through scripture.[152] Luke, therefore, in this section, demonstrates that the events of Jesus' death and resurrection fulfill the relevant Jewish scriptures.[153] The divine origin of the scriptures is not explicitly stated; the auditor knows, however, that God is the source of the prophecies. In both passages, the Lukan Jesus employs the word δεῖ (24:26, 44)[154] to emphasize that what is transpiring follows the divine plan as prophesied in scripture.[155]

The divine testimony through scripture thus functions as prophecy which has now been fulfilled by Jesus' death and resurrection.[156] As I demonstrated in the section above concerning oracles in Hellenistic writ-

---

152. 24:27: καὶ ἀρξάμενος ἀπὸ Μωϋσέως καὶ ἀπὸ πάντων τῶν προφητῶν διερμήνευσεν αὐτοῖς ἐν πάσαις ταῖς γραφαῖς τὰ περὶ ἑαυτοῦ; 24:44b–45: δεῖ πληρωθῆναι πάντα τὰ γεγραμμένα ἐν τῷ νόμῳ Μωϋσέως καὶ τοῖς προφήταις καὶ ψαλμοῖς περὶ ἐμοῦ, τότε διήνοιξεν αὐτῶν τὸν νοῦν τοῦ συνιέναι τὰς γραφάς.

153. The specific scriptures from which the Lukan Jesus draws are not mentioned. Green argues that this is irrelevant, stating that "the truth to which all the Scriptures point has now been realized" (Green, *Luke*, 857). Tannehill (*Luke*, 286) provides three possibilities for these general references to scripture; Luke is referring: (i) to all scripture; (ii) to a central truth contained in scripture in general; or (iii) to a prophetic pattern seen throughout the OT. Agreeing with Tannehill's first possibility, see Crüsemann, "Schrift und Auferstehung," 152; Wright, "Resurrection," 148. Maxey argues that the intent of the narrator at this point is to suggest that the reader should study the scriptures for him- or herself in order to substantiate Jesus' claims; Maxey, "Road to Emmaus," 121. On the centrality of the "proof from prophecy" theme in Luke 24, see Schubert, "Structure and Significance," 165–86. Schubert argues that the theme of proof-from-prophecy is what binds together the three disparate traditions from which Luke has drawn in composing this account.

154. Most scholars argue that there is no evidence in Jewish scripture prior to Luke's gospel of a suffering Messiah, rendering 24:26 somewhat enigmatic. For a representative listing of scholars who take this position, see Doble, "Luke 24.26, 44," 268 n. 1. Doble himself argues that one can indeed find such a model when one considers the Psalter as a whole.

155. On the significance of divine necessity in Luke-Acts, see Squires, *Plan of God*; Cosgrove, "Divine ΔΕΙ," 168–90; see also Talbert, "Promise and Fulfillment," 96–97. As noted above, enough citations of the Jewish scriptures are explicitly described as being the words of God (or the Holy Spirit) that an auditor of Luke-Acts would understand all references to Moses, the prophets, and the Psalms to be divine testimony. This is similar to another passage, in which the Lukan Jesus cites a prophecy that "must" be fulfilled; see Luke 22:37. Here, Jesus quotes Isa 53:12 and tells his disciples that it is necessary that this prophecy concerning him be fulfilled (τοῦτο τὸ γεγραμμένον δεῖ τελεσθῆναι ἐν ἐμοί).

156. Hays's comment is apposite: "Scripture forms the hermeneutical matrix within which the recent shattering events in Jerusalem become intelligible" (Hays, "Gospels," 416).

ings, here the contemporary events and the prophecies found in scripture serve to mutually interpret one another.[157] Jesus' death and resurrection are therefore sanctioned through divine testimony as being part of God's plan, first seen in the Jewish scriptures. But to recognize this requires one who is able correctly to interpret the relevant scriptures in light of what has happened. Thus, Jesus is portrayed in a positive light as the one who has the ability to do this.[158] Contrariwise, the disciples are portrayed as the ones who are in need of such an interpreter. They fail to understand what has happened[159] until Jesus explains it to them through references to the scriptures.

Acts 1:15–16

The citation of scripture in this passage (1:15–26) is in association with the apostles' selection of the successor to Judas.[160] The context is one of prayer; in 1:14 the narrator states: οὗτοι πάντες [the eleven apostles, named in 1:13] ἦσαν προσκαρτεροῦντες ὁμοθυμαδὸν τῇ προσευχῇ. Peter takes up

---

157. On this as it pertains to Luke 24, see L. Johnson, *Luke*, 399, and Green, *Luke*, 844.

158. The auditor, at this point, is not surprised. This is a portrayal of Jesus that began in 4:16, and has been reinforced throughout the gospel. Green, commenting on the theme of fulfillment of scripture, which, according to him, is central to this passage, states that the fulfillment motif "draws attention both to Luke's perspective on the prophetic role of the Scriptures and to the necessity of interpreting them faithfully"; see Green, *Luke*, 842–43.

159. This theme was first seen when Jesus made his initial statements in Luke 9 concerning his impending death and resurrection; see above on the divine voice at the transfiguration.

160. Concerning the significance of having twelve apostles, see L. Johnson, *Acts*, 38. Johnson argues that Judas's betrayal of Jesus and subsequent death has caused a rift in the original group that serves as the reconstituted people of God. Johnson also maintains that the significance of the passage is seen in its placement; it effectively interrupts the sequence of the promise of the Holy Spirit (Luke 24:49; Acts 1:5, 8) and the fulfillment of this prophecy in Acts 2. Menoud maintains that Judas's *betrayal* of Jesus must be justified through scripture, not his death per se; see Menoud, "Additions," 133–48. Haenchen, "Judentum und Christentum," 162, commenting on 1:21, argues that for Luke, it is imperative that a group of witnesses from the time of Jesus' baptism up to his resurrection be maintained.

the leadership role in this setting,[161] stating within his speech[162] to the one hundred twenty gathered (1:15) that ἔδει πληρωθῆναι τὴν γραφὴν ἥν προεῖπεν τὸ πνεῦμα τὸ ἅγιον διὰ στόματος Δαυὶδ περὶ Ἰούδα τοῦ γενομένου ὁδηγοῦ τοῖς συλλαβοῦσιν Ἰησοῦν (1:16). Through Peter's introduction to the citations in 1:20, it is clear that the quotation of scripture has a divine origin.[163] The scripture is described as προεῖπεν τὸ πνεῦμα τὸ ἅγιον διὰ στόματος Δαυὶδ.

The texts that Peter cites come from Ps 68:26 LXX (Γενηθήτω ἡ ἔπαυλις αὐτοῦ ἔρημος καὶ μὴ ἔστω ὁ κατοικῶν ἐν αὐτῇ; 1:20a) and Ps 108:8 LXX (Τὴν ἐπισκοπὴν αὐτοῦ λαβέτω ἕτερος; 1:20b).[164] The first citation serves to demonstrate that Judas's death was prophesied by David in the psalms, and thus this divine testimony functions as a fulfilled prophecy. The second citation concerns a future event, and is best understood as a divine command[165] to replace Judas. Together, the two citations, given that they are cited within a deliberative speech, function as a means to persuade those gathered that they must act in order to replace Judas. The citations also function as God's approval of the apostles as they reflect on Judas's betrayal of Jesus. Even this heinous event is not outside of God's purview,[166] and before beginning their mission (cf. 1:8), the apostles are to follow the divine instructions for the restoration of their group of twelve.[167]

---

161. Parsons, *Acts*, 31, correctly recognizes the irony of Peter, the one who denied Jesus (cf. Luke 22:54–62), encouraging the remaining apostles to replace Judas, the one who betrayed Jesus.

162. The speech should be considered deliberative; Peter is encouraging the group to act on the selection of one to replace Judas. See Kennedy, *Rhetorical Criticism*, 116.

163. L. Johnson, *Acts*, 35, refers to Jesus' statement in Luke 24:44 (on this, see above) and argues that for Luke, all scripture is prophetic and therefore has the Holy Spirit as its source.

164. For deviations of these citations from the MT, see Nellessen, "Tradition und Schrift," 215–17. See also L. Johnson, *Acts*, 36.

165. Note the aorist imperative, λαβέτω.

166. Recognized by Talbert, *Reading Acts*, 13, due to the use of δεῖ in 1:16, 21. Parsons (*Acts*, 32) also sees δεῖ as the key word in Peter's speech; he maintains that the imperfect ἔδει in 1:16 points back to Judas's death, while the present δεῖ in 1:21 refers to the contemporary issue of Judas's successor.

167. Clearly the divine testimony through the citation of scripture also serves to elevate Peter in the auditor's eyes, especially following his betrayal of Jesus, narrated in Luke 22. Through his correct application of scripture, Peter is now "restored" and should be considered a reliable character (for a similar argument, see Tannehill, *Acts*, 20. Tannehill maintains that Peter has now assumed this role in Jesus' absence). This will be further emphasized in Acts 2, continuing through Acts 15. Simultaneously, these citations serve to demonstrate God's disapproval of Judas's actions.

Acts 2:14–36

Within Peter's Pentecost speech[168] are multiple references to the Jewish scriptures. The speech is triggered by the crowd's assertion that the apostles are intoxicated, given their behavior after the anointing of the Holy Spirit. The speech therefore refutes this claim, and in turn serves to explain the phenomenon that has just occurred.[169] Within the speech, Peter makes reference to scripture in: 2:17–21 (Joel 3:1–5 LXX); 2:25–28 (Ps 15:8–11 LXX); and 2:34 (Ps 109:1 LXX). In the first citation from Joel, Luke makes the divine origin of the passage explicit: within the citation he inserts λέγει ὁ θεός (2:17), which is found neither in the MT nor in the LXX. The other citations are attributed to David. With regard to these, the auditor is already aware that the Spirit spoke through David (cf. 1:16 and comments above); therefore, implicitly, these citations are also attributed to the speech of the Holy Spirit.

The citation from Joel serves to cast the events of Pentecost as the fulfillment of Joel's prophecy. Therefore, rather than being drunk, what the apostles have experienced is the outpouring of the Holy Spirit in fulfillment of Joel's words.[170] Ps 15:8–11 LXX[171] is employed as scriptural proof

---

168. Talbert actually sees two speeches here; 2:14–15 explain what is not happening (the apostles are not drunk), and 2:16–36 explain what is happening and its ramifications (Talbert, *Reading Acts*, 27). Kennedy (*Rhetorical Criticism*, 117) considers this one speech; he does distinguish between those sections which are judicial (vv. 14–21—the charge of drunkenness is countered; vv. 22–36—Peter's audience is accused of killing Jesus) and deliberative (vv. 37–40—a call to repentance) in nature.

169. L. Johnson, *Acts*, 53, draws a possible analogy to the work of the priest at Delphi. Just as the priest would interpret the Pythia's speech for the suppliant, so here Peter interprets the glossolalia. He recognizes an important difference, however: Peter does not interpret what was said through the glossolalia (i.e., he does not provide a translation); rather, he explains why it is happening.

170. Parsons (*Acts*, 42) states, "The Joel prophecy serves as the authoritative interpretation of the Pentecost event." Steyn argues, somewhat implausibly, that the genitive construction in the sentence ἐκχεῶ ἀπὸ τοῦ πνεύματός μου in Acts 2:17 should be understood as God pouring out an object from within his spirit. Steyn goes on to say that this object is God's power, which results in the apostles' ability to prophesy. See Steyn, "ἐκχεῶ ἀπὸ τοῦ πνεύματος," 365–71; for a counter-argument see, e.g., Culy and Parsons, *Acts*, 34, who maintain that the partitive genitive prepositional phrase is most likely due to the nature of the verb ἐκχέω. Cf. Dillon, "Prophecy," 544–56, who maintains that Luke, through this speech and Peter's speech at the temple in Acts 3, portrays the apostles' preaching as "the eschatological renewal of prophecy," through which "the voice of the risen Christ is heard, through the testimony of his witnesses" (ibid., 544).

171. Fenske attempts to refute Haenchen's argument that Luke is dependent on

The *Topos* of Divine Testimony in Luke/Acts

of Peter's statement in 2:24, namely that Jesus' resurrection was prophesied in the psalms.¹⁷² Thus, this citation functions as a prophecy which interprets contemporary events as well. Finally, Ps 109:1 LXX is cited in order to substantiate Peter's claim in 2:33; Jesus is the one who has ascended into heaven, not David, and is responsible for the outpouring of the Holy Spirit.¹⁷³ Once again, a prophecy given through the psalms has been fulfilled through Jesus' resurrection.

In general, the divine testimonies through the citation of scripture in this speech contribute to the overall purpose of the speech, that of explaining the giving of the Holy Spirit. Looking closer, they do so as formerly-received prophecies which are now fulfilled through the events of Pentecost.¹⁷⁴ Thus, the citations serve to provide a divine sanction on the giving of the Spirit, an event which itself involves divine testimony, as I will demonstrate in chapter six. The auditor, therefore, is provided with two divine testimonies, the doubling of which serves to reinforce the divine nature of the events which are transpiring in the narrative.¹⁷⁵ This multiplicity of evidence of the legitimacy of the giving of the Spirit emphasizes the significance of Pentecost within the greater narrative context.

Secondarily, through the speech and the use of divine testimony via citations, Peter is portrayed as an authoritative interpreter of the scriptures.¹⁷⁶ Two pieces of evidence give credence to this claim. First, Luke

---

Psalm 15 LXX to make his point (rather than the Hebrew; see Haenchen, *Apostelgeschichte*, 144–45), maintaining that Luke's reference to David's tomb in 2:29 points in the direction of the Hebrew text; see Fenske, "Aspekte Biblischer Theologie," 54–70.

172. Parsons notes that the implied speaker of Ps 15:8–10 LXX in 2:25–28 is the messiah himself. Thus the situation is the same here as in the citation of Joel, where Luke explicitly attributes the citation to God by inserting λέγει ὁ θεός into the text; see Parsons, *Acts*, 45. This is *contra* G. Trull ("Peter's Interpretation," 432–48), who claims that the citation from the psalm is "a direct prophecy from David concerning the Messiah's resurrection" (ibid., 448).

173. L. Johnson, *Acts*, 54, helpfully remarks that the citation of Joel explains what happened at Pentecost, while the citations from the psalms serve to interpret the cause of the phenomenon.

174. Grant, "Cover Versions," 27–49, argues that the psalms lend themselves well to reinterpretation due to their "ahistorical" nature.

175. See Parsons, *Acts*, 43; *contra* A. Johnson, "Resurrection," 146–62, who argues that the only witness to the resurrection of Jesus at this point in Peter's speech is the public testimony (cf. 2:32) of the apostles who had experienced the giving of the Holy Spirit at Pentecost.

176. Specifically focusing on Peter's citation and interpretation of the psalms in this speech, Moessner ("Two Lords," 215–32) draws attention to Jesus' statement in Luke 24:44–45 that he would "open the minds" of the apostles so that they might

states the introduction to the speech in the following way: Σταθεὶς δὲ ὁ Πέτρος σὺν τοῖς ἕνδεκα ἐπῆρεν τὴν φωνὴν αὐτοῦ καὶ ἀπεφθέγξατο αὐτοῖς (2:14). The verb ἀποφθέγγομαι is commonly used in reference to inspired speech, and therefore depicts Peter as a reliable spokesperson.[177] Second, the results of the speech are proof of its effectiveness. In 2:41, Luke reports that approximately 3000 were baptized, confirming the persuasiveness of the speech and the skill of the orator who delivered it.

Acts 3:12-26

In this speech, following the healing of the lame man at the temple (3:1-11),[178] there are three references to scripture. The first is a general reference to what God had said through the prophets (ὁ δὲ θεὸς ἃ προκατήγγειλεν διὰ στόματος πάντων τῶν προφητῶν παθεῖν τὸν Χριστὸν αὐτοῦ ἐπλήρωσεν οὕτως; 3:18). In this case, the divine origin of the fulfilled prophecy is made clear. The second reference is to what Moses said, namely that God would eventually call a prophet to whom all must listen and be obedient (3:22-23; cf. Deut 18:15-20[179]). Third, Peter cites a promise that God gave to Abraham (3:25; cf. Gen 12:3).[180] All three are employed as evi-

---

understand all the scriptures, specifically including the psalms (cf. Luke 24:44). Therefore, Peter now understands the messianic significance of the psalms due to this experience.

177. See Parsons, *Acts*, 41.

178. Kennedy, *Rhetorical Criticism*, 118-19, argues that the speech is both judicial (3:12-18, in which Peter argues that God is responsible of the healing of the lame man) and deliberative (3:19-26, in which there is a call to repentance). See also Soards, *Speeches in Acts*, 39. Talbert, *Reading Acts*, 35, divides the speech into two sections as well. Talbert rightly recognizes the connection of the speech to the healing of the lame man; 3:12-16 therefore deals with how the healing was accomplished, while 3:17-26 is concerned with the repercussions of the discussion in 3:12-16. Fitzmyer, *Acts*, 281, states that the catalyst of the speech was "a misunderstanding" on the part of the people concerning the man's healing that needed to be corrected.

179. So Parsons, *Acts*, 61. L. Johnson, *Acts*, 70, argues that Luke has combined citations from Deut 18:15-19 and Lev 23:29 (see esp. ἐξολεθρευθήσεται in Acts 3:23 and Lev 23:29, which does not appear in Deut 18:15-20).

180. As L. Johnson (*Acts*, 70) recognizes, this promise is made multiple times in Genesis; cf. 12:3; 18:18; 22:18; 26:4. Léonas, "Acts 3,25-26," 149-61, argues against the universal (i.e., Pauline) interpretation of 3:25-26 adopted by most commentators (see his list, 149 n. 1). Léonas, *contra* this stance, argues that the promise is actually only to Israel. He then concludes, however, that while this is perhaps the meaning in the narrative, Luke intended his audience to understand a more universal message of salvation. Léonas is clearly not correct on this point; Luke's narrative is meant to be

The *Topos* of Divine Testimony in Luke/Acts

dence within the speech in an effort to persuade the audience.[181] The first is evidence for Jesus' death (and indirectly for the responsibility for it of those in the audience);[182] the last two references are evidence that God has raised up Jesus to bless all humanity.

The divine testimony in this speech functions on multiple levels. In general, as stated above, it makes contributions as evidence in both the judicial (explaining the healing of the lame man) and deliberative (the call to repentance) portions of the speech. Secondarily, in the first reference, Peter states that the scriptures were fulfilled despite the people's ignorance of them. Thus, the divine testimony serves as a fulfilled prophecy despite the misunderstanding (or, in this case, a lack of understanding) of such, a common function as I have shown. In this way, the divine testimony in 3:18 is used to demonstrate God's disapproval of those who were ignorant of the prophecies in scripture.[183] The other two references, in supporting Peter's call to repentance, are cited as prophecies that have been fulfilled. The reference to Deut 18/Lev 23 also contains a warning, namely that the people are to listen to the prophet that God raises up.[184] Overall, the divine testimony specifically provides legitimation for the healing of the lame

---

persuasive in and of itself. It is, therefore, not logical that the narrative would contradict the point being communicated to the audience. For a more balanced approach to the universal/particular question raised here, see Schlosser, "Moïse," 26.

181. For the importance of the rhetorical setting (Peter at the temple) of the speech and its intended audience, see Haraguchi, "Call for Repentance," 267–82. Haraguchi argues that because Peter is standing at the temple when he gives this speech, it constitutes a call to repentance for all of Israel, not just the audience physically present.

182. Here the Lukan Peter is associating the healing of the lame man to Jesus' resurrection, whom God raised. See Talbert, *Reading Acts*, 38–39; see also L. Johnson, *Acts*, 73. Tannehill, *Acts*, 53, shows the progression of thought as Jesus' death (3:14–15a), to his resurrection (3:15b), to the healing (3:16). The reference to the prophets, therefore, connects the people's ignorance to Jesus' death; in other words, their ignorance of the earlier prophecies was instrumental in this chain of events.

183. Parsons (*Acts*, 60) argues that Peter makes this statement as part of an invective against his audience. I agree with Parsons, and thus can argue that the divine testimony is part of this invective. As Johnson points out, however, despite their ignorance, repentance is still possible for those listening to Peter (L. Johnson, *Acts*, 73). Cf. Tannehill, *Acts*, 57; Tannehill notes that just as the apostles, too, were ignorant at one time (here he cites Luke 24), but were restored, so here. Heimerdinger, "Unintentional Sins," 269–76, argues that guilt or innocence is not the issue. The real issue here, according to Heimerdinger, is that the people have sinned, and what they now must do in order to avoid the punishment (hence the call to repentance).

184. L. Johnson, *Acts*, 73, terms this a "threat."

man, and therefore to the apostles and Christian movement in general, thus supporting Peter's call on his audience to repent.

Acts 4:25–26

The divine testimony through the citation of scripture is found here in the context of the apostles'[185] prayer which takes place after Peter and John are released by the Jewish council following the healing of the lame man (3:1–11). In their prayer, the apostles address God as creator (4:24)[186] and then preface a citation from the Psalms with this clause: ὁ τοῦ πατρὸς ἡμῶν διὰ πνεύματος ἁγίου στόματος Δαυὶδ παιδός σου εἰπών (4:25a).[187] The citation is thus given divine origins within this prayer.[188] The citation itself is from Ps 2 LXX, and is recorded in 4:25b-26: Ἱνατί ἐφρύαξαν ἔθνη καὶ λαοὶ ἐμελέτησαν κενά; παρέστησαν οἱ βασιλεῖς τῆς γῆς καὶ οἱ ἄρχοντες συνήχθησαν επὶ τὸ αὐτὸ κατὰ τοῦ κυρίου καὶ κατὰ τοῦ Χριστοῦ αὐτοῦ. Clearly, the psalm is being interpreted messianically,[189] with Jesus' death primarily in view, but secondarily, the apostles' sufferings at the hands of the leaders. Luke, therefore, connects the divine testimony of the psalm to the present persecution of the apostles.

---

185. The text literally states that Peter and John ἦλθον πρὸς τοὺς ἰδίους (4:23) and is therefore somewhat enigmatic. See L. Johnson, *Acts*, 83, who renders πρὸς τοὺς ἰδίους as "to their associates." Dupont, *Études*, 521, argues that only the apostles are in view, in that their prayer is for the apostolic ministry in which they are engaged.

186. Wahlde ("Acts 4,24–31," 237–44) argues that the prayer is in a chiastic form, the frame of which is the sovereignty of God and the center of which is 4:26c, 27. Thus the center point emphasizes the people's opposition to the Lord and to Jesus.

187. Wahlde lists several issues with the rendering of this clause in the UBS and Nestle-Aland GNT, including: the separation of ὁ from εἰπών; the separation of τοῦ πατρὸς ἡμῶν from Δαυίδ; God speaking through the Holy Spirit; and the lack of διὰ preceding στόματος. In order to understand better the "peculiar wording" of this text, von Wahlde proposes that the text was originally structured in a chiastic fashion (thus introducing the citation from the Ps 2 that follows), in which ὁ and εἰπών constitute A/A', τοῦ πατρὸς ἡμῶν and παιδός σου comprise B/B', and διὰ πνεύματος ἁγίου and στόματος Δαυίδ form C/C'. See Wahlde, "Problems," 265–67.

188. This is similar to the "narrative layers" that Parsons recognizes in Acts 2, at which point, concerning Peter's citation of the prophet Joel, Parsons cleverly states that "Luke said that Peter said that Joel said that God said" (*Acts*, 42). In this passage, the chain is: "Luke said that the apostles said that God said that David, through the Holy Spirit, said."

189. See Talbert, *Reading Acts*, 46; L. Johnson, *Acts*, 90; Parsons, *Acts*, 66; and Haenchen, *Apostelgeschichte*, 185.

The *Topos* of Divine Testimony in Luke/Acts

The divine testimony functions here as the fulfillment of prophecy, in which an earlier, prophetic statement is applied to a contemporary situation.[190] Through the divine testimony, Luke demonstrates that even the apostles' struggles with the religious leaders have divine sanction and are therefore part and parcel of their apostolic ministry. This interpretation is confirmed at the end of the prayer: first, καὶ δεηθέντων αὐτῶν ἐσαλεύθη ὁ τόπος ἐν ᾧ ἦσαν φυνηγμένοι (4:31a); on this, see the previous chapter); second, their prayer is answered in that they indeed ἐλάλουν τὸν λόγον τοῦ θεοῦ μετὰ παρρησίας (4:31b). Likewise, the opponents of the apostles are portrayed negatively as opposing God's work through his agent Jesus.[191]

Acts 7:2–60

OT citations and allusions constitute a large part of Stephen's speech in Acts 7. To analyze each one in detail would be beyond the scope of the present study. It is possible, however, to analyze this speech and determine the overall function of divine testimony through the various citations of the Jewish scripture. It is to this analysis that I now turn.

Stephen's speech is in response to the high priest's question: Εἰ ταῦτα οὕτως ἔχει (7:1). ταῦτα refers to the charges leveled against Stephen, namely from false witnesses who claim Stephen is saying that Ἰησοῦς ὁ Ναζωραῖος οὗτος καταλύσει τὸν τόπον τοῦτον [i.e., the temple] καὶ ἀλλάξει τὰ ἔθη ἃ παρέδωκεν ἡμῖν Μωϋσῆς (6:14). Stephen's speech is in response to these charges, refuting them by making a counter charge against his accusers. Thus, the speech is considered to be a judicial speech.[192] As part of this refutation, in the speech Stephen summarizes portions of Israel's history; within these summaries he constantly quotes from and alludes to the Jewish scripture.[193]

---

190. See Fitzmyer, *Acts*, 306. L. Johnson, *Acts*, 90, argues that Luke at this point employs midrash in order to apply the earlier prophecy to the contemporary situation.

191. Tannehill, *Acts*, 71, correctly notes that through the citation, those who opposed Jesus and those now opposing the apostles are one in the same. Further, for the auditor, this is not a great leap in that the Sanhedrin was involved in both situations.

192. Kennedy, *Rhetorical Criticism*, 121.

193. For a complete list of scripture quotations referenced in the speeches in Acts (those prefaced by introductory formulae), see Soards, *Speeches in Acts*, 60n139. According to Soards, there are ten such quotations in Stephen's speech. Of course, there are many more allusions and passages which summarize sections of the OT narrative as well. For an exhaustive treatment of the OT in Stephen's speech, see Richard, *Acts 6:1—8:4*, 33–155.

Divine Testimony through Utterances in Luke-Acts

In the speech, scripture is often cited as having divine origins. For example, in 7:2, 3, the citation of Gen 12:1 is prefaced with Ὁ θεὸς τῆς δόξης ὤφθη τῷ πατρὶ ἡμῶν Ἀβραάμ . . . καὶ εἶπεν πρὸς αὐτόν.[194] In 7:6, a reference to Gen 15:13 is introduced by the phrase, ἐλάλησεν δὲ οὕτως ὁ θεός. In 7:7, a summary of Gen 15:14-16, Luke inserts the words ὁ θεὸς εἶπεν.[195] God's speech to Moses is also emphasized; at the burning bush, Moses heard the φωνὴ κυρίου (7:31), and an angel spoke with him on Mt. Sinai (7:38). Finally, Moses ἐδέξατο λόγια ζῶντα δοῦναι ἡμῖν (7:38); in the context, it is clear that the λόγια ζῶντα are from God. From these examples,[196] it is clear that God is the source of the citations that Stephen presents as the basis of his refutation of the charges, and that divine testimony through God's speech is integral to the argument made in the speech.

The divine testimony through the citation of scripture in Stephen's speech functions as the main aspect of Stephen's defense. Through the use of scripture, Stephen demonstrates that God first spoke to Abraham, making a promise to him, which was eventually fulfilled in the time of Moses (7:17). Moses, however, as God's messenger, was rejected by the people, both in Egypt (7:27) and in the wilderness (7:39). Finally, according to Stephen, the people were also disobedient to Moses[197] when Solomon built the temple, thus rejecting the worship of God in the tabernacle in favor of a building.[198] Stephen's refutation through a counter accusation comes to

---

194. Kim ("Quotations," 352) makes the claim that this citation in the context of the speech represents "the *ipsissima verba* of God."

195. Reinmuth has studied Luke's use of references to Genesis in this speech (esp. 7:2-17) and compares this to Ps.-Philo's use of the same, attempting to determine the "Bedeutung der Genesis in der Textwelt beider Autoren." Reinmuth concludes that for both authors, the Genesis narrative demonstrates God's election of Israel, and that Israel is now in a time between God's giving of his promise and the fulfillment of that promise. See Reinmuth, "Beobachtungen," 552-69.

196. I must note that the fact that the Lord is speaking is found in most of these references in their original contexts. Luke has, however, often transposed the reference to God speaking to a different part of the citation, thus highlighting the fact that God is indeed speaking through the scripture being cited. A good example of this is the citation of Isa 66:1 LXX in 7:49-50. In Isa 66:1 LXX, the citation is prefaced with οὕτως λέγει κύριος, the usual method of introducing a prophetic oracle in the OT. In 7:49-50, however, λέγει κύριος has been removed from the beginning and placed in the middle of the citation (in 7:49).

197. Pervo, *Acts*, 179, understands Moses at this point in the speech to be a metonym for Torah. Thus, what is emphasized is the disobedience of the people.

198. Talbert, *Reading Acts*, 63. This is accomplished through a citation of Isa 66:1. Kilgallen, "Function," 173-93, argues that Stephen (and therefore Luke) is not antitemple; rather, it is Stephen's accusers' understanding of the temple as a place that can contain God that is at issue.

The *Topos* of Divine Testimony in Luke/Acts

a climax in 7:52,[199] at which point he associates those charging him with those in Israel's past who have rejected God's messengers and message. The divine testimony through the citation of scripture serves, therefore, to portray Stephen's accusers as following in the line of their ancestors, demonstrating their impiety by rejecting divine prophecies and killing Jesus (7:52).[200] This is reinforced by the next sentence: οἵτινες ἐλάβετε τὸν νόμον εἰς διαταγὰς ἀγγέλων, καὶ οὐκ ἐφυλάξατε (7:53).

Conversely, Stephen is portrayed positively both prior to and immediately after the speech (and therefore, during). In 6:14, Stephen's face is described ὡσεὶ πρόσωπον ἀγγέλου. After the speech, the auditor learns that Stephen is πλήρης πνεύματος ἁγίου (7:55a),[201] and that he has a vision of Jesus standing at the right hand of God (7:55b).[202] This vision would have

---

199. As noted by Parsons, *Acts*, 106.

200. Kilgallen, "Function," 180, considers the main point of Stephen's accusation to be in 7:51, namely that his accusers have rejected the Spirit, the source of the prophecy through which God has spoken throughout history. See also Sylva, "Meaning," 261–75, who makes a similar point (see esp. ibid., 274). Sweeney ("Stephen's Speech," 185–210) maintains that the emphasis of the speech is found in its salvation-historical aspects; it is therefore not a polemic against the temple as scholars have understood it to be in the past. Kilgallen, in another essay on Stephen's speech, argues that the speech serves to explain to Theophilus the theological significance of the destruction of the Jerusalem temple; see Kilgallen, "Speech," 293–97. Sterling ("'Opening the Scriptures,'" 199–225) argues that the function of the speech is to justify the spread of the Christian movement outside of Jerusalem. Parsons correctly recognizes and highlights the element of syncrisis in the speech as a whole; through references to the Jewish scriptures, Stephen is contrasting his listeners to those who were obedient to God's directives throughout the history of Israel (i.e., Abraham, Joseph, Moses), and aligning them with those who were disobedient to those whom God sent, and therefore disobedient to God. His listeners have continued this pattern of behavior by killing Jesus, and thus continue to be disobedient to God by killing his appointed messenger. See Parsons, *Acts*, 107–8.

201. Kennedy argues that Luke's comment concerning Stephen being full of the Spirit refers to Stephen's condition throughout the speech; see Kennedy, *Rhetorical Criticism*, 121.

202. Chibici-Revneanu cogently argues that, given the "seated" language in Ps 109:1 LXX and its widespread use in the NT, one should expect variant readings for ἑστῶτα in this verse. She explains the lack of variants by appealing to ancient martyr traditions, in which martyrs are consistently portrayed as standing in God's presence. See Chibici-Revneanu, "Ein himmlischer Stehplatz," 459–88. Maxwell argues that Stephen's speech is never completed; instead, the vision of Jesus standing demonstrates his (exclusive) authority to judge Stephen. Ultimately, Maxwell contends that the incomplete (from a rhetorical perspective) speeches in Acts serve to elicit the audience's participation in the narrative. See Maxwell, "Role of the Audience," 171–80.

Divine Testimony through Utterances in Luke-Acts

been understood by the auditor as yet another instance of divine testimony, and serves to legitimate Stephen's refutation of the charges against him.[203]

Acts 8:32–33

I have already described the overall context of this passage in my previous discussion of direct divine speech; specifically, the analysis at that point concerned the commands given to Philip by the angel and the Holy Spirit. A third instance of divine testimony, in this case through the citation of scripture, occurs in this passage. When Philip, as directed by the Spirit, approaches the chariot in which the eunuch is riding, he hears the eunuch reading from the prophet Isaiah.[204] The eunuch then asks Philip about whom the prophet is writing, thinking it is either about the prophet himself, or someone else. The narrator then continues to say that Philip, ἀρξάμενος ἀπὸ τῆς γραφῆς ταύτης, explains the good news of Jesus to the eunuch,[205] who is subsequently baptized.[206]

---

203. Kennedy, *Rhetorical Criticism*, 122, rightly comments that the vision is "proof of the rightness of Stephen's cause both for himself and for the readers of Acts."

204. Isaiah is not specifically mentioned. The passage quoted in 8:32–33 is from a Greek version of Isa 53:7–8. Luke does have the eunuch recognize that he is reading a prophetic text; see 8:34, in which the eunuch asks: περὶ τίνος ὁ προφήτης λέγει τοῦτο; περὶ ἑαυτοῦ ἢ ἑτέρου τινός; Fitzmyer, *Acts*, 413, compares the Greek translation of Isa 53 here to the MT and finds the Greek version "inaccurate." Talbert, *Reading Acts*, 76–77, argues that there are three scenes within the Philip/eunuch episode. Scene two (30c–35) is structured chiastically, with the Eunuch inviting Philip into the chariot and the recitation of the passage at the center.

205. By doing so, Philip is doing as Jesus before him (see Luke 4:16; cf. 24:13–35) and as Paul will do later (see Acts 13:13–43). All three cite Isaiah in speeches. On this, see O'Toole, "Philip," 25–34. See also Talbert, *Reading Acts*, 77–78, who includes a helpful chart illustrating the parallels between the apostles in Acts and Jesus.

The interpretation of the passage, however, is never explained; it is simply stated that it occurred. Parsons takes issue with Hooker's argument that Luke specifically began and ended the citation from Isa 53 so as to avoid any reference to vicarious suffering (see Hooker, *Jesus and the Servant*). Parsons, on the other hand, argues that the citation is structured in order to highlight the humiliation and exaltation motifs seen in the Greek version of Isa 53:7–8. For Parsons, this is significant because the eunuch, as a culturally marginalized person, could relate to the one to whom the prophet refers. This is complemented by an intertextual echo (ἀρξάμενος ἀπὸ) to Luke 24, a passage in which Jesus' suffering is associated with the Gentiles hearing the gospel. See Parsons, "Isaiah 53 in Acts 8," 104–19. For a similar argument, see Parsons, *Body and Character*, 123–41.

206. After Philip baptizes the eunuch (8:38), Philip simply disappears (8:39). This

The *Topos* of Divine Testimony in Luke/Acts

The divine testimony through the citation of Isaiah functions as the fulfillment of prophecy; in this case, what is written in Isa 53 is considered to be a prophecy of Jesus' suffering and death.[207] Philip uses this scripture (and others, presumably; see 8:35) to explain the events of Jesus' death and resurrection.[208] The divine testimony through fulfilled prophecy therefore legitimates the conversion of the eunuch, a significant new step in the spread of the gospel.[209]

Acts 13:33–35, 41

The divine testimony through quotation of scripture found here is within the context of a speech, as seen earlier in Acts 1, 2, 3, and 7.[210] Here, it is Paul who is giving a sermon, in the synagogue in Antioch of Pisidia, during a service on the Sabbath (Acts 13:14).[211] Paul's sermon can be viewed

---

serves to legitimate the entire account, especially the eunuch's baptism. Cf. Schreiber, "Beobachtungen," 65.

207. Brueggemann references this passage in his argument for the polyvalency of biblical texts. Brueggemann recognizes the Christian reading of this passage from Isaiah as valid; he argues, however, that this reading does not negate other (i.e., Jewish) readings of the text; see Brueggemann, "Dialogue," 383–98.

208. O'Toole makes the argument that the citation of Isa 53:7-8 LXX reinforces Luke's portrayal of Jesus as the servant of Yahweh who faces his death in humility and without protest. In addition, the phrase ὅτι αἴρεται ἀπὸ τῆς γῆς ἡ ζωὴ αὐτοῦ in 8:33 is a reference to Jesus' resurrection. See O'Toole, "How Does Luke Portray Jesus," 328–46.

209. As L. Johnson, *Acts*, 159, rightly recognizes, this is not the beginning of the Gentile mission. Johnson bases his argument on the lengthy narrative in Acts 10:1–11:18 (continued in Acts 15), which serves to explain and justify the conversion of Cornelius and his household. Thus, the conversion of the Ethiopian eunuch represents a new movement of the gospel, but not the initiation of the mission to the Gentiles. Haenchen, *Apostelgeschichte*, 263–64, is of the same opinion; he considers this narrative to be a step between the mission to the Samaritans and the mission to the Gentiles. A. Smith performs a narrative-critical analysis of this passage and concludes by noting several connections of this account to the greater context of which it is a part: (i) it is one example of several in Acts of God's desire to welcome non-Jews into the Christian community; (ii) it is to be understood as God's ability to overcome persecution and benefit humanity; (iii) the gospel is open to all, even powerful, wealthy non-Jews. A fourth point (it is actually the first stated) is that Luke contrasts Philip's willingness to evangelize the Ethiopian with Peter's unwillingness to go to Cornelius. This, however, is overstated by Smith. See A. Smith, "'Do You Understand,'" 48–70.

210. Also Acts 4, in that the apostles' prayer can also be considered a speech.

211. Talbert, *Reading Acts*, 119, demonstrates that Paul's sermon fits well with what is known of Jewish synagogue services in the first century. Elements of such services included the recitation of the Shema, prayers, a priestly blessing, a reading from the

as a speech, composed of the following sections: v. 16b—*exordium*; vv. 17-25—*narratio*;[212] v. 26—*probatio*; vv. 27-37—demonstration, or proofs; vv. 38-41—*peroratio*.[213] Given this structure, three of Paul's citations fall in the section of the speech in which proofs are elaborated. As proofs, the divine testimony serves to persuade Paul's audience of the validity of the issue being argued, articulated in the *probatio*: ἡμῖν ὁ λόγος τῆς σωτηρίας ταύτης ἐξαπεστάλη (13:26).

How do the citations function as proofs? Paul cites Greek versions of Ps 2:7 in 13:33, Isa 55:3 in 13:34, and Ps 15:10 in 13:35.[214] The point Paul is making is seen in his statement in 13:32-33a: καὶ ἡμεῖς ὑμᾶς εὐαγγελιζόμεθα τὴν πρὸς τοὺς πατέρας ἐπαγγελίαν γενομένην, ὅτι ταύτην ὁ θεὸς ἐκπεπλήρωκεν τοῖς τέκνοις ἡμῖν. The passages cited thus serve as prophecies which were fulfilled through Jesus' resurrection (13:33). The citations are given a divine origin in that they were promised by God "to our fathers," as well as fulfilled by God. Therefore, Jesus' resurrection[215] is interpreted through the lens of previously received promises from God,

---

Torah, a reading from the Prophets, and finally a short sermon.

212. Within the *narratio*, Paul specifically states that God is a witness (ᾧ καὶ εἶπεν μαρτυρήσας), giving direct testimony concerning David as ἄνδρα κατὰ τὴν καρδίαν μου (13:22). Also in the *narratio*, John the Baptist is called as a "corroborating" witness (προκηρύξαντος Ἰωάννου πρὸ προσώπου τῆς εἰσόδου αὐτοῦ βάπτισμα μετανοίας παντὶ τῷ λαῷ Ἰσραήλ; 13:24); see Parsons, *Acts*, 195. I would add that for the authorial audience, John is a reliable witness, as he has been sanctioned through numerous instances of divine testimony.

213. See Parsons, *Acts*, 191-92, who follows Kennedy, *Rhetorical Criticism*, 124-25, with some modifications. For an alternate schema, see Talbert, *Reading Acts*, 120, who argues that the sermon is in three sections, each prefaced with an address, i.e., 16b-25 (Ἄνδρες Ἰσραηλῖται καὶ οἱ φοβούμενοι τὸν θεόν); 26-37 (Ἄνδρες ἀδελφοί, υἱοὶ γένους Ἀβραὰμ καὶ οἱ ἐν ὑμῖν φοβούμενοι τὸν θεόν); 38-41 (Ἄνδρες ἀδελφοί). Sandt offers a third, four-part proposal: 17-25—a summary of Israel's history; 26-31—kerygma; 32-37—promise/fulfillment; 38-41—conclusion; see Sandt, "Quotations," 26-58.

214. L. Johnson, *Acts*, 238, argues that this is a "midrashic argument" with two, associated main points: (i) Jesus has been raised from the dead; (ii) this is a fulfillment of prophecy.

215. O'Toole maintains that Jesus' resurrection is the focus of 13:13-52, and that through the fulfillment of prophecy (i.e., Jesus' resurrection) the promise of resurrection is extended to those hearing Paul's speech (as well as subsequent auditors of this passage). See O'Toole, "Christ's Resurrection," 361-72.

which have now been fulfilled.²¹⁶ In this way Luke displays God's approval of these events through God's testimony.²¹⁷

In 13:41, however, the citation of Hab 1:5 does not function as a prophecy fulfilled by current events. Rather, it is cited as a warning to those who are listening to Paul.²¹⁸ Paul prefaces his statement by saying, οὖν μὴ ἐπέλθῃ τὸ εἰρημένον ἐν τοῖς προφήταις. By attributing this to one of the prophets, the Lukan Paul retains the prophetic nature of the citation; it serves, however, to reinforce the importance of his message to his listeners. The significance of this warning is then seen in the ensuing narrative. In 13:42–43, Luke describes the positive response of some of those who heard Paul's sermon. Thus, they are portrayed in a positive light, having taken the divine warning seriously. In vv. 44–47, however, the auditor learns of those who did not, rejecting Paul's message (including the warning). This will lead to Paul and Barnabas turning their attention to the Gentiles, which is based on divine testimony through a command.

Acts 13:47

Acts 13:44–52 is a short narrative, the point of which is to demonstrate the rejection of Paul and Barnabas's message by the Jews.²¹⁹ In vv. 44–45, the auditor learns of the opposition posed by some of the Jews due to their

---

216. This is not the only reference to fulfillment in this passage. In 13:27, the Lukan Paul touches on a theme to which I have already called attention. In chapter 3, Peter argues that Jesus was put to death because of the people's ignorance of prophecy. Here, Paul makes the same claim; see Talbert, *Reading Acts*, 121. See also deSilva, "Paul's Sermon," 32–49, who argues that one of the themes in this sermon, which is found throughout the narrative of Luke-Acts, is that of "the ignorance of those who opposed Jesus and the fulfillment of God's plan in spite of, or rather through, that very lack of recognition" (ibid., 49).

217. Additionally, one can also say that Paul as a missionary is validated as well. Just as Jesus is the Messiah foretold by God through divine testimony, Paul, as interpreter of those scriptures, is also validated by God. Thus, Luke demonstrates a line of continuity: Israel—Jesus—Paul. On this point, see Sterling, "'Do You Understand,'" 101–18.

218. Wall ("Habbakkuk 1:5," 247–58) notes that ὑμῖν has been added to the LXX of Hab 1:5, thus emphasizing the contemporary force of the warning (see esp. ibid., 250).

219. Talbert's structure (13:1—14:28) is illuminating (*Reading Acts*, 116). He demonstrates that this section is in an A (13:4–5)/B (13:6–12)/A' (13:13–43)/B' (13:44–52)/A" (14:1–7)/B" (14:8–18, 19–23) pattern, in which the A sections narrate Paul and Barnabas's interaction with the Jews, and the B sections are those in which they turn to the Gentiles. The section I am considering here is therefore one in which the mission turns to the Gentiles, after the rejection of the message by the Jews.

ζῆλος (13:45). Therefore, Paul and Barnabas inform the Jews that they will now concentrate on evangelizing the Gentiles (13:46). Paul justifies this stance through the citation of Isa 49:6, stating: οὕτως γὰρ ἐντέταλται ἡμῖν ὁ κύριος, Τέθεικά σε εἰς φῶς ἐθνῶν τοῦ εἶναί εἰς σωτηρίαν ἕως ἐσχάτου τῆς γῆς (13:47). Luke clearly identifies the citation as having a divine source (ἐντέταλται ἡμῖν ὁ κύριος).[220] The function of the divine testimony is also clear; due to the Jews' rejection of the gospel, Paul and Barnabas are commanded by God[221] to turn to the Gentiles. The divine testimony thus serves as God's approval of this move, and simultaneously condemns the Jews for their rejection of Paul and Barnabas's message. The divine warning, given in 13:41, goes unheeded by some.

Acts 15:15–18

This instance of divine testimony through the citation of scripture occurs in the context of the Jerusalem council, specifically in James's speech, which follows those of Peter and Paul and Barnabas. The issue over which the council deliberates is described in 15:1–5. The question before the council is the obedience to the Jewish law of new Gentile converts.[222] Peter first recounts his experience of what God has accomplished among the Gentiles;[223] the auditor is already familiar with Peter's experience (cf. 10:1—11:18). Peter therefore argues against the necessity of obedience to the law (15:7–11). Paul and Barnabas speak next, describing what God was doing among the Gentiles (15:12). Finally, James speaks, affirming what Peter has described, and further stating: καὶ τούτῳ συμφωνοῦσιν οἱ λόγοι τῶν προφητῶν, καθὼς γέγραπται (15:15). What follows is a citation

---

220. Rese notes the perfect form of the verb, correctly explaining that with the perfect, Luke is emphasizing a past event that has implications in the present. Rese then questions to which event in the past is the Lukan Paul referring. His answer is Paul's experience on the way to Damascus in Acts 9. See Rese, "Funktion," 77.

221. Tannehill, *Acts*, 173: "a command of the Lord."

222. Concerning this passage, Segal argues that the debate over inclusion of the Gentiles portrayed in Acts 15 can be found in contemporary Jewish sources as well, which, according to Segal, "should not surprise us." On the other hand, he goes on to say, surprisingly (by his admission), that "the accepted position in rabbinic literature is that one does not need to be Jewish to be saved." See Segal, "Acts 15," 63–87 (quotations from 67).

223. Talbert, *Reading Acts*, 130: Peter's speech constitutes an "argument from experience." Cf. Parsons, *Acts*, 212–13.

The *Topos* of Divine Testimony in Luke/Acts

primarily from Amos 9:11–12 LXX (15:16–18).²²⁴ The divine nature of this citation is not explicitly stated; as I have already argued, however, due to the numerous citations previously attributed to God and/or the Holy Spirit, the auditor is assured of the divine nature of these words.

James's point in citing the passage from Amos is to establish that what Peter (and, by inference, Paul and Barnabas) has described is the fulfillment of what Amos prophesied.²²⁵ Thus, once again, divine testimony through the quotation of scripture functions within a fulfillment schema, in which the contemporary event of Gentiles receiving the Holy Spirit is interpreted through a reference to prophecy.²²⁶ Peter's work among the

---

224. Parsons, *Acts*, 213, argues that Μετὰ ταῦτα ἀναστρέψω in the citation in 15:16 is an allusion to Jer 12:15–16, and that γνωστὰ ἀπ' αἰῶνος (15:18) is a reference to Isa 45:21. L. Johnson, *Acts*, 265, considers the allusion to Isa 45:21 "weak." Richard ("Use of Amos," 37–53) argues that changes such as mentioned here (i.e., the addition of Μετὰ ταῦτα, and the changing of "possess" in the MT to "seek" in the Greek text [see below]) are ways in which Luke has molded the citation to apply it and the speech in which it is found to the greater narrative context. Stowasser ("Am 5,25–27," 47–63) tentatively makes the suggestion that Luke has made use of a pre-Lukan testimony source for the Amos citations in Acts, and that the early Christians shared with other contemporary Jewish groups (such as the Qumran community) concepts concerning the interpretation of these prophetic books; he goes on to say, however, that while the means may have been the same, the ends were quite dissimilar.

225. Talbert, *Reading Acts*, 131; Parsons, *Acts*, 212–13: "another authority: scripture." See also Ådna, "Heilige Schrift," 18. The way in which this is accomplished is somewhat complicated. Talbert, *Reading Acts*, 131, argues that the part of the citation recorded in vv. 16–17a equates the resurrection of Jesus with the restoration of David's house. Second, vv. 17b–18 refers to the conversion of the Gentiles, equating this with the nations seeking God. L. Johnson, *Acts*, 265, demonstrates the importance of the LXX version that Luke quotes; from the MT of Amos 9:11–12, Johnson translates "that they may possess the remnant of Edom and all nations who are called by my name" (compare to the NRSV translation of Acts 15:17: "so that all other peoples may seek the Lord—even all the Gentiles over whom my name has been called"). Johnson argues that those who translated the Hebrew text into Greek supplied "they will seek" for the Hebrew translated as "they may possess," and "mankind" for "Edom." In the resulting citation, Luke himself supplied "the Lord" as the object of their seeking. Haenchen, *Apostelgeschichte*, 388–89, terms the Hebrew text of Amos 9:11–12 "unbrauchbar," and continues by stating that "er widerspräche ihr [der Argumentation] sogar." Bauckham also recognizes the substitution of "seek" for "possess," but argues that this is an alternate reading, rather than a translator's mistake. He further argues that the selection of the Amos text is key for this context; according to Bauckham, all other related texts could be understood in the sense that Gentiles can only be accepted as proselytes. Here, in Amos, the understanding is that Gentiles are accepted as Gentiles. See Bauckham, "James," 415–80.

226. Jervell (*Luke and the People of God*, 192) points out that James does not refer to Peter and Cornelius, nor does he reference "signs and wonders" (cf. 15:12). Scripture

Gentiles, as well as that of Paul and Barnabas, receives divine sanction,[227] as well as Peter, Paul, and Barnabas themselves. It should be noted that this is in effect a re-establishment of the validity of their work. God has already positively testified to Peter's interaction with the Gentiles through the interrelated dreams Peter and Cornelius received. Likewise, the work of Paul and Barnabas was initiated through divine testimony (13:1–3; see above), and their decision to turn to the Gentiles was through a divine command (13:47; again, see above). Thus the evidence through divine testimony continues to accumulate as the narrative continues.

Acts 23:5

In Acts 23, Paul is defending himself before the Sanhedrin in Jerusalem;[228] thus the scene portrays Paul on trial. In the speech (the recording of which begins in 23:1), Paul addresses the council and immediately declares his innocence: Ἄνδρες ἀδελφοί, ἐγὼ πάσῃ συνειδήσει ἀγαθῇ πεπολίτευμαι τῷ θεῷ ἄχρι ταύτης τῆς ἡμέρας (23:1).[229] After this statement, the high priest orders that Paul be punched in the mouth, upon which Paul lashes out at the high priest: Τύπτειν σε μέλλει ὁ θεός, τοῖχε κεκονιαμένε· καὶ σὺ κάθῃ κρίνων με κατὰ τὸν νόμον, καὶ παρανομῶν κελεύεις με τύπτεσθαι (23:3).[230] When questioned as to the propriety of his statement to the high priest, Paul apologizes for his outburst, stating: Οὐκ ᾔδειν, ἀδελφοί, ὅτι ἐστὶν ἀρχιερεύς· γέγραπται γὰρ ὅτι Ἄρχοντα τοῦ λαοῦ σου οὐκ ἐρεῖς κακῶς (23:5).[231] The text that Paul quotes is a Greek translation of Exod 22:28.

---

is the sole authority at this point. Contrast this with Fitzmyer, *Acts of the Apostles*, 551, who avers that James "bolsters" Peter's argument through his citation of scripture.

227. See L. Johnson, *Acts*, 268, who understands the Jerusalem council to be a significant turning point in the overall narrative of Acts. One of the emphases noted by Johnson is that the council "legitimates in formal fashion the Gentile mission."

228. Talbert, *Reading Acts*, 195, calls this a "defense."

229. Schubert ("Final Cycle," 1–16) argues that a major theme of Paul's speeches in Acts 22–26 is the establishment of his innocence. Parsons, *Acts*, 314, interprets Paul's statement as an affirmation of his obedience to pursue the calling he received on the way to Damascus.

230. L. Johnson, *Acts*, 397, points out that the verb παρανομέω carries a stronger connotation than simply "breaking the law." Thus, he translates with the word "flouting," emphasizing the disregard the high priest shows for the law. The specific law that Ananias disregards is unclear; Talbert, *Reading Acts*, 195, argues for Deut 1:16–17, which is a call for impartiality in rendering judgment. Fitzmyer, *Acts*, suggests Lev 19:15, which speaks of judging correctly.

231. Paul's statement raises an interesting question: did he truly not recognize the

The *Topos* of Divine Testimony in Luke/Acts

The divine testimony through scripture in this speech of Paul's is in the form of a command, and ultimately serves as part of Paul's defense in support of his claim of innocence. Clearly the divine testimony within the narrative context portrays Paul as desiring to be obedient to the law,[232] while simultaneously the high priest is characterized as having no regard for the law.[233] Paul's innocence, stated at the outset of the speech, is reinforced through his stated desire to be obedient to God's commands, while the mockery of the trial is emphasized when the high priest, in defiance of the law, orders that Paul be struck.

Acts 28:26–27

The last instance of divine testimony in Luke-Acts is the citation of a passage from Isaiah in Acts 28:26–27. Paul is in Rome (28:16), and is described as having discussions with the Jews, διαμαρτυρόμενος τὴν βασιλείαν τοῦ θεοῦ πείθων τε αὐτοὺς περὶ τοῦ Ἰησοῦ ἀπό τε τοῦ νόμου Μωϋσέως καὶ τῶν προφητῶν ἀπὸ πρωῒ ἕως ἑσπέρας (28:23).[234] Paul's message receives a mixed response; some of the Jews believe him, while others do not (28:24). As the meeting breaks up, Paul states: Καλῶς τὸ πνεῦμα τὸ ἅγιον ἐλάλησεν διὰ Ἠσαΐου τοῦ προφήτου πρὸς τοὺς πατέρας ὑμῶν (28:25), and follows this introduction with a citation of Isa 6:9–10 LXX. The divine origin of the citation from Isaiah is clear, as Paul attributes Isaiah's words to the Holy Spirit speaking through the prophet.[235]

---

high priest? Scholarly opinion varies. For example, Fitzmyer, *Acts*, 714, argues that due to Paul's prolonged absence from Jerusalem, he did not, in fact, recognize that he was speaking with the high priest (see also: Haenchen, *Apostelgeschichte*, 566; Wenkel, "Speech-Acts," 81–93). Parsons, *Acts*, 314–15, maintains that Paul in this situation would have certainly recognized the high priest; therefore, his statement is ironic, in that Ananias is not behaving in a fashion which is appropriate for a high priest.

232. Tannehill, *Acts*, 286, maintains that Paul quotes the this scripture in order to demonstrate his respect for the office of the high priest, and therefore ultimately to portray Paul as not being "anti-Jewish."

233. L. Johnson, *Acts*, 397, terms Paul's statement a "prophetic criticism" of the high priest.

234. Here, one notes that again, scripture is being used in a persuasive situation. This is similar to the Lukan Jesus, who instructs the disciples in Luke 24 through reference to the law, prophets, and psalms.

235. Concerning the early Christian usage of the word καλῶς, see Bovon, "(Act 28 25)," 226–32. Bovon argues that καλῶς here emphasizes that what Luke is citing constitutes the words of the Holy Spirit, not of the prophet Isaiah.

Divine Testimony through Utterances in Luke-Acts

The function of the divine testimony through the citation of Isaiah is also clear. Here, the divine testimony is a formerly received prophecy which is now being fulfilled through the currently unfolding events. Through the citation from Isa 6, Luke is arguing that the Jews' refusal to believe Paul's message was foretold by the prophet and is now being fulfilled.[236] Thus, Paul is portrayed as God's obedient servant,[237] the one who has gone "to this people" and brought them the gospel,[238] which they have heard but refused to understand. The Jews who refuse to believe are therefore characterized negatively, as those who hear but do not understand. This interpretation is reinforced by Paul's statement in 28:28: γνωστὸν οὖν ἔστω ὑμῖν ὅτι τοῖς ἔθνεσιν ἀπεστάλη τοῦτο τὸ σωτήριον τοῦ θεοῦ· αὐτοὶ καὶ ἀκούσονται. Because of the Jews' rejection of the gospel, it has gone out to the Gentiles.

---

236. L. Johnson, *Acts*, 476, argues that the citation from Isa 6 places blame squarely on the Jews, rather than Paul or God. One sees this in the fact that in the LXX version of Isa 6:10, the imperatives in the Hebrew original have been changed to finite verbs (for example, *hashmen* has been translated as ἐπαχύνθη); see Fitzmyer, *Acts of the Apostles*, 795. For a different perspective, see Lehnert, "Absage an Israel," 315-23, who claims that Paul's citation of Isa 6:9-10 is a rhetorical ploy, through which Luke is attempting to call his Jewish readers to repentance, leaving the state of the Jews an unanswered question. For a similar argument, see van de Sandt, "Acts 28,28," 341-58. Tannehill is more pessimistic; while he sees hints in the narrative of Luke-Acts which point to the continued possibility of the Jews coming to repentance (including its conclusion, which Tannehill describes thusly: "[F]illed with a tension that expresses the unresolved tension in the plot at this point [i.e., the Jews' refusal to recognize God's messiah opposed to God's continued desire for Israel to repent]"), overall the story of the Jews in Luke-Acts is a tragic one. See Tannehill, "Israel in Luke-Acts," 69-85, quotation from 83. Finally, see Uemura, "Isaiah 6:9-10," 23-57, who maintains that Isa 6:9-10 in its Isaianic context was not a prophecy meant to reject the original auditors. Luke, however, as other NT authors, applies it as a "hardening prophecy" in order to demonstrate the separation of Jews and Christians.

237. This idea is reinforced when one considers the context and structure of the narrative in which this passage is found. Talbert, *Reading Acts*, 221-22, demonstrates that the narrative in 28:17-31 unfolds in three scenes (vv. 17-22, 23-28, 30-31), in which the emphasis is Paul's interactions with Jews in Rome. The first scene, according to Talbert, is structured chiastically, with 28:18 at the center of the chiasm, thus emphasizing Paul's innocence. One could therefore argue that scenes one and two both speak to Paul's innocence of wrongdoing; in scene one this is brought out structurally and through Paul's statement in 28:18, while in scene two Luke employs divine testimony to show that Paul's actions were in obedience to God's plan.

238. Parsons, *Acts*, 364, rightly draws attention to the fact that of all the citations of Isa 6 in the NT, Luke alone includes the phrase Πορεύθητι πρὸς τὸν λαὸν τοῦτον καὶ εἰπόν (28:26).

The *Topos* of Divine Testimony in Luke/Acts

In sum, through the analysis of these examples of the *topos* of divine testimony through the citation of and references to the Jewish scriptures in Luke-Acts, one can see that the *topos* functions in the same manner as the *topos* of divine testimony through utterances in the examples from Hellenistic writings above. Here, I have shown that the citation of scripture serves primarily as prophecies which are fulfilled by contemporary events. This occurs whether they are understood or not. Quotations of scripture also function, however, as a means of defense of a character or to influence other characters to make a decision. Scripture is cited as divinely issued commands and warnings, and as explanations of other events in the narrative. Also, as oracles could be manipulated by unscrupulous characters, and rightly interpreted by devout characters, so it is with scripture citations in Luke-Acts as well. Therefore, it is safe to conclude that oracles and citations of scripture would have been understood as divine testimony by ancient audiences.

Summary of Findings from Luke-Acts and Comparison to the Data from Greco-Roman Narratives

Having surveyed numerous examples of the *topos* of divine testimony through utterances in Hellenistic literature and Luke-Acts, I can now make some concluding statements as to how this *topos* would have been understood by the auditors of Luke-Acts. First, I have shown that the *topos* of divine speech occurs in Hellenistic writings in the form of direct speech by the gods, divine speech through inspired characters, and through oracles. This is also the case in Luke-Acts; divine speech is heard directly from God, from angels sent by God, or directly from the Holy Spirit. Divine speech is also spoken by inspired characters, those "filled with the Holy Spirit." Finally, I argued that the citation of the Jewish scriptures in Luke-Acts is analogous to the reference to oracles in Hellenistic writings, in that both are considered divine speech, and that both are cited in similar ways.[239]

The similarities extend to the placement within the narrative and function of the *topos* of divine testimony through utterances as well. Regarding placement, divine testimony through utterances often occurs at significant moments in the narrative and serves to explain movements

---

239. As argued above, both oracles and scripture are sometimes prefaced with an introductory statement. Oracles are quoted in some instances and other times either paraphrased or mentioned; this is also the case with the citations of scripture in Luke-Acts.

Divine Testimony through Utterances in Luke-Acts

in the plot. Particularly in Luke-Acts, divine testimony through the citation of scripture often occurs in speeches, which are strategically placed throughout the narrative and can serve to explain extraordinary occurrences which have transpired in the story. Also, in many cases, divine testimony through utterances occurs in the context of prayer and/or worship.

The results of the analysis of the data should best be envisioned as a taxonomy in the form of a matrix. Assuming this image, the rows of the matrix are the ways in which the gods testify through speech (i.e., directly, through an intermediary, through oracles/scripture). The functions of the *topos* (the columns of the matrix), as I have demonstrated, include divine guidance, warnings, persuading a group of people of the validity of a certain action, the defense of a character, and the explanation of a divine act which occurred earlier in the narrative. Divine speech also serves as prophecies which have been fulfilled through events in the narrative, whether a character rightly understands the prophecy or not. In both the Hellenistic writings and Luke-Acts, divine testimony functioned as a prophecy of the future greatness and achievement of the subject of the prophecy. Divine speech, particularly oracles and scripture, must be properly interpreted by characters, and can also be manipulated by characters for their own purposes. I have demonstrated through the analyses of examples from Hellenistic writings and Luke-Acts that these functions are common to both, and would therefore have been readily understood by the auditors of Luke-Acts

The overarching function of the *topos* is, however, one of characterization. In chapter two, I demonstrated through the examples from speeches and treatises that divine testimony was used to praise one's ally or vilify an opponent. That is also the case here. Divine testimony through utterances serves to demonstrate the piety and/or impiety of the characters in the narrative. Fulfilled prophecies, for example, serve to legitimate those events which fulfill them, and thus sanction the characters who are the subject of those prophecies.[240] Likewise, a character who is able to discern the proper meaning of an oracle or text from scripture is portrayed positively, while characters who are ignorant of the meaning or, worse, attempt to manipulate the meaning of an oracle or scripture for their own purposes are disparaged. In this way, the *topos* of divine testimony through utterances functions in the same way that I demonstrated in chapter two: the

---

240. This is generally the case. A prophecy can also serve as the disapproval of a character when that prophecy predicted the impious or blasphemous action that takes place.

175

testimony of the deity is used to shed light on the character of the subject of the testimony, allowing the auditor to experience the divine perspective of the character in question.

5 • The *topos* of Divine Testimony through Deeds in Hellenistic Narratives

IN THE PREVIOUS TWO chapters I demonstrated that divine testimony through utterances functions in Hellenistic literature as well as in Luke-Acts to highlight the piety (or impiety) of a character or characters. Significantly, this was the same function for the *topos* determined through the analysis of ancient forensic and deliberative speeches. I now turn my attention to the *topos* of divine testimony through deeds. The analysis that follows will be organized around Cicero's statement in *Top.* 20.76–77, in which he generally describes how the gods actually testify through their deeds. As noted previously, Cicero states:

> The testimony of the gods is covered thoroughly enough by the following: first, utterances, for oracles get their name from the fact that they contain an utterance (*oratio*) of the gods; secondly, things in which are embodied certain works of the gods. First, the heavens themselves and all their order and beauty; secondly, the flight of birds through the air and their songs; thirdly, sounds and flashes of fire from the heavens, and portents given by many objects on earth, as well as the foreshadowing of events which is revealed by the entrails (of sacrificial animals). Many things also are revealed by visions seen in sleep.

From this statement come these categories: the heavens; the flight and singing of birds; sounds and fire from heaven; examination of entrails; and dreams and visions. In each category, examples from the extra-biblical sources surveyed in chapter three will be provided and examined in order to determine how the particular instance of the *topos* is functioning in the narrative. This will require a careful investigation of the narrative context in each case. As was the case earlier, the results of the analysis can

The *Topos* of Divine Testimony in Luke/Acts

be envisioned as a taxonomy in the form of a matrix. Here, however, the "rows" of the matrix are the various forms of divine testimony through deeds. The "columns" of the matrix are the assorted functions of the *topos* in the narrative in which the instances of divine testimony appear. This means, for example, that dreams (or visions) of divine origin can function as a warning, but also serve in other narratives as providing divine guidance to a character. What will be demonstrated through the analysis is that in these narratives the gods testify through many different methods to achieve various ends. It is to these examples of the *topos* of divine testimony that I now turn.

Divine Testimony through Objects and Events in the Heavens

In this category are found those testimonies of the gods which appear in the heavens. These can include such natural phenomena as eclipses and comets (which are often attributed to the direct workings of the gods), but also encompasses such things as apparitions which appear in the sky.[1]

Diodorus Siculus gives an account of an eclipse[2] that is interpreted later in the narrative to be a negative testimony from the gods. Because of losses in the field and a plague that had broken out among the troops, the leaders of the Greek forces meet to decide their next move. There is disagreement within the group; Demosthenes urges a return to Athens, while Nicias argues that they should stay. Demosthenes prevails, and the Greeks prepare to escape back to Athens.

> But when they were about to sail on the following day, on the night of the day before, the moon was eclipsed. Consequently Nicias, who was not only by nature a superstitiously devout man but also cautious because of the epidemic in camp, summoned the soothsayers. And when they declared that the departure must be postponed for the customary three days, Demosthenes and the others were compelled, out of respect for the deity, to accede. (*Hist.* 13.12.6)

While waiting to leave, the Greeks are defeated by the Syracusans and subsequently surrender (*Hist.* 13.13.1–19.3). The Syracusans, after performing

---

1. For prodigies and omens involving phenomena in the sky in the works of Livy, Tacitus, and Suetonius, see F. Kraus, "Omens, Portents, and Prodigies," 55–79.
2. See also Plutarch, *Nic.* 23.6.

Divine Testimony through Deeds in Hellenistic Narratives

sacrifices,[3] have a debate which concerns the fate of the captured Greeks. After Diocles recommends killing the prisoners, Nicolaüs gives an impassioned speech in which he interprets the events to be the punishment of the gods:

> The people of the Athenians have received a punishment their own folly deserved, first of all from the hands of the gods and then from us whom they have wronged. (*Hist.* 13.21.1)[4]

An auditor, then, given this context, must understand the eclipse as the gods' negative testimony concerning the Greeks and their actions against the Syracusans. By causing the eclipse, the gods forced the Greeks to remain in Sicily; subsequently, they were soundly defeated in battle. The interpretation of the testimony on a narrative level is retrospectively carried out through a speech by another character in the narrative.

An example of heavenly portents is found in Plutarch's *Life* of Julius Caesar, and occurs after the murder of Caesar.[5] In this instance, Plutarch describes two signs from the heavens, as well as an apparition seen by Brutus:

> Among the events of man's ordering, the most amazing was that which befell Cassius; for after his defeat at Philippi he slew himself with that very dagger which he had used against Caesar; and among events of divine ordering, there was the great comet, which showed itself in great splendor for seven nights after Caesar's murder, and then disappeared; also, the obscuration of the sun's rays [for one year] . . . But more than anything else the phantom which appeared to Brutus showed that the murder of Caesar was not pleasing to the gods. (*Caes.* 69.3–6)

---

3. "Now at that time the whole city of Syracuse offered sacrifices to the gods" (*Hist.* 13.19.4).

4. Nicolaüs argues for mercy for the prisoners, as the Athenians have already been punished by the gods.

5. Portents associated with the death of the hero are common in ancient literature. For example, the following are found in Plutarch's *Lives*: Alcibiades's dream before his death (*Alc.* 39:1–4); an oracle commands that the bones of Theseus should be collected, and an eagle points out where they were buried on the island of Scyros (*Thes.* 36.1–2); Numa's empty coffin is exposed by a heavy rain (400 years after his death; see *Num.* 22.4–5); and the statement concerning Demosthenes that "it was not due to poison, but to the honour and kindly favour shown him by the gods, that he was rescued from the cruelty of the Macedonians by a speedy and painless death" (*Dem.* 30.4).

The *Topos* of Divine Testimony in Luke/Acts

Divine testimony demonstrating lack of favor concerning Caesar's murder is provided by a human act (Cassius's suicide)[6] and three occurrences of testimony from the gods. Two of these testimonies occur in the heavens, namely the comet which appeared for seven nights, and the darkening of the sun for an entire year.[7] It is not necessary for the reader to interpret these signs; the narrator states that the testimonies, especially the specter that appeared to Brutus, were of "divine ordering [τῶν θείων]" and provided to show the displeasure of the gods (οὐ γενομένην θεοῖς ἀρεστήν). Therefore, the reader explicitly understands that the gods disapprove of those who murdered Julius Caesar; conversely, the signs are simultaneously an implicit affirmation of Caesar. Thus the gods' testimonies in this case serve to divinely sanction Caesar, while his murderers are condemned.[8]

A second example of the gods testifying through an eclipse is Plutarch's account of the death of Pelopidas.[9] In this example, the eclipse serves as a portent of Pelopidas's death. The context is one in which Alexander of Pherae is looting and pillaging Thessalian cities. The Thessalians, therefore, call on Thebes to send an army led by Pelopidas. As Pelopidas sets out with his troops, Plutarch states that "the sun was eclipsed and the city was covered in darkness in the day-time" (*Pel.* 31.2). This is interpreted to be a bad omen; the soothsayers even attempt to prevent Pelopidas from going out with the army.[10] The audience learns, however, that Pelopidas's anger against the actions of Alexander was so great that he was compelled to go out and oppose him.[11] Pelopidas indeed is killed in the ensuing action, but Alexander is routed (*Pel.* 32.7).

---

6. But even this human act is related in a way such that the auditor might be persuaded that more than just a simple coincidence is at work. Plutarch points out that Cassius's suicide was carried out with the same weapon with which he murdered Caesar; his editorial comment is that this event was "θαυμασιώτατον" (*Caes.* 69.3), a standard reaction to the miracles of Jesus (cf., e.g., Luke 8:25; 9:43 [here the amazement is directed toward God after Jesus exorcises a demon]; 11:14; 24:12).

7. Plutarch notes that the lack of sunlight and warmth adversely affected the fruit crop during this year (*Caes.* 69.5).

8. Suetonius also references the comet at Caesar's death, but nothing further. He writes: "For at the first of the games which [Caesar's] heir Augustus gave in honour of his apotheosis, a comet shone for seven successive days, rising about the eleventh hour, and was believed to be the soul of Caesar, who had been taken to heaven" (*Jul.* 88).

9. A similar narrative is found in Diodorus Siculus, *Hist.* 15.80.1–6.

10. Pelopidas "set out, although the seers forbade it, and the rest of the citizens disapproved; for the eclipse was thought to be a great sign from heaven, and to regard a conspicuous man" (*Pel.* 31.3).

11. Pelopidas, however, takes only three hundred cavalry with him; originally,

Divine Testimony through Deeds in Hellenistic Narratives

Plutarch follows the account of Pelopidas's death with an extensive encomium (*Pel.* 33–34), and even states, "The death of Pelopidas brought great grief to his allies, but even greater gain" (*Pel.* 35.1), due to the continued pursuit and eventual defeat of Alexander. The function of the divine testimony, therefore, must be evaluated in this context. Pelopidas is given a clear sign from the gods that he would lose his life in the engagement with Alexander. His self-sacrificing character is therefore emphasized when he, despite the direct warning of the eclipse, goes out with a volunteer army of three hundred soldiers and engages Alexander, who is ultimately defeated.[12] This demonstration of character through testimony in conjunction with action is then reinforced through the encomium that follows.

In the Annals of Tacitus, Nero is negatively characterized through this particular *topos* of divine testimony. In his *Annales*, Tacitus writes that during Nero's reign, "a comet blazed into view—in the opinion of the crowd, an apparition boding change to monarchies" (*Ann.* 22).[13] Later, lightning strikes at a banquet while Nero is eating in the town of one of his rival's (Plautus) ancestors. This is interpreted to mean that Plautus would ascend to the throne. Nero subsequently dispatches Plautus to Asia, after which Tacitus states,

> Nero's passion for extravagance brought him some disrepute and danger: he had entered and swum in the sources of the stream which Quintus Marcius conveyed to Rome; and it was considered that by bathing there he had profaned the sacred waters and the holiness of the site. The divine anger was confirmed by a grave illness which followed. (*Ann.* 32)

---

seven thousand soldiers had been assigned to him. The narrator informs that Pelopidas "did not think it meet to use compulsion with men who were apprehensive and fearful, nor to run extreme hazard with seven thousand citizens, but devoting himself alone to the Thessalians, and taking with him three hundred of the cavalry who were foreigners and who volunteered for the service, set out" (*Pel.* 31.3).

At this point it is interesting to compare Plutarch's account with that of Diodorus. Here, Diodorus states, "Although in this interpretation [the soothsayers] were foretelling the death of Pelopidas, he not withstanding set out for the campaign, *drawn on by Fate* [ὑπὸ τοῦ χρεὼν ἀγόμενος]" (*Hist.* 15.80.3; my emphasis). Thus, in Diodorus's account, the human element of Pelopidas is somewhat muted, while in Plutarch, Pelopidas's character is heightened through his decision to continue on to the battle despite the warning from the gods.

12. This is reminiscent of Paul in Acts 21; there, Paul receives warnings through inspired characters that he was heading into imminent danger if he continued his journey to Jerusalem.

13. It is interesting that Tacitus attempts to distance himself from the omen by noting that the comet is a portent "in the opinion of the crowd."

Here, the original portent of a comet, allegedly signaling the gods' displeasure with Nero's reign, is confirmed through various means. A second portent in the form of a lightning strike occurs, after which Nero reveals his character by sending his rival into exile. A further demonstration of his character follows when Nero profanes waters considered sacred; he is then afflicted with an illness, which is explicitly attributed to the gods' anger. Thus the original testimony of a comet, which is to some degree ambivalent,[14] is subsequently explained by further instances of the gods' testimony.

In Josephus's account of the fall of Jerusalem portents are seen in the sky.[15] Josephus characterizes those people remaining in the temple as "deluded by charlatans and pretended messengers of the deity," who were encouraging the people to remain in the temple precincts and await God's help there (B.J. 6.288). These people, however, "disregarded the plain warnings of God" (B.J. 6.288). Josephus then continues by describing seven different portents, the first three of which are situated in (or originate from) the heavens:

> So it was when a star, resembling a sword, stood over the city, and a comet, which continued for a year. So again when, before the revolt and the commotion that led to war, at the time when the people were assembling for the feast of unleavened bread . . . at the ninth hour of the night, so brilliant a light shone round the altar and the sanctuary that it seemed to be broad daylight; and this continued for half an hour. (B.J. 6.288).

After telling of two further portents,[16] Josephus lists a sixth, which also appears in the heavens:

> For before sunset throughout all parts of the country chariots were seen in the air and armed battalions hurtling through the clouds and encompassing the cities. (B.J. 6.298-99)[17]

---

14. In its narrative context, the comet is only said to mean that change in rulers was prophesied. The reason for the change is not given.

15. This passage was analyzed in chapter three; specifically, there I discussed a divine voice that emanated from the temple.

16. A cow meant for sacrifice gave birth to a lamb within the temple walls, and a huge gate moves on its own (B.J. 6.292-96).

17. This is similar to a passage in 2 Macc; when Antiochus leads his army into Egypt, the narrator states: "And it happened that, for almost forty days, there appeared over all the city golden-clad cavalry charging through the air, in companies fully armed with lances and drawn swords—troops of cavalry drawn up, attacks and counterattacks made on this side and on that, brandishing of shields, massing of spears, hurling

Divine Testimony through Deeds in Hellenistic Narratives

Finally, as seen in chapter three, the seventh portent consists of a voice which announces, "We are departing hence" (*B.J.* 6.299–300).[18]

Josephus explicitly states that these particular portents were warnings from God. Therefore the portents serve as God's testimony through prophecy to the people in the temple precinct that they should escape before the destruction of the temple. The people, however, do not listen, being "deluded" by those unable to understand the plain meaning of the portents.

In sum, ancient literature provides several examples of the *topos* of divine testimony through deeds which involve objects and events in the heavens. Comets, eclipses, and apparitions in the sky belong in this category. It has been shown that these instances of the gods' testimony function in their respective narratives in various ways, including as demonstrations of the gods' disfavor with an event that has already taken place, or as warnings that concern current or future events. The testimony in question is sometimes interpreted by further deeds of the gods (see the example from Tacitus) or a speech by a character in the narrative (Nicolaüs in Diodorus's *Hist.*). But in each case, this testimony functions in its narrative context to shape the auditors' perceptions of a character or group.

Divine Testimony through Birds

Often one finds that the gods testify through birds.[19] This can involve the direction of flight of a particular bird, the singing of birds, or simply the appearance of birds at a significant moment. These significant moments are often at the death of a character, but can also occur at the birth of the character or at the beginning of a noteworthy period in a person's life. As before, in each case below, the example of the gods' testimony will be described and examined for its rhetorical function within the narrative context.

The gods often testify through birds at significant moments in the narrative; an example this is found in Livy's *Historiae*. The immediate context in which the *topos* is found is that of a battle between the Romans and

---

of missiles, the flash of golden trappings, and armor of all kinds. Therefore everyone prayed that the apparition might prove to have been a good omen" (2 Macc 5:2–4).

18. For a similar list of portents in the same historical context, see Tacitus, *Hist.* 5.13.

19. For portents including birds in the works of Livy, Tacitus, and Suetonius, see F. Kraus, "Omens, Portents, and Prodigies," 96–107.

the Gauls. A large soldier from the Gallic army challenges the Romans to one-on-one combat. Marcus Valerius takes up the challenge. Here, Livy elaborates:

> But the human interest of the combat was eclipsed by the intervention of the gods; for the Roman was in the very act of engaging, when suddenly a raven alighted on his helmet, facing his adversary. This the tribune [Marcus Valerius] first received with joy, as a heaven-sent augury, and then prayed that whosoever, be it god or goddess, had sent the auspicious bird might attend him with favor and protection. Marvelous to relate, the bird not only held to the place it had once chosen, but as often as the combatants closed, it rose on its wings and attacked the enemy's face and eyes with beak and talons, till he was terror-struck with the sight of such a portent, and bewildered at once in his vision and his mind, was dispatched by Valerius,—whereupon the raven flew off towards the east and was lost to sight. (*Hist.* 7.26.3–5)

That the raven is from the gods is explicitly stated.[20] Livy also notes here that when the bird alights on the soldier's helmet, the soldier reacts by praying for the god's (or goddess's) protection on the battlefield, thus confirming the heaven-sent testimony.

Once the Gaul is overcome, the rest of the Roman army is inspired by Marcus Valerius's victory, and the Gallic army is routed; Livy states: "Both gods and men helped in that battle, and they fought it out with the Gauls to a conclusion that was never doubted, so clearly had each side foreseen the result implicit in the outcome of the single combat" (*Hist.* 7.26.8). The raven clearly represents the gods' prophetic testimony that the Roman would overcome his Gallic opponent. In the greater context, however, the testimony serves as an affirmation of the Romans over and against the Gauls.

A second example of this *topos* comes from Plutarch's *Life* of Numa, as seen in the following passage:

> But when the insignia of royalty were brought to [Numa], he bade the people pause, and said his authority must first be ratified by Heaven. Then taking him the augers and priests, he

---

20. Levene, *Religion in Livy*, 216–17, compares this passage to other ancient accounts of the same event; he concludes that no other ancient writer emphasizes the divine aspect of this incident as does Livy. See also MacDonald, "Style of Livy," 159, who comments on this account that "[t]he combat loses its vivid details so that the reader may feel the force of divine intervention." MacDonald goes on to argue that Livy has adapted the "archaic robustness" of his source to suit the style preferred in his day.

ascended the Capitol, which the Romans of that time called the Tarpeian Hill. There the chief of the augurs turned the veiled head of Numa towards the south, while he himself, standing behind him, and laying the right hand on his head, prayed aloud, and turned his eyes in all directions to observe whatever birds or other omens might be sent from the gods. Then an incredible silence fell upon the vast multitude in the forum, who watched in eager suspense for the issue, until at last auspicious birds appeared and approached the scene on the right. Then Numa put on his royal robes and went down from the citadel to the multitude, where he was received with glad cries of welcome as the most pious of men and most beloved of the gods. (Plutarch, *Num.* 7.2–3)

It is important to understand the greater context in which this passage is found. The people of Rome previously entreated Numa to assume the throne, because "there was none other on whom both parties could unite" (*Num.* 6.1). The people persisted and their case was bolstered by "auspicious omens," which Plutarch does not describe. Eventually, Numa acquiesces, "and after sacrificing to the gods, set out for Rome" (*Num.* 7.1). Already, one sees Numa's piety in that he does not fail to offer sacrifices to the gods before assuming power. On his way to Rome, the people, including the Roman senate, rejoice at his arrival, "filled with a wondrous love of the man" (*Num.* 7.1). Thus, Plutarch records the testimony of others, including that of Roman statesmen, which serves to enhance the reader's view of Numa's character.[21]

But Numa is still not convinced. In the passage reproduced above, Plutarch informs his readers that Numa will not be satisfied until the gods themselves place their stamp of approval on his new position of authority through "birds or other omens" which "might be sent from the gods." The scene is crafted to promote the drama of the moment; an "incredible silence [σιγὴ δὲ ἄπιστος] fell upon the vast multitude" assembled in the forum, and those present "watched in eager suspense [κατεῖχε καραδοκούντων]" for what would happen next. The gods do, "at last," send an omen through an auspicious flight of birds. Numa is then celebrated as "most pious of men" and "most beloved of the gods." Thus, through the adoration of the people, especially the Roman politicians, and the flight of birds, Plutarch establishes Numa as the people's and, more significantly, the gods' choice to be ruler over Rome.

21. As previously mentioned in chapter two, in his discussion of appropriate *topoi* for arguing a thesis, Theon includes "the evidence of famous men, poets and statesmen and philosophers." See Theon, *Progymnasmata* 122 (Kennedy 57).

The *Topos* of Divine Testimony in Luke/Acts

In his *Life* of Augustus, Suetonius lists several portents that surrounded the birth and early childhood of Augustus; this list is found fairly late in the narrative. Suetonius writes:

> Having reached this point, it will not be out of place to add an account of the omens which occurred before he was born, on the very day of his birth, and afterwards, from which it was possible to anticipate and perceive his future greatness and uninterrupted good fortune. (*Aug.* 2.94.1)

Augustus's birth and early childhood is therefore characterized as momentous through the various testimonies of the gods. The assorted ways the gods testify before Augustus's birth include: lightning (fire from heaven) striking the city wall of Velitrae, the city of Augustus's family;[22] an undescribed portent is seen in Rome, "which gave warning that nature was pregnant with a king for the Roman people" (*Aug.* 2.94.3); a snake comes to Atia, Augustus's mother, while asleep in the temple of Apollo; when she awakes a snake-like image is on her body which will not wash off. Suetonius states, "In the tenth month after that Augustus was born and was therefore regarded as the son of Apollo" (*Aug.* 2.94.4).[23] Other auspicious events occur on the day of Augustus's birth, including "a pillar of flame" that "sprang forth from the wine that was poured over the altar," so high "that it rose above the temple roof and mounted to the very sky" (*Aug.* 2.94.5),[24] and a dream that Octavius has in which his son appears to him as a god-like figure.[25]

When Augustus was a young boy and had just learned to talk, Suetonius tells his readers that he told croaking frogs to be quiet at his grandfather's country home, and they obeyed him (*Aug.* 2.94.7). A second incident from Augustus's childhood includes an omen involving an eagle. Suetonius writes:

---

22. *Aug.* 2.94.2; Suetonius adds: "[B]ut at last long afterward the event proved that the omen had foretold the rule of Augustus."

23. Following this event Atia also dreams "that her vitals were borne up to the stars and spread over the whole extent of land and sea, while Octavius dreamed that the sun rose from Atia's womb" (*Aug.* 2.94.4). This "double-dream" is a pattern that will be discussed in the section below concerning divine testimony through dreams.

24. This flame is seen when Octavius's priests consult the gods concerning the birth of Octavius's son.

25. This passage is cited by Talbert as a typical example of the description of prodigies and omens that were associated with the subject of ancient biographies. See Talbert, "Prophecies," 133.

> As [Augustus] was breakfasting in a grove at the fourth milestone on the Campanian road, an eagle surprised him by snatching his bread from his hand, and after flying to a great height, equally to his surprise dropped gently down again and gave it back to him. (*Aug.* 2.94.7)[26]

No divine agency is directly assigned to the bird. The context, however, demands that one understand the bird as being the gods' testimony to the future greatness of Augustus. Because this portent is found in such a long list (which is introduced by the narrator as a list of omens which speak to the future greatness of Augustus) of omens,[27] some of which take place in sacred spaces or during religious rites, it is clear that the eagle also is the gods' testimony to the future greatness of Augustus. Thus, the divine testimony functions as prophecy, and as the gods' stamp of approval on the future ruler.

A further example of a bird serving as the testimony of the gods also comes from Suetonius, this time from his *Life* of Claudius. The occasion is the beginning of Claudius's term of service as consul:

> It was only under his nephew Gaius, who in the early part of his reign tried to gain popularity by every device, that [Claudius] at last began his official career, holding the consulship as his colleague for two months; and it chanced that as he entered the Forum for the first time with the fasces,[28] an eagle that was flying by lit upon his shoulder. (*Claud.* 5.7.1)

What is lacking here is any mention of the cultic events with which instances of divine testimony are so often associated. However, earlier in

---

26. A similar story is told by Dionysius of Halicarnassus about Lucumo, the son of Damaratus, who goes to Rome and stands on the hill of Janiculum. When he does, an eagle swoops down and grabs his cap from his head, but then very politely replaces it. This is considered a portent of royalty as well as a "prediction of the gods" (Dionysius of Halicarnassus, *Ant. rom.* 3.47.1–48.1). See also another account from Dionysius (*Ant. rom.* 4.63.1–2), in which the fall of Tarquinius is portended through two eagles which build a nest and hatch young. Vultures come and kill the hatchlings, driving the eagles away, an omen of the imminent ousting of Tarquinius. Cf. Livy, *Hist.* 1.56.4 for a similar account.

27. Other omens are explained after this one, including more dreams, young Augustus's toga being ripped, and a tree that miraculously grows out of another palm tree which Julius Caesar would not allow his troops to cut while making camp (*Aug.* 2.94.10–11).

28. The fasces were a symbol and implement of Roman power, and included a bundle of wooden rods surrounding an axe. Cf. Livy, *Hist.* 3.36.3–6. For the origins and significance of the fasces, see A. Marshall, "The Fasces," 120–41.

the story of Claudius, in explaining the details of his birth, Suetonius mentions that Claudius was born "the very day when an altar was first dedicated to Augustus in that town" (*Claud.* 5.2.1). Therefore, the auditor has a somewhat subtle hint that the gods look favorably on Claudius. Thus, in this case, when the eagle perches on Claudius's shoulder, the auditor is not surprised at this testimony of the gods.[29]

The eagle serves to bolster Suetonius's encomium[30] of Claudius, which begins in the passage preceding this one and continues afterwards.[31] In the encomium, Suetonius gives several examples of the greatness of Claudius, including examples from the political sphere[32] and his personal life.[33]

Simultaneously, Claudius is being positively compared to Gaius, who "tried to gain popularity by every device." Claudius is described as being lauded by the people without trying: "[S]everal times [Claudius] presided at the shows in place of Gaius, and was greeted by the people now with 'Success to the emperor's uncle!' and now with 'All hail to the brother of Germanicus!'" (*Claud.* 5.7.2). Thus, the *topos* of divine testimony through birds in this instance assists in portraying Claudius in a positive light, and as a foil to Gaius.

In several cases birds make appearances at the death of a character. An example of this is found in Plutarch's *Life* of Cato the Younger. In this example, the *topos* of divine testimony helps one understand a deeper meaning to a comment that could be understood as a simple statement of time.

---

29. Also, one must think back to the account previously discussed of the eagle which snatched Augustus's breakfast away and then returned it. There, although not directly noted by the narrator, the auditor would have to understand that the eagle was a testimony from the gods. Birds which do marvelous, out-of-character things would certainly have been perceived as acting on the desires of the gods.

30. In this case I am not implying that Suetonius has written a formal encomium of Claudius. Rather, the passage in which the *topos* of divine testimony appears is a consistent praise of Claudius.

31. The material directly following the incident with the eagle demonstrates the obstacles Claudius had to overcome. For example, he was mocked by his peers at formal dinners (*Claud.* 5.8), but faced even more significant struggles in his political and family life (*Claud.* 5.9).

32. Claudius was twice selected by the equestrians as patron; he was elected by the senate to be a priest of Augustus; when his house was destroyed in a fire the senate voted to have it rebuilt from public funds (Suetonius, *Claud.* 5.6.1–2).

33. Suetonius notes that Claudius was an heir to Tiberius, inheriting a third of his estate (*Claud.* 5.6.2).

> And now the birds were already beginning to sing,[34] when he fell asleep again for a little while. And when Butas came and told him that the harbours were very quiet, he ordered him to close the door, throwing himself down upon his couch as if he were going to rest there for what remained of the night. But when Butas had gone out, Cato drew his sword from its sheath and stabbed himself below the breast. (*Cat. Min.*, 70.4–5)

In this passage, Plutarch sympathetically narrates the suicide of Cato.[35] Cato has admitted his defeat at the hands of Caesar and has overseen the sending off of his forces. He has nothing left to contribute to Rome; therefore, he decides to end his life. But Cato waits until the troops are safely away before he takes his life. Due to an injured hand (ironically, Cato hurt his hand striking his servant), he struggles to commit the act; in the end, however, he overcomes this obstacle and takes his life, even pushing aside the physician who attempted to prevent him from killing himself.

Thus Cato's suicide is described as a noble act. Plutarch desires for his readers to view Cato in a positive light; he was a noble statesman for Rome who was in control of his life until the end. The singing of the birds before his suicide, rather than simply being a temporal marker showing that the night was almost over, also provides a testimony of the gods' legitimation for his choice of death.[36]

A second example of divine testimony through birds at the time of a character's death is in Suetonius's *Life* of Julius Caesar. In this *Life*, Suetonius describes a scene which preceded Caesar's murder. Suetonius begins the section with the statement: "Now Caesar's approaching murder was foretold to him by unmistakable signs [*evidentibus prodigiis*]" (*Jul.* 81.1).

34. "Ἤδη δὲ ὄρνιθες ᾖδον." This could be translated as a statement that the birds began to sing at this moment (considering ᾖδον to be an ingressive imperfect; see Wallace, *Greek Grammar*, 544), or that they were already singing, giving it more of a temporal force, describing when the action took place (i.e., in the morning).

35. Concerning the various attitudes of the Greco-Roman philosophical schools regarding suicide, see Droge and Tabor, *Noble Death*, 17–51.

36. Tacitus relates a passage concerning the suicide of Otho which also involves a bird. He writes, "While I must hold it inconsistent with the dignity of the work I have undertaken to collect fabulous tales and to delight my readers with fictitious stories, I cannot, however, dare to deny the truth of common tradition. On the day of the battle at Bedriacum, according to the account given by the people of that district, a bird of unusual appearance settled in a much-frequented grove near Regium Lepidum, and neither the concourse of people nor the other birds which flew about it frightened it or drove it away, until Otho had committed suicide; then it disappeared from view. And they add that when people reckoned up the time, they found that the beginning and end of this marvel coincided with Otho's death" (*Hist.* 2.50).

Suetonius then provides a list of various events that are interpreted to be portents of Caesar's murder. Within this list one reads:

> Again, when he was offering sacrifice, the soothsayer Spurinna warned him to beware of danger, which would come not later than the Ides of March; and on the day before the Ides of that month a little bird called the king-bird flew into the Hall of Pompey with a sprig of laurel, pursued by others of various kinds from the grove hard by, which tore it to pieces in the hall. (*Jul.* 81.3)

It is significant that this portent is found in the context of religious expression; the event concerning the bird directly follows the description of Spurinna offering a sacrifice. This is a clue to the auditor that what occurs is indeed from the gods. Also significant is the type of bird which is killed—the "king-bird" (*avem regaliolum*)—and that it carried a sprig of laurel in its mouth—the royal crown of the emperor. Thus it is clear that Caesar is the subject of the gods' testimony through the birds.[37]

In the ensuing narrative, Suetonius states that Caesar "entered the House in defiance of portents, laughing at Spurinna and calling him a false prophet, because the Ides of March were come without bringing him harm" (*Jul.* 81.4). Thus one has the impression that Caesar is not aligned with the will of the gods' and is therefore being negatively characterized by the prophetic divine testimony. Later, however, Suetonius makes an evaluation of Caesar's death, weighing various opinions that surrounded it (*Jul.* 86–87). In the end, he argues (with the majority) that Caesar had no desire for a "lingering kind of end" and rather wanted to die a sudden death. Therefore, ultimately, Caesar's desires are demonstrated to be in line with the testimony provided by the gods through the birds.[38]

A third and final example of divine testimony through the flight of birds associated with a character's death is found in the *Martyrdom of Polycarp*. The setting of the divine testimony is Polycarp's final moments;

---

37. This is reinforced by a further instance of divine testimony; both Caesar and Calpurnia have dreams that night which allude to Caesar's impending demise (*Jul.* 81.3).

38. A bird plays a prominent role in Suetonius's account of the death of Augustus as well. Augustus's death, much like Caesar's, is preceded by many portents. One of these Suetonius describes thusly: "As he was bringing the lustrum to an end in the Campus Martius before a great throng of people, an eagle flew several times about him and then going across to the temple hard by, perched above the first letter of Agrippa's name" (*Aug.* 2.92.1). Note that here, as was seen in the case of Caesar, the eagle appears within a context of a sacrifice of propitiation (cf. Rolfe's note at this point in his translation).

Divine Testimony through Deeds in Hellenistic Narratives

he has been tied to a pole and the pyre prepared (*Mart. Pol.* 13). As his executioners finish binding Polycarp, he prays (*Mart. Pol.* 14).[39] After his prayer, the fire is lit, but, extraordinarily, it fails to burn his body. Indeed, rather than the flames consuming Polycarp's body, there is an aroma of perfume which emanates from him (*Mart. Pol.* 15).[40] Because the flames do not burn him, one of the soldiers stabs him with a knife. When he does so, two more remarkable events occur: a dove flies out from his body (*Mart. Pol.* 16.1),[41] and so much blood flows from the wound that it quenches the fire.

The flight of the dove is therefore described in conjunction with many other supernatural events in the immediate context of its narration.[42] An ancient auditor would have readily understood the flight of the dove to be a divine testimony of Polycarp's innocence and the divine approval of his life.[43] This idea is seen in the narrator's comments which follow the description of these events:

---

39. Here, again, one finds the divine testimony occurring in a context of prayer and worship.

40. The text specifically states that Polycarp's body was in the midst of the flames and was like "baking bread or like gold and silver being refined in a furnace" (*Mart. Pol.* 15.2).

41. There is a great deal of scholarly controversy concerning the words περιστερὰ καὶ in the clause ἐξῆλθεν περιστερὰ καὶ πλῆθος αἵματος (*Mart. Pol.* 16.1). The crux of the issue is that these two words are not recorded by Eusebius, and are therefore considered to be later additions by most scholars; see, e.g., Schoedel (*Polycarp*, 72), who argues, "There is almost universal agreement that this was added later (probably by ps-Pionius)." See also Conzelmann, *Bemerkungen*, for whom the fact that these two words are not found in Eusebius is decisive. See also, however, Buschmann, *Martyrium des Polykarp*, 312–15, who reviews the evidence for both exclusion and inclusion of these two words. Buschmann argues for inclusion because: all the Greek manuscripts of this document do include the phrase (with the exception of Eusebius, of course); and, as he argues, the dove early in the history of Christianity was a symbol of the Holy Spirit, and would therefore have been appropriate in the context of Polycarp's martyrdom. Finally, in Ehrman's LCL Greek text and translation, he includes the words as original.

42. There are several examples of divine testimony throughout *Mart. Pol.*, one of which is a divine voice which encourages Polycarp as he faces his accusers (*Mart. Pol.* 9; on this, see the chapter on divine testimony through utterances in extra-biblical narratives and biographies). Also, Polycarp has a vision (on visions as divine testimony, see below) of his pillow being burned, and interprets this as God's will for him to be burned (δεῖ με ζῶντα καυθῆναι; *Mart. Pol.* 5.2; 12.3). As I have shown, and as is the case here, divine testimony often occurs in "clusters."

43. The flight of the dove also invokes images of the dove at Jesus' baptism (see, e.g., Luke 3:21–22 and comments below), thus being an example of the *imitatio Christi* so prevalent in this document. But an ancient auditor, who was unfamiliar with this

> [A] dove came forth, along with such a quantity of blood that it extinguished the fire, striking the entire crowd with amazement that there could be so much difference between the unbelievers and the elect. One of the latter was this most astounding Polycarp... For every word that came forth from his mouth was fulfilled and will be fulfilled. (*Mart. Pol.* 16.1–2)

The dove then serves to portray Polycarp's death as a "good death," the death of an innocent martyr. This is in keeping with the portrayal of Polycarp throughout the narrative.

As can be seen through these examples, birds often appear as the testimony of the gods at momentous occasions in the lives of those being described. These occasions are frequently the birth and/or death of the protagonist. In the accounts of a person's death, the testimony of the gods through birds normally signals the gods' approval of the character, which is supported by other contextual clues in the narrative. When a bird appears in the account of a birth, it generally signals the gods' prophecy of a great career for the one being born. Thus, as in the appearance of a bird at a character's death the testimony acts as the gods' sanction of that particular character. This is also the case when birds appear at significant moments in the narrative. What is also noteworthy is that birds often appear in conjunction with some type of religious observance, be it a sacrifice or prayer. Finally, birds can and often do appear as the gods' testimony along with other forms of the *topos* of divine testimony.

Divine Testimony through Sounds and Fire (from Heaven)

In this category I will consider examples of the *topos* of divine testimony through sounds,[44] including storms, and fire.[45] Fire can be sent from the heavens in the form of lightning, as discussed in chapter two. But as will be demonstrated, other forms of fire also serve as the gods' testimony.[46]

---

tradition, would nonetheless have understood the dove emerging from Polycarp's body to be a testimony of the deity.

44. Voices could also be considered here; voices, however, are most often a deity speaking to a character, and were considered under direct speech of the gods in chapter three.

45. For storms (including thunder and lightning) as omens in the works of Livy, Tacitus, and Suetonius, see F. Kraus, "Omens, Portents, and Prodigies," 35–49.

46. E.g., the flame that shot from the altar during Octavius's sacrifice, as seen in

Divine Testimony through Deeds in Hellenistic Narratives

Storms are included as they are often given divine origin and contain the rumblings of thunder. These forms of the *topos* can serve as approval (or disapproval) of a person or that person's mission, as a warning, or as punishment, especially in the case of lightning and storms.

An example of fire from the heavens comes from Plutarch's *Life* of Timoleon. In the narrative, Timoleon was readying his forces to sail to Sicily; before they sail, however, "the priestesses of Persephone fancied they saw in their dreams that goddess and her mother making ready for a journey, and heard them say that they were going to sail with Timoleon to Sicily" (*Tim.* 8.1). Here, as in other instances of this *topos*, one sees that within the immediate context there is an allusion to some type of religious rite or act; in this example, Plutarch mentions that the priestesses of the goddess Persephone had a dream[47] concerning Timoleon. They also specifically state that they heard the goddess say that she would accompany Timoleon on his journey to Sicily. The auditor, therefore, has explicit clues in the narrative that the gods show approval for Timoleon and his mission.

Timoleon then traveled to Delphi and offered his own sacrifices; while in the presence of the Pythia, Timoleon received a sign:

> [A] fillet which had crowns and figures of Victory embroidered upon it slipped away and fell directly upon the head of Timoleon, so that it appeared as if he were being crowned by the god and thus sent forth upon his undertaking. (*Tim.* 8.2)[48]

Again, the context is one of religious ceremony. The narrator provides the specific information that Timoleon is being sent by the deity on his mission to Sicliy. Given this divine send-off, Timoleon then sets sail for Sicily. Once out on the ocean,

> [t]he heavens seemed to burst open on a sudden above his ship, and to pour forth an abundant and conspicuous fire. From this a torch lifted itself on high, like those which the mystics bear, and running along with them on their course, darted down upon precisely that part of Italy towards which the pilots were steering. (*Tim.* 8.3)

---

the previous section discussing divine testimony through birds.

47. Note well that, once again, there is a confluence of various forms of the *topos* of divine testimony.

48. For the opposite testimony using the laurel wreath, cf. Suetonius, *Galb.* 7.18.3; here, while Galba is offering a sacrifice, "the garland fell from his head." This is considered a portent of Galba's imminent death (see 7.18.1). See also Suetonius, *Vit.* 8.9.1; Vitellius's crown falls into a stream after beginning his march against Otho.

Timoleon's seers interpreted this as the fulfillment of the vision seen earlier by the priestesses, and "that the goddesses were taking part in the expedition and showing forth the light from heaven" (*Tim.* 8.4). Plutarch summarizes the account by stating, "Such, then, were the signs from Heaven which encouraged the expedition" (*Tim.* 9.1).[49]

It is clear that this instance of divine testimony is in support of Timoleon's actions. What is significant in this case is that a prophecy, received by the priestesses through a vision (another example of the *topos*) and substantiated by a second sign in Delphi, is ultimately fulfilled through the flame of fire from heaven which comes over the ship and eventually leads Timoleon to his intended destination. Therefore, through a combination of various methods of divine testimony, Timoleon and his mission are the objects of the gods' approval. What is also significant is the narrator's comment that Timoleon's soothsayers interpret the flame to be a fulfillment of the original prophecy received by the priestesses through their dream.[50] Often, testimony from the gods must be interpreted by human beings in order for their full testimonial value to be appreciated.

Another example of a torch-like apparition in the sky is found in Plutarch's *Life* of Caesar, specifically related to his battle against Pompey. Once again, this testimony of the gods is prefaced with a description of Caesar offering sacrifices:

> As he was holding a lustration and review of his forces and had sacrificed the first victim, the seer at once told him that within three days there would be a decisive battle with the enemy. (*Caes.* 43.3)

Significantly, when Caesar asks his soothsayer about the sacrifice, the seer replies that the sacrificial victim[51] portended that "the gods indicate a great change" (*Caes.* 43.4); therefore, it is up to Caesar to interpret the true meaning of the testimony of the gods. This statement emphasizes the importance of human interpretation of the gods' testimony, but it also serves

---

49. This same incident is found in Diodorus of Siculus, *Hist.* 16.66.3–5. Diodorus's account includes the flame over Timoleon's ship, as well as the priestesses' dream of Persephone (and Demeter) and their willingness to accompany Timoleon. Timoleon's sacrifice in Delphi, however, is not mentioned. Diodorus states that the torch was a sign that "Heaven came to the support of [Timoleon's] venture and foretold his coming fame and the glory of his achievements" (*Hist.* 16.66.3–5).

50. "The soothsayers declared that the apparition bore witness to the dreams of the priestesses [τοῖς ὀνείρασι τῶν ἱερειῶν μαρτυρεῖν]" (*Tim.* 8.4).

51. This is a reference to the *topos* of divine testimony through the entrails of sacrificial animals, a topic which I will address below.

Divine Testimony through Deeds in Hellenistic Narratives

to heighten the drama of the account. The auditor, however, is not left ignorant of the gods' intentions; the narrator then tells of a second, more explicit divine testimony:

> Moreover, on the night before the battle, as Caesar was making the round of his sentries about midnight, a fiery torch was seen in the heavens, which seemed to be carried over his camp, blazing out brightly, and then to fall into Pompey's. And during the morning watch it was noticed that there was actually a panic confusion among the enemy. (*Caes.* 43.5–6)

Caesar indeed achieves victory over Pompey when he does attack. Plutarch adds, "There were many portents of the victory" (*Caes.* 47.1), which included a tree that grew up out the floor at the base of a statue of Caesar in the temple of Victory in Thralles (*Caes.* 47.1–2).[52]

What follows the account of Pompey's defeat is an extended encomium of Caesar, in which he is lauded for: setting the Thessalians and Cnidians free; providing a tax rebate to the citizens of Asia; crying when he receives Pompey's royal ring; and treating prisoners in a humane fashion (*Caes.* 48.1–3). Finally, Plutarch's concluding statement in this section reads:

> And to [Caesar's] friends in Rome he wrote that this was the greatest and sweetest pleasure that he derived from his victory, namely, from time to time to save the lives of fellow citizens who had fought against him. (*Caes.* 48.4)

The *topos* of divine testimony would therefore have been heard by the ancient audience to be a part of this encomium of Caesar. The sign certainly prophesies his victory, as it is received prior to the battle. In the greater context, however, the sign serves as an element of the author's praise of Caesar.

In the next two examples, flames appear from the heads of characters in the narrative. While these flames do not necessarily have their origins in the heavens, through the context in which they are presented it is clear that they represent the testimony of the gods. The first involves the circumstances surrounding the birth of Tullius, the son-in-law of King

---

52. For another account of this tree, see Caesar, *Bell. civ.* 3.105; cf. also Plutarch's *Life* of Pompey (*Pomp.* 68.1–3). In this account, the night before the divine testimony is seen, Pompey has an ambiguous dream because of which "[o]n some accounts he was encouraged, but on others depressed" (*Pomp.* 68.2). As the sacrifice which Caesar performed before the torch appears, Pompey's dream requires human interpretation in order to determine how the gods are testifying.

Tarquinius. Tullius would eventually become king after the death of Tarquinius. The account here is that found in Dionysius of Halicarnassus.[53]

Dionysius begins by narrating the circumstances which surrounded the conception of Tullius, which he admits "raises the circumstances attending it to the realm of the fabulous";[54] he also states, however, that "we have found it in many Roman histories" (*Ant. rom.* 4.2.1). In this account, a phallus appears in the hearth of the palace, "on which," Dionysius tells his readers, "the Romans offer various other sacrifices and also consecrate the first portions of their meals" (*Ant. rom.* 4.2.1). Tarquinius also sees the prodigy, and then consults his soothsayers. Tanaquil, who is described as "not only wise in other matters but also inferior to none of the Tyrrhenians in her knowledge of divination" (*Ant. rom.* 4.2.2), tells the king that whoever would have sexual relations with the apparition would bear "a scion superior to the race of mortals" (*Ant. rom.* 4.2.2). Tarquinius confirms this interpretation, and decides that Ocrisia, the woman who originally saw the apparition while offering a sacrifice, should be the mother of this child. Through this course of events, the child Tullius is conceived and born.

The next scene in the narrative is prefaced by Dionysius thusly:

> This fabulous account, although it seems not altogether credible, is rendered less incredible by reason of another manifestation of

---

53. Levene lists the following documents in which accounts of this event are found: Cicero, *Div.* 1.121; Ovid, *Fast.* 6.631–36; Florus 1.1.6.1; Plutarch, *Fort. Rom.* 10; *De Vir. Ill.* 7; Servius, *ad Aen.* 2.683; Zonaras 7.9. It is also included by Livy, *Hist.* 1.39.1–4. Levene notes the emphasis that Livy, in his account, places on the role that Tanaquil plays in the interpretation of the apparition; she also prophesies that Servius will aid Tarquin in the future. See Levene, *Religion in Livy*, 142–43.

54. See Kajanto (*God and Fate*, 33), who comments on Livy's version of this account. According to Kajanto, because Livy gives a second, more fabulous version of the story, it demonstrates that "the story of the miracle is told by Livy only because it is a familiar legend." What is significant for this study, however, is that the author includes it in the narrative, regardless of the author's opinion of its validity. See also the comments of J. Linderski, "Roman Religion," 54: "Equally wide off the mark is the opinion of Kajanto (p. 101) to whom it is 'obvious' that according to Livy 'the course of events was mainly determined by human beings and not by gods and fate.' This is a very un-Roman opinion for in Rome *dei hominesque* formed an inseparable whole. The solid rock of Livy's presentation of Roman *religio* is the priestly tradition as transmitted or invented by the annalists and antiquarians, and still largely observed in the cult of the gods in Livy's own time." See also Lown, "Miraculous," 41, who recognizes that when Livy is relating certain supernatural occurrences, he often distances himself from the account through the use of introductory phrases, such as "it is said." Lown, however, affirms what I am arguing here: "At the same time, [Livy] *does* repeat the prodigies conscientiously, thereby, it seems, accepting the *possibility* of them as expressions of the divine will" (emphasis in original).

Divine Testimony through Deeds in Hellenistic Narratives

the gods relating to Tullius which was wonderful and extraordinary. (*Ant. rom.* 4.2.1)

According to Dionysius, while the previous account may seem fantastic and difficult to believe, he brings other evidence to bear in an attempt to persuade his audience of the credibility of his account.[55] And the evidence he presents is a second instance of divine testimony:

> For when [Tullius] had fallen asleep one day while sitting in the portico of the palace about noon, a fire shone forth from his head. This was seen by his mother and by the king's wife, as they were walking through the portico, as well as by all who happened to be present with them at the time. The flame continued to illumine his whole head till his mother ran to him; and with the ending of his sleep the flame was dispersed and vanished. (*Ant. rom.* 4.2.2)

Clearly, as Dionysius presents this event in support of the divine conception of Tullius, one can consider the origins of the flame to be divine. Dionysius also strengthens the evidentiary value of the event through multiple witnesses to it. Therefore, the flames which surround Tullius's head are the gods' testimony to Tullius's future greatness, and serve as evidence of such in this narrative.

A second, similar account is found in Livy in his description of the Romans' battle against the Carthaginians in Spain in the third century BCE (*Hist.* 25.39.1–16). In this narrative, the Roman commander, Lucius Marcius, leads the Romans to victory, overrunning two camps of the Carthaginians. Livy then surveys several historians in order to communicate the magnitude of the victory.[56] Livy summarizes this short section by stating, "In all of [the various historians' accounts] great is the name of Marcius the general" (*Hist.* 25.39.16), thus informing the reader of his opinion of Marcius. Following this statement, one reads:

---

55. In *Ant. rom.* 1.48.1, Dionysius enjoins his readers to determine for themselves the credibility of the account that follows. Josephus also uses this technique; see, e.g., *Ant.* 1.108: "[W]hile Hesiod, Hecataeus, Hellanicus, Acusilaus, as well as Ephorus and Nicolas, report that the ancients lived for a thousand years. But on these matters let everyone decide according to his fancy"; cf. *Ant.* 2.348; 3.81, 268, 322. The statement made here, however, is different. In the present passage, Dionysius is not content to allow his readers to make up their own minds. He seeks further evidence in an effort to persuade them.

56. Slightly different numbers of the enemy killed and captured are provided by the various historians, as well as the actual details of how the battle was fought.

> And to his real fame they add even marvels; that as he was speaking a flame burst from his head without his knowledge, causing great alarm among the soldiers who stood around him. (*Hist.* 25.39.16)

Livy goes on to say that as a memorial of this defeat of the Carthaginians, "there was in the temple a shield called the Marcian, bearing a likeness of [the Carthaginian general; cf. *Hist.* 25.37.8] Hasdrubal" (*Hist.* 25.39.17). Thus, there is an extremely distant allusion to a religious context in which the victory is celebrated; this allusion and the testimony of the gods are therefore mutually supportive.

This instance of the *topos* serves to allow the reader to understand the gods' approval of Marcius. Earlier in the narrative, when Livy introduces Marcius, he is described in glowing terms. Livy writes:

> While it seemed that the armies had been wiped out and all Spain lost, a single man repaired their shattered fortunes. In the army was Lucius Marcius . . . an active young man of much more spirit and talent to be expected in the station in which he had been born. (*Hist.* 25.37.1–2)[57]

Livy's encomium of Marcius includes his training at the hands of Gnaeus Scipio,[58] his unanimous election by the soldiers to be their commander, and finally his statement that "the soldiers carried out all his commands, not only with energy, but also in no dejected spirit" (*Hist.* 25.37.3–7). Given this high praise of Marcius, the divine testimony through fire described above only serves to increase the standing of Marcius in the auditors' eyes.[59]

Storms and tempests constitute a subset within this category of divine testimony by sounds and fire from heaven. I place storms in this category

---

57. Note that in Theon's description of the preliminary exercise of encomium he suggests the following as a possible method of praising the individual: "It is also praiseworthy if someone from a humble home becomes great . . . It is also worth admiring a workman or someone from the lower class who makes something good of himself" (Theon, *Progymnasmata* 111 [Kennedy, ed. and trans., 52]).

58. Gnaeus Scipio is described as having "made an army that was not to be despised out of soldiers gathered up from the flight and in part withdrawn from garrison towns" (*Hist.* 25.38.4).

59. Another event involving flames is narrated by Dionysius of Halicarnassus (*Ant. rom.* 5.46.2). In a scene describing the Romans in battle against the Sabines, the Romans receive encouragement through several portents from the gods. One in particular, however, gives the Romans confidence that they will prevail in the battle. Dionysius describes this omen as javelins that had flames coming from them. See also Livy, *Hist.* 22.1–13.

Divine Testimony through Deeds in Hellenistic Narratives

because in their description one normally finds lightning and thunder, as well as wind and rain. Storms are often portrayed as portents of the gods' displeasure with a character or group of people; their overall function in the narrative, however, can be somewhat more complicated.

Dionysius of Halicarnassus records the possible occurrence of a storm as punishment with which he ultimately takes issue. At the end of his account of Tullus Hostilius, Dionysius describes the king as

> worthy of exceptional praise for his boldness in war and his prudence in the face of danger, but, above both these qualifications, because, though he was not precipitate in entering upon a war, when he was once engaged in it he steadily pursued it until he had the upper hand in every way over his adversaries. (*Ant. rom.* 3.35.1)

Dionysius informs his auditors that the king eventually perished, along with his family, in a house fire. He then explores the reasons for the house fire:

> Some say that his house was set on fire by a thunderbolt, Heaven having become angered at his neglect of some sacred rites ... but the majority state that the disaster was due to human treachery. (*Ant. rom.* 3.35.2)

Here one clearly sees the ancient attitude that lightning from heaven was a form of negative divine testimony, a form of punishment. This, however, Dionysius must reject, due to his view of Hostilius as such as laudable person.

In Suetonius's *Life* of Otho, a storm is presented as a negative portent at the time that Otho rose to power. In this account, Suetonius is consistent in his condemnation of Otho. He portrays Otho as extorting the funds necessary to bankroll his plot against the emperor (*Otho* 5.2), having Galba and Piso murdered (6.3), and lying to the senate afterwards, saying that the people were the impetus for taking the throne (7.1). Suetonius states:

> It is said that he had a fearful dream that night, uttered loud groans, and was found by those who ran to his aid lying on the ground beside his couch; that he tried by every kind of expiatory rite to propitiate the shade of Galba, by whom he dreamt that he was ousted and thrown out; and that next day, as he was taking the auspices, a great storm arose and he had a bad fall. (*Otho*, 7.2)

In the context of an invective against Otho, multiple instances of divine testimony are used to cast Otho in a negative light. A dream, a storm, and even an auspicious fall are understood by the audience to be the displeasure of the gods with Otho. As has been shown before, the storm is mentioned as Otho is "taking the auspices," leaving little doubt as to its divine nature.

Another illustration[60] in which a storm is given divine origin is found in Plutarch's *Life* of Galba. In the account, Galba abruptly decides to appoint Piso as Caesar. Piso is described as "a young man in whose predisposition to every virtue the traits of gravity and decorum were most conspicuous" (*Galb.* 23.2). But just as Galba begins to move to the camp to make his announcement,

> great signs from heaven accompanied him on his way, and after he had begun to pronounce and read his address to his soldiers, there were many peals of thunder and flashes of lightning, and much darkness and rain pervaded both the camp and the city, so that it was plain that the act of adoption was inauspicious and was not favoured or approved by the heavenly powers. (*Galb.* 23.2)

One might assume that the storm is used here to demonstrate the gods' lack of enthusiasm for Galba's choice. On the surface it seems to be a negative sign from the gods, through which they reject Galba's decision by way of their testimony contained in the storm. The context, however, speaks against this interpretation of the testimony. Above I noted that Piso was described as a virtuous man, who is nearly beyond reproach. Therefore, it does not make sense that the gods would reject such a man. Instead, the storm signals that the gods were not pleased with "the *act* of adoption," as opposed to Piso himself.[61] Later in this account, the reader learns that because Galba chose to name Piso as Caesar, both men lost their lives to Otho's treachery (*Galb.* 24.1). Therefore, the disfavor which the gods express through their storm testimony is that treachery will be unleashed

---

60. Other examples include Dionysius of Halicarnassus *Ant. rom.* 3.35; Suetonius, *Claud.* 5.66 (an omen of Claudius's death occurs when the tomb of his father is struck by lightning); Suetonius, *Galb.* 1 (in the last year of Nero's reign the temple of the Caesars is hit by lightning, removing all the heads from the statues); Suetonius, *Dom.* 8.15.2 (eight months of lightning follow Domitian's decision that his sons should succeed him).

61. In Tacitus's account of this event, Otho gives a speech in which he states, "Comrades, you saw how even the gods by a wonderful storm [*notabili tempestate*] expressed their disapproval of this ill-starred adoption" (*Hist.* 1.38).

Divine Testimony through Deeds in Hellenistic Narratives

through the act of adoption, and good men will lose their lives. It is simultaneously an affirmation of the character of Piso, and a condemnation of Otho.

In Plutarch's *Life* of Alexander there is an account of a storm for which no divine origin is given. If one accepts that generally storms are the gods' testimony of their displeasure, the storm helps the reader to understand the character of Alexander. The context of the passage is Alexander's military campaign against Porus, in India. Alexander, "on a dark and stormy night," crossed the river Hydaspes with some of his infantry and his best cavalry to an island, which was near Porus's positions. Plutarch states,

> Here rain fell in torrents, and many tornadoes and thunderbolts dashed down upon his men; but nevertheless, although he saw that many of them were being burned to death by the thunder-bolts, he set out from the islet and made for the opposite banks. (*Alex.* 60.4)

Despite the terrible conditions, Alexander leads his army to a great victory over Porus. The storm plays a significant role in the narrative. The storm certainly made Alexander's campaign more difficult, thus demonstrating that he is a brave leader, willing to do battle in any conditions in order to win victory. Assuming, however, that Plutarch's auditors would have understood the storm to be a negative reaction from the gods,[62] Alexander is portrayed as battling not only a human opponent, but also the gods. Even though the gods are not assisting him, and indeed seem to be working against him, he is still capable of winning a victory.

It is appropriate to contrast this to an account from the *Life* of Julius Caesar, the hero to whom Alexander is compared in the *Lives*. Caesar, in a moment of frustration and impatience, decides to hide himself in a boat, disguised as a slave, in order to go to Brundisium to meet the enemy. As the boat moves down the river Aoüs, a storm blows in from the sea.

> [T]he river therefore chafed against the inflow of the sea, and the opposition of its billows, and was rough, being beaten back

---

62. No agency is assigned to the storm in this account. The underlying sense here is that storms often function explicitly as negative signs from the gods. In Plutarch this idea is prevalent; see the storm in the *Life* of Galba noted above. One also finds storms as the negative testimony of the gods in the *Lives* of Romulus (storms break out at his death) and Fabius (when Hannibal arrives in the vicinity of Rome, storm signs from heaven appear, along with other portents). Therefore, a storm, even if it is not explicitly stated that it was sent from the gods, would be understood by ancient auditors as a negative sign.

with a great din and violent eddies, so that it was impossible for the master of the boat to force his way along. (*Caes.* 38.4)

When the captain decides to turn the boat around, Caesar reveals himself and says, "Come, good man, be bold and fear naught; thou carryest Caesar and Caesar's fortune in thy boat" (*Caes.* 38.5–6). The oarsmen attempt to row through the storm, but they find it impossible, and Caesar must reluctantly order the captain to turn around.

Upon his return to shore, Caesar's soldiers are upset that he did not trust them enough to take them with him. Thus, the soldiers' testimony serves to cast aspersions on Caesar's character. However, the fact that Caesar is not able to overcome the storm is even more damning. The gods' testify through the storm against Caesar's decision to proceed without his soldiers. Considering Alexander's experience in the storm, Plutarch makes his point against Caesar that much more forcefully.

Another example of a storm which expresses divine displeasure is found in Philo's *De vita Mosis*, occurring in his version of the punishment of Korah, Dathan, and Abiram (Num 16). In the biblical account, Korah, Dathan, and Abiram, along with their households, disappear when the earth opens up underneath them (Num 16:31–33). Immediately after this event, two hundred fifty additional men are killed by fire which "came out from the Lord" (πῦρ ἐξῆλθεν παρὰ κυρίου; Num 16:35).[63] In Philo's retelling, the sense is the same as that found in the original narrative; the details, however, are slightly different. After Korah, Dathan, and Abiram fall into the earth, the additional men are killed by thunderbolts (κεραυνοὶ κατασκήψαντες αἰφνίδιον). The divine origins of the thunderbolts are not in question; following this statement, Philo writes: "The quick succession of these punishments and their magnitude in both cases clearly and widely established the fame of the prophet's godliness, to the truth of whose pronouncements God Himself had testified" (*Mos.* 2.284).

In this case, the description reflects the usage of the *topos* of divine testimony as seen in other examples. The two hundred fifty men are the victims of the anger of God, displayed through a storm. Philo explicitly informs his auditors that God has testified to Moses' piety. What he doesn't say, but is made clear through the narrative, is that this is certainly a testimony against those who are disobedient to God's will. In this example, as in others already discussed, the characterization through divine testimony is multi-dimensional.

---

63. This is a direct translation of the MT: *v'esh yats'ah me'et yhvah*

Divine Testimony through Deeds in Hellenistic Narratives

Josephus, in his retelling of the Israelites' crossing of the Red Sea, includes elements of divine testimony through thunder and lightning which are not found in the original account in Exod 14. Significantly, prior to the crossing, Moses prays to God, asking him for protection from the Egyptians (*Ant.* 2.334-37).[64] After praying, Moses strikes the water with his staff, and the Israelites begin crossing the sea. The Egyptians pursue them and enter the sea, at which point the waters close upon them. Josephus adds, however, the following to the biblical narrative:

> Rain fell in torrents from heaven, crashing thunderbolts accompanied the flash of lightning [βρονταὶ σκληραὶ προσεξαπτομένης ἀστραπῆς], aye and thunderbolts were hurled [κεραυνοὶ δὲ κατηνέχθησαν]. In short, there was not one of those destructive forces which in token of God's wrath combine to smite mankind that failed to assemble then. (*Ant.* 2.343-44)

The storm that accompanies the inundation of the Egyptian army is clearly of divine origin,[65] and it is equally as clearly attributed to God's anger towards the Egyptians.

Josephus has embellished his account in such a way to include an element of divine testimony. First, he has placed the Israelites' crossing and the subsequent destruction of the Egyptians in a context of prayer not found in the original account. Second, Josephus has added the element of the storm, which he specifically attributes to God's wrath.[66] In this way, the audience understands the storm (as well as Josephus's comments which follow) as God's testimony against the Egyptians; the storm demonstrates his disapproval of Israel's enemies and their attempt to prevent the Israelites from crossing the sea.

Given these examples of the *topos* of divine testimony through sounds and fire from heaven, I can now summarize the findings concerning how this *topos* functions in these narratives. Fire from the gods can serve as a means of the gods' approval of a character; this was demonstrated through the example of Plutarch's *Timoleon* and *Caesar*. In the case of Timoleon,

---

64. Josephus has added this prayer to the account; it is not in the original text in Exodus. L. Feldman rightly recognizes that some type of interaction with God is implied at this point in the biblical text; in Exod 14:15, God asks Moses, "Why do you cry out to me?" See Feldman, *Judean Antiquities*, 227-28.

65. For example, κατηνέχθησαν is most likely a divine passive.

66. *Contra* Feldman, *Judean Antiquities*, 229, who argues that the annihilation of the Egyptians is "presented . . . in naturalistic rather than supernatural terms." Feldman does correctly note that a storm also accompanies the destruction of the Egyptian army at the Red Sea in Pss 18:12-14; 77:16-20.

the fire was the fulfillment of an earlier prophecy; for Caesar, the fire in the sky prophesied his defeat of Pompey. Fire surrounding a person's head was also seen as testimony of the gods' approval of a character, which can be prophetic in nature. Storms are generally viewed as a method of the gods' punishment.

This testimony also frequently occurs in conjunction with other forms of the *topos*. It is often necessary to interpret the testimony, which, in the case of Plutarch's account of Caesar, is accomplished through other testimonies.

Divine Testimony through Dreams and Visions

There are a plethora of examples of dreams, visions, and apparitions in ancient narratives.[67] Many are true dreams, occurring while the subject is asleep. Others are simply visions which occur when the subject is awake.[68] Again, as before, I will examine these dreams in the narrative context in which they are found in order to attempt to ascertain the function of the gods' testimony through the dream or vision.[69] I will explore several examples of this form of the *topos* of divine testimony.

[67]. For dreams and ghostly apparitions in the works of Livy, Tacitus, and Suetonius, see F. Kraus, "Omens, Portents, and Prodigies," 139–61.

[68]. For the categorization of dreams, see Hanson, "Dreams and Visions," 1410–12. In studying the form of dream-vision reports, Hanson argues that there are three basic categories, which he terms: "audio-visual dream-vision," an experience in which the one impacted by the dream-vision receives information through hearing and seeing; "auditory dream-vision," in which one only hears another speaking to him or her (there is, however, normally a reference to sight on the part of the one who received the dream-vision); "visual dream-vision," in which the one receiving the dream only sees and does not hear any type of speech. On the lack of clarity between dreams and visions and the fluidity of the terminology in the ancient world, see Hanson, "Dreams and Visions," 1407–9.

[69]. Dreams were of great interest to the ancients; see, e.g., Artemidorus's work *Onirocritica*, in which Artemidorus discusses dreams and their interpretation, even providing numerous examples. See also Philo, *De somniis*; in this work, Philo discusses the dreams that God gave to Jacob and Joseph (as well as others who receive dreams in the account of Joseph) in Genesis. A great deal of modern scholarship has lately centered on dreams and how they function in Jewish and Greco-Roman narratives. For example, Hanson ("Dreams and Visions," 1413–14) argues that dream-visions in ancient narratives "often function to direct or redirect the movement of the narrative, and not simply that of the dreamer, though they may coincide." Gnuse (*Dreams*, 101–27) reviews dreams in the Greco-Roman world and classifies them in four categories: (i) auditory only (see Hanson's "auditory dream-vision" above); (ii) "visual symbolic" dreams, in which the dream contains some type of imagery that

Divine Testimony through Deeds in Hellenistic Narratives

The gods often testify concerning the founding of a new city or cult,[70] and dreams can function as this form of the *topos*. In Diodorus Siculus's legendary history of the founding of Rome,[71] he includes a section from

---

must be interpreted to some degree; (iii) "audio-visual" dreams (Hanson's "audio-visual dream-vision"); (iv) dreams involving healing. While his classification scheme is surely correct, Gnuse's overview does not include more specific information on how dreams function in these narratives (which, it must be stated, is not his purpose in this section). Within each category Gnuse helpfully includes many examples of each type of dream. Flannery-Dailey (*Dreamers*, 58–108) has compiled an extensive taxonomy of dreams in the Greco-Roman world in order to demonstrate that there were a set of common "patterns and motifs" available to Jewish authors whose works contained dream reports. Flannery-Dailey argues that dreams in Greek prose works functioned for the most part to "impart unusual *knowledge, healing* and *divine sanction* or their opposites" (*Dreamers*, 76; cf. 82–83). Regarding Latin writers, Flannery-Dailey notes a spectrum of attitudes towards dreams, concentrating on the writings of Cicero, Juvenal, and Suetonius. For my purposes, her comments on dreams in Suetonius are instructive; she notes that through dreams the gods express their approval or disapproval at significant junctures in a character's childhood. Dreams can also link the act of healing with the gods' sanction of a character (here she specifically mentions the *Life of Vespasian*; Flannery-Dailey *Dreamers*, 95). Brenk, in analyzing the dreams found in Plutarch's *Lives*, places these dreams into three categories: (i) symbolic dreams, which must be interpreted; (ii) visions of the future; (iii) oracular dreams, in which a course of action for the future is revealed; see Brenk, *In Mist Apparelled*, 215. J. Miller (*Convinced*, 21–63) surveys dreams and visions in Greco-Roman (23–39) and Jewish (40–60) contexts. His assessment focuses on both the positive and negative attitudes towards dreams and visions in the ancient world. He argues that the evidence for the divine origin of dreams in the ancient world is not clear-cut, and that many writings express a skeptical attitude toward the revelatory nature of dreams. This stance is important for his overall study, which focuses on the role that human beings assume in the human action of interpretation of these phenomena in Luke-Acts. Therefore, it seems that Miller has over-emphasized the minority of ancient writings which do not attribute dreams and visions to divine communication. For a survey of ancient attitudes towards dreams (including scientific, philosophical, and theological) see P. Miller, *Dreams*, 39–73. Miller argues that in antiquity, dreams represented a "fitting technology" for communication with the divine. She also maintains that this attitude was so prevalent that "Cicero's naturalist views seem marginal to the temper of the times" (*Dreams*, 51; cf. my discussion of Cicero's views of divination in chapter 2). See also Gnuse, in his discussion of the same: "Generally the masses, especially in the Hellenistic era, took dreams seriously, while dissent was limited to the writings of a few intelligentsia" (*Dreams*, 116).

70. This should certainly be considered a new direction in the narrative, a particular function of dreams in ancient narratives as emphasized by Hanson, "Dreams and Visions," 1413–14.

71. Mention of this dream is also found in Cicero, *Div.* 1.43. See also Kragelund, "Dreams," 53–95, who mentions this dream specifically as an example of a dream associated with the founding of a city (ibid., 53n3).

the *Chronicle* of Eusebius. In this section, the story of Ascanius's (the son of Aeneas) founding of the city of Alba Longa is narrated. Citing the Roman historian Fabius as the source of the story, it is said that Aeneas received an oracle, telling him to follow a four-footed animal to a place where he should build a city. Some time later, Aeneas is about to sacrifice a sow, when she suddenly runs away and gives birth to thirty piglets on a hilltop. He remembers the oracle, and decides to found a city on that hill in obedience to the oracle. But he then has a dream, which is described in the following way:

> But in his sleep he saw a vision [ἰδόντα δὲ κατὰ τὸν ὕπνον ὄψιν] which strictly forbade him to do so and counseled him to found the city thirty years hence, corresponding to the number of the farrow of pigs, and so he gave up his design. (*Hist.* 7.5.4–5)[72]

In obedience to the dream, Aeneas gives up on the idea of founding the city; thirty years later, in fulfillment of the dream, his son Ascanius does found a colony on that hill.

In this narrative there are several instances of the *topos* of divine testimony (including an oracle, the sow and her pigs, and the dream). In its context, the dream serves as a direct command from the gods,[73] to which Aeneas is obedient. The dream thus serves multiple purposes: it provides divine sanction for the founding of Alba Longa; it demonstrates Aeneas's piety through his obedience to the gods; and it also serves to show Aeneas's son Ascanius as obedient to the gods, as his father before him was.

In Livy's *Historiae*, a dream also functions as a command, but plays a significant role later in the narrative, in which the dream is used in a speech in order to attempt to convince the Roman senate to build a temple. The context is provided by Livy in the opening statement of the section: "It so happened that at Rome preparations were making to repeat

---

72. In Dionysius's account of this same event, Aeneas receives this same command from a voice while he is awake (see *Ant. rom.* 1.56.3). Dionysius goes on to say, however, that "others say . . . a great and wonderful vision of a dream appeared to him in the likeness of one of his country's gods [ἐπιστῆναι μεγάλην τινὰ καὶ θαυμαστὴν ἐνυπνίου τῶν θεῶν τινι τῶν πατρίων εἰκασθεῖσαν ὄψιν] and gave him the advice just before mentioned" (*Ant. rom.* 1.56.5).

73. Again, the clues provided in the narrative assure the auditor that the dream is of divine origin. Aeneas first receives an oracle; then the sow, an intended sacrificial victim, leads Aeneas to the hilltop, at which time she supernaturally produces a brood of thirty piglets. Also, Aeneas is "astounded at this strange happening [τό τε παράδοξον θαυμάσαντα]."

Divine Testimony through Deeds in Hellenistic Narratives

the Great Games" (*Hist.* 2.36.1).[74] Livy then goes on to explain why the games had to be repeated.[75] When the games were originally held, a slave, being beaten by his master with a whip, was driven through the crowd during the pre-games celebration. Later, a plebeian by the name of Titus Latinius "dreamt that Jupiter said that the leading dancer at the games had not been to his liking; that unless there were a sumptuous repetition of the festival the City would be in danger; that Latinius was to announce this to the consuls" (*Hist.* 2.36.2).[76] Out of potential embarrassment, the plebeian does not immediately act on the dream; but soon thereafter his son dies, and the dream is repeated. Once again, he fails to act; this time, he is afflicted with a disease, and the dream is repeated a third time. Finally, convinced of the validity of the message from Jupiter, the plebeian is carried to the Forum where he recounts the message of the dream. The man is miraculously healed of his disease, and the senate agrees to repeat the games (*Hist.* 2.36.3–37.1).[77] In this example one sees a dream, repeated three times and clearly of divine origin, which on one level serves as a warning, but ultimately is referenced in a deliberative application in the Forum.[78]

A second example of the *topos* of divine testimony through dreams used as a means of persuasion concerns a dream that Themistocles had while in exile and prior to seeking asylum in Persia, as narrated by Plutarch. In the passage, one learns that Themistocles has a bounty on his head (*Them.* 26.1), and therefore runs to Aegae, where he has a friend, Nicogenes. Plutarch notes that "after the dinner, which followed a certain sacrifice," Nicogenes's children's tutor became "rapt and inspired" and recited a verse: "Night shall speak, and night instruct thee, night shall give

---

74. Ogilvie (*Commentary on Livy*, 327), mentions that games were traditionally held in celebration of a past victory. Here, Olgilvie mentions that Cicero attributes these particular festivals to battles won by Postumius Cominius; see Cicero, *Div.* 1.55, in which this dream is discussed.

75. Ogilvie, *Commentary on Livy*, 327, notes that religious rites were repeated when some issue arose during those rites. These issues included instances in which the rite was not carried out correctly or was in some way conducted irreverently.

76. Here we have an instance of the *topos* actually serving multiple functions. To the character of the plebeian, the dream serves as a warning. But as will be shown, the plebeian ultimately uses the dream to convince the senate of the need to repeat the games.

77. In 2.37.1 Livy writes, "Games of the greatest possible splendor were decreed by the senate."

78. Cf. Plutarch, *Cor.* 24.2; Dionysius of Halicarnassus, *Ant. rom.* 7.68–69.

The *Topos* of Divine Testimony in Luke/Acts

thee victory" (*Them.* 26.2).[79] Later that night, Themistocles has a dream, which Plutarch describes in the following way:

> And in the night that followed, Themistocles, as he lay in bed, thought he saw in a dream that a serpent wound itself along over his body and crept up to his neck, then became an eagle as soon as it touched his face, enveloped him with its wings and lifted him on high and bore him a long distance, when there appeared as it were a golden herald's wand, on which it set him securely down, freed from helpless terror and distress. (*Them.* 26.2–3)[80]

Later, Themistocles has an opportunity to plead his case before the Persian king,[81] seeking the king's protection. Themistocles begins his speech before the king by noting that the Greeks' pursuit of him is evidence that he is a friend of the Persians. Plutarch then continues: "After these words Themistocles spoke of divine portents in his favour, enlarging upon the vision which he saw at the house of Nicogenes" (*Them.* 28.3).[82] Thus, while the dream which Themistocles experiences at the house of Nicogenes is certainly prophetic, it is later recalled by Themistocles in the narrative as a means of persuasion, in this case a means of self-defense. Themistocles attempts to curry favor with the Persian king by citing the testimony of the gods.

Dreams can also function as simple warnings or guidance from the gods, encouraging the recipient to avoid the possible danger foretold in

---

79. This is an example of divine testimony through inspired speech, a topic which was discussed in chapter three.

80. This is clearly a symbolic, prophetic dream (as is Nicogenes's inspired speech), but has a second function as in other examples. Ultimately, the dream will be used by Themistocles in his own defense. Plutarch does not explicitly describe the dream as having divine origins. Clues, however, do exist in the narrative that lead the reader in this direction. First, Plutarch states that the events occurred "μετὰ τὸ δεῖπνον ἐκ θυσίας τινος," thus providing a cultic setting in which one quite often finds instances of the *topos* of divine testimony. Also, F. Frost claims that the dream was "auspicious," noting that the snake turns into an eagle, the royal insignia of the Persians; as evidence, Frost cites Xenophon, *Cyr.* 7.1.4: "And [Cyrus] gave orders to keep an eye upon his ensign and advance in even step. Now his ensign was a golden eagle with outspread wings mounted upon a long shaft. And this continues even unto this day as the ensign of the Persian king." See Frost, *Plutarch's* Themistocles, 212.

81. Before which Persian king is not clear. Plutarch cites Thucydides and Charon of Lampsacus, who claim the king was Artaxerxes, the son of Xerxes. But he also notes that Ephorus, Dinon, Clitarchus, and Heracleides (among unnamed others) maintain it was Xerxes himself. Plutarch tells his readers that he is of the opinion that Thucydides was correct (see *Them.* 27.1).

82. Themistocles also references an oracle; this was discussed in chapter 3.

Divine Testimony through Deeds in Hellenistic Narratives

the dream. An example of such a dream is also from Plutarch's *Life* of Themistocles. Plutarch tells his auditors that Themistocles is traveling to the coast "to deal with Hellenic affairs"; meanwhile, one learns that Epixyes, a Persian, is plotting to kill Themistocles when he stops for the night at a village by the name of Lion's Head. But the day before he is to arrive in Lion's Head, Themistocles receives a dream:

> But while Themistocles was asleep at midday before, it is said that the Mother of the Gods appeared to him in a dream and said: "O Themistocles, shun a head of lions, that thou mayest not encounter a lion. And for this service to thee, I demand of thee Mnesiptolema to be my handmaid." (*Them.* 30.1–2)

In this case the dream is explicitly attributed to a deity. After praying to the goddess, Themistocles resumes his journey and indeed bypasses Lions Head, making camp in another place. Along the way, one of his pack animals had fallen into a river, so that Themistocles's servants had to hang his tent up to dry. The Pisidians choose this time to attack, in the darkness mistakenly thinking that Themistocles must be in the tent. The attackers are apprehended, and Themistocles is spared. Thus the goddess's warning is fulfilled, and Themistocles is affirmed by her testimony through the dream-warning.

Having received this warning from the goddess and thus avoided capture, Themistocles, out of a sense of gratitude, builds a temple in Magnesia to the goddess. In this way the goddess's approval is complemented by a portrayal of Themistocles as a pious man, willing to acknowledge and give thanks for the goddess's favor shown to him.

The recipients of dreams are not always the one for whom the dream is meant. In Suetonius's *Life* of Galba, Galba hears of a rebellion in Gaul. Galba is called upon to quell the rebellion; he receives letters asking him "to make himself the liberator and leader of mankind" (*Galb.* 7.9.2).[83] Suetonius continues by mentioning several instances of divine testimony which motivate Galba to take on this task:

> He was encouraged too, in addition to most favourable auspices and omens, by the prediction of a young girl of high birth, and the more so because the priest of Jupiter at Clunia, directed by a dream, had found in the inner shrine of his temple the very same prediction, likewise spoken by an inspired girl two hundred years before. And the purport of the verses was that one

---

83. Note the rhetorical use of hyperbole in this statement; on *superlatio*, see *Rhet. Her.* 4.33.44. Cf. Quintilian, *Inst.* 8.6.67–76.

day there would come forth from Spain the ruler and lord of the world. (*Galb.* 7.9.2)

The end result of the divine testimony is that Galba would become emperor. The priest's dream plays a crucial role. Through the dream, the priest is directed to an older prophecy which matches and thus substantiates the "prediction of a young girl of high birth," which was recently received. The dream, therefore, does not contain the actual prophecy, but serves as divine guidance to the prophecy.

In Plutarch's *Life* of Alexander a dream plays a prominent role in the birth narrative of Alexander. As in the previous example, the dream is not received by the character to which it refers. In this case, the parents of the subject of the dream receive the dream. Thus, in the narrative two dreams are described, those of Alexander's parents. On the night before the consummation of Philip's marriage to Olympias, Olympias dreamed

> that there was a peal of thunder and that a thunder-bolt fell upon her womb, and that thereby much fire was kindled, which broke into flames that traveled all about, and then was extinguished. (*Alex.* 2.3–4)

Here one notices the confluence of multiple forms of the *topos*, thus signaling a truly momentous event. By the description of thunder and fire, one can know that this dream is of divine origin. It is also significant that the dream occurs within the context of Alexander's birth and beginnings.[84] Finally, the description of Olympias's dream is followed by the account of a dream that Philip, her husband, had:

> At a later time, too, after the marriage, Philip dreamed that he was putting a seal upon his wife's womb; and the device of the seal, as he thought, was the figure of a lion. (*Alex.* 2.4–5)

Both dreams point to "a son whose nature would be bold and lion-like" (*Alex.* 2.5–6). Through this double-dream motif,[85] Plutarch emphasizes the divine favor that Alexander will enjoy later in his life. Thus, the gods testify by giving their sanction to Alexander's future life.

---

84. Theon includes a "good birth" as an important *topos* when writing an encomium; see Theon, *Progymnasmata* 111 (Kennedy, ed. and trans., 51).

85. For examples of double-dreams in antiquity (which Wikenhauser considers parallels to Acts 9:10–16 and Acts 10:1—11:18), see Wikenhauser, "Doppelträume," 100–111. On the significance of double-dreams (and examples), see Hanson, "Dreams and Visions," 1414–19. Hanson argues that double dreams will result in a "circumstance of mutuality" and are found in significant movements in the plot of the narrative.

Divine Testimony through Deeds in Hellenistic Narratives

Another significant double-dream is found in Dionysius's *Antiquitates romanae* and concerns the legendary founding of Rome. Aeneas, having arrived from Europe with his army, first sacrifices the sow which led him to the hill on which he was called to settle. He then arrays his army against the local king, Latinus. Latinus is terrified at the sight of Aeneas and his army, and is confident of defeat. He allows his troops to rest before attacking Aeneas the next day. During that night, however,

> a certain divinity of the place appeared to him in his sleep and bade him receive the Greeks into his land to dwell with his own subjects, adding that their coming was a great advantage to him and a benefit to all the Aborigines alike. (*Ant. rom.* 1.57.4)

At the same time that Latinus was receiving this testimony from the gods, Aeneas was having a similar experience:

> And the same night Aeneas' household gods appeared to him and admonished him to persuade Latinus to grant them of his own accord a settlement in the part of the country they desired and to treat the Greek forces rather as allies than as enemies. (*Ant. rom.* 1.57.4)

The narrator then comments on the significance of the double-dream: "Thus the dream hindered both of them from beginning an engagement" (*Ant. rom.* 1.57.4). Later in the narrative, the auditor learns that indeed, a treaty is made between the two groups.[86] The double-dream thus serves as the gods' direction to both Aeneas and Latinus at a significant moment, reconciling these two potential enemies.

Josephus narrates a double-dream as a part of his account of Alexander's conquest of Palestine; these dreams also serve to resolve a potential conflict between two parties. As Alexander marches on Jerusalem, Jaddus, the high priest, becomes frightened, because he had formerly sworn allegiance to the Persians (*Ant.* 11.326). He therefore orders a sacrifice, praying to God for his protection. That night, Josephus informs his auditors, Jaddus had a dream,[87] in which God tells him that he should welcome Alexander's arrival, and that God would indeed protect him and the people of Jerusalem.

---

86. "Aeneas having accepted [Latinus's] proposal, a treaty was made between the two nations and confirmed by oaths to this effect" (*Ant. rom.* 1.59.1).

87. Κατακοιμηθέντι δὲ μετὰ τὴν θυσίαν ἐχρημάτισεν αὐτῷ κατὰ τοὺς ὕπνους ὁ θεὸς (*Ant.* 11.327).

When Alexander is in the vicinity of Jerusalem, Jaddus, obedient to the vision, goes out to meet him, together with the priests and some of the Jerusalemites.[88] When Alexander sees Jaddus and the others in their priestly raiment, he comes to them and, surprisingly to some, bows before them.[89] When asked why he showed such submission to the high priest, especially when it was normal for others to show *him* obeisance, Josephus reports Alexander saying,

> It was not before [Jaddus] that I prostrated myself but the God of whom he has the honor to be high priest, for it was he whom I saw in my sleep dressed as he is now, when I was at Dium in Macedonia, and, as I was considering with myself how I might become master of Asia, he urged me not to hesitate but to cross over confidently, for he himself would lead my army and give over to me the empire of the Persians. Since, therefore, I have beheld no one else in such robes, . . . I believe that I have made this expedition under divine guidance. (*Ant.* 11.334–35)

The meeting of Alexander and Jaddus, therefore, as Josephus reports it, is quite amicable and even sacred, rather than antagonistic and violent, as expected.

In this account, Josephus attributes the extraordinary outcome of this meeting to God's intervention through divine testimony. The report of Jaddus's dream is in the setting of worship and prayer the day before.[90] Josephus explicitly reports that God is the source of Jaddus's dream, as is the case of Alexander's dream. The two "interlocked" dreams serve to demonstrate God's desire that these two parties be reconciled; it is through these dreams that the expected violence and pillaging are avoided. But not only does the event receive divine sanction; through the divine testimony

---

88. Josephus describes the welcome as ἱεροπρεπῆ, emphasizing its sacred character in comparison to other similar events in which the arrival of a political figure is celebrated. Also, Josephus adds that the meeting took place at Σαφείν, which means "lookout." The place was given this name because from it, Jerusalem and the temple were visible.

89. Josephus explains that the "Phoenicians and the Chaldeans who followed along thought to themselves that the king in his anger would naturally permit them to plunder the city and put the high priest to a shameful death" (*Ant.* 11.330). After Alexander greets Jaddus, Josephus continues: "[B]ut the kings of Syria and the others were struck with amazement at his action and supposed that the king's mind was deranged" (*Ant.* 11.332).

90. Gnuse, *Dreams*, 186, goes so far as to claim that Jaddus had the dream while in the temple. This, however, is not explicitly stated in the account, in which one finds the temporal clause κατακοιμηθέντι δὲ μετὰ τὴν θυσίαν.

of the dreams, Jaddus and Alexander are portrayed as characters who are obedient to the divine direction they receive in their dreams.

Often dreams must be interpreted to discern the exact testimony the gods are revealing through the dream. Diodorus Siculus, in recounting the events of the war between Athens and Sparta in the late fifth century, tells of an impending naval battle, with Callicratidas leading the Spartans, and Thrasybulus as general of the Athenians. Before the battle, the soothsayers argue against fighting. On the Spartan side,

> the head of the victim, which lay on the beach, was lost to sight when the waves broke on it, and the seer accordingly foretold that the admiral would die in the fight. (*Hist.* 8.97.5)

Callicratidas, however, is undeterred by the auspicious sacrifice, stating: "If I die in the fight, I shall not have lessened the fate of Sparta" (*Hist.* 8.97.5). On the Athenian side, Thrasybulus

> dreamed that he was in Athens and the theatre was crowded, and that he and six of the other generals were playing the *Phoenician Women* of Euripides, while their competitors were performing the *Suppliants*; and that it resulted in a "Cadmean victory"[91] for them and they all died, just as did those who waged the campaign against Thebes. (*Hist.* 8.97.6)

This dream requires interpretation, which is accomplished by Thrasybulus's seer. The seer states that the dream foretold victory for the Athenians in the battle, but that they would lose seven generals as a result. The Athenian generals press on with their plans for the battle, but only proclaim that the gods have prophesied victory for the Athenians; they do not allow the other prophecy to be mentioned.

In a speech to his troops, Callicratidas acknowledges that he will die in the fight, but this serves to inspire his forces (*Hist.* 8.98.1). The speech and the ensuing account of the battle serve to portray Callicratidas in a positive light. Through the speech, Callicratidas demonstrates that he is willing to enter the battle, even though he knows it will cost him his life. This is reinforced by the narrator's comments: "But Callicratidas especially, since he had heard from the seer of the end awaiting him, was eager to compass for himself a death that would be renowned" (*Hist.* 8.98.3). Later, one reads, "It was at this time, we are told, that Callicratidas, after

---

91. Cf. *Hist.* 22.6: "A 'Cadmean Victory' is a proverbial expression. It signifies that the victors suffer misfortune, while the defeated are not endangered because of the magnitude of their dominion."

fighting brilliantly and holding out for a long time, finally was worn down by numbers, as he was struck from all directions" (*Hist.* 8.98.5). Thus, Callicratidas dies a good death, foretold to him through divine testimony, interpreted by one of his seers.

The Athenian generals, whose deaths were foretold through Thrasybulus's dream, did, however, not die in the naval engagement. The prophecy is fulfilled later in the narrative. News of the victory reaches Athens, but the Athenians also learn that their generals failed to properly bury those soldiers who were killed in action. Therefore, the seven generals responsible are put on trial and executed (*Hist.* 13.101–102).[92]

In this account one finds "interlocked" divine testimony, through sacrificial animals to the Spartans and a dream to Thrasybulus. Both testimonies must be interpreted to be understood correctly, and in each case this interpretation comes through a soothsayer. The testimony to Callicratidas allows the reader to understand his death as a "good" death; the testimony to the Athenians is a sign of the gods' approval of the Athenians' purposes in the war.[93]

Given these examples of dream-visions, it is appropriate to attempt to make some summary statements concerning the data. First, most of the dreams in these examples are found in contexts in which multiple divine testimonies occur. Some dreams are explicitly stated as being of divine origin, while for others one must rely on the context of the narrative to understand them as divine testimonies (for example, Themistocles's dream of the serpent which turns into an eagle occurs after performing a sacrifice). In some cases the one who receives the dream is the subject thereof, but it is also possible that a character receives a dream concerning someone else. Multiple dreams are also possible, including one person receiving the same dream more than once, or multiple people receiving a dream about a common person or event.

---

92. At the end of the trial, one of the generals, Diomedon (Diomedon is described by the narrator as "thought by all to excel both in justice and in the other virtues" [*Hist.* 13.102.1]), makes this statement: "Men of Athens, may the action which has been taken regarding us turn out well for the state; but as for the vows which we made for the victory, inasmuch as Fortune has prevented our paying them, since it is well that you give thought to them, do you pay them to Zeus the Saviour and Apollo and the Holy Goddesses; for it was to these gods that we made vows before we overcame the enemy" (*Hist.* 13.102.2). The narrator then states that Diomedon's death was "unjust," and that he should be praised for only thinking of the state and not himself at this time (*Hist.* 13.102.3).

93. But it also serves, albeit indirectly, to portray Diodomen in a positive light, through his trial and speech.

Divine Testimony through Deeds in Hellenistic Narratives

Dreams function as commands, warnings, and the demonstration of the approval of the gods. They often occur at significant turns of plot within the narrative and help to explain the change in the course of action. They can assist in understanding a previous testimony, or can be used in an attempt to convince another character of the validity of a particular choice. In the case of Aeneas and Latinus (as well as Alexander and Jaddus), reconciliation of potential enemies is achieved through the testimony of the gods through dreams. Finally, dreams often require some type of interpretation.

Divine Testimony through Signs and Portents in Creation

This category is somewhat general; many instances of divine testimony in ancient narratives could potentially be considered to be communicated through signs and portents in nature. In this section I will concentrate on examples that involve earthquakes and animals.[94]

Earthquakes figure prominently in ancient narratives, most often as the gods' testimony against a person or group of people in the form of punishment. In his history, Diodorus Siculus describes a massive earthquake in Sparta, which caused houses to collapse "uninterruptedly over a long period," so that "no little property was ruined by the quake" (*Hist.* 11.63.2–3).[95] The earthquake is given an explicitly divine origin: "And although [the Lacedaemonians] suffered this disaster because some god, as it were, was wreaking his anger upon them" (*Hist.* 11.63.3). In the narrative, the earthquake serves as the cause of a war between Sparta and the Helots and Messenians, who take advantage of Sparta's weakened condition and attack the Spartans. Also, King Archidamus of Sparta rises above the devastation of the earthquake to rally the Spartans:

> The king of the Lacedaemonians, Archidamus, by his personal foresight not only was the saviour of his fellow citizens even

---

94. On earthquakes as omens in the works of Livy, Tacitus, and Suetonius, see F. Kraus, "Omens, Portents, and Prodigies," 49–53. For portents involving animals (other than birds), see ibid., 107–18.

95. Note the use of litotes (λιτότης; in Latin, *deminutio*) in the description of the damage (οὐκ ὀλίγον δὲ τῶν κατὰ τὰς οἰκίας χρημάτων ὁ σεισμὸς ἐλυμήνατο). According to the author of *Rhet. Her.*, "*deminutio* occurs" when "we moderate and soften the statement" of some "exceptional advantage" (4.38.50). Thus, litotes/*deminutio* is the purposeful understatement of a particular condition.

during the earthquake, but in the course of the war also he bravely fought the aggressors. For instance, when the terrible earthquake struck Sparta, he was the first Spartan to seize his armour and hasten from the city into the country, calling upon the other citizens to follow his example. The Spartans obeyed him and thus those who survived the shock wave were saved and these men King Archidamus organized into an army and prepared to make war upon the revolters [i.e., the Helots and Messenians]. (*Hist.* 11.63.3)

No reason for the wrath of the gods is provided; auditors do understand, however, that Archidamus has made the best of a terrible situation.

In a second example from Diodorus Siculus (*Hist.* 15.49.1–6), an earthquake is seen as testimony of the gods' anger; in this case, it is clear why the god (Poseidon) is displeased. Diodorus tells of an Ionian festival honoring Poseidon (τὰ Πανιώνια) that for many years took place near Mycalê. Due to wars being fought in this region, the festival had to be moved to Ephesus. The Ionians send a delegation to Delphi, and through an oracle they are ordered to take a copy of the sacred altar located at Helicê.[96] The Ionians obey the oracle and send a group to Achaïa; the Achaeans agree to allow them to make a copy of the altar. The people of Helicê, however, remembered an oracle that they had received which prohibited the Ionians from sacrificing at the altar of Poseidon, and also argued that the altar belonged to them. Therefore, the Achaeans had no right to allow the Ionians to have dealings with the altar. The Ionians ignore the delegation from Helicê, and perform their sacrifices. In retaliation, the Helicians "scattered the sacred possessions of the Ionians and seized the persons of their representatives, thus committing sacrilege" (*Hist.* 15.49.3).

It is at this point that Poseidon weighs in on the matter through an earthquake. Diodorus describes the scene thusly:

> It was because of these acts, they say, that Poseidon in his anger brought ruin upon the offending cities through the earthquake and the flood. That it was Poseidon's wrath that was wreaked upon these cities they allege that clear proofs are at hand [φάσιν ἐμφανεῖς ἀποδείξεις ὑπάρχειν]: first, it is distinctly conceived that authority over earthquakes and floods belongs to this god, and also it is the ancient belief that the Peloponnese was an habitation of Poseidon; and this country is regarded as sacred in a way to Poseidon, and, speaking generally, all the cities in the

---

96. Diodorus adds this clarifying comment concerning Helicê, "which was situated in what was then known as Ionia, but is known now as Achaïa" (*Hist.* 15.49.1).

Divine Testimony through Deeds in Hellenistic Narratives

Peloponnese pay honour to this god more than to any other of the immortals. (*Hist.* 15.49.4)

Diodorus thus allows for the possibility that the earthquake is a proof of the wrath of Poseidon. In this way it is his testimony against the impiety of the Helicians in their (mis)handling of the sacred objects belonging to the Ionians.[97]

In Suetonius's *Life* of Galba, an earthquake serves as a portent (along with several other divine testimonies) of the imminent murder of Galba. Suetonius describes Galba's procession to assume the throne; he prefaces the account with the statement, "Many prodigies in rapid succession from the very beginning of his reign had foretold Galba's end exactly as it happened" (*Galb.* 7.18.1).[98] An earthquake then occurs, along with a strange noise: "Again, as he entered the city, and later the Palace, he was met by a shock of earthquake and a sound like the lowing of a kine" (*Galb.* 7.18.1).[99] After these prodigies, Suetonius describes other, "even clearer signs" (*Galb.* 7.18.2).[100] Concerning the earthquake, it is one of many of the gods' testimonies that demonstrate their displeasure over Galba's reign, thus casting divine aspersions on Galba as emperor.[101]

---

97. This event is also found in Pausanias's description of Achaia, with a similar emphasis on the earthquake as a testimony of Poseidon's wrath: "But later on the Achaeans of the place removed some suppliants from the sanctuary and killed them. But the wrath of Poseidon visited them without delay; an earthquake promptly struck their land and swallowed up, without leaving a trace for posterity to see, both the buildings and the very site on which the city stood" (Pausanias, *Descr.* 24.6).

98. These prodigies include a sacrificial ox which escapes and sprays blood on Galba, and a guard, in trying to protect Galba during this incident, who almost stabs him with his weapon (*Galb.* 7.18.1).

99. See also Tacitus, *Hist.* 1.27–41.

100. These include: a dream in which Fortune displays her anger over Galba consecrating a necklace to Venus instead of placing it on her statue in Tusculum as he had originally intended; Galba then goes to make propitiation to Fortune in Tusculum, where his men find warm ashes on the altar and a young man dressed in black beside it; while making sacrifices his laurel wreath falls off his head; the sacred chickens used for augury fly away; finally his chair in two different settings is misplaced.

101. That the earthquake is a condemnation of Galba as emperor is confirmed when one reaches the end of Suetonius's *Life* of Galba. Suetonius describes Galba's physical appearance thusly: "He was of average height, very bald, with blue eyes and a hooked nose. His hands and feet were so distorted by gout that he could not endure a shoe for long, unroll a book, or even hold one. The flesh on his right side too had grown out and hung down to such an extent, that it could with difficulty be held in place by a bandage" (*Galb.* 7.21.1). His prodigious eating habits are also criticized, to the degree that "in winter time [he] was in the habit of taking food even before daylight" (*Galb.*

The *Topos* of Divine Testimony in Luke/Acts

A further example of the gods' testimony through earthquakes comes from Plutarch's *Life* of Agesilaus. In this section of the *Life* (3.3–5), Lysander is promoting Agesilaus as king of Sparta in the wake of Agis's death. Lysander references an oracle which mentions that the Spartans should avoid a "maimed royalty"; he interprets this oracle to be referring to the fact that Agesilaus's opponent, Leotychides, was an illegitimate child. Plutarch then adds: "And Agesilaus declared that Poseidon also had borne witness to the bastardy of Leotychides [τὸν Ποσειδῶ καταμαρτυρεῖν τοῦ Λεωτυχίδου τὴν νοθείαν], for he had cast Agis forth from his bedchamber by an earthquake, and after this more than ten months elapsed before Leotychides was born" (*Ages.* 3.5). In this case, a character directly invokes the witness, through an earthquake, of the god Poseidon against Leotychides in an effort to convince the Spartans that naming Leotychides as king would be in disobedience to an oracle.[102] Here, therefore, the *topos* of divine testimony is used by a character in order to try to persuade other characters of the validity of his position and influence their future behavior.

In his retelling of the Philistines' attack on the Israelites gathered at Mizpah (1 Sam 7), Josephus has added an earthquake[103] to the biblical account which would have been understood by his auditors as a divine testimony. Josephus's narrative is introduced as in 1 Sam 7; when the Israelites hear of the Philistines' impending attack, they become scared, and Samuel offers a sacrifice to God and prays (*Ant.* 6.25; cf. 1 Sam 7:7–9). In his account, Josephus expands upon the original passage (ἐπήκουσεν αὐτοῦ κύριος;[104] 1 Sam 7:9b) by stating that "God hearkened to his prayers, and, accepting the sacrifice in gracious and befriending spirit, gave them assurance of victory and triumph" (*Ant.* 6.25).

In the account of the battle as found in 1 Sam, the text states that "the LORD thundered with a mighty voice [ἐβρόντεσεν κύριος ἐν φωνῇ μεγάλῃ][105] that day against the Philistines and threw them into confusion; and they were routed before Israel" (1 Sam 7:10b). Josephus, however, describes the battle thusly:

7.22.1). Also, his sexual appetites come under fire: "He was more inclined to unnatural desire, and in gratifying it preferred full-grown, strong men" (*Galb.* 7.22.1).

102. Oracles, are, of course, another form of the *topos* of divine testimony. Therefore, here, as in many other instances, oracles and other forms of the *topos* are combined.

103. As well as other elements; see the discussion which follows.

104. The MT reads: *vay'anehu yhwah*

105. This follows the MT exactly.

Divine Testimony through Deeds in Hellenistic Narratives

> God vexed [the Philistines] with an earthquake [αὐτοὺς ὁ θεὸς κλονεῖ σεισμῷ], rocking and making tremulous and treacherous the ground beneath them... Next He deafened them with thunderclaps [ἔπειτα βρονταῖς καταψοφάσας], made fiery lightning [διαπύροις ἀστραπαῖς] to flash around them as it were to burn out their eyes, struck the arms from their hands, and so turned them weaponless to flight. (*Ant.* 6.27)

Josephus has added details which ancient auditors would have understood to be God's testimony against the Philistines. The thundering voice of God in the MT is now loud thunderclaps, which are accompanied by lightning bolts. Also, an earthquake occurs, which causes the Philistines to be unsteady and even fall into the resulting chasms.[106] These elements of divine testimony function to demonstrate God's disapproval of the Philistines' attack, and as tangible demonstrations of his assurance of victory to the Israelites (cf. *Ant.* 6.25 above).

The shaking of the earth, however, is not always a divine testimony which serves as a punishment of a character in the narrative. In Josephus's description of Daniel's reception of his second vision (also narrated in Dan 8), Daniel feels the earth shake immediately before he sees the vision. In the account in Dan 8, the introduction is quite simple: "In the third year of the reign of King Belshazzar a vision [ὅρασις][107] appeared to me, Daniel" (Dan 8:1). In 8:2, the auditor learns that Daniel is in Susa, by the river Ulai. The content of the vision is then described. In Josephus's account, however, he states:

> For [Daniel] says that when he was in Susa, the metropolis of Persia, and went out into the plain with his companions, there was a sudden shaking and trembling of the earth [κλόνου τῆς γῆς ἐξαίφνης γενομένου], and he was left alone by his friends, who fled, and in confusion he fell on his face and his two hands, whereupon someone touched him and at the same time bade him arise and see what was to happen to his countrymen in the future after many generations. (*Ant.* 10.269)

Following this introduction, Josephus describes the vision itself, which is very similar to what is found in the book of Daniel. Within the description

---

106. Begg (*Judean Antiquities*, 103) recognizes these embellishments as well, and argues that Josephus here emphasizes the irony of the Israelites' apparent helplessness before the battle (*Ant.* 6.24), and God's rendering of the Philistines helpless during the battle.

107. MT: *hazon*

of the vision, its origins are explicitly attributed to God.[108] The interpretation which follows is also said to have come directly from God.[109]

In this example, Josephus has described an instance of divine testimony (the vision to Daniel from God) and embellished the original account with a second occurrence of divine testimony, namely, some type of earthquake-like phenomenon,[110] which causes those with him to flee. Given the divine origins of the other elements in the narrative (the vision, the touch Daniel feels, the command to "arise and see"), and the fear expressed by Daniel's companions, it is clear that the shaking of the earth is also of divine origin. Here, however, the shaking of the earth does not denote God's anger; on the contrary, it is a sign of God's presence[111] and should be understood as God's sanction of Daniel as one who can be trusted with a vision and its interpretation from God.

The gods often testify through the behavior of animals. The wolf and its significance for Mars are found in Livy's account of a battle between the Romans and a large force made up of Gauls and Samnites. Livy reports that as the two armies faced each other, a wolf chased a deer in the space between the two armies. The deer turned and ran into the lines of the Gauls and Samnites, while the wolf went the opposite direction, into the Roman lines. The Gauls kill the deer in their midst, but the Romans allow the wolf to pass unharmed. When this occurs, one of the Roman soldiers calls out:

> That way flight and slaughter have shaped their course, where you see the beast lie slain that is sacred to Diana; on this side the wolf of Mars, unhurt and sound, has reminded us of the Martian race and of our Founder. (*Hist.* 10.27.8-9)

The appearance of the wolf and deer are portrayed as more than coincidence in the narrative; this is confirmed by their behavior when the wolf breaks off the chase and they go their separate ways. Through the soldier's

---

108. "From these, he writes, there arose another smaller horn which God, who revealed these things to him [αὐτῷ ὁ ταῦτα ἐπιδεικνὺς θεός], told him would grow and make war on his nation" (*Ant.* 10.271). The detail of God's revelation has been added to the original account.

109. "This, Daniel writes, is what he saw in the plain of Susa, and he relates that God interpreted to him the form of the vision as follows [κρῖναι δ' αὐτῷ τὴν ὄψιν τοῦ φαντάσματος ἐδήλου τὸν θεὸν οὕτως]" (*Ant.* 10.272).

110. It must be noted that Josephus does not use the Greek word σεισμός here; from the context, however, it is clear that the earth is moving in some way.

111. Contra Begg and Spilsbury, *Judean Antiquities*, 310, who tentatively state that the earthquake is Josephus's addition, "perhaps for dramatic effect."

statement, the Gaul's killing of the deer is portrayed as an impious act, while the Romans allowing the wolf to pass is a sign of their piety.[112] Given the eventual outcome of the battle, the testimony could also be understood as prophetic. The Romans subsequently win the battle, apparently aided by the gods.[113]

Plutarch's (and others') account of the birth of Romulus and his brother Remus is filled with fantastic events which involve animals. Plutarch provides multiple accounts of the origins of Romulus and Remus; what is consistent in these accounts is the miraculous feeding of the infant boys by a wolf and birds (*Rom.* 2.6; 3.2). For the purposes of this study, the second account (3.2) is the more significant. Here, the only difference to the first account is that rather than "all sorts of birds" feeding the two babies, it is said that a woodpecker helps in their feeding. Plutarch provides the significance for the reader:

> Now these creatures [the wolf and the woodpecker] are considered sacred to Mars, and the woodpecker is held in especial veneration and honour by the Latins, and this was the chief reason why the mother was believed when she declared that Mars was the father of her babes. (*Rom.* 3.2)

Here we have an instance of divine testimony through a sign in the created order. Also, Plutarch ensures that his readers understand the high standing that both the wolf and the woodpecker have, not only among the Romans, but also with Mars. Thus, the fact that these particular animals attended to Romulus and Remus at their birth is a noteworthy divine affirmation of their future lives.

Snakes also make many appearances as testimony of the gods. In most cases snakes are understood as the gods' condemnation of a character. In Livy's history of Rome, he tells the story of Gracchus, who offers a sacrifice before leading his troops to Beneventum, as ordered. Livy begins the account with the statement that "[A]s Gracchus was sacrificing before leaving Lucania, an unfavourable portent occurred" (*Hist.* 25.16.1). The auspicious portent is that two snakes appear and eat the liver of the

---

112. See Levene, *Religion in Livy*, 235–36: "[Livy] thus shows the good omen to be a direct result of the Romans' own behaviour, their sparing of the '*Martius lupus*' contrasted with the Gauls' slaying of the '*sacram Dianae feram*' (10.29.9). Once again, then, we see a victory associated with piety."

113. In his account of the battle proper, Livy states: "From that moment [the death of the Roman general Decius] the battle seemed scarce to depend on human efforts" (*Hist.* 10.29.1).

sacrificial animal. Gracchus's augurs encourage him to repeat the sacrifice; when he does, the same thing happens. This strange occurrence is repeated a third time (*Hist.* 25.16.2–3).

Following the failed sacrifices, Gracchus is deceived by Flavus, a Lucanian, who had professed loyalty to Rome but subsequently decided to switch his allegiance to the Carthaginians. Flavus lures Gracchus into a trap, in which Gracchus is killed along with some of his men. Gracchus, however, is portrayed as dying bravely, fighting ferociously in the face of overwhelming odds. The Carthaginians desire to take him alive, but Gracchus puts up such resistance it is impossible to do so without suffering a significant loss (*Hist.* 25.16.5–24). Thus, at the end of his life, Gracchus is seen by the audience as a noble, brave man, but one who cannot escape the "unfavourable portent" of the snakes.

A second example of divine testimony involving snakes is found in Plutarch's *Life* of Tiberius. As Tribune, Tiberius finds himself in conflict with the Roman senate over his desire for agrarian reform and a perceived lust for power. Near the time of his murder, Tiberius experiences unfavorable omens through the augural birds.[114] Tiberius then recalls an omen that he had experienced some time in the past:

> He had a helmet which he wore in battle, exceptionally adorned and splendid; into this serpents crawled unnoticed, laid eggs there and hatched them out. For this reason Tiberius was all the more disturbed by the signs from the birds. (*Ti. C. Gracch.* 17.2)

Following this are more portents of impending disaster.[115] In spite of these testimonies, Tiberius presses on to the assembly, where he is eventually murdered (*Ti. C. Gracch.* 19.6). Therefore, the snakes in this passage contribute to the negative prophecy of the gods. Specifically, Tiberius recalls a testimony of the gods through snakes that he had received sometime in the past which substantiated other, more current testimonies.

This example, as seen in the previous account of Gracchus, involves a character who is portrayed in a complementary manner but nonetheless cannot escape the evil prophesied by the gods in so many ways. Tiberius's

---

114. The birds refuse to eat the food they are given; only one will even leave the cage (even when the augur shook the cage to try and force them out), but this one "would not touch the food, but raised its left wing, stretched out its leg, and then ran back into the cage" (*Ti. C. Gracch.* 17.1).

115. Tiberius stubs his toe going out of the house. He then notices ravens fighting on the roof of a house he passes on the way to the assembly; as they fight they knock a stone off the roof which falls at Tiberius's feet (*Ti. C. Gracch.* 17.3).

reforms are portrayed as positive, while his opponents are portrayed as being scared of his power. This reading of the *Life* of Tiberius is confirmed by two pieces of evidence. First, in questioning Tiberius's friend Blossius after Tiberius's death, "he admitted that he had done everything at the bidding of Tiberius" (*Ti. C. Gracch.* 20.3). When asked, "What then, if Tiberius had ordered thee to set fire to the Capitol?" Blossius eventually answers, "If such a man as Tiberius had ordered such a thing, it would also have been right for me to do it; for Tiberius would not have given such an order if it had not been for the interest of the people" (*Ti. C. Gracch.* 20.4). Blossius's life is spared, thus legitimating his testimony.

Second, the senate, which had opposed Tiberius's reform movement, after his death tried "to conciliate the people now that matters had gone so far, no longer opposed the distribution of the public land, and proposed that the people should elect a commissioner in place of Tiberius" (*Ti. C. Gracch.* 21.1). Thus, Tiberius's reforms, supported by the people, are eventually enacted after his death.

To summarize, divine testimony through signs and portents in creation can be a display of the anger of the gods, but can also demonstrate their favor. In the examples here the testimony normally occurs concurrent with the events with which the gods desire to show their favor or disapproval; in one case, however, a character recalled a testimony received at an earlier time which helped to interpret a later testimony. Also, I have shown an example of this form of the *topos* being used in an attempt to persuade others. As with other forms of divine testimony, sometimes it is explicitly attributed to the gods, and in other cases this must be inferred.

Divine Testimony through the Examination of Entrails

In many of the examples of the *topos* of divine testimony through the gods' deeds analyzed above the examination of entrails has played a role (see, e.g., Suetonius, *Jul.* 81; Plutarch, *Caes.* 43; Livy, *Hist.* 25.16; Diodorus Siculus 8.97). From these examples one receives a sense of the function of the *topos* in this form. Therefore, I will restrict myself in this section to only two more explicit examples of this form of divine testimony, which functions as affirmation of those the gods favor as well as condemnation of those they do not.

In Plutarch's *Life* of Alexander, while Alexander lays siege to the city of Tyre, his priest Aristander performs a sacrifice in order to discern the will of the gods concerning the fate of the city. The entrails show that the city will be taken that same month; the sacrifice was performed, however, on the last day of the month. In order to ensure that the prophecy will be fulfilled, Alexander orders the date to be changed from the thirtieth to the twenty-third, because he was "always eager to support [Aristander's] prophecies" (*Alex.* 25.2). The troops are encouraged, and Tyre is conquered on that day, fulfilling the prophecy. The divine testimony through the examination of the entrails of sacrificial animals in this example therefore functions as prophecy. But also through the divine testimony, Plutarch shows that the gods approve of Alexander and his plans to conquer Tyre; likewise, Alexander is portrayed as pious, as he is willing to take fairly extreme measures to ensure that the gods' prophecy is fulfilled. Thus Alexander is rewarded with victory over Tyre.

For the second example I return to Galba's adoption of Piso as narrated by Plutarch; this was originally discussed under the heading "Sounds and Fire from Heaven." In this *Life*, shortly after Galba carries out the adoption of Piso as Caesar, Plutarch indicates that some of Otho's cronies "went round corrupting the soldiers" (*Galb.* 24.1). Thus, the auditor is already negatively predisposed toward Otho. Plutarch then reports:

> On that day, shortly after dawn, Galba was sacrificing in the Palatium in the presence of his friends; and as soon as Umbricius, the officiating priest, had taken the entrails of the victim in his hands and inspected them, he declared not ambiguously, but in so many words, that there were signs of a great commotion, and that peril mixed with treachery hung over the emperor's head. Thus the god all but delivered Otho over to arrest. (*Galb.* 24.2–3)

The testimony of the gods through the entrails is, again, a form of prophecy. It is necessary for the priest to interpret the testimony, which he does somewhat ambiguously. The narrator, however, clearly interprets the gods' testimony as a negative attitude toward Otho, and the testimony is used to implicate Otho in his plot to murder Galba. The auditor's suppositions concerning Otho's shady character are confirmed; likewise, because the gods are against Galba's enemy, implicitly they are for Galba.

Divine testimony through the entrails of sacrificial animals is prophetic in nature. It requires an interpreter, normally the augur performing the sacrifice. On the narrative level, the narrator can serve as the interpreter for the reader.

Divine Testimony through Deeds in Hellenistic Narratives

Summary of Divine Testimony through Deeds—Extra-biblical Data

I will now attempt to summarize the data collected from this survey of instances of divine testimony through deeds in ancient narratives. I will begin by drawing some conclusions concerning common ways in which these examples of divine testimony have been structured within the narratives in which they are found, and follow with an encapsulation of how divine testimony functions within the narratives.

Often, the testimony of the gods through deeds appears at significant moments within the narrative and is used to help explain the direction a single character or group of people takes in the plot. Also, as seen in the previous chapters concerning divine testimony through utterances, frequently in the immediate context of the description of the testimony there is some type of religious expression depicted. This religious expression is most often one of prayer to the gods or an act of sacrifice to the gods. Generally, the testimony is directly attributed to the gods, but there are cases in which the auditor must rely on clues within the narrative to discern that the gods are actually testifying. In the majority of cases there are multiple testimonies, of either the same or differing forms, within the same narrative context. Testimonies, such as dreams or other portents, can be repeated more or less verbatim. Very often characters are required to interpret the testimony that the gods have furnished. Similar to this, there are cases in which a testimony serves to confirm another testimony. Finally, it is almost always introduced "at the moment"; in other words, the narration of the testimony of the gods occurs at a significant moment in the plot of the narrative. There are cases, however, in which the testimony has occurred sometime in the past (of which the auditor may or may not have been aware), and is recalled at a later, more auspicious moment.[116] Thus the character requires a new situation to understand the full significance of a testimony he or she has received in the past from the gods.

Concerning the function of divine testimony through deeds, through these examples one notices the *topos* functioning in several ways. Generally, the gods' testimony serves as warnings, commands, encouragement, and prophecies of coming events. When one considers the narrative context in which they occur, one sees that in addition to these general functions, the divine testimony serves to sanction some characters and

---

116. See, e.g., Plutarch's account of Tiberius, who remembers an omen of snakes nesting in his helmet. He had received this testimony some time in the past (*Ti. C. Gracch.* 17.2), and it helps to explain his current situation.

The *Topos* of Divine Testimony in Luke/Acts

display the disapproval of the gods for others. In extreme cases, the gods' testimony is actually used to punish a character. In many instances, one testimony can legitimate one character while at the same time discredit another. A divine testimony that is pronounced upon a character can be used later by the character in some type of persuasive situation, often within a speech. Also, a testimony from a god provides a character with an opportunity to align him or herself with that prophecy, thus demonstrating the character's piety (or lack thereof).[117]

What is important to consider here is that there is not a one-to-one relationship between a certain form of divine testimony through deeds and a certain function; dreams, for example, can serve as warnings, commands, encouragement, or actually to influence two parties to come to the same idea. Storms can also serve as warnings or punishments; earthquakes can function as displays of the gods' anger or as the gods' affirmation of a character. The significance of this form of the *topos* is the same as that determined through the analysis of ancient speeches and the examination of divine testimony through utterances: the over-arching function of the *topos* of divine testimony through deeds in ancient narratives is a means of characterization, demonstrating the gods' favor or displeasure for characters and/or their actions.

The gods' testimony is used to persuade others, regardless of the type of deed. Therefore, in considering the use of divine testimony in Luke-Acts, it is important to remember this range of functions within the narrative, and to consider how the different forms of divine testimony are used in these works. What will be demonstrated is that divine testimony functions in very similar ways when one considers the full range of functions seen here.

---

117. For an extreme example, Alexander at Tyre receives the prophecy that he will conquer Tyre in that month, and changes the calendar to ensure that he remains in the will of the gods!

6 • The *topos* of Divine Testimony through Deeds in Luke-Acts

IN THIS CHAPTER, I will proceed as in the previous one. I will use the same categories of divine deeds as in the analysis of the extra-biblical material, namely the form of the gods' testimony through deeds as described by Cicero, and consider examples of this type of testimony as seen in Luke-Acts. These will be analyzed with an eye towards how the divine testimony is presented within the narrative context and a determination made as to the function(s) of the testimony in the overall plot of the narrative. Before beginning the analysis, a few clarifying statements are in order. First, it will be readily apparent that many of these examples will not neatly fit into a single category. As will be shown, Luke tends toward the ancient convention of including multiple testimonies of different form in the description of one event, thus disallowing a neat and tidy classification.[1] Similarly, there is sometimes a great deal of difficulty in understanding what exactly is being described, especially in the case of dreams, visions, theophanies, and angelophanies. The categories here are only to facilitate the analysis of the data; at the end of the day, it would be possible to consider some of these examples under a different heading. Here, however, the summary from the last section is helpful: because a certain form of divine testimony through deeds does not always function in the same way in every narrative, the classification is of lesser importance than the way in which the testimony functions.

---

1. In extreme cases, of which there are multiple examples, a divine testimony through a particular deed is coupled with direct speech from God. In these cases, I will emphasize the deed aspect of the testimony here, as I have already examined divine utterances in chapter four.

The *Topos* of Divine Testimony in Luke/Acts

DIVINE TESTIMONY THROUGH OBJECTS AND EVENTS IN THE HEAVENS

I stated earlier that this form of the *topos* of divine testimony through deeds can include such natural phenomena as eclipses and comets which are found in the sky. This short section will examine examples of this use of the *topos* in Luke-Acts, of which there are two.

Luke 21:11, 25

In this passage, Jesus responds to two questions put to him by some of those with him in the temple. Their questions (τότε οὖν ταῦτα ἔσται, καὶ τί τὸ σημεῖον ὅταν μέλλῃ ταῦτα γίνεσθαι; Luke 21:7) concern the destruction of the temple that Jesus predicts in 21:6, specifically when it will occur and by what sign (τί τὸ σημεῖον) will they know that it is about to occur.[2] Jesus' immediate response is found in v. 11: σεισμοί τε μεγάλοι καὶ κατὰ τόπους λιμοὶ καὶ λοιμοὶ ἔσονται, φόβητρά τε καὶ ἀπ' οὐρανοῦ σημεῖα μεγάλα ἔσται. Here one notes that Jesus connects the destruction of the temple with "great signs from heaven [ἀπ' οὐρανοῦ σημεῖα μεγάλα]," along with large earthquakes on the earth. In v. 25, he makes a somewhat similar statement, telling the people that preceding the coming of the Son of Man there will be σημεῖα ἐν ἡλίῳ καὶ σελήνῃ καὶ ἄστροις, καὶ ἐπὶ τῆς γῆς συνοχὴ ἐθνῶν ἐν ἀπορίᾳ ἤχους θαλάσσης καὶ σάλου; again, as in v. 11, the coming of the Son of Man will be portended by signs in the heavens and on the earth.

Within these statements of Jesus' one hears echoes of Josephus's description of the fall of Jerusalem discussed in the previous chapter.[3] There,

---

2. Maddox, *Purpose of Luke-Acts*, 118, notes that technically, the answer that Jesus gives does not answer the questions posed to him. He argues that the questions are actually answered by Jesus' statement in 21:20–24, which speaks of the destruction of Jerusalem.

3. See McCasland, "Portents," 323–35. Given the portents in Josephus, McCasland maintains that Jewish and Gentile auditors of the gospels would have fully comprehended the heavenly signs which are associated with Jesus' death in the gospels. In the context of that passage, I also noted a similar passage in 2 Macc 5, as well as Tacitus, *Hist.* 5.13. This connection has been noted by several scholars; see, e.g., L. Johnson, *Luke*, 321; Klein, *Lukasevangelium*, 647 n. 42. The OT apocalyptic background has also been referenced; see I. H. Marshall, *Luke*, 765; Green, *Luke*, 740; Bock, *Luke 9:51—24:53*, 1667, 1682–83. See also Dodd, "Fall of Jerusalem," 69–83. Dodd argues that Luke has not simply redacted Mark in light of historical events surrounding the Romans' conquest of Jerusalem in 70 CE. Dodd maintains that Luke's portrayal of these events has been influenced by the OT prophets' descriptions of the fall of Jerusalem to the Babylonians.

Divine Testimony through Deeds in Luke-Acts

I argued that the divine testimony through portents in the sky functioned as a prophetic warning to the people in Jerusalem. Here, they function in a similar fashion. Jesus, speaking authoritatively as a prophet,[4] tells the people that the fall of Jerusalem and his coming will be accompanied by God's testimony through signs in the heavens and on the earth; therefore, they should be ready for these two events.

But there is a second, less explicit function of the divine testimony through signs in the heavens in this passage, especially seen in 21:11. Green recognizes two points of focus in Luke 20:1—21:4; these are: (i) the authority that has been given to Jesus by God; and (ii) the perceived authority on the part of the Jewish leaders in Jerusalem and God's lack of approval for them.[5] Through Jesus' prediction of the fall of Jerusalem and his own return through the *topos* of divine testimony, he is portrayed to the ancient auditor as the authoritative prophet, one who is able to understand how God is interacting with the world. At the same time, the divine testimony serves to discredit his opponents, in this case the religious leaders associated with the temple. I have already demonstrated in chapter two how divine testimony was used in the law courts to portray a client in a positive light, and to cast a negative light on an opponent. This was seen in the examples from histories and biographies previously analyzed, and can be noticed here as well.

---

4. L. Johnson, *Luke*, 325, along with many others, notes the emphasis on Jesus as a prophet in this passage. He argues that Luke is writing after the historical fall of Jerusalem, in an environment in which Christians are being persecuted. Jesus, in the greater context in which this passage is found, predicts the persecution of Christians, the destruction of Jerusalem, and his parousia. Because the implied reader already knows that the first two have occurred, the reader can be assured of the veracity of the third prediction.

5. Green, *Luke*, 731. Talbert, *Reading Luke*, 221–22, sees a warning in four parts to the religious leaders in Jerusalem in 19:45—20:18; (i) the religious leaders have failed in their duty to tend to the needs of the people of God (19:45–46); (ii) the religious leaders who have failed will be replaced (19:47a); (iii) the religious leaders fail to recognize the true source of their authority, namely God, and have assumed their own authority (20:1–19); and (iv) because of these issues the religious leaders must be replaced (20:16). Bloomquist ("Rhetorical Argumentation," 173–209), through an intertextual analysis of 19:47—21:38, also finds a focus on the authority of Jesus as compared to the hypocrisy of the religious leaders. Bloomquist argues that Jesus' familiarity with the signs seen in 21:11, 25, sets him apart as holding true authority.

The *Topos* of Divine Testimony in Luke/Acts

Luke 23:44–45

In this passage, narrating the death of Jesus, the narrator makes this comment: Καὶ ἦν ἤδη ὡσεὶ ὥρα ἕκτη καὶ σκότος ἐγένετο ἐφ' ὅλην τὴν γῆν ἕως ὥρας ἐνάτης τοῦ ἡλίου ἐκλιπόντος, ἐσχίσθη δὲ τὸ καταπέτασμα τοῦ ναοῦ μέσον (Luke 23:44–45). The unusual darkness is emphasized through the temporal statement that it was already the sixth hour, and that the darkness lasted three hours. Thus the reader understands that this darkness is not a natural occurrence. The source of the darkness is explained to be through an eclipse of the sun.[6] There is an accompanying occurrence which reinforces the testimony through the eclipse; simultaneously the veil of the temple is divided down the middle. Thus, as was shown in previous examples to be the norm in Greco-Roman narratives, the death of Jesus elicits testimony from God, which serves to characterize both him and those who put him to death.[7]

Within the immediate context one also finds the theme of prayer. Directly following the statement of the divine testimony, Jesus cries out: "Πάτερ, εἰς χεῖράς σου παρατίθεμαι τὸ πνεῦμά μου" (23:46), an echo of LXX Ps 30:6. Therefore, through the emphasized unusual nature of the darkness, the multiple actions so characteristic of divine testimony, and Jesus' prayer in the immediate context, the auditor is assured that the eclipse of the sun is the work of God, and not a natural occurrence.

In this passage one is reminded of the eclipse of the sun that occurred at the death of Caesar discussed earlier.[8] In the case of Caesar, I argued that the darkening of the sun was a testimony of the gods' displeasure over Caesar's death (thus portraying Caesar as being in favor with the gods), as well as a condemnation of his murderers. Here, I find the same function of the divine testimony. Again, events and statements within the immediate context are helpful. In 23:47, after the centurion, who is standing at the

---

6. A variant in 23:45 helps to emphasize the unusual nature of the eclipse. In A C³ W Δ Θ and Ψ (among other witnesses), τοῦ ἡλίου ἐκλιπόντος is replaced by καὶ ἐσκοτίσθη ὁ ἥλιος. Metzger maintains that this would be an easier reading than τοῦ ἡλίου ἐκλιπόντος, thus justifying τοῦ ἡλίου ἐκλιπόντος as the more likely reading. See Metzger, *Textual Commentary*, 155. Fitzmyer, *Luke X-XXIV*, 1512, notes that Luke adds the reason for the darkness ("the sun's light failed") in v. 45a to Mark's account in Mark 15:33–40a (cf. Matt 27:45–55a).

7. Several scholars mention that it is usual for signs to accompany the death of the protagonist in Greco-Roman literature. See, e.g., Green, *Luke*, 824–25; Talbert, *Reading Luke*, 253.

8. In Plutarch's account of Caesar's death, however, the sun's intensity was lessened and it lasted for an entire year.

cross overseeing Jesus' crucifixion, observes these things,⁹ he ἐδόξαζεν τὸν θεὸν λέγων, "Ὄντως ὁ ἄνθρωπος οὗτος δίκαιος ἦν. By praising God after experiencing τὸ γενόμενον, the centurion attributes the death of Jesus and the events surrounding it to God himself. And when he states that Ὄντως ὁ ἄνθρωπος οὗτος δίκαιος ἦν, he is reinforcing through words what the auditor has already experienced through the divine testimony of the eclipse.

The words of the centurion certainly relate to Jesus' innocence. The entire passage up to this point has emphasized his lack of guilt as he endures various trials (cf. 23:4, 14, 22 [Pilate]; 23:15 [Herod]; 23:40–41 [thief]),¹⁰ therefore portraying the death of Jesus as an innocent martyr.¹¹ Thus the divine testimony, given its forensic sense, contributes to the audience's perception that Jesus truly is innocent. The audience has heard from disparate characters within the narrative that Jesus is innocent; at this point they hear from God.

But scholars also recognize, perhaps more significantly, that Jesus dies as a righteous, obedient son.¹² Through his death he is portrayed as "the Messiah who through his life and death brings healing and salvation to the people,"¹³ whose death God will vindicate through the resurrection.¹⁴ The divine testimony through the eclipse assists in this portrayal of Jesus, especially when seen in conjunction with earlier instances of divine testimony in Jesus' career.¹⁵ God's testimony at Jesus' death thus reinforces

9. Exactly to what the centurion is reacting in the text is somewhat ambiguous; the participial clause preceding the centurion's reaction and statement simply states Ἰδὼν δὲ ... τὸ γενόμενον.

10. Tannehill, *Luke*, 198, in discussing Pilate's role in Jesus' death, argues that the focus of 23:13–25 is Jesus' innocence.

11. Talbert, *Reading Luke*, 252–53, lists four meanings for Jesus' death in Luke's gospel, the first of which is Jesus as the "model martyr." The other three include Jesus' death as a "covenant sacrifice," the fulfillment of prophecy and thus concord with God's plan, and his death as the "unredeemed firstborn."

12. See Talbert, *Reading Luke*, 253, who argues that Jesus' death is primarily the death of a righteous person, and secondarily the death of an innocent person. See also Johnson, *Luke*, 382, and Matera, "The Death of Jesus," 481–82. For a comparison of Jesus' death to the death of Socrates, through which it is argued that "Jesus dies well and nobly," see Kloppenborg, "*Exitus clari viri*," 106–20. See also Sterling, "Mors Philosophi," 383–402.

13. Johnson, *Luke*, 384.

14. Talbert reads Luke's account of Jesus' passion as a theodicy; see Talbert, *Reading Luke*, 252: "God does not leave the righteous one abandoned."

15. Here I am thinking specifically of God's spoken testimony at Jesus' baptism (see discussion on Luke 3:21–22 below) and at the transfiguration (Luke 9:28–36; I treated this passage in a previous chapter on divine testimony through utterances).

what the audience has been hearing throughout the narrative through diverse testimonies of God, portraying Jesus as the righteous, beloved Son of God.

Finally, in considering the testimony to Jesus' righteousness and his wrongful death, one must also consider the negative testimony of the eclipse and the ensuing portrayal of those responsible for that wrongful death. Matera argues that the centurion's praise of God functions to demonstrate that Jesus, "not the religious leaders, stands in right relationship to God."[16] The eclipse also functions to reinforce this aspect of Jesus' death. As seen in Plutarch's account of Caesar's death (and in others), the testimony serves as a negative portrayal of those responsible for the death of one favored by the gods. So it is here, as well.

In sum, it can be readily seen that divine testimony through events in the heavens (i) is found in Luke-Acts as it is in other ancient narratives and biographies; and (ii) this particular form of the gods' testimony functions in similar ways in Luke-Acts, including God's warnings of a future event, or a testimony of God's disfavor with an event that has already taken place. Significantly, as seen throughout this study, the function of this form of divine testimony in Luke-Acts is to affirm or discredit a character in the narrative.

Divine Testimony through Birds

In Luke-Acts, birds are often mentioned; however, they are the subjects of sayings of Jesus (Luke 9:58; 12:24), appear in parables (Luke 8:5; 13:19), appear in Peter's vision (Acts 10:12; 11:6), or are mentioned as sacrificial victims (Luke 2:24). There are no narratives which describe the singing of birds; only Luke 3:21–22, the account of Jesus' baptism, describes a bird in flight.

> Ἐγένετο δὲ ἐν τῷ βαπτισθῆναι ἅπαντα τὸν λαὸν καὶ Ἰησοῦ βαπτισθέντος καὶ προσευχομένου ἀνεῳχθῆναι τὸν οὐρανὸν καὶ καταβῆναι τὸ πνεῦμα τὸ ἅγιον σωματικῷ εἴδει ὡς περιστερὰν ἐπ' αὐτόν, καὶ φωνὴν ἐξ οὐρανοῦ γενέσθαι· σὺ εἶ ὁ υἱός μου ὁ ἀγαπητός, ἐν σοὶ εὐδόκησα. (Luke 3:21–22)[17]

16. Matera, "The Death of Jesus," 485.

17. Similar descriptions of this event are also found in Mark 1:10–11 and Matt 3:16–17. Fuchs notes that recently some scholars have suggested that Luke and Matthew have drawn their accounts of Jesus' baptism from Q, rather than Mark. Fuchs argues, however, that the agreements between Luke and Matthew are better explained

Divine Testimony through Deeds in Luke-Acts

The descent of the dove in this passage, clearly a symbol for the descent of the Holy Spirit, would most certainly have been understood by an ancient auditor as an instance of divine testimony through the flight of birds.

The narrative occurs at a pivotal moment in the account of Jesus' ministry. Jesus' birth and childhood have been described;[18] Jesus is now on the verge of beginning his earthly ministry.[19] The context of prayer is also emphasized. Only in Luke's gospel is Jesus described as being in prayer at his baptism (Ἐγένετο δὲ ἐν τῷ βαπτισθῆναι ἅπαντα τὸν λαὸν καὶ Ἰησοῦ βαπτισθέντες καὶ προσευχομένου).[20] Finally, as was seen in the analysis of ancient narratives above, this form of divine testimony through the flight of a bird is combined with another form of divine testimony, in this case through utterances.

That the bird is of divine origins is beyond question. First, within the narrative the auditor learns that "the heaven was opened [ἀνεῳχθῆναι τὸν οὐρανὸν]" before the descent of the dove. Next, one learns that it is actually the Holy Spirit which descends; the bird image serves only as a description of the divine event.[21] Third, the divine voice is also assigned a heavenly origin: "a voice came from heaven [καὶ φωνὴν ἐξ οὐρανοῦ γενέσθαι]." Thus it is clear that it is God who is testifying through both the image of the bird and the voice.

---

by a deutero-Markan source, rather than Q. See Fuchs, "Agreements," 5–34; for the same claim, argued from different passages, cf. idem, "Die Sadduzäerfrage," 83–110; idem, "Mehr als Davids Sohn," 111–28.

18. The birth account, of course, is replete with the testimony of the gods and would have been considered the standard method of portraying the beginning of the life of a hero in ancient biography. This topic will be considered in the category of dreams and visions. On the influence of the divine on the early careers of the subjects of ancient biographies, see esp. Talbert, "Prophecies," 129–41; see also idem, "Miraculous Conceptions and Births," in 79–86.

19. L. Johnson (*Luke*, 70) argues that this passage, along with the genealogy of Jesus in Luke 3:23–38, answers the question, "Who is Jesus?"

20. Tannehill also makes this point. He helpfully notes that prayer and revelation are often combined in Luke-Acts. See Tannehill, *Luke*, 56. See also Green, *Luke*, 185; Talbert, *Reading Luke*, 42. Cf. Werline, *Pray Like This*, 124, who also makes this observation; Werline, however, points out that Luke in this scene has also combined the reception of the Spirit with prayer and revelation. Plymale (*Prayer Texts*, 112) argues that Luke often includes prayer "before events that prove to be significant manifestations of God's saving activity." At this point, Plymale does not specifically mention this passage, but 3:21–22 would certainly qualify as such a manifestation.

21. Nolland notes that the description through the Greek word ὡς represents the "language of approximation"; Nolland, *Luke 1–9:20*, 161.

The *Topos* of Divine Testimony in Luke/Acts

The function of the testimony is also clear, given the examples of divine testimony noted earlier.[22] Through the sending of the Holy Spirit, described as the flight of a bird "in bodily form like a dove [σωματικῷ εἴδει ὡς περιστερὰν]," God is empowering[23] his son Jesus for his impending

---

22. The examples analyzed in the previous chapter demonstrate the significance of birds as testimonies of the gods at important points in the narrative. Talbert discusses the example of Numa at his coronation as found in Plutarch's *Life* of Numa as an apt parallel for Jesus' baptism. Given this episode in the life of Numa in which the flight of birds played such a noteworthy role, Talbert states: "In such a thought-world the Lukan narrative would be viewed as an omen of Jesus' status. Exactly what that status was can be discerned from the bird involved, a dove, and the interpreting voice from heaven"; see Talbert, *Reading Luke*, 42. Regarding the dove, Talbert cites the work of Goodenough, *Pagan Symbols*. In this volume, Goodenough, examining art and literary objects, demonstrates that in early Greece, the dove was a symbol of erotic love, but later came to be seen as a symbol of "divinity and divine love and life" (ibid., 31), in addition to its association with the departed soul of a deceased person (34). He concludes this section by stating: "The bird, especially the dove, has come in many situations to suggest an association with soul, immortality, and love, three conceptions which are really one since the first two mean life directly, and since also love is life." In early Christianity, Goodenough argues that the emphasis on love continued, and that the dove represented the love shared by God and humanity, and therefore the future hope of immortality which could only be realized through that love (41). Others have attempted to ascertain the meaning behind the dove imagery. Keck ("Spirit and the Dove," 41–67) argued that the phrase ὡς περιστερὰν in Mark 1:10 (Keck studied the dove imagery in all four gospels, as well as in extra-biblical sources) is "ambiguous" in reference to its grammatical function, because it is a Greek translation of the Hebrew *kywnh*, which is adverbial in nature and originally described the action (as opposed to the physical appearance) of the Spirit. As this Jewish tradition was picked up in Christian circles, "the Jewish simile was no longer understood or recalled, and was reified into a phenomenon" (ibid., 63). Gero ("Spirit as a Dove," 17–35) argues that the gospel tradition represents a conflation of two earlier traditions, one from the Gospel of Hebrews (which represents a pre-Marcan tradition) in which the Spirit descends on Jesus, and a second from the 24th Ode of Solomon, in which a dove descends on the Messiah. Dörrfuß ("'Wie eine Taube,'" 7–13) provides a third suggestion; he claims, similar to Keck, that ὡς περιστερὰν is a Greek expression for the Hebrew *kywnh*, but more specifically from the words of Ben Zoma in a commentary on Gen 1:2. Thus this image, in conjunction with God's statement of approval of Jesus, serves to project the dove as a messenger of the relationship between Father and Son. Poon ("Background," 33–49), provides the most comprehensive survey of sources from the OT, the ancient world, and first-century (and later) Judaism. He concludes, based primarily on rabbinic evidence, that the dove imagery serves to connect Jesus with Israel. See also Manns, "La symbolique animale," 255–67; Manns surveys Jewish literature as well as patristic references to Jesus' baptism, concluding that the dove as the Holy Spirit is simply a symbolic attempt to represent the mystery of God, which cannot be adequately described.

23. Talbert, *Reading Luke*, 41–42, argues that Luke shares this perspective with Mark; in Luke, however, the empowerment is directly connected to prayer, while in

mission, and at the same time is sanctioning this mission. This is complemented by the words spoken by the heavenly voice which expresses the love God has for his son.[24]

This function of divine testimony through the flight and singing of birds aligns well with the findings from ancient narratives. There, I argued that birds appear at significant moments in the narratives, and that birds are often used as the gods' testimony of their preference for an individual or group of characters. Here, at Jesus' baptism, it is no different. The testimony of God through the flight of the dove (and confirmed through God's direct testimony through speech), occurring in the context of prayer, is a direct affirmation of Jesus and his impending ministry.

Divine Testimony through Sounds and Fire (from Heaven)

In this section, as before, I will consider those passages in Luke-Acts which mention fire from heaven as well as storms. From this discussion I hope to demonstrate that these types of divine testimony do indeed appear in Luke-Acts and that they function in the same manner as in the examples already discussed.

Luke 9:52–56

The narrative context of Luke 9:52–56 is the beginning of Jesus' journey to Jerusalem, narrated in Luke 9:51—19:44. The journey is announced in 9:51; 9:52–56 is the opening section of 9:51—10:24.[25] According to

---

Mark it is associated with the act of baptism.

24. Klein, *Lukasevangelium*, 170, maintains that the voice is the predominant focus of the passage (the "zentrale Aussagung"), while the events described by the rest of the passage, including the flight of the dove, are "Begleiterscheinungen." Given the results of the analysis in this study, I would argue, however, that both forms of divine testimony are equal in the statement which they are making, namely the legitimation and sanction of Jesus and his mission. Certainly the words spoken by the heavenly voice are clearer and require less interpretation. But the dove descending on Jesus would have been no less powerful a statement of testimony to an ancient auditor. Green, *Luke*, 187, argues that the divine voice is "providing an unimpeachable sanction of Jesus with regard to his identity and mission."

25. See Talbert, *Reading Luke*, 121. Talbert sees an A / B / A´ pattern, the A (9:52–56) and A´ (10:1–24) elements dealing with Jesus sending out his disciples, while the core of the chiasm (B; 9:57–62) is concerned with the cost of following Jesus as one of

The *Topos* of Divine Testimony in Luke/Acts

Talbert, this section of text is concerned with explaining "guidelines to govern missionary behavior."[26] In this short passage, Jesus sends his disciples into a Samaritan village to prepare for his arrival; the Samaritans, however, are not amenable to Jesus' visit. James and John then ask Jesus if they should call down fire from heaven to destroy the village (Κύριε, θέλεις εἴπωμεν πῦρ καταβῆναι ἀπὸ τοῦ οὐρανοῦ καὶ ἀναλῶσαι αὐτούς; Luke 9:54). Jesus, however, rebukes them and goes on to find a more hospitable place.

This passage is almost universally considered to be an echo of Elijah's destruction of two groups of fifty soldiers through fire from heaven, as found in 2 Kgs 1.[27] The discussion here is therefore not to try to find a 'better' interpretation of this passage by viewing it through the lens of divine testimony; rather, my intent is to argue that a Greco-Roman auditor with no knowledge of the Elijah incident would also have been able to ascertain a similar meaning from the passage, given the prevalence of divine testimony in the ancient world.

I have demonstrated that divine testimony through fire from heaven, especially in the case of lightning, is seen as punishment of the ods, and therefore an extremely negative testimony toward the recipient. That is certainly the function of the fire here, as in the context of 2 Kgs 1.[28] Thus an ancient auditor would likewise have understood James and John's question to be one of, "Shouldn't these Samaritans be punished for not welcoming you?"

The function of this divine testimony is seen in multiple ways. Primarily, Jesus is cast in a positive light by his refusal to allow the divine testimony to occur.[29] Jesus, in declining to invoke the divine testimony, overturns the convention of the gods punishing those who are deemed impious. Secondarily, the disciples are portrayed as not understanding Jesus' mission and therefore what it means to be a disciple of Jesus.[30] They

---

his disciples.

26. Talbert, *Reading Luke*, 121.

27. See, e.g. Nolland, *Luke 9:21—18:34*, 536; Green, *Luke*, 405–406; Fitzmyer, *Luke I-IX*, 827, 830. The most complete treatment of this position is found in Brodie, "Departure," 96–109. Brodie argues that Luke has intentionally imitated the passage from the LXX and modified it through abbreviation and improvement to suit his purposes.

28. Tannehill, *Luke*, 251, associates the fire here with the fire of judgment.

29. Green, *Luke*, 406, claims that Jesus represents an "anti-type" of Elijah in this passage. Dochhorn ("Die Verschonung," 359–78) maintains that Jesus' refusal to destroy the village is "due to soteriological reasons"; the suffering he must endure is not compatible with this type of response.

30. This reinforces what for Green is a major theme of the travel narrative, namely

are not in harmony with the one they are following, and are thus rebuked by him.

Acts 2:1–13

The overall context of Acts is significant here. Talbert has demonstrated that there are two main missionary movements in Acts. The first (Acts 2–12) is inaugurated by the coming of the Holy Spirit, which I will consider below. The second (Acts 13–28), is initiated with an equally significant event, the calling of Saul (Acts 9).[31] Therefore, Acts 2:1–4 is found at a pivotal point in the narrative; as I have shown, divine testimony is quite common at such turns in the plot.

In the immediate context of this passage, the disciples are gathered together in obedience to Jesus' command to remain in Jerusalem until they receive "the promise of the Father" (Acts 1:4). They also know, through Jesus' words, that they will be empowered to fulfill their vocation as worldwide witnesses (μάρτυρες) when the Holy Spirit comes (Acts 1:8). The disciples are also portrayed as being in prayer as they wait (cf. Acts 1:14), thus supplying the normal context of piety that so often sets the stage for the testimony of the gods.

Here, too, at Pentecost, in the context of the disciples at prayer, God testifies through a loud noise from heaven (καὶ ἐγένετο ἄφνω ἐκ τοῦ οὐρανοῦ ἦχος ὥσπερ φερομένης πνοῆς βιαίας; Acts 2:2) as well as tongues of fire which appear over each of the disciples (καὶ ὤφθησαν αὐτοῖς διαμεριζόμεναι γλῶσσαι ὡσεὶ πυρός, καὶ ἐκάθισεν ἐφ' ἕνα ἕκαστον αὐτῶν; Acts 2:3). Therefore, in the context of a group of people praying, God testifies in two different ways: through a loud noise and tongues of fire.[32]

---

the "obduracy" of the disciples. See Green, *Luke*, 394–99, 406.

31. The fact that the second movement, found in Acts 13–28, is initiated by an event which takes place in Acts 9 is an example of Lucian's chain-link principle, as noted by Talbert, *Reading Acts*, 82; Parsons, *Acts*, 17. Lucian states that "when [a historian] has finished the first topic he will introduce the second, fastened to it and linked with it like a chain . . . ; always the first and second topics must not merely be neighbors but have common matter and overlap" (Lucian, *How to Write History*, 55).

32. Most commentators recognize the allusions to the giving of the Law at Sinai in Exodus. See, e.g., Talbert, *Reading Acts*, 23; Parsons, *Acts*, 37; L. Johnson, *Acts*, 46; Fitzmyer, *Acts*, 233–34; Pervo, *Acts*, 61. A somewhat tempered acceptance is offered by Witherington, *Acts*, 131. Talbert, followed by Parsons, goes the furthest in this association. Talbert argues that the feast of Pentecost had come to be associated with the giving of the Law, and that this scene should therefore be considered "typological writing," in that Luke is therefore drawing on these images in describing the giving

The *Topos* of Divine Testimony in Luke/Acts

The divine origin of these events is clearly stated by the narrator; the loud noise is ἐκ τοῦ οὐρανοῦ. The auditor thus understands that both the loud noise and the fire are divine manifestations, and serve as testimonies on behalf of the disciples. These divine testimonies are then confirmed through a further event, the speaking in different languages and/or the understanding of those languages by the crowds assembled in Jerusalem (cf. Acts 2:5–12).

Therefore, the first significant event in the Book of Acts following Jesus' ascension is accompanied by two instances of divine testimony and a confirmatory sign.[33] This is clearly a major movement in the plot of Acts, and its significance is signaled by the use of the *topos* of divine testimony.[34] Here, in Acts 2, it would be possible for an ancient auditor to have understood God's testimony as functioning as it did in the example of fire from the head of L. Marcius or Servio Tullius, or the fire hovering over Timoleon's ship as described by Plutarch.[35] Just as the gods show their approval of Timoleon's mission to Sicily through an accompanying flame over his ship, here, through the testimony of the loud noise and tongues of fire, God is sanctioning the mission of the disciples to be witnesses for Jesus.[36]

---

of a new covenant. For arguments against the connection between Acts 2:1–13 and the giving of the Law at Sinai, see Lohse, "Bedeutung," 422–36; and I. H. Marshall, "Significance," 347–69. Lohse prefers to interpret the Pentecost event in Acts under the rubric of promise-fulfillment, as does Marshall.

My point concerning this passage is not to attempt to overthrow the scholarly consensus of the theophanic imagery as seen on Mt. Sinai in Exodus in Luke's description. I am simply trying to point out other, perhaps more subtle, allusions in the text that would have been available to ancient auditors familiar with divine testimony through fire from heaven in the Greco-Roman milieu.

33. The use of divine testimony is not limited to the loud noise like wind and the coming of the Spirit like tongues of fire. As is quite usual, the meaning of the divine testimony is then explained through a speech, in this case by Peter in Acts 2:14–36. Within the speech, Peter uses the *topos* of divine testimony through utterances (citing Jewish scripture) as part of his explanation/proof. This use of the *topos* was discussed in chapter four. See also Parsons, *Acts*, 43.

34. Parsons, *Acts*, 37–38, also notes the use of ekphrastic language in the description of the wind and fire, arguing that this, too, signals to the auditor a momentous event in the plot of the narrative.

35. On L. Marcius, see above on Livy, *Hist.* 25.39.16; for S. Tullius, see above on Dionysius of Halicarnassus, *Ant. rom.* 4.2.2 (cf. Livy, *Hist.* 1.39.2). The stories concerning L. Marcius and S. Tullius as found in Livy are listed as parallels to this passage by Horst, "Hellenistic Parallels," 49–60. Plutarch's account of Timoleon is not listed, however, by Horst.

36. Also important is that the incident in Plutarch's account of Timoleon is seen by the soothsayers as a fulfillment of prophecy. In Peter's speech following Pentecost,

This is also comparable to Jesus' baptism in Luke 3.[37] In addition to the purpose of demonstrating God's approval of the disciples and their mission, the divine testimony also functions as the fulfillment of the prophecy in Luke 3:16; 24:49; Acts 1:4–5, and 1:8.[38] This reinforces the portrayal of Jesus as a reliable prophet which has already been seen in Luke's gospel.

Acts 27:1—28:10

In my analysis of the use of this form of the *topos* in the Greco-Roman and Jewish histories and lives, I decided to treat storms in this category of divine testimony and provided examples of storms from the gods which were considered testimonies of punishment. Clearly, there are storm scenes in Luke-Acts that should be considered under this heading. Here, I will limit myself to the storm which occurs during Paul's sea voyage to Rome, narrated in Acts 27:1—28:10.

It is important to consider the overall context of Acts in which the sea voyage occurs. Paul has undergone trials in Jerusalem (21:17—23:11) and Caesarea (before Felix, 24:1–27; before Festus, 25:1–27; before Agrippa, 26:1–32), and is now on his way to stand trial in Rome. At the end of all these proceedings, Paul has been found to be innocent (cf. Agrippa's statement in 26:31: Οὐδὲν θανάτου ἢ δεσμῶν ἄξιον πράσσει ὁ ἄνθρωπος οὗτος; he then adds this statement: Ἀπολελύσθαι ἐδύνατο ὁ ἄνθρωπος οὗτος εἰ μὴ ἐπεκέκλητο Καίσαρα [26:32]).[39] Therefore, the context of Paul's innocence is extremely important to keep in mind when reading the account of the sea voyage.[40]

Paul, therefore, having demanded an audience before the Roman emperor (25:11), is assigned to a Roman centurion and placed on a ship, heading west along the Asian coast. In 27:9, the auditor learns that it is

---

in which he explains the divine testimony to the crowd, Peter argues that the events of Pentecost are also the fulfillment of prophecy. I considered this in some detail in chapter four.

37. Several commentators rightly see the parallels between this event and the events surrounding Jesus' baptism; see, e.g., Tannehill, *Luke*, 57; Green, *Luke*, 186; Talbert, *Reading Luke*, 44. In both situations, God sends the Holy Spirit and thus testifies through different means to the legitimacy and significance of the mission of both Jesus and the disciples.

38. Talbert, *Reading Acts*, 24–25.

39. See also 23:29; 25:25.

40. See Talbert, *Reading Acts*, 218, who also notes the significance of the narrative up to this point.

past the season for safe sea travel; because of this, Paul makes a prediction: Ἄνδρες, θεωρῶ ὅτι μετὰ ὕβρεως καὶ πολλῆς ζημίας οὐ μόνον τοῦ φορτίου καὶ τοῦ πλοίου ἀλλὰ καὶ τῶν ψυχῶν ἡμῶν μέλλειν ἔσεσθαι τὸν πλοῦν (27:10). Note well that no divine agency is given for this prophetic statement.[41] In the ensuing narrative, the auditor will learn that this prophecy of Paul's is only partially correct. Paul's prediction is ignored, and the ship sets sail once again (27:12).[42]

The storm and its effects are described in 27:13–44; its intensity is heightened by a reference to the sun and stars in 27:20a: μήτε δὲ ἡλίου μήτε ἄστρων ἐπιφαινόντων ἐπὶ πλείονας ἡμέρας, χειμῶνός τε οὐκ ὀλίγου ἐπικειμένου. The violence of the storm also adversely affects the attitude of those on board the ship: λοιπὸν περιῃρεῖτο ἐλπὶς πᾶσα τοῦ σῴζεσθαι ἡμᾶς (27:20b). At this point, it seems as if Paul's prediction will come to pass. The auditor, however, learns that Paul has received a vision, a testimony from God, in which Paul learns two things: (i) he must (note the use of δεῖ in 27:24) reach his goal of having an audience with the emperor; and (ii) God has guaranteed that all the crew will be saved along with him. Therefore, through the divine testimony of a vision, the source of which is explicitly divine,[43] Paul's initial prediction of loss of ship and even life is revised to reflect God's testimony to Paul through the vision. God's testimony in the immediate context thus serves primarily as an encouragement to Paul, that he and the others on the ship will survive the storm.[44] At the same time, it functions as a divine sanction of Paul's decision to go to Rome to appear before the emperor.[45]

As the narrative unfolds, the auditor learns that this is indeed the case. Paul, however, is not a passive observer as God brings him and those

---

41. Talbert, *Reading Acts*, 213, notes that Paul's statement is based purely on knowledge of the current season and the bad weather associated with it.

42. As the narrative continues, the narrator's statement in 27:9 proves to be more ominous: Ἱκανοῦ δὲ χρόνου διαγενομένου καὶ ὄντος ἤδη ἐπισφαλοῦς τοῦ πλοὸς διὰ τὸ καὶ τὴν νηστείαν ἤδη παρεληλυθέναι.

43. The vision was of an angel (παρέστη γάρ μοι ταύτῃ νυκτὶ τοῦ θεοῦ οὗ εἰμι [ἐγώ], ᾧ καὶ λατρεύω, ἄγγελος; 27:23), who acts as a spokesperson for God.

44. Parsons, *Acts*, 356. S. Praeder ("Acts 27:1—28:16," 700–701, 705) argues that Paul's prophecy that all will survive the shipwreck is a deviation from conventional Greco-Roman sea voyage accounts. For the purposes of this study, it is significant that Paul's statement to the crew to this effect is based upon an instance of divine testimony, thus emphasizing to the ancient auditor familiar with these stories God's favor shown to Paul through the testimony of the vision.

45. Paul repeats the revised prophecy at 27:34: οὐδενὸς γὰρ ὑμῶν θρὶξ ἀπὸ τῆς κεφαλῆς ἀπολεῖται.

Divine Testimony through Deeds in Luke-Acts

on the ship through the storm. Rather, Paul must take measures in order to ensure that all indeed survive the shipwreck. For example, at a certain point during the storm, some of the sailors attempt to escape from the ship; Paul realizes through the vision that it is important that all stay on the ship (27:27–32),[46] and he convinces the sailors to remain on board. Paul is therefore portrayed as being in harmony with the divine testimony he has received, working to bring about its fulfillment.[47] Later, the crew of the ship is negatively portrayed through their desire to escape the ship. At another point, the soldiers plot to kill the prisoners, but the centurion intercedes on the prisoners' behalf (27:42–43). Therefore, he, too, is cast in a favorable light, as his actions are determined by the divine testimony given to Paul.

After the shipwreck, those who had been on board the ship are stranded on Malta, where they are warmly received by the natives. While gathering wood for a fire, a snake bites Paul on the hand. As has been shown in the examples in the previous chapter, snakes are often used as negative testimony from the gods. The natives' reaction is in line with this perception. They say to one another, Πάντως φονεύς ἐστιν ὁ ἄνθρωπος οὗτος ὃν διασωθέντα ἐκ τῆς θαλάσσης ἡ δίκη ζῆν οὐκ εἴασεν (28:4), thus revealing their opinion that the storm and the snake are of divine origin. Here, as in Plutarch's account from the *Life* of Alexander (see previous chapter), the perception on the part of the natives (and perhaps the ancient auditors) is that the storm represents some type of divine condemnation.[48]

In this passage, the direct divine testimony of a vision to Paul, along with the overcoming of the "trials" of storm and snake bite, both examples

---

46. Pervo, *Acts*, 660, argues that the significance of all being saved from the shipwreck symbolizes the message of God's universal salvation that Paul proclaims.

47. At this point one is reminded of Plutarch's account of Alexander at Tyre, discussed earlier in the previous chapter (*Alex.* 25).

48. Talbert and Hays rightly point out that this is a "category 3" storm; they describe this category as a storm of other than divine cause but with a divine outcome. Talbert and Hays, "Theology of Sea Storms," 270. See also Talbert, *Reading Acts*, 215.

Luke 8:22–25 is the account of Jesus calming a storm while he and the disciples cross the lake. Similar to the account in the life of Alexander, a divine agent is not given for the storm. However, the storm functions in a similar manner as in Acts 27 and the Alexander account; it is an obstacle. But in Luke, instead of Jesus and the disciples safely navigating through the storm to the other side (overcoming the obstacle, as Paul and Alexander do), Jesus *removes* the storm. Viewing the account through the *topos* of divine testimony, one sees that not only is Jesus capable of not allowing the storm to have a negative effect on him, he is able to completely master the storm. The disciples' reaction (8:25) may also reflect the storm as a divine testimony; if the disciples saw the storm as a negative sign from supernatural powers, who is this Jesus who has mastery even over these powers responsible for the storm?

of an "implied," negative divine testimony, serve as divine affirmations of Paul's innocence.[49] Also, through the vision, Paul's piety and trust in God is highlighted. Because of the vision, Paul is willing to revise his first prediction, made without having heard from God. In the narrative, Paul is also willing to do whatever is necessary to remain in God's will, revealed through the testimony of the dream. Paul intervenes when some of the sailors attempt to escape from the ship (27:30–32), and encourages the crew to eat (27:33–34) in order that they might survive the impending shipwreck.[50]

I argued earlier that fire from heaven in the Greco-Roman narratives functioned as punishment as well as divine affirmation of characters, depending on the context. Storms in these narratives displayed the displeasure of the gods, but also allowed characters to show their resilience in overcoming obstacles. In the examples from Luke-Acts, one recognizes that this form of the *topos* is familiar to Luke, and it would have been heard by Greco-Roman auditors in similar ways. John and James seek to punish the Samaritan village through fire from heaven. The image of fire at Pentecost, however, also serves to affirm and sanction the disciples' newly empowered vocation as witnesses, ἕως ἐσχάτου τῆς γῆς (Acts 1:8). The storm in Acts 27 is understood on a narrative level by characters as the punishment of some god or gods (along with the bite of a snake); Paul, however, overcomes both of these as demonstrations of his innocence.

---

49. Talbert, *Reading Acts*, 210–11, 216. Talbert argues persuasively that the purpose of the passage is twofold, namely to demonstrate: (i) Paul's innocence; and (ii) that God's plan cannot be thwarted. As I argue here, it should be recognized that Paul's actions after the dream demonstrate his efforts to align himself with the divine plan. He is certainly not simply a passive observer of what God is doing. On the innocence of Paul, see also L. Johnson, *Acts*, 466; Tannehill, *Acts*, 341. Cf. also Clabeaux, who maintains that Luke uses the incidents of shipwreck and snakebite to portray Paul's death, which is comparable to Jesus' death. Both are accused, and both are found to be innocent. Clabeaux, however, overreaches in his argument, claiming that Paul's shipwreck and the fire on the beach are linked to John's prophecy of Jesus, who would baptize with the Holy Spirit and fire. See Clabeaux, "Maltese Viper," 604–10.

50. The centurion assigned to Paul is also similarly portrayed. When the soldiers decide to kill the prisoners, he prevents them from doing so. The centurion is described as βουλόμενος διασῶσαι τὸν Παῦλον (27:43), and is therefore cast in a favorable light in the narrative.

Divine Testimony through Deeds in Luke-Acts

Divine Testimony through Dreams and Visions

There are several examples of dreams and visions in Luke-Acts. I will consider many of these passages here, while others which could be analyzed under this category were examined in chapter three, in which divine testimony through utterances was the subject.[51]

Luke 1:8–23, 26–38

In Luke 1:8–23, one finds the usual context for an occurrence of divine testimony. Zechariah, a priest (1:5),[52] is on duty in the temple, and his lot is drawn to enter into the sanctuary and offer incense to the Lord (1:8–9).[53] Meanwhile, the auditor learns that there is a group of people outside the sanctuary in prayer (1:10). Here one notices what has been previously seen: the act of divine testimony occurs within the context of a person (or, in this case, persons) engaged in some type of religious ritual. In this particular example, the effect is heightened by the parallel actions of Zechariah the priest and the prayer of the people.[54]

While Zechariah is at the altar, he is visited by the angel of the Lord, who speaks to him.[55] Later in the narrative, when he emerges and meets

---

51. For example, the angelophany to the shepherds in Luke 2 and Jesus' transfiguration in Luke 9 were addressed in that chapter.

52. He and his wife Elizabeth are further described in the following manner: ἦσαν δὲ δίκαιοι ἀμφότεροι ἐναντίον τοῦ θεοῦ, πορευόμενοι ἐν πάσαις ταῖς ἐντολαῖς καὶ δικαιώμασιν τοῦ κυρίου ἄμεμπτοι (Luke 1:6). This serves to reinforce Zechariah's and Elizabeth's piety.

53. This and the reference to Jesus' blessing of the disciples in Luke 24 frame the narrative. Both the offering of incense and the blessing of the congregation are elements of the Jewish Tamid service of worship. Hamm, in making this connection, argues that Luke thus makes a strong connection between Christian faith (and discipleship) and worship. Hamm, "Tamid Service," 215–31.

54. *Contra* Coleridge, *Birth of the Lukan Narrative*, 33, who argues that Zechariah's performance of his duties is never described; therefore, the angelophany has no connection to Zechariah's actions as a priest. Coleridge does admit, however, that it is significant that Zechariah is in the temple when Gabriel appears. Green, *Luke*, 73, associates the vision with the prayers of the people, noting that this is common in Luke's gospel.

55. Gnuse, while stopping short of arguing for literary dependence, notes the parallels between this dream-vision report and the dream-visions of Jaddus the High Priest and Hyrcanus the High Priest, as described by Josephus; see Gnuse, "Temple Theophanies," 457–72.

the people who have been waiting for his blessing,⁵⁶ the audience learns that the people who had been in prayer ἐπέγνωσαν ὅτι ὀπτασίαν ἑώρακεν ἐν τῷ ναῷ. Therefore, it is confirmed that Zechariah has received a testimony from God, through the angel of the Lord, in the form of a vision.

The content and function of the testimony is primarily prophetic, but also contains encouragement and a command. It is prophetic in that the angel states that a son will be born to Zechariah and Elizabeth, who have been previously described as being προβεβηκότες ἐν ταῖς ἡμέραις αὐτῶν (1:7); in addition, Elizabeth has been unable to have children (1:7).⁵⁷ Therefore, what the testimony prophesies is truly remarkable. The prophecy, however, goes further. Gabriel describes to Zechariah the career of their soon-to-be-born son, which is summarized in 1:17: ἑτοιμάσαι κυρίῳ λαὸν κατεσκευασμένον.⁵⁸ The vision encourages Zechariah in that the angel tells him that his prayers have been heard. The command within the vision is quite simple. Zechariah and Elizabeth are directed to name their son John.

Due to their personal circumstances and the extraordinary nature of the divine testimony, Zechariah reacts accordingly: he questions what the angel tells him (1:18). For his doubt, Zechariah is punished by being struck dumb (1:19–20). At this point, one is reminded of the dream of Titus Latinus, narrated by Livy in *Hist.* 2.36 and discussed earlier. In a similar situation, Titus Latinus refused to take a vision from Jupiter seriously, and was punished with a physical ailment. But the similarities do not end at this point. When the prophesied son is born, Zechariah confirms Elizabeth's statement to those with them at the baby's circumcision that their son is to be named John. At this point, Zechariah's ability to speak is restored, and he immediately praises God. Just as Titus Latinus was healed when he was finally obedient to the command in his dream from Jupiter, so Zechariah is healed by his demonstration of obedience in naming his son as the angel commanded.

---

56. Nolland, *Luke 1–9:20*, 33.

57. Shuler, along with many other scholars, recognizes the parallels between Zechariah and Elizabeth and Abraham and Sarah. He argues that this is a rhetorical device Luke uses to portray Zechariah and Elizabeth favorably, ultimately also elevating their son, John. See Shuler, "Rhetorical Character," 179–80.

58. D. Miller, considering the reception history of Mal 3 in Sirach, 4Q521, and the LXX, concludes that Luke links Jesus with Elijah as seen in 1–2 Kgs, while associating John with Elijah as found in Mal 3:22–24; see D. Miller, "Messenger," 1–16.

Divine Testimony through Deeds in Luke-Acts

Soon after Zechariah's vision of Gabriel, Mary has a similar vision.[59] In the vision the angel Gabriel prophesies the birth of a son to Mary. This divine testimony through a vision also serves to encourage Mary; the angel tells her that she has found favor with God (εὗρες γὰρ χάριν παρὰ τῷ θεῷ; 1:31). The prophecy of the birth of her son, however, is somewhat different from the prophecy to Zechariah. This son is described in more favorable terms than the son who is to be born to Zechariah and Elizabeth. Jesus will be called "Son of the Most High" (υἱὸς ὑψίστου κληθήσεται; 1:32),[60] while John is to be a great prophet.[61] Thus there is an implicit syncrisis between the two sons,[62] the births of whom are prophesied, in which the divine testimony of the angel to both Zechariah and Mary plays a prominent role.

The significance of these visions is clear. First, they are placed side-by-side in the narrative so that the auditor can clearly compare the two figures being prophesied (as well as the ones receiving the visions).[63] Second, Talbert has cogently argued that this type of material (i.e., prophecies, portents, and extraordinary elements surrounding the birth and childhood of a person) is common in Greco-Roman biography, and serves to illuminate the divine nature of the protagonist's birth and early childhood, thus providing the background for the description of the subject's career as an adult.[64] Through these interrelated testimonies from God, the extraordinary birth of the "Son of the Most High" is prophesied. The divine nature of John's birth adds to the overall portrayal of the divine circumstances of

---

59. Technically, there is no dream-vision vocabulary used to describe this experience. It is, however, so similar to Zechariah's experience that the auditor is compelled to consider this as a dream-vision (for example, in both cases it is the angel Gabriel; also, in each instance Gabriel tells the recipient of the vision not to fear, and prophesies the birth of a child). For a helpful discussion of dream-vision terminology (and lack thereof) in Luke-Acts, see J. Miller, *Convinced*, 8–14.

60. Kuhn argues that Luke demonstrates literary dependence on 4Q246 (*Aramaic Apocalypse*) in the use of this term; see Kuhn, "'One like a Son of Man,'" 22–42.

61. Green, *Luke*, 51; cf. Tannehill, *Luke*, 25. L. Johnson, *Luke*, 38, lists several other ways in which the prophecy of Jesus is different than that of John; most significantly, John prepares a people and has a role which is limited in time (1:17), while Jesus will rule over the people and will do so forever (1:33).

62. On the syncrisis between John and Jesus and ancient rhetoric, see Shuler, "Rhetorical Character," 77–79. Shuler surveys the data in the rhetorical handbooks by Cicero and Quintilian, and its application in the work of Plutarch.

63. J. Miller, *Convinced*, 110, expresses it well; in the narrative there are "interwoven layers of experience."

64. See Talbert, "Prophecies." See also L. Johnson, *Luke*, 35, who maintains that supernatural elements in the narrative demonstrate Luke's familiarity with Hellenistic literary conventions.

Jesus' birth and childhood.[65] But the divine testimony also functions in a somewhat more subtle manner.

First, the reactions of Zechariah and Mary to the visions are recorded, through which the auditor is able to gauge their obedience to their respective visions, and therefore their piety. Having been described as a faithful servant of the Lord, Zechariah's reputation, through his expression of doubt and subsequent punishment, is tarnished to some degree. In the end, however, Zechariah is restored in the eyes of the auditor through his demonstration of faith in the vision. Mary, however, is portrayed as completely obedient to the vision.[66] Second, and more significantly, Talbert has argued that John "functions as the prototype of the Christian evangelist."[67] As a Christian evangelist, John has been sanctioned through divine testimony. One would expect that subsequent evangelists in the mold of the prototype would have to be sanctioned as well. I have already demonstrated that divine testimony serves this function in Acts 2; I will now turn to other examples of this same function.

Acts 9:1–19a; 22:1–29; 26:1–23

In this section I will consider Saul's encounter with Jesus while on the road to Damascus along with the vision Ananias receives in conjunction with Saul's experience. Because the account of this experience is repeated twice in the ensuing narrative, I will treat all of these vision accounts here, including 22:17–21, which is not heard in the original account in Acts 9. I will show that there are multiple forms of divine testimony which help to shape this section of the narrative.

In the discussion of Acts 2:1–4 above, I drew attention to the fact that there are two main missionary thrusts in Acts, and that Acts 9 served as the introduction to the second (narrated in Acts 13–28). Therefore, the passage I am about to consider is extremely significant, as it serves as the

---

65. This is reinforced by the interlocking nature of Zechariah's vision and Gabriel's visit to Mary.

66. Her question in 1:34 has been interpreted in various ways as different from Zechariah's question. For example, Coleridge, *Birth of the Lukan Narrative*, 65, argues that Mary exhibits "puzzlement," while Zechariah shows that he doubts the angel.

67. Talbert, *Reading Luke*, 29–31. He is a prototype in that he is a prophet who is filled with the Spirit; he is sent by the Lord, and finally he prepares the people for the Lord's arrival.

Divine Testimony through Deeds in Luke-Acts

introduction to Paul's mission to the Gentiles.[68] Thus it will come as no surprise that divine testimony is found in this introduction.[69]

The immediate context is also important in what it does not say. As has been shown, within the immediate context of most instances of divine testimony one finds a character or characters engaged in some type of religious ritual. Here, that is not the case. Indeed, up to this point Saul has been portrayed in the opposite fashion regarding his behavior towards followers of Jesus. He is, through various references, characterized as increasing in vehemence against the Christian movement.[70] This will prove to be significant for the analysis of divine testimony in this passage.

In Acts 9, Saul is pictured as on his way to Damascus, ἔτι ἐμπνέων ἀπειλῆς καὶ φόνου εἰς τοὺς μαθητὰς τοῦ κυρίου (9:1), with the authorization of the high priest to bring any who were part of "the Way" (τῆς ὁδοῦ) back to Jerusalem. On the journey, Saul encounters Jesus, which is described thusly: ἐξαίφνης τε αὐτὸν περιήστραψεν φῶς ἐκ τοῦ οὐρανοῦ (9:3). This lightning-like flash of light is accompanied by the voice of Jesus, who issues a command to Saul. Thus there are multiple forms of divine testimony in this passage, namely the flash of light and the speech of Jesus.[71] Both deserve attention.

As I have demonstrated in the examples above, thunder and lightning are often found as negative testimonies from the gods; i.e., they are punitive in nature.[72] So it is here. Saul is suffering a divine punishment

---

68. Its significance is also demonstrated in that the basic account is narrated three times. See Talbert, *Reading Acts*, 82. Haenchen (*Apostelgeschichte*, 276) argues that the triple redundancy of this report demonstrates that God was clearly in control of Paul's destiny to become a missionary. Witherington, *Acts*, 309, states that "the effect [of the thrice narrated call narrative] is meant to be collective, cumulative, and supplemental to each other."

69. Fitzmyer, *Acts*, 419, argues for the significance of this account as the transformation of the protagonist for the entire second half of Acts.

70. See Witherup, "Functional Redundancy," 70–75. Witherup rightly recognizes that in the portrayal of Saul in Acts 7:58; 8:1, 3, Saul goes from a passive observer of persecution of Christians, to giving consent to their persecution, and finally to the point of active participation.

71. I have placed this discussion under the category of dreams/visions because later, when Paul describes his experience to King Agrippa in Acts 26:19, he tells Agrippa he was obedient τῇ οὐρανίῳ ὀπτασίᾳ. Also, in 9:12, the text states: εἶδεν ἄνδρα [ἐν ὁράματι] Ἀνανίαν ὀνόματι. ἐν ὁράματι is not found in P[74], ℵ, and A (among others); Metzger, *Textual Commentary*, 319, however, argues that this omission may be due to the same phrase appearing in 9:10, even though the referent there is Ananias's vision.

72. See, e.g., the account of Tullus Hostilius in Dionysius of Halicarnassus (*Ant. rom.* 3.35.1), in which Dionysius argues against the cultural assumption that lightning

The *Topos* of Divine Testimony in Luke/Acts

in the form of blindness from the flash of heavenly lightning (9:8–9).[73] The difference, however, is that Saul is not being punished for the sake of punishment; rather, Saul is being punished in order that he might be reformed and become a witness for Jesus.[74] The punishment/restoration aspect of this passage is reinforced when one considers the argument that Saul is here undergoing a symbolic death and resurrection.[75]

The voice of Jesus in the Christophany is the second divine testimony in the account. Jesus first asks Saul why he is persecuting him; he then orders Saul to go into the city to await further orders (9:6). Here, the divine testimony functions as a command, a common function. Saul is obedient and is led into Damascus by his traveling companions (9:8b).

In Damascus, the reader learns of a third divine testimony. While Saul is in Damascus, Ananias, a disciple of Jesus, also receives a vision in which he is ordered to go to Saul and lay hands on him so that his sight might be restored (9:12). Thus the vision to this point functions as a command. When Ananias balks,[76] however, due to Saul's reputation, the vision becomes prophetic, through which the Lord tells Ananias: Πορεύου, ὅτι σκεῦος ἐκλογῆς ἐστίν μοι οὗτος τοῦ βαστάσαι τὸ ὄνομά μου ἐνώπιον ἐθνῶν τε καὶ βασιλέων υἱῶν τε Ἰσραήλ· ἐγὼ γὰρ ὑποδείξω αὐτῷ ὅσα δεῖ αὐτὸν ὑπὲρ

---

striking Tullus's house was a punishment for his impiety.

73. Hamm ("Paul's Blindness," 63–72) considers the imagery drawn from Isaiah in Acts 13:6–12 and argues that Saul is an example of "Israel's blind resistance" to "the straight way of God" (ibid., 70). Therefore, Hamm concludes that Paul's blindness is indeed punitive. See also Hedrick, "Paul's Conversion/Call," 419, who argues that Paul's blindness is not natural, but rather a divine act (citing OT examples in n. 14) and Acts 13:9–11. Haenchen disagrees, however, arguing that Saul's blindness is simply a natural outcome of the bright light. Haenchen notes that in 22:9, it is recorded that everyone with Paul saw the light as well. To explain their lack of blindness, Haenchen simply states: "Daß nach 22:9 auch die anderen das Licht gesehen haben, hat Lukas übersehen"; *Apostelgeschichte*, 271. Others who argue against Saul's blindness being punitive include Fitzmyer, *Acts*, 426 (for Fitzmyer, Saul's blindness is a sign of his helplessness; cf. Conzelmann, *Acts*, 72).

74. L. Johnson, *Acts*, 167, and Talbert, *Reading Acts*, 89, draw attention to the parallels with the account of Apollonius in 4 Macc 4:1–14. Brenk, "Greek Epiphanies," 355, argues that epiphanies in Greek literature often function to "check the excesses of those favored by the divinity."

75. See Horton, *Death and Resurrection*, 51–55. Horton argues that Saul is in darkness for three days, is completely helpless, and eschews food and water for three days. The combination of these factors leads Horton to his conclusion.

76. Ananias is, however, a reliable character, despite his initial refusal to do as the Lord commands. L. Johnson, *Acts*, 167, states that evidence of this is Ananias's initial response to the vision: Ἰδοὺ ἐγώ, κύριε (9:10).

τοῦ ὀνόματός μου παθεῖν (9:15-16).⁷⁷ The interlocking nature of the testimonies to Saul and Ananias adds significance to the moment.⁷⁸ Also, as in the double-dream of Aeneas and Latinus (Dionysius of Halicarnassus, *Ant. rom.* 1.57.4), the two visions function to bring Saul and Ananias together, thus reconciling potential enemies.⁷⁹ The divine nature of the encounter is confirmed and emphasized when Ananias lays his hands on Saul and Saul regains his sight (9:18).

In Acts 22 and 26, Paul recalls this experience in the context of defense speeches (Acts 22, before the people in Jerusalem; Acts 26, before Agrippa). These contexts are significant; in his own defense Paul invokes the vision he received on the way to Damascus as a method of trying to convince his audience of the legitimacy of his mission to the Gentiles. In Acts 22, Paul recalls his vision on the way to Damascus in the *narratio* of the speech. Commenting on this speech, Parsons rightly notes that "the *narratio* does not rise to the level of proofs against the specific charges leveled against [Paul]."⁸⁰ It is, nonetheless, striking that the vision is part of Paul's defense. For the ancient auditor, it would have been clear that Paul is calling on the testimony of God himself as the basis for his calling to the mission to the Gentiles.

Also noteworthy is that in this same speech Paul actually recalls a second vision⁸¹ (ἐν ἐκστάσει; 22:17) in which Jesus orders Paul to leave Jerusalem quickly to avoid persecution and that he would send Paul to the Gentiles. Paul describes this vision as occurring προσευχομένου μου ἐν τῷ ἱερῷ, thus supplying the conventional context of prayer and worship. In the previous context in which Paul places it (i.e., Paul in Jerusalem), the divine testimony would have served as a command. But here in Paul's

---

77. Talbert (*Reading Acts*, 89-90) and Parsons (*Acts*, 125) recognize the chiastic structure of 9:1-31. 9:15-16 are at the center of this chiasm, emphasizing the importance of Paul's commissioning.

78. See Talbert, *Reading Acts*, 88, who maintains that while Saul's conversion may be in doubt, the narrative works to affirm the validity of it. One way in which this is accomplished is through the vision to Ananias.

79. The double-dream of Aeneas and Latinus is listed as a potential parallel to both Acts 9:10-16 and Acts 10:1—11:18 by Wikenhauser, "Doppelträume," 101-2. Wikenhauser, however, focuses on the fact that it is a double-dream and carries the parallel no further.

80. Parsons, *Acts*, 310.

81. Chronologically, this vision in Paul's *narratio* occurs after he leaves Damascus and is in Jerusalem. The auditor, however, hears about this vision for the first time in the context of Paul's defense.

speech in Jerusalem, it, too, is recalled in defense of Paul's calling by Jesus to go to the Gentiles.[82]

The vision Paul received on the way to Damascus is evoked a third time in Paul's speech before Agrippa in Acts 26. Again, the vision here is used as a part of Paul's defense of his actions toward the Gentiles. Two additional points are worth making here. First, Paul explicitly states in this speech that οὐκ ἐγενόμην ἀπειθὴς τῇ οὐρανίῳ ὀπτασίᾳ. Through this statement he attempts to portray himself as in harmony with the divine will revealed through the vision. Second, Paul's blindness is no longer a part of the *narratio*. Thus, the emphasis now falls on the end result of the punishment, i.e., Paul as a witness for the gospel to the Gentiles.[83] This idea is reinforced when one considers that in the original vision to Ananias, Jesus tells Ananias that Paul σκεῦος ἐκλογῆς ἐστίν μοι (9:15). In 22:15, however, Ananias tells Paul that he ἔσῃ μάρτυς αὐτῷ πρὸς πάντας ἀνθρώπους ὧν ἑώρακας καὶ ἤκουσας. This idea is repeated in 26:16; here the words are directly from Jesus to Paul: εἰς τοῦτο γὰρ ὤφθην σοι, προχειρίσασθαί σε ὑπηρέτην καὶ μάρτυρα ὧν τε εἶδές με ὧν τε ὀφθήσομαί σοι. Thus Paul is described in Acts 9 as an instrument; later in the narrative he is a witness. And the authorial audience understands him to be a legitimate witness, because he has been authorized through divine testimony.

Acts 10:1—11:18

The account of Peter and Cornelius is similar to the one previously examined. Two independent characters receive visions which cause these characters to interact. As in Acts 9, this occurs at a key moment in the narrative: the gospel moves from Jewish circles to the Gentiles, and by the end of this account this is accepted by the church. Thus the spread of the gospel to the Gentiles is sanctioned.[84] As I will demonstrate, divine

---

82. J. Miller, *Convinced*, 230, argues that Paul here "invents" a new vision which is rhetorically more fitting to the situation. Miller notes that Paul does not state what actually happened (in Acts 9:29–30), i.e., that he was run out of Jerusalem by a mob which desired to see him dead.

83. Witherup, "Functional Redundancy," 75–80. notes that in the repetition of this vision account, Paul's role in the experience increases while the other elements (Ananias's intervention, Paul's companions, Paul's blindness/helplessness) decreases. Witherup argues that the repetition with changes serves to focus ever increasingly on Paul's vocation as a witness.

84. See Talbert, *Reading Acts*, 92, who argues that through the repetition of the visions in this section Luke places the emphasis on God's approval of the reception of the Holy Spirit by the Gentiles.

testimony plays a major role in the legitimation of this new phase of the life of the church.

Both Cornelius and Peter receive visions in this section of Acts, and both vision accounts are repeated multiple times. Before it is reported that either one receives a vision, each one is portrayed in an act or acts of piety. The description of Cornelius is found in Acts 10:2-3; here, the auditor learns that Cornelius is εὐσεβὴς καὶ φοβούμενος τὸν θεόν. He is also ἐλεημοσύνας πολλὰς τῷ λαῷ καὶ δεόμενος τοῦ θεοῦ διὰ παντός. Thus the stage is set for him to receive a testimony from God, which is described in 10:3-6. The source of the divine testimony is not in doubt; Cornelius receives a vision of an ἄγγελον τοῦ θεοῦ (10:3). The divine testimony through the vision functions as both encouragement (Αἱ προσευχαί σου καὶ αἱ ἐλεημοσύναι σου ἀνέβησαν εἰς μνημόσυνον ἔμπροσθεν τοῦ θεοῦ [10:4b]) and a command (καὶ νῦν πέμψον ἄνδρας εἰς Ἰόππην καὶ μετάπεμψαι Σίμωνά τινα ὅς ἐπικαλεῖται [10:5]). The encouragement is confirmation of Cornelius's piety; Cornelius demonstrates his understanding of and obedience to the angel's order by immediately sending two of his servants to Joppa to find Peter.

Peter, prior to receiving his vision, is portrayed as being in prayer on the roof of the house in which he is staying (10:9).[85] He, too, receives a vision, which also includes a command. The vision is of a large sheet with many animals descending from heaven (10:11-12), and a voice commands him: Ἀναστάς, Πέτρε, θῦσον καὶ φάγε (10:13). After Peter protests, a second command is issued: ἃ ὁ θεὸς ἐκαθάρισεν, σὺ μὴ κοίνου (10:15). The vision is repeated three times (10:16).[86] The divine nature of the dream is clear; before the sheet appears the text states that Peter saw τὸν οὐρανὸν ἀνεῳγμένον (10:11). Also, Peter certainly understands the vision to be from God; he protests the first command by stating, Μηδαμῶς, κύριε, ὅτι οὐδέποτε ἔφαγον πᾶν κοινὸν καὶ ἀκάθαρτον (10:14).

Peter at first does not understand the dream, but while he muses over it the two men sent by Cornelius arrive. The Holy Spirit then speaks directly to Peter, ordering him to go with the men (10:19-20). Peter is obedient to

---

85. Talbert, *Reading Acts*, 91, argues that this passage is found in a larger thought unit, namely 9:32—11:18, which describes three separate incidents which pertain to Peter. It is significant that the two events prior to Peter's reception of the vision in Acts 10 are also instances of divine intervention: (i) the healing of Aeneas (9:32-35); and (ii) the raising of Dorcas from the dead (9:36-43). I have noted earlier that divine testimony often occurs in "clusters"; this passage follows the convention.

86. Fitzmyer, *Acts*, 455, maintains that the vision is repeated three times in order to enhance its importance.

the divine command, showing hospitality to the men and going with them the next day (10:23). By the time Peter arrives at Cornelius's house, he has understood that the original vision he received was not about eating food; rather, the dream was a command to Peter not to consider the Gentiles (or anyone else) κοινὸν ἢ ἀκάθαρτον (10:28).[87] Peter then preaches a sermon (10:34–43),[88] with the result that Cornelius and his household receive the Holy Spirit (10:44). For the purposes of this study, it is important to note that an emphasis in Peter's sermon is on the act of testimony and witness.[89] The divine testimony through these dreams thus serves to authenticate Peter's role as an authoritative witness.

These "interlocking" visions[90] lead to Cornelius's (as well as others') conversions (10:44–48) and the realization that the Gentiles may also receive the Holy Spirit (10:45). Through the divine testimony, both Peter and Cornelius are shown to be obedient to the leading of God through the visions (and the Holy Spirit, in the case of Peter). Also, Peter is portrayed as a reliable interpreter of the vision, as his vision was a symbolic vision,[91] which he indeed misunderstood when he first saw it. Through the divine leading and human interaction between Peter and Cornelius, including the recounting of the visions,[92] Peter comes to a right understanding of what God is telling him.[93]

---

87. Parsons, *Acts*, 150, argues that Peter's interpretive statement in 10:28 has two effects, one which is overt, and a second that is somewhat understated. First, Peter in 10:28 demonstrates that he now understands that the vision was not about food, but about people. Rather than a command to eat any food, it was God's statement that Peter could associate with Gentiles. The second, less obvious interpretation, is seen in the shift from κοινὸν καὶ ἀκάθαρτον (10:14) to κοινὸν ἢ ἀκάθαρτον (10:28). Through the change in conjunction, Peter recognizes that Jews and Gentiles are defiled in different but connected ways. A Jew is defiled through contact with Gentiles, while a Gentile is defiled but what he or she eats. Parsons concludes: "Peter claims God has revealed to him that he is to refrain from calling any Jew 'common' for associating with Gentiles, or any Gentile 'unclean' because of diet."

88. J. McDonald, "Rhetorical Issue," 59–73, argues that Peter's sermon is an outcome of the authoritative visions received by Peter and Cornelius.

89. See Fitzmyer, *Acts*, 465–66; see also Talbert, *Reading Acts*, 97, who lists a A/B/C/C'/B'/A' structure for this sermon. The C (10:39a)/C' (10:41–42) elements correspond to the theme of witness.

90. A theme not unlike the dual dreams of Alexander's mother and father reported in Plutarch's *Life* of Alexander.

91. Fitzmyer, *Acts*, 453.

92. For a schematization of the repetitions in this passage, see Barthes, "L'Analyse structurale," 33–34.

93. *Contra* Haenchen, *Apostolgeschichte*, 307–8. Haenchen argues that Luke has

Divine Testimony through Deeds in Luke-Acts

But this does not exhaust the function of this particular instance of God's testimony. In Acts 11, Peter is called on by the believers in Jerusalem to explain why he had eaten with Gentiles (11:3). In his defense speech[94] before the elders, Peter recalls the vision that he received while on the roof (11:5–10). Thus, Peter recalls God's testimony as an argument in his favor, arguing that he was led by God to associate with the Gentiles. Peter also tells his audience of Cornelius's dream (11:13–14), giving further evidence of the divine source of his actions.[95] Therefore, both visions are used in this speech as arguments for the validity of the movement of the gospel to the Gentiles. In addition to the visions, Peter recalls a previous instance of divine testimony, namely the giving of the Holy Spirit at Pentecost.[96]

Acts 16:9–10 / Acts 18:9–10 / Acts 23:11

These three short passages describe God's testimony to Paul through visions. All three lack the usual context of prayer or acts of worship of God that normally accompanies instances of divine testimony. In these visions,

---

over-emphasized the working of God in this incident to the point that human decision making is no longer present. He writes, "Nicht in menschlichen Entscheidungen verwirklicht sich der göttliche Wille, nicht durch menschliche Entscheidungen hindurch, sondern zwischen die menschlichen Handlungen schieben sich übernatürliche Eingriffe ein." For the opposite position, similar to what I am arguing, see Tannehill, *Acts*, 128–29.

94. Parsons, *Acts*, 157.

95. Witherup, "Cornelius," 45–66, argues that the function of the repetition of Cornelius's and Peter's vision is to reduce the role of Cornelius in the narrative and elevate the role of the Holy Spirit and Peter as a witness. He sees the main point of emphasis in 10:34, at which point the text states: Ἀνοίξας δὲ Πέτρος τὸ στόμα εἶπεν. Witherup considers the phraseology significant, in that it emphasizes Peter's role as a witness.

96. A character recalling an earlier instance of divine testimony to explain a current situation is a theme to which I have already called attention. See, for example, Plutarch's report of Tiberius, who, when he receives ominous omens through augural birds, remembers an earlier instance of divine testimony through snakes which nest in his helmet (Plutarch, *Ti. C. Gracch.* 17.2).

Talbert, *Reading Acts*, 100, lists six different arguments that Peter uses in this speech. They include his own vision (vv. 5–10), the direction of the Holy Spirit (vv. 11–12a), Cornelius's vision (vv. 13–14), the giving of the Holy Spirit to Cornelius and his household (vv. 15–17), the words of Jesus (vs. 16), and "communal discernment" (11:12b). E. M. Humphrey ("Collision," 65–84) makes the claim that the visions and vision reports throughout this passage are employed as non-technical proofs and are thus an "integral part of the argumentation." Humphrey's comment is directed at the whole of 10:1—11:18, not just Peter's speech in 11:1–18.

The *Topos* of Divine Testimony in Luke/Acts

Paul is given direction and/or encouragement concerning his calling to be a witness for Jesus. All three deserve attention.

Acts 16:9-10 is found in a greater thought unit (16:6—17:15) which describes Paul's mission to Macedonia. Previous to this, Paul, while in Antioch, had decided to return to those congregations in which he and Barnabas had preached the gospel on the journey described in Acts 13-14 (15:36).[97] Due to a split with Barnabas over the role of John Mark (15:37-39), Paul and Silas set off on this return journey. Acts 16:6-8 is significant in this context; here the auditor learns that the Holy Sprit is actually preventing Paul and Silas from entering into certain regions; for the first time in the narrative since his calling, the Holy Spirit seems to be working against Paul.

Acts 16:9-10, however, brings this into focus. In this passage, Paul sees a vision at night (καὶ ὅραμα διὰ [τῆς] νυκτὸς τῷ Παύλῳ ὤφθη) of a man from Macedonia, calling to him to come to Macedonia. The divine agency for this vision is not explicitly stated; from the immediate context, however, it is clear that it has divine origins.[98] In 16:5-8, the Holy Spirit is described as directly controlling Paul's actions;[99] given this vision, it is clear that the Holy Spirit, which earlier hindered Paul's work, now gives him guidance to go into Macedonia.[100] Thus the vision is the Holy Spirit's testimony, through which the Holy Spirit gives Paul direction,[101] a conventional function for this *topos* as I have demonstrated (see, e.g., Themistocles's dream as narrated by Plutarch, *Them.* 30).

---

97. J. Miller, *Convinced*, 104-5, rightly emphasizes the lack of divine guidance in Acts 15:36. According to the narrative, it is purely Paul's decision to return to visit the congregations established in Acts 13-14.

98. *Contra* J. Miller, *Convinced*, 106, who argues that a divine origin is lacking for this dream-vision; Miller, rather, emphasizes the human element of interpretation that is necessary to understand the vision.

99. It is control through obstruction. Koet views 16:6, 7, 8-10 as describing three separate revelations to Paul through the Spirit; because vv. 8-10 is cast as a dream-vision, he makes the leap to assume that the Spirit is blocking Paul's movements through other dream-visions. The multiplicity of dream-visions thus adds to the significance of this moment in the narrative. This seems, however, to be reading too much into the text. See Koet, "Schatten des Aeneas," 154-57.

100. Fitzmyer, *Acts*, 577-78. According to Fitzmyer, the dream-vision explains the previous action of the Spirit in 16:5-8.

101. Pervo offers numerous parallels from ancient literature in which a protagonist receives a vision from a "personified people or province" that provides direction for the one who receives the vision; he further argues (as I do here) that this motif would alert the reader to the fact that the hero's next move is being dictated through a revelation of divine origin. See Pervo, *Acts*, 391.

Divine Testimony through Deeds in Luke-Acts

The ensuing narrative confirms this interpretation. Paul meets Lydia, who is converted (16:11-15). He then exorcises a demon from a young girl (16:16-18), and is supernaturally rescued from prison in Philippi through an earthquake, after which the jailer and his family are converted (16:19-40). Thus, in multiple ways, the direction of the Holy Spirit is confirmed.[102]

Therefore, the divine testimony through the vision functions primarily as divine guidance for Paul and his group. But it also serves to demonstrate Paul's ability to understand rightly God's direction for his mission. In 16:10, the auditor learns that the group is συμβιβάζοντες ὅτι προκέκληται ἡμᾶς ὁ θεὸς εὐαγγελίσασθαι αὐτούς [i.e., the Macedonians]. The verb συμβιβάζω implies that the vision had to be interpreted,[103] and the subsequent actions and results of Paul and his group confirm that the vision was rightly interpreted. Therefore, Paul is shown through the narrative to be reliable in his understanding of the Holy Spirit's direction.

Acts 18:9-10, the narration of a dream-vision to Paul, is a part of Acts 18:1-17, a thought unit in which Paul's preaching is met with both acceptance and resistance.[104] The dream-vision in this passage occurs after one hears that the Jews have resisted Paul's preaching (18:5-8). What is significant in the immediate context is Paul's statement in 18:6 to the Jews who are resisting him: Τὸ αἷμα ὑμῶν ἐπὶ τὴν κεφαλὴν ὑμῶν· καθαρὸς ἐγώ. Through this statement, Paul is asserting his innocence of wrong-doing.[105]

The dream (ἐν νυκτὶ δι' ὁράματος; 18:9) is explicitly attributed to the Lord: εἶπεν δὲ κύριος . . . τῷ Παύλῳ (18:9). The content of the dream is encouragement, a command, and prophecy;[106] Paul should not fear (Μὴ

---

102. *Contra* J. Miller, who evaluates Paul's missionary efforts in Acts 16 as having "lackluster success"; see J. Miller, *Convinced*, 106. Miller bases this statement on his opinion that 16:9-10 does not provide the divine guidance that Paul normally receives. I argue here that 16:9-10 indeed is divine guidance, and that what occurs in Acts 16 is confirmation of that guidance, rather than "lackluster success."

103. BDAG provides this definition: "to draw a conclusion in the face of evidence, conclude, infer." See Bauer et al., *Greek-English Lexicon*, 957. L. Johnson, *Acts*, 290, correctly notes the balance here between human interpretation and divine guidance. He writes: "On the one side there is the role of human calculation . . . On the other side, there is divine intervention and guidance." See also Tannehill, *Acts*, 195.

104. Talbert, *Reading Acts*, 158. Talbert includes 18:18a as the conclusion to the thought unit.

105. Following Koet, "Close to the Synagogue," 178-88. Koet interprets Paul's gesture of shaking the dust from his clothes, along with his words, as "a declaration of innocence" (ibid., 181-82). See also Talbert, *Reading Acts*, 160.

106. Hubbard argues persuasively that this dream-vision (along with many others in Luke-Acts) constitutes a commissioning of Paul. See Hubbard, "Role of Commissioning Accounts," 187-98.

The *Topos* of Divine Testimony in Luke/Acts

φοβοῦ), but rather is to continue to preach the gospel (ἀλλὰ λάλει καὶ μὴ σιωπήσῃς; 18:9). The reason that Paul should be encouraged is found in 18:10: διότι ἐγώ εἰμι μετὰ σοῦ; the prophecy is that οὐδεὶς ἐπιθήσεταί σοι τοῦ κακῶσαί σε. Paul demonstrates his obedience to the vision by remaining in Corinth for eighteen months, preaching the Gospel (18:11).[107] The fulfillment of the prophecy of protection is found in the account of the Jews' accusations concerning Paul and Gallio's dismissal of the same (18:12–17).[108]

Therefore, this instance of divine testimony through a dream serves to direct and sanction Paul's continued work in Corinth. God tells Paul that he is with Paul, thus giving divine legitimation to Paul's work. Paul's obedience to the divine directive in the dream demonstrates his desire to be in line with God's purposes.[109] Finally, given the forensic aspect of the *topos* of divine testimony, the dream especially serves to confirm Paul's statement of innocence in 18:6. Paul states his innocence, and the dream is the Lord's testimony to the validity of that declaration.

The vision to Paul narrated in 23:11 takes place at the end of Paul's defense before the Sanhedrin (22:30—23:10), and before a long section dealing with Paul's trials before Felix, Festus, and Agrippa. Commentators are almost universal in considering this verse a conclusion to Paul's speech before the Sanhedrin.[110] Talbert, however, argues that this verse introduces the next section (23:11—26:32), in which Paul's innocence is repeatedly affirmed.[111] Here I will argue that the divine testimony through a vision to Paul does indeed proclaim Paul's innocence, which is then confirmed through the narrative that follows this passage.

Paul's hearing before the Sanhedrin (22:30—23:10)[112] ends in an uproar, with the Pharisees and Sadducees arguing amongst themselves. Paul

---

107. Thus fulfilling the prophecy in the dream to speak openly.

108. Talbert sees a prophecy-fulfillment schema here. The dream-vision serves as the prophecy; the fulfillment is found in two stages: (i) Paul's preaching in 18:11; and (ii) the confirmation of the Lord's protection in 18:12–17. Talbert, *Reading Acts*, 161.

109. Conversely, the testimony also serves as a negative testimony against those who are opposing Paul. By their opposition, they demonstrate their lack of sensitivity to what God is doing through Paul.

110. See, e.g., Haenchen, *Apostelgeschichte*, 567; Parsons, *Acts*, 317; L. Johnson, *Acts*, 399; Tannehill, *Acts*, 292; Fitzmyer, *Acts*, 715; Dunn, *Acts*, 301; Bock, *Acts*, 668; Gaventa, *Acts*, 317; Conzelmann, *Acts*, 191; Jervell, *Apostelgeschichte*, 552; Pesch, *Apostelgeschichte*, 2:239; Polhill, *Acts*, 466.

111. Talbert, *Reading Acts*, 197.

112. Paul's speech is recognized by scholars as a self-defense; Tannehill, however, adds that Paul's witness for Christ is also on trial here. See Tannehill, *Acts*, 292.

Divine Testimony through Deeds in Luke-Acts

is subsequently ushered out of the proceedings. The auditor then learns that the Lord speaks to Paul that night: Τῇ δὲ ἐπιούσῃ νυκτὶ ἐπιστὰς αὐτῷ ὁ κύριος εἶπεν (23:11a). Clearly the dream (understanding Τῇ δὲ ἐπιούσῃ νυκτὶ to mean a dream) is divine in origin. The dream serves simultaneously to encourage Paul (Θάρσει) and to prophesy that he will indeed arrive in Rome (ὡς γὰρ διεμαρτύρω τὰ περὶ ἐμοῦ εἰς Ἰερουσαλὴμ οὕτω σε δεῖ καὶ εἰς Ῥώμην μαρτυρῆσαι), thus giving divine sanction to a statement made to this effect by Paul earlier in the narrative (see 19:21). It is important to note that the idea of witness is repeated twice in 23:11, thus emphasizing Paul's role as a witness for the Lord.

The divine testimony through a dream to Paul therefore functions as the Lord's divine sanction of Paul's vocation as a witness.[113] Through the dream, the auditor understands that Paul will surely arrive in Rome; it has been divinely ordained. When one considers the forensic aspect of the *topos* of divine testimony, one understands that here the Lord himself has proclaimed Paul innocent of the preceding charges, and therefore also innocent of any subsequent charges throughout the rest of the narrative.[114] As a witness for Jesus, Paul is reliable due to the divine calling and sanction of his vocation. Human trials can only serve to confirm this innocence.

In these examples, one notices a great deal of similarity to the dreams found in the survey of Greco-Roman narratives already considered. Dream-visions, as other forms of this *topos*, often occur in the context of religious expression of some type. Dream-visions in some cases are symbolic, requiring interpretation on the part of a character or characters. Many times dreams concerning the same event are received by two characters, who then must interact in order for the ultimate function of the dreams to be realized. A dream itself can occur multiple times, or the report of a dream is repeated at other points in the narrative. Repetition can occur in the context of some type of speech, in which a character uses his or her dream to persuade other characters. In all these ways dream-visions appear similarly in Luke-Acts as in Greco-Roman narratives.

Dream-visions also function similarly as well within their respective narratives. Divine dreams are received by characters in order to give them guidance, warnings, encouragement, and affirmation. Dual dream-visions also function in both sets of data to bring reconciliation to two potential

---

113. Fitzmyer, *Acts*, 715, states that the dream gives approval to Paul's speech before the Sanhedrin; "Paul's courage is to be rewarded."

114. Talbert recognizes the importance of the theme of Paul's innocence throughout the rest of Acts. Acts 23–26 are especially concerned with Paul's innocence before human authorities. See Talbert, *Reading Acts*, 197.

enemies. Finally, and most significantly, dream-visions function to give divine sanction to the actions of a character (and condemn those opposing that character). Further positive portrayal of a character is achieved when the character must overcome obstacles in order to remain aligned with the divine will received in the dream-vision.

Divine Testimony through Signs and Portents in Creation

In this section I will consider two examples of this form of the *topos*, both involving the movement on the earth. I will show that both are instances of divine testimony; the context, however, must inform the interpretation of each testimony.

Acts 4:31

The greater context of Acts 4:31 is the release of Peter and John after being questioned by the temple leadership in the aftermath of the healing of the lame man outside the temple. God has therefore already performed a sign through Peter (τὸ σημεῖον τοῦτο τῆς ἰάσεως; 4:22), and the community is in prayer.[115] Thus the context for this instance of divine testimony is conventional; it occurs along with other instances of divine intervention, and while the recipients are engaged in prayer and worship.[116]

The occurrence of the testimony is through the shaking of the house in which the community was praying (καὶ δεηθέντων αὐτῶν ἐσαλεύθη ὁ τόπος ἐν ᾧ ἦσαν συνηγμένοι; 4:31a). The divine testimony is in direct answer to the prayer of the community;[117] in the prayer they ask God that he would make them bold to preach (δὸς τοῖς δούλοις σου μετὰ παρρησίας πάσης λαλεῖν τὸν λόγον σου; 4:29). After their prayer and the shaking of the place in which they were gathered, ἐπλήσθησαν ἅπαντες τοῦ ἁγίου πνεύματος, καὶ ἐλάλουν τὸν λόγον τοῦ θεοῦ μετὰ παρρησίας (4:31b). The

---

115. Pervo argues that prayers are, in effect, speeches, examples of "deliberative rhetoric addressed to the deity"; see *Acts*, 121.

116. A third important aspect to the context is that divine testimony through utterances is found in 4:24, in which the Holy Spirit is said to have spoken through David, followed by a quotation from scripture. I dealt with this passage in chapter four.

117. Parsons, *Acts*, 67.

Divine Testimony through Deeds in Luke-Acts

divine testimony therefore serves to sanction the continued witness of the community to Jesus.[118]

Acts 16:24-40

In this passage, Paul and Silas are in prison in Philippi, a result of Paul's exorcism of a prophetic spirit from a slave girl in that city. As already shown, they are in Philippi due to a direct command through a vision to go to Macedonia. In the immediate context, the auditor hears that Κατὰ δὲ τὸ μεσονύκτιον Παῦλος καὶ Σίλας προσευχόμενοι ὕμνουν τὸν θεόν, ἐπηκροῶντο δὲ αὐτῶν οἱ δέσμοι (Acts 16:25). As seen in other examples, Paul and Silas are thus portrayed as praying and praising God, providing the auditor with the context of religious expression that so often accompanies an instance of the *topos* of divine testimony.

Following this statement, a major earthquake occurs: ἄφνω δὲ σεισμὸς μέγας (16:26a). The significance of the earthquake is heightened by the suddenness (ἄφνω) of its occurrence and that it is μέγας. The impact of the earthquake is heightened by the description of its effects: ὥστε σαλευθῆναι τὰ θεμέλια τοῦ δεσμωτηρίου, ἠνεῴχθησαν δὲ παραχρῆμα αἱ θύραι πᾶσαι, καὶ πάντων τὰ δεσμὰ ἀνέθη (16:26b).[119] Although no divine origin is specifically assigned to the earthquake in the narrative, from the context described above it is clear to the auditor that this is an instance of divine testimony.[120] The earthquake occurs while Paul and Silas are praying and praising God, and it is a major earthquake which serves to open the doors of the jail (again, παραχρῆμα) and free all the prisoners from the chains which bound them.

---

118. On this particular prayer in Acts 4:24-30, see Karris, *Prayer*, 77-78. Karris favorably compares this prayer to one which Josephus has Moses pray (*Ant.* 4.40-50). Karris notes that, as here in Acts 4, after Moses prays, an earthquake occurs (*Ant.* 4.51). The parallel, however, is not exact; through the earthquake in Josephus's account, in answer to Moses' prayer, God punishes the disobedient through the earthquake. The earthquake in Acts 4:31 is in affirmation of the community.

119. Parsons argues that Paul having to yell in a loud voice (ἐφώνησεν δὲ Παῦλος μεγάλῃ φωνῇ λέγων, Μηδὲν πράξῃς σεαυτῷ κακόν, ἅπαντες γάρ ἐσμεν ἐνθάδε; 16:28) is evidence of the magnitude of the earthquake; Parsons, *Acts*, 233-34.

120. *Contra* J. Miller, who argues that there is no divine agency associated with the earthquake (*Convinced*, 104). Miller is correct that divine agency is not explicitly assigned to the earthquake; as I argue here, however, the context demands it. Many scholars associate the earthquake with a theophany; see, e.g., Talbert, *Reading Acts*, 146; Parsons, *Acts*, 233.

The *Topos* of Divine Testimony in Luke/Acts

In the examples from Greco-Roman histories and biographies examined in chapter five, I argued that earthquakes were often viewed as the gods' negative testimony toward a person or group of people (see on Diodorus Siculus, *Hist.* 11.63.2–3; 15.49.1–6; cf. Suetonius, *Galb.* 7.18.1–2). I would argue that the earthquake is functioning in the same way in this passage. The authorial audience knows, by means of the earlier instance of divine testimony through a vision to Paul, that Paul and Silas have been directed into this region for the purposes of evangelism.[121] Therefore, for Paul and Silas to be in prison would be recognized as a human attempt to thwart the mission. The earthquake as punishment of those who are making this attempt thus makes sense on a narrative level.

This interpretation is bolstered by two pieces of evidence. First, the reaction of the jailer is one of great fear, to the point that he is on the verge of committing suicide.[122] The narrative explicitly states that the jailer draws his sword, νομίζων ἐκπεφευγέναι τοὺς δεσμίος.[123] But even after Paul reassures him that none of the prisoners have escaped, the jailer is described thusly: καὶ ἔντρομος γενόμενος προσέπεσεν τῷ Παύλῳ καὶ [τῷ] Σίλᾳ (16:29). The word ἔντρομος connotes a state of terror on the part of the jailer;[124] it is also found in Stephen's speech to describe Moses' reaction at being in God's presence at the burning bush (Acts 7:32).[125] The jailer also falls at Paul and Silas's feet, a sign of his humility before them.[126] Thus, the jailer is characterized as perhaps attributing the divine testimony of the earthquake to Paul and Silas, and furthermore believing that he will be punished. This idea is reinforced through the jailer's question: Κύριοι, τί με δεῖ ποιεῖν ἵνα σωθῶ (16:30).

There is, perhaps a double-entendre through the use of the verb σῴζω which the ancient audience may have understood. According to Louw and Nida, σῴζω can mean "rescue from danger and to restore to a former state

---

121. Note the narrator's first-person statement in 16:10: συμβιβάζοντες ὅτι προσκέκληται ἡμᾶς ὁ θεός εὐαγγελίσασθαι αὐτούς.

122. L. Johnson, *Acts*, 303, argues that the jailer's attempted suicide is "because he is fearful of retribution" and due to the "shame at having failed his responsibility."

123. At this point the auditor is reminded of the fate of the guards when Peter is freed from prison; see Acts 12:18–19; on this, see Parsons, *Acts*, 233.

124. BDAG, 341, states that ἔντρομος "pert. to being in a quivering condition because of exposure to an overwhelming or threatening circumstance."

125. Cf. also Luke 8:48 and Acts 9:6, in which the verbal form (τρέμω) of this adjective is used to describe a character's fear at being in Jesus' presence.

126. Cf. Luke 8:47; here, the woman with the flow of blood who is healed by Jesus falls (trembling in fear; see note above) at his feet. Cf. Luke 8:28.

of safety and well being," and is used in Acts in this way (cf. 7:25; 27:34). But it can also mean "to cause someone to experience divine salvation."[127] Given Paul's response to the jailer (Πίστευσον ἐπὶ τὸν κύριον Ἰησοῦν, καὶ σωθήσῃ σὺ καὶ ὁ οἶκός σου; 16:31), this second meaning is certainly in play.[128] In the Third Gospel, Luke takes advantage of the semantic range of this verb; in the account of the healing of the ten lepers, Jesus tells the one leper, who has returned to thank him after his healing, ἡ πίστις σου σέσωκέν σε. In this context, the word clearly connotes the physical healing of the leper; in the greater context, however, the auditor understands that more than physical healing is in view.[129] Here in Acts 16, the auditor understands through Paul's response to the jailer that the jailer is inquiring after divine salvation; the earthquake and his reaction to it, however, allow for the possibility that the jailer is seeking to avoid the punishment that the earthquake implies.

This interpretation is reinforced through a second piece of textual evidence. In the ensuing narrative, Paul and Silas are allowed to go free by the magistrates, who inform the police of their decision. The Greek text (NA27) reads:

Ἡμέρας δὲ γενομένης ἀπέστειλαν οἱ στρατηγοὶ τοὺς ῥαβδούχους λέγοντες, Ἀπόλυσον τοὺς ἀνθρώπους ἐκείνους.

The Western Text, however, reads thusly at this point:

Ἡμέρας δὲ γενομένης *συνῆλθον οἱ στρατηγοὶ ἐπὶ τὸ αὐτὸ εἰς τὴν ἀγορὰν καὶ ἀναμνησθέντες τὸν σεισμὸν τὸν γεγονότα ἐφοβήθησαν καὶ* ἀπέστειλαν τοὺς ῥαβδούχους λέγοντες, Ἀπόλυσον τοὺς ἀνθρώπους ἐκείνους.[130]

The words in italics are additions to the Western text; they indicate that the authorities were in fear due to the earthquake. Through this addition one notes that early in the reception history of this passage the idea of divine judgment was indeed associated with the earthquake.[131]

---

127. On σῴζω as a verb of rescue, see Louw and Nida, *Greek-English Lexicon*, 241 (§21.18); on σῴζω as a verb of salvation in a religious sense, see Louw and Nida, *Greek-English Lexicon*, 242 (§21.27).

128. Parsons argues that the jailer's question is an "inquiry of faith"; see Parsons, *Acts*, 234.

129. See Talbert, *Reading Luke*, 193–94.

130. See Boismard and Lamouille, *Le Texte occidental*, 183. Cf. Tannehill, *Acts*, 199, who notes the Western Text addition and adds that the authorities could have potentially associated the earthquake with judgment for imprisoning Paul and Silas.

131. Cf. also Acts 12, in which Herod takes action against the Christian movement

The *Topos* of Divine Testimony in Luke/Acts

Given this reading of the text and the background of earthquakes as punishments from the gods, the ancient auditor could have understood the earthquake as a divine testimony against those who are attempting to prevent the divinely sanctioned (through a vision) spread of the gospel into Macedonia and beyond. The earthquake also allows Luke to characterize Paul and Silas as turning this ancient convention on its head; Paul and Silas choose not to escape when the opportunity is afforded them. Rather, they stay and present the gospel to the Philippian jailer. Thus, rather than carrying out the judgment on the jailer, Paul and Silas offer him salvation, not from the earthquake, but salvation through faith in Christ, for him and his family. Therefore, through the obedient servants Paul and Silas, the gospel does impact Macedonia, as God has decided.

In this section it is clear to see that context must inform the interpretation of divine testimony. In the first example from Acts 4, the shaking of the house in which the community is praying is an affirmation of their desire to be witnesses for Jesus.[132] In the case of the earthquake in Philippi, examples from Greco-Roman narratives help to understand the divine testimony of an earthquake as a punishment of those opposing Paul and Silas in their vocation as witnesses. Thus, this form of the *topos* functions in similar ways to those seen earlier.

SUMMARY OF FINDINGS FROM LUKE-ACTS AND COMPARISON TO THE DATA FROM GRECO-ROMAN NARRATIVES

Given these two surveys of the use of the *topos* of divine testimony through deeds, it is appropriate now to draw some conclusions concerning how this *topos* would have been understood in Luke-Acts. In a very general sense, there is a great deal of correlation concerning this *topos*. Earlier, I used the illustration of a matrix to describe divine testimony in ancient histories and biographies: the rows were the ways in which the gods testified through deeds, and the columns were the different purposes the divine testimonies served in the narrative. The data from this analysis of Luke-Acts indicates that the functions of divine testimony exhibited in Luke-Acts would fit within this matrix. The different ways in which the gods testify through deeds, as described by Cicero, all appear in

---

by imprisoning Peter; by the end of the chapter, he is the subject of grisly, divine judgment.

132. Cf. the example from Josephus, *Ant.* 10, discussed earlier, in which the shaking of the earth is a divine affirmation of Daniel.

Divine Testimony through Deeds in Luke-Acts

Luke-Acts, with the exception of the investigation of entrails of sacrificial animals. More importantly, how the *topos* appears in the narratives and how it functions are very similar in both sets of data. In the following I will detail areas of agreement that have been seen.

In the examples from Greco-Roman histories and biographies, I noted that the testimony of the gods through deeds often appears at significant moments in the narratives. This, as I have demonstrated, occurs in Luke-Acts as well. Also, divine testimony was seen to occur in "clusters"[133] in the histories and biographies; there are often multiple forms of divine testimony within the narrative of a single event. This is certainly the case in Luke-Acts as well.[134] In the Greco-Roman examples, divine testimony most often occurs when characters are engaged in some type of prayer, worship, or religious rite through which they are seeking divine direction. This is also seen in Luke-Acts, with prayer playing a prominent role. Another point of similarity is that characters must often interpret the divine testimony; this can occur in conjunction with other characters or through a speech. In speeches, divine testimony can also be used in an attempt to be persuasive. Within these speeches, I have shown that a divine testimony which was received just prior to the speech can be discussed, but also testimonies which occurred much earlier in the narrative are mentioned. In all these ways a Greco-Roman auditor would have similarly heard the *topos* of divine testimony through deeds in Luke-Acts.

The ways in which this *topos* functions within the narrative is also similar. As has been seen, in both surveys, the *topos* in its various forms serves to warn, encourage, and direct the behavior of characters within the narrative. It can also function to bring characters together, and even reconcile potential enemies. Fundamental to the application of divine testimony through deeds, however, is the sanction and legitimation of some characters, while other characters (most often those who oppose those favored by the gods or God) are vilified. Even when, for example, God testifies to Paul that he must appear before the emperor in Rome (Acts 27:24), Paul nevertheless must overcome the trials of a storm, shipwreck, and snakebite and thus demonstrate his obedience to the vision which he has received.

---

133. This term is used by Lown, "Miraculous," 37: "[O]f what I would choose to call, for lack of a better term, 'cluster' miraculous happenings."

134. I have already demonstrated this in the chapter analyzing divine testimony through utterances; one example of this phenomenon was the account of Jesus' baptism.

The *Topos* of Divine Testimony in Luke/Acts

But the application of the *topos* of divine testimony through deeds is not applied exactly in Luke-Acts as it is in the Greco-Roman narratives surveyed in chapter five. For example, as mentioned above, in Luke-Acts there is no recorded instance of the examination of the entrails of animals. This is perhaps due to the fact that the act of sacrifice, essential to the practice of extispicy,[135] was also fundamental to the practice of the Law within Judaism.[136] It is therefore possible that Luke, portraying the beginnings of the Christian movement as being thoroughly grounded in Judaism, would have avoided using this form of the *topos* in order to preserve the Jewish background of his protagonists.[137]

Despite this minor disagreement, the over-arching function of the *topos* of divine testimony through deeds in Luke-Acts is the same as its usage in extra-biblical narratives. As demonstrated in chapter two, this *topos* was used in ancient law courts and political speeches in an attempt to persuade the audience of the piety or impiety of a client or opponent. Thus, ancient auditors familiar with this *topos* from forensic and deliberative situations would have best understood the *topos* of divine testimony through deeds in these narrative contexts as that of the portrayal of characters. Through these surveys from ancient narratives and Luke-Acts, it can be readily seen that the *topos* of divine testimony through deeds functions as it does in forensic and deliberative situations: to praise protagonists and to disparage antagonists in the narratives.

---

135. See the examples discussed in chapter five above. In those examples, a priest or auger is responsible for sacrificing the animal in order to examine its entrails.

136. See, e.g., Mary and Joseph offering a sacrifice after Jesus' birth in Luke 2:24.

137. The selection of Judas's successor in Acts 1 could have been determined through extispicy. This is accomplished, however, through the casting of lots (Acts 1:26), which was practiced by the Jews.

7 • Conclusion

Summary of the Results of the Study

Given the preceding analyses, I am now in a position to summarize the findings of this study. In general, I have set out to demonstrate that the *topos* of divine testimony, as defined by the authors of the ancient rhetorical handbooks, and as applied by orators and philosophers in Greco-Roman speeches and treatises, can be found in Hellenistic histories and biographies. Further, ancient auditors of these works would have heard and understood the instances of this *topos* to function in a comparable way to its function in speeches and treatises, namely, to demonstrate the gods' approval of a character or characters. Because Luke-Acts is a product of the first-century literary milieu, and shares affinities with the aforementioned genres, I have argued that auditors of Luke-Acts would also have understood many of the events in Luke-Acts to be examples of the *topos* of divine testimony through utterances or deeds, through which God displays God's approval of some characters and disapproval of others.

In the second chapter of this study, I attempted to define the concept of *topos* by surveying the data found in the ancient rhetorical handbooks, concentrating on those treatises written by Aristotle, Cicero, Quintilian, and Theon. The results of that survey were that the definition of *topos* is somewhat unspecific. For Aristotle, a *topos* constitutes the structure of an argument; in the works of Quintilian and Cicero, a *locus* is more the content of an argument, rather than its form. For these two rhetoricians, a *locus* is a place in which arguments can be found and applied to specific forensic and deliberative situations.[1] These arguments can be either intrinsic to the case being argued, or external to it. Theon demonstrates that

---

1. Cicero and Quintilian both distinguish between *loci* and *locos communes*. A *locus* is a source for arguments which can be applied to any rhetorical issue, while a common *locus* is a self-contained argument for or against a particular theme.

The *Topos* of Divine Testimony in Luke/Acts

he is familiar with this concept of *topos* as well, using the term *topos* to refer to a particular line of argumentation used in composing the various preliminary exercises described in his treatise. I then concluded this section by arguing that definitions of *topos* put forth in NT scholarship have to this point neglected to include these external *topoi*, which are proofs drawing from oaths, documents, and the testimony of witnesses.

Having established a case for considering a *topos* to be an external source of proofs, I drew attention to a particular form of the topos, that of divine testimony. Because a *topos* can be a source of proofs external to the case being argued, a major source of such proofs is that of witnesses. Cicero argues that the most reliable witness is one who is virtuous; the most reliable witnesses, therefore, are the gods, because, according to Cicero, they are virtuous by nature.[2] Cicero goes on to say that the gods testify both through words and deeds, and further delineates the deeds through which the gods testify into several different categories.[3] The second half of chapter two concentrated on analyzing examples of divine testimony through words and deeds found in speeches and philosophical treatises. Through these examples it was clear that divine testimony was indeed called upon by ancient orators as proof, and was most often used to demonstrate the approval of the gods of the clients whom they were representing, or to show the gods' disapproval of their opponents. Finally, I attempted to show that this type of testimony would have been considered quite persuasive in its first-century cultural milieu.

Having, therefore, established that the *topos* of divine testimony was considered a source of persuasive, external proofs in Greco-Roman culture, I then turned my attention to Hellenistic narratives and biographies, in search of this *topos* in works of these genres. Before doing so, I first established the validity of analyzing such works for rhetorical features, arguing that these works were by nature meant to be persuasive to ancient auditors,[4] so that it was not surprising to find elements of argumentation in them. I then analyzed the use of divine testimony through speech in these narratives, finding that the gods testified through direct speech, through inspired humans, and through the giving and receiving of oracles. This analysis further demonstrated that each of these forms of this *topos*

---

2. Cicero is not the only rhetorician to discuss divine testimony; this idea is found in *Rhet. Her.*, the writings of Quintilian, and in the treatise *Art of Political Speech*.

3. *Top.* 20.76–77.

4. Biographies, for example, were written in order to provide examples of virtue for the audience. Histories, too, were written so that the audience might understand the mistakes made in previous generations in order to avoid the same in the future.

functions in many different ways within the narrative contexts in which the examples are found; divine testimony through the speech of the gods, for example, is used to encourage characters, to give guidance or warnings, in deliberative speeches to convince other characters of a course of action, and as a means of defense in trial settings. Divine testimony can also be used to explain an extraordinary incident which occurred earlier in the narrative. The *topos* in this form also serves as prophetic statements, which have been fulfilled through events in the narrative; these prophecies are sometimes fulfilled despite a character's misunderstanding of them. Divine testimony in the form of prophecy can be rightly interpreted by wise characters, or manipulated by unscrupulous characters; lastly, prophetic statements often serve to predict the future prominence of a character.

The common denominator in all of these different functions, however, was that divine testimony through speech served to demonstrate the piety or impiety of a character or characters, as was shown in the examples from speeches and treatises. For example, a character who was the subject of a fulfilled prophecy was generally seen in the narrative to be a part of the gods' plan and was thus being positively characterized.[5] Another example is found in the interpretation of the testimony of the gods; characters are shown to be wise when they can properly interpret the gods' speech or oracles. Contrariwise, characters who do not understand or attempt to manipulate the gods' testimony for selfish means are portrayed as impious and the subject of the gods' disapproval.

This analysis of the use of divine testimony through utterances provided a snapshot of the "horizon of expectations" an ancient auditor of Luke-Acts would have had regarding this form of the *topos*. Through the investigation of several passages in Luke-Acts, I was able then to demonstrate that direct speech from God or the Holy Spirit, speech through inspired intermediaries (those "filled with the Holy Spirit"), and especially citations of Jewish scripture would have been understood in much the same way as found in the Hellenistic writings previously investigated.[6] These forms of divine speech in Luke-Acts functioned in the same ways within the narrative, and ultimately would have been understood by ancient auditors as a means of characterization, legitimating Jesus and his

---

5. This was not always the case; the context was the determining factor for how the auditors would have understood the divine testimony.

6. At this point, I argued that the reference to and citation of scripture in Luke-Acts would have been understood by the ancient audience in an analogous fashion to the reference to and citation of oracles in Hellenistic histories and biographies.

apostles, and disparaging those who oppose them. I will provide a more detailed summary of these findings below.

I then moved from the *topos* of divine testimony through speech to divine testimony through deeds of the gods. In this case, the analysis was organized around Cicero's description of this *topos*, in which he lists the different actions through which the gods can testify; these include: objects and events in the sky; birds and their flight; sounds and fire emanating from the sky; dreams and visions; signs and portents on the earth; and the examination of entrails. The analysis of ancient histories and biographies revealed that all of these forms of divine testimony were represented, and that they functioned within these narratives in similar ways to the *topos* of divine testimony through speech. Specifically, divine testimony through acts of the gods functioned as warnings, commands, encouragement, and prophecies of future events. But more generally, divine testimony through the gods' actions also served, as seen in the analysis of the *topos* of divine testimony through speech, to display the piety or impiety of characters in the narrative. The gods can even go so far as to punish a character through their deeds, giving ultimate expression to their disapproval. As before, the testimony rendered by the gods can be used later in the narrative as evidence in a speech in an attempt to persuade those hearing the speech of the validity of a certain course of action.

In the subsequent analysis of Luke-Acts, I was able to show that all of the forms of the *topos* of divine testimony through the gods' actions described by Cicero were found in Luke-Acts, with the single exception of the examination of the entrails of sacrificial animals. And these forms of the *topos* functioned in the same way in Luke-Acts as they did in the extrabiblical writings examined. Through the various testimonies, characters are encouraged, warned, commanded, and receive prophetic statements from God. Thus the characters in the narrative are affirmed and legitimated by God, or are portrayed as being enemies of God and his work through Jesus and the apostles.

The analysis of Luke-Acts in both chapters was organized by category of divine testimony. Therefore, from a narrative standpoint, the passages might seem as if they were treated in a somewhat random order. To understand fully how divine testimony (through both word and deed) is functioning throughout the narrative, it would be perhaps enlightening to review the findings from these passages in the order in which they occur in the narrative.

Conclusion

The *topos* of divine testimony is predominant throughout the intertwined birth narratives of Jesus and John in Luke's gospel. The births of both John and Jesus are prophesied through divine dreams to Zechariah and Elizabeth (Luke 1:8–23, 26–38); following the naming of John, Zechariah prophesies through inspired speech concerning John's appointed task as a herald for Jesus (1:67–79). Likewise, the birth of Jesus is announced through a divine testimony; in this case it is angels who proclaim Jesus' birth to the shepherds (2:8–20). Significantly, the shepherds then act as witnesses, whose testimony amazes the people who hear it (Luke 2:18). At Jesus' presentation in the temple, through divine testimony, his parents are portrayed as obedient to the law (2:21–24), supporting the encomium of Jesus by proving the piety of his parents. Simeon, much like Zechariah earlier, then prophesies concerning the future significance of Jesus through inspired speech (2:25–35). John, fulfilling his role as a messenger, prophesies the coming of Jesus through the citation of the scripture (3:4–6). Many of these instances of divine testimony serve to emphasize the importance of John, and therefore the even greater significance of Jesus, for whom John is a precursor.

At Jesus' first appearance in the narrative as an adult,[7] Jesus is affirmed through two forms of divine testimony (3:21–22). First, the Holy Spirit is described as descending on him in the form of a dove; second, a heavenly voice expresses God's approval of Jesus through direct speech. Now full of the Holy Spirit, the Spirit leads Jesus into the wilderness, where he is tempted by Satan (4:1–13). In this narrative, divine testimony again plays a prominent role. Jesus answers Satan's temptations to abdicate his sonship by citing scripture, therefore proving himself to be obedient to the divine commands therein. Also, in his last temptation, Satan attempts to manipulate the meaning of Ps 90:11–12 LXX in order to test Jesus, thereby being portrayed as one who does not take care to understand divine speech correctly, and is thus discredited.

Up to this point in the narrative, divine testimony has served to reassure the auditor of Luke-Acts that John, and especially Jesus, have divine approval. John's prophesied role has been fulfilled; he has gone out and announced to the people the coming of the savior, prophesied through God's testimony through the angel Gabriel, Zechariah, the angels in the fields outside of Bethlehem, and Simeon. Jesus himself has received divine sanction at his baptism and in the wilderness. Thus, the expectation of the

---

7. This is assuming that Luke 3:23 can be understood to refer approximately to the time of Jesus' baptism.

auditor, due to the divine testimonies throughout this section, is that Jesus will play a significant role in the rest of the narrative. The culmination of this expectation is found in Luke 4:16–30, in which Jesus himself inaugurates his ministry in the synagogue in Nazareth by stating that his work is the fulfillment of prophecy.

Throughout the rest of the gospel, instances of divine testimony serve to portray the main characters. In Luke 7, Jesus explains the significance of John to some of his followers by stating that he is the fulfillment of prophecy. He goes on to say that John, as important as he is, is the least in the kingdom, thus emphasizing the importance of all people. Also in this passage, those baptized by John are compared with those who refused, thus implicitly demonstrating the impiety of those who refuse to follow the one to whom God has testified through prophecy.

In Luke 9, Jesus is once again sanctioned through divine testimony, this time through a divine voice at the time of his transfiguration (9:28–36). This is significant, as Jesus has just told his disciples of his impending arrest, death, and resurrection (9:22). The divine testimony therefore serves specifically as divine approval of Jesus' obedience to God's plans for his future.[8] This testimony also serves as a divine command, ordering the disciples to pay attention to what Jesus is saying. This then becomes a question in the auditors' minds: will the disciples indeed be obedient and faithful? For the most part, the question will be answered negatively until the end of the gospel.

An example of the disciples' lack of ability to hear and understand Jesus is seen almost immediately following the transfiguration. When Jesus is rejected by a Samaritan village, James and John ask if they should request God's punishment through fire from heaven (an example of divine testimony) to be inflicted on the Samaritans (9:52–56). Jesus reprimands them, demonstrating his superior understanding of God's desires, simultaneously revealing to the audience that the disciples lack this understanding.

Divine testimony serves to differentiate Jesus from others in the narrative. In Luke 10:25–37, a lawyer challenges Jesus concerning his interpretation of the law, specifically Lev 19:18. Jesus is able to interpret rightly what it means to love one's neighbor, demonstrating his ability to understand God's desires expressed in the law. Conversely, the lawyer demonstrates his inability to do so. A similar situation occurs in Luke 20:27–40 and 41–47. Here, in vv. 27–40, Jesus meets the challenge of the

---

8. Note the "divine necessity" in 9:22, expressed through the word δεῖ.

Conclusion

Sadducees, interpreting the law in order to show them their error in their refusal to believe in the resurrection of the dead. Likewise, in vv. 41–47, Jesus points out the failings of the scribes in their lack of understanding of the messiah. In these two passages, Jesus proves himself to be superior in understanding what God has testified through scripture to those who represent the religious elite of his time.

Jesus once again sets himself apart from his opponents through his predictions in Luke 21:11, 25. Through these prophetic warnings, which involve God's testimony through signs in the heavens, Jesus demonstrates his authority as a prophet through his knowledge of how and when God will act in the future. Simultaneously, within the narrative context in which this passage is found, the failure of the religious elite of Jesus' day to care for the people is contrasted to Jesus' authority.

Several instances of divine testimony serve to explain Jesus' death and resurrection. An ancient auditor would have readily understood the eclipse mentioned in Luke 23:44–45 as God's displeasure over Jesus' death. Jesus' empty tomb is then explained by two divine beings to the women who discover it as the fulfillment of divinely-given prophecy. Jesus himself then explains, through reference to scripture, his death and resurrection to his followers, who finally understand. Thus, divine testimony is once again seen at a major turning-point in the narrative. First, Jesus' death and resurrection are portrayed as being the fulfillment of the divine plan as seen in the Jewish scriptures. Second, Jesus' followers, after failing to perceive what he has been telling them on the way to Jerusalem concerning his death and resurrection, do comprehend the significance of what has occurred.

This portrayal of the disciples is continued in Acts. Through the angels' words in Acts 1:1–14, Jesus' ascension is explained and the disciples are given a promise that he will return. In the meantime, the disciples are to wait for the promised Holy Spirit. During this period, Peter is portrayed as an authoritative interpreter of scripture, as he explains to the other disciples that Judas's death was the fulfillment of two passages from the Psalms. According to Peter, God had predicted Judas's betrayal of Jesus, and through his testimony has commanded that Judas be replaced, which is accomplished. The disciples, Peter in particular, are now seen as comprehending God's will and acting in accordance with it.

The promised Holy Spirit is given in Acts 2:1–13, and the event is described in terms of divine testimony. The coming of the Spirit is depicted as a loud noise from heaven and flames of fire over the heads of the disciples. Through this, Luke expresses God's approval of the disciples as his witnesses. Immediately following this event, Peter has an opportunity to act as a witness, explaining the events of Pentecost through his speech in Acts 2:14–36. The argument of the speech is centered on God's testimony through scripture, interpreting the events of Pentecost to be the fulfillment of prophecy, and serving as the basis for Peter's call to repentance on the part of his listeners.

The depiction of the disciples as obedient, competent witnesses continues through Acts 3–4. In these chapters, Peter uses divine testimony to convince the people that the healing of the lame man was the work of God, as well as reminding the people that Jesus was killed due to their ignorance of what God had said through scripture. The disciples are therefore contrasted with the people as those who truly understand what God has done and is doing. This continues in Acts 4:5–12, in which Peter utters inspired speech in his own defense in order to explain the healing of the lame man to the council; he is specifically described as speaking with παρρησία. Even the persecution suffered by the disciples is interpreted as the fulfillment of God's testimony through prophecy; in 4:25–26 the harassment of the disciples by the religious leaders is explained through divine testimony. Finally, at the end of Acts 4, at the conclusion of their prayer, the followers of Jesus are affirmed in their witness by God's testimony through the shaking of the house in which they were praying (4:30).

This affirmation of Jesus' followers in the face of persecution is also seen in the following chapters. In Acts 5, some of the apostles are imprisoned, but are subsequently freed by an angelic being, thus providing God's testimony of the apostles' innocence, as well as God's approval of the their continued witness despite persecution by their opponents. Stephen is accused of blasphemy in Acts 6, and his defense (Acts 7), much like Peter's earlier, is based largely on God's testimony through scripture. Although Stephen is martyred, he receives God's approval through a vision of Jesus in heaven, enraging his opponents.

In Acts 8, Philip's encounter with the Ethiopian eunuch is orchestrated through divine testimony through direct commands from the Holy Spirit. Philip is an obedient witness, explaining to the eunuch through the fulfilled prophecies of Isaiah (Isa 53:7–8) the good news of Jesus. Thus, a movement of the gospel into Ethiopia is confirmed for the auditor by the *topos* of divine testimony.

In the next chapters of Acts, a major shift in the work of the apostles is determined and subsequently sanctioned through divine testimony.

Conclusion

In Acts 9, Saul, on his way to Damascus to arrest followers of Jesus, is convinced through two visions, one to him and one to Ananias, to cease persecuting the fledgling church and to become a witness for Jesus. Peter and the Roman centurion Cornelius likewise receive visions, which bring them together (Acts 10:1—11:18) and serve to demonstrate God's approval of the gospel being received by the Gentiles. In both of these instances, divine testimony is the vehicle through which an ancient auditor would have understood this major shift in the proclamation of the gospel, from being exclusively preached to the Jews to being available to the Gentiles as well.

In Acts 12, Peter is once again proved innocent through a testimony from God; in this case, much like the narrative in Acts 5, Peter is delivered from prison by an angelic being. Herod, responsible for Peter's incarceration, is thus portrayed as an enemy of the gospel, which is confirmed by Herod's death at the end of Acts 12. In Acts 13, Paul and Barnabas are set apart through testimony by the Holy Spirit for a specific work (13:1-3); their witness meets opposition on the island of Cyprus, which Paul resists through inspired speech, proving the legitimacy of the work to which they were called (13:9-12). Later, while in Antioch in Pisidia, Paul persuades his audience that Jesus' resurrection is the fulfillment of God's testimonies by citing passages from the Psalms and Isaiah (13:33-35). He goes on to reference Hab 1:5 as a prophetic warning to his audience, the fulfillment of which is found in 13:44-52. In this passage, some of the Jews reject the message of Paul and Barnabas, thus demonstrating their lack of regard for God's testimony. Paul subsequently cites Isa 49:6 as a divine command to him and Barnabas to continue their work among the Gentiles. Through the *topos* of divine testimony, Paul and Barnabas are portrayed as obedient to God's commands, while those who reject their message are shown to be lacking in their regard towards God's desires.

In Acts 15, James cites Amos 9:11-12 (Acts 15:16-18) as proof that what Peter, Paul, and Barnabas are doing is in fulfillment of what God has prophesied. Once again, divine testimony serves as God's sanction of the work of the apostles. Later, Paul, now with Silas, is directed by testimony through the Holy Spirit to enter Macedonia in order to preach the gospel. Their work in this region is further sanctioned by divine testimony; in Acts 16:24-40, Paul and Silas are freed from prison through an earthquake. The earthquake would have been understood by an ancient audience as divine approval of Paul and Silas, but also as disapproval of those who would hinder the spread of the gospel.

The *Topos* of Divine Testimony in Luke/Acts

For Paul, the pattern of preaching the gospel and meeting resistance continues. In Corinth, when Paul encounters resistance to the gospel from some of the Jews, he declares his innocence and his intention to preach to the Gentiles (18:6). Shortly thereafter, Paul has a dream in which the Lord speaks to him and encourages him to stay. This dream serves as God's approval of Paul's decision to stay in Corinth and focus on the Gentiles; more significantly, however, it is also God's testimony to Paul's innocence, a theme with which the rest of Acts will deal. In Acts 21:4 and 21:10–12, Paul is warned through inspired speech that his persistence in going to Jerusalem (see 19:21) will result in imprisonment. Paul, however, demonstrates his obedience to the divine plan and continues on. As he meets opposition, he defends himself before the people of Jerusalem by relating the vision from the Lord he received on the way to Damascus (22:6–16), along with a second vision he received in the temple in Jerusalem (22:17–21). In this way, God's testimony through dreams is used as evidence of Paul's innocence of wrongdoing.

This pattern of defense through divine testimony continues in Acts 23. Here, in a defense speech before the council, Paul is accused of insulting the high priest. In his argument, he cites the law in order to show that he is normally obedient to the law and therefore innocent of wrongdoing; in this case he simply did not recognize the high priest. After his appearance before the council, Paul receives yet another vision (23:11), in which God testifies that Paul will be his witness in Rome. Through the vision, the auditor understands that Paul is indeed innocent of the accusations against him, and has been declared so by God's testimony. Having been moved to Caesarea, Paul must then plead his case before Agrippa (26:1–23). Once again, he relates the vision he received on his way to Damascus, invoking God's testimony through that vision as part of his defense.

Finally, Paul finds himself on the way to Rome, confirming what Paul decided ἐν τῷ πνεύματι in 19:21 and what God told him in the vision in 23:11. On the voyage there, he must endure a terrible storm, during which he has another vision, through which God testifies that Paul will survive the journey to Rome, along with the rest of the passengers (27:24–26). Paul, however, must demonstrate his obedience to the vision by keeping the crew on the ship. When they are finally shipwrecked on Malta, Paul receives a bite on the hand from a snake. The islanders reflect the opinion of the ancient audience when they remark that Paul must be guilty of something, having endured a sea storm and a snake bite. From the previous instances of divine testimony, however, the auditors of Luke-Acts know that God has already declared Paul innocent, and that he will indeed make it to Rome. His survival of storm and snake bite serves to reinforce his innocence.

At the conclusion of the narrative, Paul is indeed in Rome. Again, Paul follows his pattern of preaching to the Jews first, and as before, some respond positively, while some reject his message. Paul therefore resolves to turn to the Gentiles; at this point, the Lukan Paul once again invokes divine testimony through the citation of Isa 6:9–10, through which he argues that the Jews' refusal to accept his testimony to Jesus is the fulfillment of prophecy and therefore God's declaration of their guilt.

One sees, therefore, that the main characters in the combined narrative of Luke-Acts are described throughout by God's testimony. Jesus, even before his birth, is shown to enjoy God's favor through testimony to multiple, less important characters, such as John's parents, Jesus' parents, and John himself. God testifies directly to Jesus' significance at his baptism, at the transfiguration, and finally at his death[9] and resurrection. In the same way, Peter, in Acts, is legitimated through the reception of the Holy Spirit,[10] by his understanding that the Jewish scriptures are being fulfilled by present events, through dreams and visions, and through being sprung from jail by God's messenger. Likewise, Paul is commissioned through a divine vision, is constantly given guidance through the same means, and also demonstrates his concord with God's will through his invocation of scripture as fulfillment of prophecy, commands, and warnings.[11]

Just as the protagonists are portrayed as enjoying God's favor through divine testimony throughout the narrative, the antagonists are constantly depicted as resisting God's plan. Jesus' opponents are shown to have no understanding and/or regard for the prophecies concerning him (or the scriptures in general); their guilt is confirmed through his death and subsequent resurrection. This characterization continues in Acts, in which the opponents of the apostles are depicted similarly through instances of divine testimony. Their attempts to obstruct the apostles' missionary work

---

9. All of which provides supporting evidence for the centurion's statement: Ὄντως ὁ ἄνθρωπος οὗτος δίκαιος ἦν (Luke 23:47).

10. Along with, obviously, the rest of the disciples.

11. For a general discussion of parallels between Luke and Acts, as well as those within the individual documents, see Talbert, *Literary Patterns*, 15–33. This discussion could be expanded to include the "supporting" characters in the narrative, such as John the Baptist (in Luke), Philip, Stephen, and James (in Acts).

are overturned, and their ignorance concerning Jesus and their opposition to God's will are shown to be the fulfillment of prophecy.[12]

In this way, evidence through God's testimony for the piety, and therefore the innocence, of the protagonists is built up over the course of the two-part narrative, the cumulative weight of which would have been readily understood by the ancient audience.[13] Likewise, the evidence against the opponents also amasses, demonstrating that those who oppose what God is doing through Jesus are guilty, guilty of the sin of impiety. Hence, when Jesus is on trial at the end of Luke, the audience is clear as to the question of his innocence. The same is true of Peter before the Sanhedrin, and Paul in his various trial scenes. Luke, acting somewhat as a lawyer, has presented repeated instances of divine testimony, demonstrating the piety of his protagonists, and contrariwise disparaging those opposing them by the same methods. Innocence and guilt have been established in the minds of the auditors.

Avenues of Future Research

This study in its present form has opened up several possibilities for future explorations of this topic. There are opportunities to increase both the breadth and depth of the study. Both of these options will be briefly elaborated.

One way in which the scope of the study could be widened is through the expansion of what exactly constitutes divine testimony. In the present study, I have consciously limited myself to instances which correspond (to varying degree) to Cicero's definition (cf. *Top.* 20.76–77) of divine testimony. One could, perhaps, make the case that the healings, exorcisms, and resuscitations performed by Jesus in Luke and his witnesses in Acts are indeed acts of divine testimony. Evidence for this is found in Acts 2:22, within Peter's speech following the events of Pentecost. The Lukan Peter explains to his audience that Jesus was a man ἀποδεδειγμένον ἀπὸ τοῦ θεοῦ εἰς ὑμᾶς δυνάμεσι καὶ τέρασι καὶ σημείοις οἷς ἐποίησεν δι' αὐτοῦ ὁ θεὸς ἐν

---

12. In Luke, this characterization extends also to Jesus' disciples. Although they are certainly not depicted as Jesus' opponents, as I have demonstrated, divine testimony is used to portray them as lacking in understanding of Jesus' mission and purpose. After their encounter with the risen Jesus, however, this is clearly no longer the case.

13. This is the basic argument of Salier, *Rhetorical Impact*, who maintains that the signs in John's gospel serve as forensic evidence which, from a narrative and rhetorical standpoint, accumulates as the narrative progresses; by the time Jesus is on trial, the auditor is convinced of his innocence.

μέσῳ ὑμῶν. δυνάμεσι καὶ τέρασι καὶ σημείοις in this statement certainly refer to Jesus' actions described throughout the Gospel of Luke, and that Luke considers Jesus to be an agent of God's power. Therefore, these signs and wonders, performed by God through Jesus and the apostles (cf. Acts 4:16, 30) are elements of God's testimony on behalf of his son Jesus, as well as the witnesses to the son.

A second manner in which the breadth of the present study could be expanded is through the investigation of other NT documents for this same phenomenon. Clearly the other gospel writers have employed the miraculous as a constitutive element within their narratives; given this study as a baseline, one could compare the function of the miraculous in those documents in an attempt to answer the question of how an ancient audience would have heard and understood the miraculous elements within them. Also, as I have done in this study, the citation of scripture in the other gospels would be an integral part of such a future investigation. While miraculous occurrences play less of a role in the epistolary literature of the NT, the citation of scripture is quite prevalent. Here, a fruitful path of research would be to consider the possibility of the Jewish scripture functioning as authoritative, and even divine, testimony, in an attempt to persuade the original audiences to which those documents were addressed.

The present study could also be expanded by increasing its depth. As I have demonstrated, the *topos* of divine testimony was primarily used as evidence in forensic and deliberative situations. I have shown that to be the case in ancient speeches, treatises, and as a similar means of characterization in narratives. The forensic nature of divine testimony, therefore, serves to undergird the trial motif that is found at the conclusion of the Third Gospel and throughout Acts. Here, the work of A. Neagoe[14] is significant. In his monograph, Neagoe argues that the trial scenes in Luke-Acts constitute an element of the author's apology for the gospel, his *apologia pro evangelio*, which is part and parcel of his stated purpose, namely, ἵνα ἐπιγνῷς περὶ ὧν κατηχήθης λόγων τὴν ἀσφάλειαν (Luke 1:4).[15] Therefore, in the Third Gospel, while Jesus himself is the defendant in the trial scenes, the actual subject of the trial is Jesus' messiahship; the issue being adjudicated is "Christianity's beliefs about Jesus."[16] The trial of the gospel continues in Acts; in Acts, however, the apostles are now the

---

14. Neagoe, *Trial of the Gospel*.
15. Ibid., 22.
16. Ibid., 90.

ones who are the defendants on trial,[17] but it is their message that is being judged.

The use of divine testimony would clearly strengthen Neagoe's thesis. As I have shown, divine testimony serves to legitimate Jesus, the defendant of the trial in the Third Gospel. Jesus' innocence is declared on a narrative level through the various instances of the *topos* of divine testimony found throughout the narrative. Those who oppose him, even the disciples to a certain degree, are portrayed negatively through the same means. Rhetorically, the *topos* serves to add significance to the implied author's voice as part of the *apologia pro evangelio*, to which Neagoe draws attention. This is performed in a way that, as demonstrated by this study, would have been found persuasive by an ancient audience.

The same can be said for Jesus' apostles in Acts. After experiencing the resurrected Jesus, at the end of the Third Gospel and the beginning of Acts, they are transformed from "opponents" of the gospel to its spokespersons. They, too, are portrayed to be legitimate proponents of the gospel through God's testimony at various strategic points in the narrative. Their opponents, however, are depicted as impious and incapable of understanding what God has done through Jesus. As in the Third Gospel, the gospel itself is thus supported through the implied author's use of the *topos* of divine testimony.

---

17. Neagoe specifically analyzes the trials of Peter, Stephen, and Paul in Part Two of his monograph (*Trial of the Gospel*, 131–218).

Bibliography

Primary Sources

Aeschines. *In Ctesiphonem.* Translated by C. D. Adams. LCL. Cambridge, MA: Harvard University Press, 1968.
Aristides. *In Defense of Oratory.* Translated by C. A. Behr. LCL. Cambridge, MA: Harvard University Press, 1973.
Aristotle. *Rhetorica.* Translated by J. H. Freese. LCL. Cambridge, MA: Harvard University Press, 1991.
———. *Topica.* Translated by E. S. Forster. LCL. Cambridge, MA: Harvard University Press, 1960.
Artemidorus. *Oneirocritica.* Translated by Robert J. White. Park Ridge, NJ: Noyes, 1975.
Cicero, M. T. *De amicitia.* Translated by W. A. Falconer. LCL. Cambridge, MA: Harvard University Press, 1971.
———. *De divinatione.* Translated by W. A. Falconer. LCL. Cambridge, MA: Harvard University Press, 1971.
———. *De domo suo.* Translated by N. H. Watts. LCL. Cambridge, MA: Harvard University Press, 1965.
———. *De haruspicum responso.* Translated by N. H. Watts. LCL. Cambridge, MA: Harvard University Press, 1965.
———. *De inventione rhetorica.* Translated by H. M. Hubbell. LCL. Cambridge, MA: Harvard University Press, 2006.
———. *De legibus.* Translated by C. W. Keyes. LCL. Cambridge, MA: Harvard University Press, 1977.
———. *De officiis.* Translated by W. Miller. LCL. Cambridge, MA: Harvard University Press, 1938.
———. *De oratore.* Translated by E. W. Sutton and H. Rackham. LCL. Cambridge, MA: Harvard University Press, 1979.
———. *In Catalinam.* Translated by C. Macdonald. LCL. Cambridge, MA: Harvard University Press, 1977.
———. *In Vatinium.* Translated by R. Gardner. LCL. Cambridge, MA: Harvard University Press, 1958.
———. *In Verrem.* Translated by L. H. G. Greenwod. 2 vols. LCL. Cambridge, MA: Harvard University Press, 1976.
———. *Orationes philippicae.* Translated by W. C. A. Ker and D R. Shackleton Bailey. 3 vols. LCL. Cambridge, MA: Harvard University Press, 1969.

Bibliography

———. *Partitiones oratoriae*. Translated by H. Rackham. LCL. Cambridge, MA: Harvard University Press, 1942.

———. *Pro Ligario*. Translated by N. H. Watts. LCL. Cambridge, MA: Harvard University Press, 1953.

———. *Pro Milone*. Translated by N. H. Watts. LCL. Cambridge, MA: Harvard University Press, 1953.

———. *Pro Sulla*. Translated by C. Macdonald. LCL. Cambridge, MA: Harvard University Press, 1977.

———. *Topica*. Translated by H. M. Hubbell. LCL. Cambridge, MA: Harvard University Press, 2006.

———. *Tusculanae disputationes*. Translated by J. E. King. LCL. Cambridge, MA: Harvard University Press, 1971.

Charlesworth, James H., editor. *The Old Testament Pseudepigrapha*. 2 vols. AB Reference Library. Garden City, NY: Doubleday, 1983–1985.

Demosthenes. *In Midiam*. Translated by J. H. Vince. LCL. Cambridge, MA: Harvard University Press, 1935.

Dilts, Mervin R., and George A. Kennedy, editors. *Two Greek Rhetorical Treatises from the Roman Empire: Introduction, Text, and Translation of the Arts of Rhetoric Attributed to Anonymous Seguerianus and to Apsines of Gadara*. Leiden: Brill, 1997.

Dio Cassius. *Roman History*. Translated by E. Cary and H. B. Foster. 9 vols. LCL. Cambridge, MA: Harvard University Press, 1969.

Dio Chrysostom. *Discourses*. Translated by J. W. Cohoon and H. Lamar Crosby. 5 vols. LCL. Cambridge, MA: Harvard University Press, 1961–1962.

Diodorus Siculus. *Bibliotheca historica*. Translated by C. H. Oldfather. 12 vols. LCL. Cambridge, MA: Harvard University Press, 1954.

Dionysius of Halicarnassus. *Antiquitates romanae*. Translated by E. Cary. 7 vols. LCL. Cambridge, MA: Harvard University Press, 1968.

———. *De Thucydide*. Translated by S. Usher. LCL. Cambridge, MA: Harvard University Press, 1974.

Isocrates. *Helenae encomium*. Translated by L. van Hook. LCL. Cambridge, MA: Harvard University Press, 1954.

Josephus. *Bellum judaicum*. Translated by H. St. J. Thackeray. 3 vols. LCL. Cambridge, MA: Harvard University Press, 1997.

Kennedy, George A., editor and translator. *Progymnasmata: Greek Textbooks of Prose Composition and Rhetoric*. Writings from the Greco-Roman World 10. Atlanta: SBL, 2003.

Kraus, Thomas J., and Tobias Nicklas, editors. *Das Petrusevangelium und die Petrusapokalypse: Die griechischen Fragmente mit deutscher und englischer Übersetzung*. Die griechische christliche Schriftsteller der ersten Jahrhunderte 11. Berlin: de Gruyter, 2004.

Livy. *Historiae*. Translated by B. O. Foster et al. 14 vols. LCL. Cambridge, MA: Harvard University Press, 1968–1979.

Longinus. *On the Sublime*. Translated by W. H. Fyfe. Revised by D. Russell. LCL. Cambridge, MA: Harvard University Press, 1995.

Lucian. *How to Write History*. Translated by K. Kilburn. LCL. Cambridge, MA: Harvard University Press, 1968.

Lycurgus. *Against Leocrates*. Translated by J. O. Burtt. LCL. Cambridge, MA: Harvard University Press, 1954.
The Martyrdom of Polycarp. In *The Apostolic Fathers*, translated by B. Ehrman, 1:355–401. 2 vols. LCL. Cambridge, MA: Harvard University Press, 2003.
Patillion, Michel, and Giancarlo Bolognesi, editors and translators. *Aelius Théon: Progymnasmata*. Paris: Belles Lettres, 1997.
Pausanias. *Graeciae description*. Translated by F. H. Jones. 4 vols. LCL. Cambridge, MA: Harvard University Press, 1977.
Philo. *De cherubim*. Translated by F. H. Colson and G. H. Whitaker. LCL. Cambridge, MA: Harvard University Press, 1929.
———. *De confusione linguarum*. Translated by F. H. Colson and G. H. Whitaker. LCL. Cambridge, MA: Harvard University Press, 1932.
———. *De somniis*. Translated by F. H. Colson and G. H. Whitaker. LCL. Cambridge, MA: Harvard University Press, 1934.
———. *De vita Mosis*. Translated by F. H. Colson. LCL. Cambridge, MA: Harvard University Press, 1935.
———. *Quod Deus sit immutabilis*. F. H. Colson and G. H. Whitaker. LCL. Cambridge, MA: Harvard University Press, 1930.
Plato. *Alcibiades major*. Translated by W. R. M. Lamb. LCL. Cambridge, MA: Harvard University Press, 1979.
———. *Apologia*. Translated by H. N. Fowler. LCL. Cambridge, MA: Harvard University Press, 1977.
———. *Charmides*. Translated by W. R. M. Lamb. LCL. Cambridge, MA: Harvard University Press, 1979.
———. *Phaedrus*. Translated by H. N. Fowler. LCL. Cambridge, MA: Harvard University Press, 1977.
Pliny the Elder. *Naturalis historia*. Translated by H. Rackham. 10 vols. LCL. Cambridge, MA: Harvard University Press, 1938.
Plutarch. *Agesilaus*. Translated by B. Perrin. LCL. Cambridge, MA: Harvard University Press, 1968.
———. *Agis et Cleomenes*. Translated by B. Perrin. LCL. Cambridge, MA: Harvard University Press, 1968.
———. *Alcibiades*. Translated by B. Perrin. LCL. Cambridge, MA: Harvard University Press, 1968.
———. *Alexander*. Translated by B. Perrin. LCL. Cambridge, MA: Harvard University Press, 1971.
———. *Caesar*. Translated by B. Perrin. LCL. Cambridge, MA: Harvard University Press, 1971.
———. *Cato Minor*. Translated by B. Perrin. LCL. Cambridge, MA: Harvard University Press, 1969.
———. *Comparatio Agesilai et Pompeii*. Translated by B. Perrin. LCL. Cambridge, MA: Harvard University Press, 1968.
———. *Comparatio Agidis et Cleomenis cum Tiberio et Gaio Graccho*. Translated by B. Perrin. LCL. Cambridge, MA: Harvard University Press, 1968.
———. *Comparatio Demosthenis et Ciceronis*. Translated by B. Perrin. LCL. Cambridge, MA: Harvard University Press, 1971.
———. *Comparatio Lycurgi et Numae*. Translated by B. Perrin. LCL. Cambridge, MA: Harvard University Press, 1967.

Bibliography

———. *Comparatio Pelopidae et Marcelli*. Translated by B. Perrin. LCL. Cambridge, MA: Harvard University Press, 1917.
———. *De Pythiae oraculis*. Translated by F. C. Babbitt. LCL. Cambridge, MA: Harvard University Press, 1969.
———. *Demosthenes*. Translated by B. Perrin. LCL. Cambridge, MA: Harvard University Press, 1971.
———. *Galba*. Translated by B. Perrin. LCL. Cambridge, MA: Harvard University Press, 1967.
———. *Lycurgus*. Translated by B. Perrin. LCL. Cambridge, MA: Harvard University Press, 1967.
———. *Numa*. Translated by B. Perrin. LCL. Cambridge, MA: Harvard University Press, 1967.
———. *Pelopidas*. Translated by B. Perrin. LCL. Cambridge, MA: Harvard University Press, 1968.
———. *Pericles*. Translated by B. Perrin. LCL. Cambridge, MA: Harvard University Press, 1916.
———. *Pompey*. Translated by B. Perrin. LCL. Cambridge, MA: Harvard University Press, 1917.
———. *Pyrrhus*. Translated by F. C. Babbitt. LCL. Cambridge, MA: Harvard University Press, 1968.
———. *Superstition*. Translated by F. C. Babbitt. LCL. Cambridge, MA: Harvard University Press, 1962.
———. *Themistocles*. Translated by B. Perrin. LCL. Cambridge, MA: Harvard University Press, 1968.
———. *Theseus*. Translated by B. Perrin. LCL. Cambridge, MA: Harvard University Press, 1967.
———. *Tiberius et Caius Gracchus*. Translated by B. Perrin. LCL. Cambridge, MA: Harvard University Press, 1949.
———. *Timoleon*. Translated by B. Perrin. LCL. Cambridge, MA: Harvard University Press, 1918.
Polybius. *The Histories*. Translated by W. R. Paton. 6 vols. LCL. Cambridge, MA: Harvard University Press, 1979.
Ps.-Cicero. *Rhetorica ad Herennium*. Translated by H. Caplan. LCL. Cambridge, MA: Harvard University Press, 1981.
Ps.-Longinus. *On the Sublime*. Translated by W. H. Fyfe. LCL. Cambridge, MA: Harvard University Press, 1973.
Quintilian. *Declamationes*. Translated by D. R. Shackleton Bailey. 2 vols. LCL. Cambridge, MA: Harvard University Press, 2006.
———. *Institutio oratoria*. Translated by D. A. Russell. 5 vols. LCL. Cambridge, MA: Harvard University Press, 2001.
Quintus Curtius. *The History of Alexander*. Translated by J. C. Rolfe. 2 vols. LCL. Cambridge, MA: Harvard University Press, 1971.
Seneca. *Ad Marciam de consolatione*. Translated by J. W. Basore. LCL. Cambridge, MA: Harvard University Press, 1970.
———. *Epistulae morales*. Translated by R. M. Gummere. 3 vols. LCL. Cambridge, MA: Harvard University Press, 1934.
———. *Naturales quaestiones*. Translated by T. H. Corcoran. LCL. Cambridge, MA: Harvard University Press, 1971.

Bibliography

Seneca the Elder. *Controversiae*. Translated by M. Winterbottom. 2 vols. LCL. Cambridge, MA: Harvard University Press, 1974.
———. *Suasoriae*. Translated by M. Winterbottom. LCL. Cambridge, MA: Harvard University Press, 1974.
Suetonius. *Divus Augustus*. Translated by J. C. Rolfe. LCL. Cambridge, MA: Harvard University Press, 1979.
———. *Divus Claudius*. Translated by J. C. Rolfe. LCL. Cambridge, MA: Harvard University Press, 1979.
———. *Divus Julius*. Translated by J. C. Rolfe. LCL. Cambridge, MA: Harvard University Press, 1979.
———. *Galba*. Translated by J. C. Rolfe. LCL. Cambridge, MA: Harvard University Press, 1979.
———. *Otho*. Translated by J. C. Rolfe. LCL. Cambridge, MA: Harvard University Press, 1979.
———. *Vespasianus*. Translated by J. C. Rolfe. LCL. Cambridge, MA: Harvard University Press, 1979.
Tacitus. *Annales*. Translated by J. Jackson. 5 vols. LCL. Cambridge, MA: Harvard University Press, 1969.
———. *Historiae*. Translated by C. H. Moore. 2 vols. LCL. Cambridge, MA: Harvard University Press, 1969.
Testament of Abraham. In *The Old Testament Pseudepigrapha*, translated by E. P. Sanders, edited by James H. Charlesworth, 1:871–902. AB Reference Library. Garden City, NY: Doubleday, 1983–1985.
Valerius Maximus. *Memorable Doings and Sayings*. Translated by D. R. Shackleton Bailey. LCL. Cambridge, MA: Harvard University Press, 2000.
Xenophon. *Cyropaedia*. Translated by W. Miller. 2 vols. LCL. Cambridge, MA: Harvard University Press, 1979.

Secondary Sources

Achtemeier, Paul. "Gospel Miracle Tradition and the Divine Man." *Int* 26 (1972) 174–97.
———. "Lucan Perspective on the *Miracles of* Jesus: A Preliminary Sketch." *JBL* 94 (1975) 547–62.
Adams, Marilyn M. "The Role of Miracles in the Structure of Luke-Acts." In *Hermes and Athena: Biblical Exegesis and Philosophical Theology*, edited by E. Stump and T. P. Flint, 235–73. Notre Dame: University of Notre Dame Press, 1993.
Ådna, Jostein. "Die Heilige Schrift als Zeuge der Heidenmission: Die Rezeption von Amos 9,11–12 in Apg 15,16–18." In *Evangelium, Schriftauslegung, Kirche*, edited by P. Stuhlmacher et al., 1–23. Göttingen: Vandenhoeck & Ruprecht, 1979.
Alexander, Loveday. "Luke's Preface in the Context of Greek Preface-Writing." *NovT* 28 (1986) 48–74.
———. *The Preface to Luke's Gospel: Literary Convention and Social Context in Luke 1.1–4 and Acts 1.1*. SNTSMS 78. Cambridge: Cambridge University Press, 1993.
Anderson, John. "A Look at Implicit Information in Rabbinical Argumentation." *Notes on Translation* 13 (1999) 13–14.

Bibliography

Auffret, Pierre. "Note sure la structure littéraire de Lc 1.68-79." *NTS* 24 (1977-1978) 248-58.
Aune, David E. *Prophecy in Early Christianity and the Ancient Mediterranean World.* Grand Rapids: Eerdmans, 1983.
Baawobr, Richard K. "Opening a Narrative Programme: Luke 4.16-30 and the Black Bagr Narrative." *JSNT* 30 (2007) 29-53.
Barthes, Roland. "L'Analyse structurale du Récit a propos d'Actes X-XI." *RSR* 58 (1970) 17-37.
Basinger, David, and Randall Basinger. *Philosophy and Miracle: The Contemporary Debate.* Lewiston: Edwin Mellen Press, 1986.
Basser, Herbert W. "The Jewish Roots of the Transfiguration." *BRev* 14 (1998) 30-35.
Bauckham, Richard. "James and the Jerusalem Church." In *The Book of Acts in Its First Century Setting,* edited by R. Bauckham, 4:415-80. Grand Rapids: Eerdmans, 1995.
Bauer, W., F. W. Danker, W. F. Arndt, and F. W. Gingrich. *Greek-English Lexicon of the New Testament and Other Early Christian Literature.* 3rd ed. Chicago: University of Chicago Press, 2000.
Beard, Mary. "Cicero and Divination: The Formation of a Latin Discourse." *JRS* 76 (1986) 33-46.
Beck, Hans. "Interne 'synkrisis' bei Plutarch." *Hermes* 130 (2002) 467-89.
Begg, Christopher T. *Judean Antiquities 5-7.* Vol. 4 of *Flavius Josephus: Translation and Commentary.* Edited by S. Mason. Leiden: Brill, 2000.
Begg, Christopher T., and Paul Spilsbury. *Judean Antiquities 8-10.* Vol. 5 of *Flavius Josephus: Translation and Commentary.* Edited by S. Mason. Leiden: Brill, 2000.
Behr, Charles A. *Aelius Aristides and The Sacred Tales.* Amsterdam: Adolf M. Hakkert, 1968.
Berger, Klaus. "Das Canticum Simeonis (Lk 2:29-32)." *NovT* 27 (1985) 27-39.
Best, Ernest. "Acts XIII. 1-3." *JTS* 11 (1960) 344-48.
Betz, Hans D. "The Early Christian Miracle Story: Some Observations on the Form Critical Problem." *Semeia* 11 (1978) 69-81.
———. *Galatians.* Hermeneia. Philadelphia: Fortress, 1979.
———. "Jesus as Divine Man." In *Jesus and the Historian: Written in Honor of Ernest Cadman Colwell,* edited by F. T. Trotter, 114-33. Philadelphia: Westminster, 1968.
Bevan, Edwyn. *Sibyls and Seers: A Survey of Some Ancient Theories of Revelation and Inspiration.* Cambridge, MA: Harvard University Press, 1929.
Bieler, Ludwig. *Theios aner: Das Bild des "Göttlichen Menschen" in Spätantike und Frühchristentum.* 2 vols. Vienna: Höfels, 1935-1936.
Bloomquist, L. Gregory. "Rhetorical Argumentation and the Culture of Apocalyptic: A Socio-Rhetorical Analysis of Luke 21." In *The Rhetorical Interpretation of Scripture: Essays from the 1996 Malibu Conference,* edited by S. E. Porter and D. L. Stamps, 173-209. JSNTSup 180. Sheffield: Sheffield Academic, 1999.
Blumenthal, Christian. "Zur 'Zinne des Tempels.'" *ZNW* 96 (2005) 274-83.
Bock, Darrell L. *Acts.* Grand Rapids: Baker, 2007.
———. *Luke.* 2 vols. Grand Rapids: Baker, 1996.
———. *Proclamation from Prophecy and Pattern: Lucan Old Testament Christology.* JSNTSup 12. Sheffield: JSOT Press, 1987.
———. "Proclamation from Prophecy and Pattern: Luke's Use of the OT for Christology and Mission." In *The Gospels and the Scriptures of Israel,* edited by C. A. Evans and W. R. Stegner, 280-307. JSNTSup 104. Sheffield: Sheffield Academic, 1994.

Bibliography

Boismard, Marie-Émile, and Arnaud Lamouille. *Le Texte occidental des Actes des Apôtres: Reconstitution et Réhabilitation.* Paris: Éditions Recherche sur les Civilisations, 1984.

Bornscheuer, Lothar. *Topik: Zur Struktur der gesellschaftlichen Einbildungskraft.* Frankfurt: Surkamp, 1976.

Bouché-Leclercq, Auguste. *Histoire de la Divination dans l'Antique.* 4 vols in 2. New York: Arno, 1975.

Bovon, François. *Luke the Theologian: Fifty-five Years of Research (1955–2005).* Rev. ed. Waco: Baylor University Press, 2005.

———. "'Schön hat der heilige Geist durch den Propheten Jesaja zu euren Vätern gesprochen' (Act 28 25)." *ZNW* 75 (1984) 226–32.

Bowden, Hugh. *Classical Athens and the Delphic Oracle: Divination and Democracy.* Cambridge: Cambridge University Press, 2005.

Brawley, Robert. *Centering on God: Method and Message in Luke-Acts.* Louisville: Westminster John Knox, 1990.

Brenk, Frederick E. "Greek Epiphanies and Paul." In *Relighting the Souls: Studies in Plutarch, in Greek Literature, Religion, and Philosophy, and in the New Testament Background,* 354–63. Stuttgart: Steiner, 1998.

———. "An Imperial Heritage: The Religious Spirit of Plutarch of Chaironeia." *ANRW* 36/1:248–349. Part 2, *Principat,* 36/1. Edited by H. Temporini and W. Haase. New York: de Gruyter, 1987.

———. *In Mist Apparelled.* Leiden: Brill, 1977.

Brodie, Thomas L. "The Departure for Jerusalem (Luke 9, 51–52) as a Rhetorical Imitation of Elijah's Departure for the Jordan (2 Kgs 1, 1–2, 6)." *Bib* 70 (1989) 96–109.

Brown, Raymond E. "The Meaning of the Manger; The Significance of the Shepherds." *Worship* 50 (1976) 528–38.

———. "The Presentation of Jesus (Luke 2:22–40)." *Worship* 51 (1977) 2–11.

Brueggemann, Walter. "Dialogue Between Incommensurate Partners: Prospects for Common Testimony." *JES* 38 (2001) 383–98.

Brunt, P. A. *Roman Imperial Themes.* Oxford: Clarendon, 1990.

Bultmann, Rudolf. *History of the Synoptic Tradition.* 2nd ed. Translated by J. Marsh. Oxford: Blackwell, 1968.

Burridge, Richard A. "The Gospels and Acts." In *Handbook of Classical Rhetoric in the Hellenistic Period: 330 B.C.–A.D. 400,* edited by S. E. Porter, 507–32. Leiden: Brill, 1997.

———. *What are the Gospels?* Society for New Testament Studies Monograph Series 70. Cambridge: Cambridge University Press, 1992.

Burriss, Eli E. "Cicero and the Religion of His Day." *CJ* 21 (1926) 524–32.

Buschmann, Gerd. *Das Martyrium des Polykarp.* Kommentar zu den Apostolischen Vätern 6. Göttingen: Vandenhoeck & Ruprecht, 1998.

Busse, Ulrich. *Die Wunder des Propheten Jesu.* Rev. ed. FB 24. Stuttgart: Katholisches Bibelwerk, 1979.

Cadbury, Henry J. *The Making of Luke-Acts.* New York: Macmillan, 1927.

Caird, G. B. *The Gospel of St. Luke.* Middlesex: Penguin, 1968.

Campbell, Douglas A. "Possible Inscriptional Attestation to Sergius Paul[l]us (Acts 13:6–12), and the Implications for Pauline Chronology." *JTS* 56 (2005) 1–29.

Bibliography

Cape, Robert W., Jr. "Persuasive History: Roman Rhetoric and Historiography." In *Roman Eloquence: Rhetoric in Society and Literature*, edited by W. J. Dominick, 212-28. London: Routlege, 1997.

Carter, Warren. "Zechariah and the Benedictus." *Bib* 69 (1988) 239-47.

Chakoian, Christine. "Luke 3:1-16." *Int* 53 (1999) 400-404.

Chatman, Seymour. *Story and Discourse: Narrative Structure in Fiction and Film*. Ithaca: Cornell University Press, 1978.

Chibici-Revneanu, Nicole. "Ein himmlischer Stehplatz: Die Haltung Jesu in der Stephanusvision (Apg 7.55-56) und ihre Bedeutung." *NTS* 53 (2007) 459-88.

Chrimes, K. M. T. *Ancient Sparta: A Re-examination of the Evidence*. Manchester: University Press, 1952.

Clabeaux, John. "The Story of the Maltese Viper and Luke's Apology for Paul." *CBQ* 67 (2005) 604-10.

Cohn-Sherbok, D. M. "Jesus' Defence of the Resurrection of the Dead." *JSNT* 11 (1981) 64-73.

Coleridge, Mark. *The Birth of the Lukan Narrative: Narrative as Christology in Luke 1-2*. JSNTSup 88. Sheffield: JSOT Press, 1993.

Combrink, H. J. B. "The Structure and Significance of Luke 4:16-30." *Neot* 7 (1974) 27-47.

Conzelmann, Hans. *Acts of the Apostles*. Translated by J. Limburg, A. T. Kraabel, and D. H. Juel. Philadelphia: Fortress, 1987.

―――. *Bemerkungen zum Martyrium Polykarps*. Nachrichten der Akademie der Wissenschaften in Göttingen 2. Göttingen: Vandenhoeck & Ruprecht, 1978.

―――. *The Theology of St. Luke*. Translated by G. Buswell. Philadelphia: Fortress, 1982.

Cope, Edward M. *An Introduction to Aristotle's Rhetoric*. London: Macmillan, 1867.

Cosgrove, Charles H. "The Divine ΔEI in Luke-Acts." *NovT* 26 (1984) 168-90.

Crahay, Roland. *La Littérature Oraculaire chez Hérodote*. Paris: Société d'Editions, 1956.

Craig, Christopher. "Audience Expectations, Invective, and Proof." In *Cicero the Advocate*, edited by J. Powell and J. Paterson, 187-213. Oxford: Oxford University Press, 2004.

Crüsemann, Frank. "Schrift und Auferstehung: Beobachtungen zur Wahrnehmung des auferstandenen Jesus bei Lukas und Paulus und zum Verhältnis der Testamente." *Kirche und Israel* 17 (2002) 150-62.

Culy, Martin M., and M. C. Parsons. *Acts: A Handbook on the Greek Text*. Waco: Baylor University Press, 2003.

Curtius, Ernst Robert. *European Literature and the Latin Middle Ages*. Translated by W. R. Trask. New York: Harper & Row, 1953.

D'Angelo, Frank J. "The Evolution of the Analytic *Topoi*: A Speculative Inquiry." In *Classical Rhetoric and Modern Discourse*, edited by R. J. Connors, L. S. Ede, and A. A. Lunsford, 50-68. Carbondale: Southern Illinois University Press, 1984.

Danker, Frederick W. *Benefactor: Epigraphic Study of a Graeco-Roman and New Testament Semantic Field*. St. Louis: Clayton, 1982.

deSilva, David A. "Paul's Sermon in Antioch of Pisidia." *BSac* 151 (1994) 32-49.

Dibelius, Martin. *From Tradition to Gospel*. Translated by B. L. Woolf. New York: Scribner's Sons, 1935.

Dillon, Richard J. "The Benedictus in Micro- and Macro-Context." *CBQ* 68 (2006) 457-80.

―――. *From Eye-Witnesses to Ministers of the Word: Tradition and Composition in Luke 24*. Rome: Biblical Institute Press, 1978.

———. "Previewing Luke's Project from His Prologue (Luke 1:1–4)." *CBQ* 43 (1981) 205–27.

———. "The Prophecy of Christ and his Witnesses According to the Discourses of Acts." *NTS* 32 (1986) 544–56.

Doble, Peter. "Luke 24.26, 44—Songs of God's Servant: David and his Psalms in Luke-Acts." *JSNT* 28 (2006) 267–83.

Dochhorn, Jan. "Die Verschonung des samaritanischen Dorfes (Lk 9.54–55). Eine kritische Reflexion von Elia-Überlieferung im Lukasevangelium und eine frühjüdische Parallele im *Testament Abrahams*." *NTS* 53 (2007) 359–78.

Dodd, C. H. "The Fall of Jerusalem and the 'Abomination of Desolation.'" In *More New Testament Studies*, 69–83. Grand Rapids: Eerdmans, 1968.

Dodds, E. R. *The Greeks and the Irrational*. Boston: Beacon, 1957.

Dörrfuß, E. M. "'Wie eine Taube': Überlegungen zum Verständnis von Mk 1,10." *BN* 10 (1991) 7–13.

Downing, F. Gerald. "Psalms and the Baptist." *JSNT* 29 (2006) 131–37.

Droge, Arthur J., and James D. Tabor. *A Noble Death: Suicide and Martyrdom among Christians and Jews in Antiquity*. San Francisco: HarperSanFrancisco, 1992.

Drouot, Gr. "Le discourse inaugural de Jésus à Nazareth: la prophétie d'un retournement (Lc 4,16–30)." *NRTh* 129 (2007) 35–44.

Dunn, James D. G. *The Acts of the Apostles*. Valley Forge, PA: Trinity, 1996.

Dupont, Jacques. *Études sur les Actes des Apôtres*. Lectio divina 45. Paris: Cerf, 1967.

Dyck, A. R. "Narrative Obfuscation, Philosophical Topoi, and Tragic Patterning in Cicero's Pro Milone." *HSCP* 98 (1998) 219–41.

Ellis, E. Earle. *Christ and the Future in New Testament History*. Leiden: Brill, 2001.

Emrich, Berthold. "Topik und Topoi." In *Toposforschung: Eine Dokumentation*, edited by Peter Jehn, 90–120. Frankfurt: Athenäum, 1972.

Engelbrecht, J. "Trends in Miracle Research." *Neot* 22 (1988) 139–61.

Feldman, Louis H. *Judean Antiquities 1–4*. Vol. 3 of *Flavius Josephus: Translation and Commentary*. Edited by S. Mason. Leiden: Brill, 2000.

Fenske, Wolfgang. "Aspekte Biblischer Theologie dargestellt an der Verwendung von Ps 16 in Apostelgeschichte 2 und 13." *Bib* 83 (2002) 54–70.

Fiebig, Paul. *Antike Wundergeschichten: Zum Studium der Wunder des Neuen Testamentes*. Bonn: Marcus & Weber, 1911.

———. *Jüdische Wundergeschichten des neutestamentlichen Zeitalters unter besonderer Berücksichtigung ihres Verhältnisses zum Neuen Testament beartetiet*. Tübingen: Mohr/Siebeck, 1911.

———. *Rabbinische Wundergeschichten des neutestamentlichen Zeitalters*. Bonn: Marcus & Weber, 1911.

Figueras, Pau. "Syméon et Anne, ou le Témoignage de la loi et des Prophètes." *NovT* 20 (1978) 84–99.

Fitzmyer, Joseph. *The Acts of the Apostles*. AB 31. New York: Doubleday, 1998.

———. *The Gospel According to Luke*. AB 28. 2 vols. Garden City, NY: Doubleday, 1985.

———. "The Use of the Old Testament in Luke-Acts." In *SBL Seminar Papers, 1992*, 524–38. SBLSP 31. Atlanta: Scholars, 1992.

Flannery-Dailey, Frances. *Dreamers, Scribes, and Priests: Jewish Dreams in the Hellenistic and Roman Eras*. Supplements to the Journal for the Study of Judaism 90. Leiden: Brill, 2004.

Bibliography

Fontenrose, Joseph. *The Delphic Oracle: Its Responses and Operations.* Berkeley: University of California Press, 1978.

Forbes, Christopher. *Prophecy and Inspired Speech in Early Christianity and its Hellenistic Environment.* Peabody, MA: Hendrickson, 1997.

Foster, Paul. "Exegetical Notes on Luke 9:28–36." *ExpTim* 118 (2007) 188–89.

———. "Polymorphic Christology: Its Origins and Development in Early Christianity." *JTS* 58 (2007) 66–99.

Frost, Frank J. *Plutarch's Themistocles: A Historical Commentary.* Princeton: Princeton University Press, 1980.

Fuchs, Albert. "Die Agreements der Perikope von der Taufe Jesu: Mk 1,9–11 par Mt 3,13–17 par Lk 3,21–22." *SNTSU* 24 (1999) 5–34.

———. "Mehr als Davids Sohn: Mk 12,35–37a par Mt 22,41–46 par Lk 20,41–44." *SNTSU* 26 (2001) 111–28.

———. "Die Sadduzäerfrage: Mk 12,18–27 par Mt 22,23–33 par Lk 20,27–40." *SNTSU* 26 (2001) 83–110.

Gaines, Robert N. "Cicero's *Partitiones oratoriae* and *Topica*: Rhetorical Philosophy and Philosophical Rhetoric." In *Brill's Companion to Cicero: Oratory and Rhetoric*, edited by J. M. May, 445–80. Leiden: Brill, 2002.

Gardner, R. "The Lex Aelia Fufia in the Late Republic." In Cicero, *Volume XIII: Orations*, translated by R. Gardner, 309–22. Cambridge, MA: Harvard University Press, 1958.

Garrett, Susan R. *The Demise of the Devil: Magic and the Demonic in Luke's Writings.* Minneapolis: Fortress, 1989.

———. "Exodus from Bondage: Luke 9:31 and Acts 12:1–24." *CBQ* 52 (1990) 656–80.

Gathercole, Simon. "The Heavenly ἀνατολή (Luke 1:78–79)." *JTS* 56 (2005) 471–88.

Gaventa, Beverly R. *The Acts of the Apostles.* Abingdon New Testament Commentaries. Nashville: Abingdon, 2003.

Gill, David W. J. "Paul's Travels through Cyprus (Acts 13:4–12)." *TynBul* 46 (1995) 219–28.

Gnuse, Robert K. *Dreams and Dream Reports in the Writings of Josephus: A Traditio-Historical Analysis.* AGJU 86. Leiden: Brill, 1996.

———. "The Temple Theophanies of Jaddus, Hyrcanus, and Zechariah." *Bib* 79 (1998) 457–72.

Genuyt, François. "L'annonce rejetée/entravée: Les commencements du ministère de Jésus en Galilée (Luc 4,14–30)." *Sémiotique et Bible* 112 (2003) 43–54.

Goar, Robert J. *Cicero and the State Religion.* Amsterdam: Hakkert, 1972.

Goodenough, Erwin R. *Pagan Symbols in Judaism.* Vol. 8 of *Jewish Symbols in the Greco-Roman Period.* Bollingen Series 37. 13 vols. New York: Pantheon, 1958.

Goodwin, Jean. "Cicero's Authority." *Philosophy and Rhetoric* 34 (2001) 38–60.

Grant, Jamie A. "Singing the Cover Versions: Psalms, Reinterpretation and Biblical Theology in Acts 1–4." *Scottish Bulletin of Evangelical Theology* 25 (2007) 27–49.

Green, Joel B. *The Gospel of Luke.* Grand Rapids: Eerdmans, 1997.

———. "Jesus and a Daughter of Abraham (Luke 13:10–17). Test Case for a Lucan Perspective on Jesus' Miracles." *CBQ* 51 (1989) 643–54.

Greenridge, A. H. "The Repeal of the Lex Aelia Fufia." *The Classical Review* 7 (1893) 158–61.

Grimaldi, William M. A. "The Aristotelian Topics." In *Aristotle: The Classical Heritage of Rhetoric*, edited by K. V. Erickson, 176–93. Metuchen: Scarecrow, 1974.

Bibliography

Güttgemanns, Erhardt. "In welchem Sinne ist Lukas 'Historiker'?: Die Beziehungen von Luk 1, 1–4 und Papias zur antiken Rhetorik." *LB* 54 (1983) 9–26.
Haenchen, D. Ernst. *Die Apostelgeschichte*. Kritisch-exegetischer Kommentar über das Neue Testament. 5th ed. Göttingen: Vandenhoeck & Ruprecht, 1965.
———. "Judentum und Christentum in der Apostelgeschichte." *ZNW* 54 (1963) 155–87.
Hamm, Dennis. "The Tamid Service in Luke-Acts: The Cultic Background behind Luke's Theology of Worship (Luke 1:5–25; 18:9–14; 24:50–53; Acts 3:1; 10:3, 30)." *CBQ* 25 (2003) 215–31.
Hanson, John S. "Dreams and Visions in the Graeco-Roman World and Early Christianity." *ANRW* 23.2:1395–427. Part 2, *Principat*, 23.2. Edited by H. Temporini and W. Haase. New York: de Gruyter, 1980.
Harnack, Adolf von. *What is Christianity?* Translated by T. B. Saunders. 2nd ed. London: Williams & Norgate, 1901.
Haraguchi, Takaaki. "A Call for Repentance to the Whole Israel—A Rhetorical Study of Acts 3:12–26." *AJT* 18 (2004) 267–82.
Hays, Richard B. "Can the Gospels Teach us how to Read the Old Testament?" *ProEccl* 11 (2002) 402–18.
Hedrick, Charles. "Paul's Conversion/Call: A Comparative Analysis of the Three Reports in Acts." *JBL* 100 (1980) 415–32.
Heibges, Ursula. "Cicero, a Hypocrite in Religion?" *AJP* 90 (1969) 304–12.
———. "Religion and Rhetoric in Cicero's Speeches." *Latomus* 28 (1969) 833–49.
Heimerdinger, Jenny. "Unintentional Sins in Peter's Speech: Acts 3:12–26." *RCT* 20 (1995) 269–76.
Hertig, Paul. "The Jubilee Mission of Jesus in the Gospel of Luke: Reversals of Fortunes." *Missiology: An International Review* 26 (1998) 168–79.
Hohmann, Hanns. "Rhetoric and Dialectic: Some Historical and Legal Perspectives." In *Dialectic and Rhetoric: The Warp and Woof of Argumentation Analysis*, edited by F. H. van Eemeren and P. Houtlosser, 41–51. Boston: Kluwer Academic, 2002.
Holladay, Carl R. *Theios Aner in Hellenistic-Judaism: A Critique of the Use of this Category in New Testament Christology*. SBLDS 40. Missoula, MT: Scholars, 1977.
Hooker, Morna. *Jesus and the Servant: The Influence of the Servant Concept of Deutero-Isaiah in the New Testament*. London: SPCK, 1959.
Hornik, Heidi J., and Mikeal C. Parsons. "Ambrogio Lorenzetti's *Presentation in the Temple*: A 'Visual Exegesis' of Luke 2:22–38." *PRSt* 28 (2001) 31–46.
Horst, Pieter W. van der. "Hellenistic Parallels to the Acts of the Apostles (2.1–47)." *JSNT* 25 (1985) 49–60.
Horton, Dennis J. *Death and Resurrection: The Shape and Function of a Literary Motif in the Book of Acts*. Eugene, OR: Pickwick, 2009.
Hoyle, Peter. *Delphi*. London: Cassell, 1967.
Hubbard, Benjamin. "Commissioning Stories in Luke-Acts: A Study of their Antecedents, Form and Content." *Semeia* 8 (1977) 103–26.
———. "The Role of Commissioning Accounts in Acts." In *Perspectives on Luke-Acts*, edited by C. H. Talbert, 187–98. Edinburgh: T. & T. Clark, 1978.
Hull, John M. *Hellenistic Magic and the Synoptic Tradition*. SBT Second Series 28. London: SCM, 1974.
Hume, David. *Enquiries Concerning Human Understanding and Concerning the Principles of Morals*. 3rd ed. Oxford: Clarendon, 1975.

Bibliography

Humphrey, Edith M. "Collision of Modes?—Vision and Determining Argument in Acts 10:1—11:18." *Semeia* 71 (1995) 65–84.
Iser, Wolfgang. *The Act of Reading: A Theory of Aesthetic Response*. Baltimore: Johns Hopkins University Press, 1978.
Jauss, Hans-Robert. *Toward an Aesthetic of Reception*. Translated by T. Bahti. Minneapolis: University of Minnesota Press, 1982.
Jervell, Jacob. *Die Apostelgeschichte*. Kritisch-exegetischer Kommentar über das Neue Testament. 17th ed. Göttingen: Vandenhoeck & Ruprecht, 1998.
———. *Luke and the People of God: A New Look at Luke-Acts*. Minneapolis: Augsburg, 1972.
Johnson, Andy. "Resurrection, Ascension and the Developing Portrait of the God of Israel in Acts." *SJT* 57 (2004) 146–62.
Johnson, Luke T. *The Acts of the Apostles*. SP 5. Collegeville, MN: Liturgical, 1992.
———. *The Gospel of Luke*. SP 3. Collegeville, MN: Liturgical, 1991.
———. "James 3:13—4:10 and the *Topos* ΠΕΡΙ ΦΘΟΝΟΥ." *NovT* 25 (1983) 327–47.
Juel, Donald. *Messianic Exegesis: Christological Interpretation of the Old Testament in Early Christianity*. Philadelphia: Fortress, 1988.
Kajanto, Iiro. *God and Fate in Livy*. Turku: Turun Yliopiston Kustantama, 1957.
Karris, Robert J. *Prayer and the New Testament*. New York: Crossroad, 2000.
Keck, Leander E. "The Spirit and the Dove." *NTS* 17 (1970) 41–67.
Kee, Howard C. *Miracle in the Early Christian World*. New Haven: Yale University Press, 1983.
Kelber, Werner. "Redaction Criticism: On the Nature and Exposition of the Gospels." *PRSt* 6 (1979) 4–16.
Kemper, Jozef A. R. "Topik in der antiken rhetorischen Techne." In *Topik: Beiträge zur interdisziplinären Diskussion*, edited by D. Breuer and H. Schanze, 17–32. Munich: Fink, 1981.
Kennedy, George A. *The Art of Persuasion in Greece*. Princeton: Princeton University Press, 1963.
———. *A New History of Classical Rhetoric*. Princeton: Princeton University Press, 1994.
———. *New Testament Interpretation through Rhetorical Criticism*. Chapel Hill: University of North Carolina Press, 1984.
Kertelge, Karl. "Die Wunder Jesu in der neueren Exegese." In *Theologische Berichte V*, edited by J. Sievi, 71–105. Zürich: Benziger, 1976.
Kilgallen, John J. "Acts 13:4–12: The Role of the *Magos*." *Estudios bíblicos* 55 (1997) 223–37.
———. "The Function of Stephen's Speech (Acts 7,2–53)." *Bib* 70 (1989) 173–93.
———. "Jesus Tempted in the Desert (Luke 4, 1–12)." *Chicago Studies* 45 (2006) 228–33.
———. "The Speech of Stephen, Acts 7:2–53." *ExpTim* 115 (2004) 293–97.
Kim, Ju-Won. "Explicit Quotations from Genesis within the Context of Stephen's Speech in Acts." *Neot* 41 (2007) 341–60.
Kimball, Charles A. *Jesus' Exposition of the Old Testament in Luke's Gospel*. JSNTSup 94. Sheffield: JSOT Press, 1994.
Klauck, Hans-Josef. *The Religious Context of Early Christianity: A Guide to Graeco-Roman Religions*. Translated by B. McNeil. Minneapolis: Fortress, 2003.
Klein, Hans. *Das Lukasevangelium*. Kritisch-exegetischer Kommentar über das Neue Testament. Vol 1/3. Göttingen: Vandenhoeck & Ruprecht, 2006.

Kloppenborg, John S. "*Exitus clari viri*: The Death of Jesus in Luke." *TJT* 8 (1992) 106-20.

Koet, Bart J. "As Close to the Synagogue as Can Be: Paul in Corinth (Acts 18,1–18)." In *Dreams and Scripture in Luke-Acts: Collected Essays*, 173–94. CBET 42. Leuven: Peeters, 2006.

———. "Im Schatten des Aeneas: Paulus in Troas (Apg 16, 8–10)." In *Dreams and Scripture in Luke-Acts: Collected Essays*, 147–72. CBET 42. Leuven: Peeters, 2006.

Kollmann, Bernd. "Images of Hope: Towards an Understanding of New Testament Miracle Stories." In *Wonders Never Cease: The Purpose of Narrating Miracle Stories in the New Testament and its Religious Environment*, edited by M. Labahn and B. J. L. Peerbolte, 244–64. Library of New Testament Studies 288. London: T. & T. Clark, 2006.

Koskenniemi, Erkki. "The Traditional Roles Inverted: Jesus and the Devil's Attack." *BZ* 52 (2008) 261–68.

Kragelund, Patrick. "Dreams, Religion and Politics in Republican Rome." *Historia: Zeitschrift für Alte Geschichte* 50 (2001) 53–95.

Kraus, Franklin B. "An Interpretation of the Omens, Portents, and Prodigies Recorded by Livy, Tacitus, and Suetonius." PhD diss., University of Pennsylvania, 1930.

Kraus, Thomas J. "'Uneducated,' 'Ignorant,' or even 'Illiterate?' Aspects and Background for an Understanding of ΑΓΡΑΜΜΑΤΟΙ (and ΙΔΙΩΤΑΙ) in Acts 4.13." *NTS* 45 (1999) 434–49.

Kuhn, Karl A. "The 'One like a Son of Man' Becomes the 'Son of God.'" *CBQ* 69 (2007) 22–42.

Kurz, William S. "Hellenistic Rhetoric in the Christological Proof of Luke-Acts." *CBQ* 42 (1980) 171–95.

Labahn, Michael. "Der Gottessohn, die Versuchung und das Kreuz: Überlegungen zum Jesusporträt der Versuchungsgeschichte in Q 4,1–13." *ETL* 80 (2004) 402–22.

Lampe, G. W. H. "Miracles in the Acts of the Apostles." In *Miracles: Cambridge Studies in their Philosophy and History*, edited by C. F. D. Moule, 164–78. London: Mowbray, 1965.

Lee, Dorothy. "On the Holy Mountain: The Transfiguration in Scripture and Theology." *Colloq* 36 (2004) 143–59.

Leff, Michael. "Commonplaces and Argumentation in Cicero and Quintilian." *Argumentation* 10 (1996) 445–52.

———. "Up from Theory: Or I Fought the Topoi and the Topoi Won." *Rhetoric Society Quarterly* 36 (2006) 203–11.

Lehnert, Volker. "Absage an Israel oder offener Schluß? Apg 28,25-28 als paradoxe Intervention." *TBei* 29 (1998) 315–23.

Lenski, Gerhard E. *Power and Privilege: A Theory of Social Stratification*. New York: McGraw-Hill, 1966.

Léonas, Alexis. "A Note on Acts 3,25–26." *ETL* 76 (2000) 149–61.

Levene, D. S. *Religion in Livy*. Leiden: Brill, 1993.

Linderski, Jerzy. "Cicero and Roman Divination." In *Roman Questions: Selected Papers*, 458–84. Stuttgart: Steiner, 1993.

———. "Roman Religion in Livy." In *Livius: Aspekte seines Werkes*, 53–70. Konstanz: Universitätsverlag Konstanz, 1993.

———. "Römischer Staat und Götterzeichen: zum Problem der obnuntiatio." In *Roman Questions: Selected Papers*, 444–57. Stuttgart: Steiner, 1993.

Bibliography

Lips, Hermann von. "Die Haustafel als 'Topos' im Rahmen der Urchristlichen Paränese: Beobachtungen anhand des 1. Petrusbriefes und des Titusbriefes." *NTS* 40 (1994) 261–80.

Litfin, Duane. *St. Paul's Theology of Proclamation: 1 Corinthians 1–4 and Greco-Roman Rhetoric.* SNTSMS 79. Cambridge: Cambridge University Press, 1994.

Littlewood, A. R. "Olympic Games." In *Encyclopedia of Ancient Greece*, edited by N. Wilson, 514–15. London: Routledge, 2006.

Lohse, Eduard. "Die Bedeutung des Pfingstberichtes im Rahmen des lukanischen Geschichtswerkes." *EvT* 13 (1953) 422–36.

Louw Johannes P., and Eugene A. Nida. *Greek-English Lexicon of the New Testament Based on Semantic Domains.* 2nd ed. 2 vols. New York: United Bible Societies, 1988–1989.

Lown, John S. "The Miraculous in Greco-Roman Histories." *Forum* 2 (1986) 36–42.

Luther, Donald J. "The Mystery of the Transfiguration: Luke 9:28–36 (37–43)." *WW* 21 (2001) 92–102.

MacDonald, A. H. "The Style of Livy." *JRS* 47 (1957) 155–72.

Maddox, Robert. *The Purpose of Luke-Acts.* Edited by J. Riches. Edinburgh: T. & T. Clark, 1982.

Maier, Gerhard. "Zur neutestamentlichen Wunderexegese im 19. und 20. Jahrhundert." In *The Miracles of Jesus*, edited by D. Wenham and C. Blomberg, 49–87. Vol. 6 of Gospel Perspectives. Sheffield: JSOT Press, 1986.

Mainville, Odette. "De Jésus à l'Église: Étude rédactionnelle de Luc 24." *NTS* 51 (2005) 192–211.

Malherbe, Abraham J. "Hellenistic Moralists and the New Testament." *ANRW* 26/1: 267–333. Part 2, *Principat*, 33/1. Edited by H. Temporini and W. Haase. New York: de Gruyter, 1992.

———. *Paul and the Popular Philosophers.* Minneapolis, Fortress, 1989.

———. *Social Aspects of Early Christianity.* Baton Rouge: Louisiana State University, 1977.

Manns, Frédéric. "La symbolique animale évoque-t-elle l'Esprit Saint?" *Lumen Vitae* 54 (1999) 255–67.

Marincola, John. *Authority and Tradition in Ancient Historiography.* Cambridge: Cambridge University Press, 1997.

Marrow, Stanley B. "Parrhēsia and the New Testament." *CBQ* 44 (1982) 431–46.

Marshall, Anthony J. "Symbols and Showmanship in Roman Public Life: The Fasces." *Phoenix* 38 (1984) 120–41.

Marshall, I. Howard. *The Gospel of Luke: A Commentary on the Greek Text.* NIGTC 3. Grand Rapids: Eerdmans, 1978.

———. "The Significance of Pentecost." *SJT* 30 (1977) 347–69.

Martin, Josef. *Antike Rhetorik.* München: Beck, 1974.

Martin, Thomas W. "What Makes Glory Glorious? Reading Luke's Account of the Transfiguration Over Against Triumphalism." *JSNT* 29 (2006) 3–26.

Matera, Frank J. "The Death of Jesus According to Luke: A Question of Sources." *CBQ* 47 (1985) 469–85.

Matthey Jacques. "Luke 4:16–30—The Spirit's Mission Manifesto—Jesus' Hermeneutics—and Luke's Editorial." *International Review of Missions* 89 (2000) 3–11.

Maxey, James. "The Road to Emmaus: Changing Expectations." *CurTM* 32 (2005) 112–23.

Maxwell, Kathy. "The Role of the Audience in Ancient Narrative: Acts as a Case Study." *ResQ* 48 (2006) 171–80.
McAdon, Brad. "Probabilities, Signs, Necessary Signs, Idia, and Topoi: The Confusing Discussion of Materials for Enthymemes in the *Rhetoric*." *Philosophy and Rhetoric* 36 (2003) 223–48.
McCasland, S. Vernon. "Portents in Josephus and the Gospels." *JBL* 51 (1932) 323–35.
McDonald, James I. H. *Kerygma and Didache: The Articulation and Structure of the Earliest Christian Message.* SNTSMS 37. Cambridge: Cambridge University Press, 1980.
———. "Rhetorical Issue and Rhetorical Strategy in Luke 10.25–37 and Acts 10.1–11:18." In *Rhetoric and the New Testament: 1992 Heidelberg Conference*, edited by S. E. Porter and T. H. Olbricht, 59–73. JSNTSup 90. Sheffield: JSOT Press, 1993.
McDonald, William F. "Clodius and the Lex Aelia Fufia." *JRS* 19 (1929) 164–79.
Menoud, Philippe H. "The Additions to the Twelve Apostles According to the Book of Acts." In *Jesus Christ and the Faith: A Collection of Studies*, translated by E. Paul, 133–48. Pittsburgh: Pickwick, 1978.
Metzger, Bruce M. *A Textual Commentary on the Greek New Testament: A Companion Volume to the United Bible Societies Greek New Testament.* 2nd ed. New York: United Bible Societies, 1994.
Miller, David M. "The Messenger, the Lord, and the Coming Judgment in the Reception History of Malachi 3." *NTS* 53 (2007) 1–16.
Miller, John B. F. *Convinced that God had Called Us: Dreams, Visions, and the Perception of God's Will in Luke-Acts.* Biblical Interpretation Series 85. Leiden: Brill, 2007.
Miller, Marvin H. "The Character of Miracles in Luke-Acts." ThD diss., Union Theological Seminary, 1971.
Miller, Patricia C. *Dreams in Late Antiquity: Studies in the Imagination of a Culture.* Princeton: Princeton University Press, 1994.
Mitchell, T. N. "The *Leges Clodiae* and *obnuntiatio*." *CQ* 36 (1986) 172–76.
Moessner, David P. "Luke 9:1–50: Luke's Preview of the Journey of the Prophet Like Moses of Deuteronomy." *JBL* 102 (1983) 575–605.
———. "The 'script' of the Scripture in Acts." In *History, Literature and Society in the Book of Acts*, edited by B. Witherington, 218–50. Cambridge: Cambridge University Press, 1996.
———. "Two Lords 'at the Right Hand'? The Psalms and an Intertextual Reading of Peter's Pentecost Speech (Acts 2:14–36)." In *Literary Studies in Luke-Acts: Essays in Honor of Joseph B. Tyson*, edited by R. P. Thompson and T. E. Philips, 215–32. Macon, GA: Mercer University Press, 1998.
Momigliano, Arnaldo. "Prophecy and Historiography." In *Essays on Ancient and Modern Judaism*, edited by S. Berti, translated by M. Masella-Gayley, 101–108. Chicago: University of Chicago Press, 1987.
Morgenthaler, Robert. *Lukas und Quintilian: Rhetorik als Erzählkunst.* Zürich: Gotthelf, 1993.
Morton, Russell. "Acts 12:1–19." *Int* 69 (2001) 67–69.
Myllykoski, Matti. "Being There: The Function of the Supernatural in Acts 1–12." In *Wonders Never Cease: The Purpose of Narrating Miracle Stories in the New Testament and Its Religious Environment*, edited by M. Labahn and B. J. L. Peerbolte, 146–79. Library of New Testament Studies 288. London: T. & T. Clark, 2006.
Neagoe, Alexandru. *The Trial of the Gospel: An Apologetic Reading of Luke's Trial Narratives.* SNTSMS 116. Cambridge: Cambridge University Press, 2002.

Bibliography

Neirynck, Frans. "Luke 4,16–30 and the Unity of Luke-Acts." In *The Unity of Luke-Acts*, edited by J. Verheyden, 358–95. Leuven: Leuven University Press, 1999.

Nellessen, Ernst. "Tradition und Schrift in der Perikope von der Erwählung des Mattias (Apg 1,15–26)." *BZ* 19 (1975) 205–18.

Neumeister, Christoff. *Grundsätze der Forensischen Rhetorik: gezeigt an Gerichtsreden Ciceros*. Munich: Max Hueber, 1964.

Nolland, John. *Luke*. WBC 35. 3 vols. Dallas: Word, 1980.

Ogilvie, Robert M. *A Commentary on Livy: Books 1–5*. Oxford: Clarendon, 1965.

Olsson, Birger. "The Canticle of the Heavenly Host (Luke 2:14) In History and Culture." *NTS* 50 (2004) 147–66.

———. "Gloria in a Multitude of Voices." *ExpTim* 117 (2005) 89–94.

Omerzu, Heike. "Die Pilatusgestalt des Petrusevangelium: Eine erzählanalytische Annäherung." In *Das Evangelium nach Petrus: Text, Kontexte, Intertexte*, edited by T. J. Kraus and T. Nicklas, 327–47. TU 158. Berlin: de Gruyter, 2007.

Ophuijsen, Jan M. van. "Where Have the Topics Gone?" In *Peripatetic Rhetoric after Aristotle*, edited by W. W. Fortenbaugh and D. C. Mirhady, 131–73. New Brunswick, NJ: Transaction, 1994.

O'Reilly, Leo. *Word and Sign in the Acts of the Apostles: A Study in Lucan Theology*. Rome: Editrice Pontificia Universita Gregoriana, 1987.

O'Toole, Robert F. "Christ's Resurrection in Acts 13,13–52." *Bib* 60 (1979) 361–72.

———. "How Does Luke Portray Jesus as Servant of Yhwh?" *Bib* 81 (2000) 328–46.

———. "Philip and the Ethiopian Eunuch (Acts VIII 25–40)." *JSNT* 17 (1983) 25–34.

Park, Chan-Woong. "Eine Untersuchung zum Bild Johannes des Täufers bei Josephus und Lukas: Ihre Darstellungen im Blick auf politische Zusammenhänge." *Yonsei Journal of Theology* 4 (1999) 59–83.

Parke, H. W. *Greek Oracles*. London: Hutchinson University Library, 1967.

Parke, H. W., and D. E. W. Wormell. *The Delphic Oracle*. 2 vols. Oxford: Blackwell, 1956.

Parker, Robert. "Greek States and Greek Oracles." In *Oxford Readings in Greek Religion*, edited by Richard Buxton, 76–108. Oxford: Oxford University Press, 2000.

Parsons, Mikeal C. *Acts*. Grand Rapids: Baker, 2008.

———. *Body and Character in Luke and Acts: The Subversion of Physiognomy in Early Christianity*. Grand Rapids: Baker Academic, 2006.

———. "Isaiah 53 in Acts 8: A Reply to Professor Morna Hooker." In *Jesus and the Suffering Servant: Isaiah 53 and Christian Origins*, 104–19, edited by W. H. Bellinger and R. Farmer. Harrisburg, PA: Trinity, 1998.

———. *Luke: Storyteller, Interpreter, Evangelist*. Peabody, MA: Hendrickson, 2007.

Pathrapankal, Joseph. "The *Nazareth Manifesto* in the Evangelizing Mission of Jesus." *Indian Theological Studies* 43 (2006) 291–308.

Patsch, Hermann. "Die Prophetie des Agabus." *TZ* 28 (1972) 228–32.

Penner, Todd. *In Praise of Christian Origins: Stephen and the Hellenists in Lukan Apologetic Historiography*. New York: T. & T. Clark, 2004.

Pernot, Laurent. "Lieu et lieu commun dans la rhétorique antique." *Bulletin de la Association Guillaume Budé* 198 (1986) 253–84.

Pervo, Richard I. *Acts*. Philadelphia: Fortress, 2009.

Pesch, Rudolf. *Die Apostelgeschichte*. EKKNT. 2 vols. Zürich: Benziger, 1986.

Phillips, Thomas E. "The Genre of Acts: Moving Toward a Consensus?" *Currents in Biblical Research* 4 (2006) 365–96.

Bibliography

Pilgaard, Aage. "The Hellenistic *Theios Aner*—A Model for Early Christian Christology?" In *The New Testament and Hellenistic Judaism*, edited by P. Borgen and S. Giversen, 101–22. Peabody, MA: Hendrickson, 1997.

Pitcher, L. V. "Characterization in Ancient Historiography." In *A Companion to Greek and Roman Historiography*, edited by J. Marincola, 1:102–17. 2 vols. Malden, MA: Blackwell, 2007.

Plymale, Steven F. *The Prayer Texts of Luke-Acts*. New York: Peter Lang, 1991.

Polhill, John B. *Acts*. NAC 26. Nashville: Broadman, 1992.

———. "Perspectives on the Miracle Stories." *RevExp* 74 (1977) 389–99.

Poon, R. S. "The Background to the Dove Imagery in the Story of Jesus' Baptism." *Jian Dao* 3 (1995) 33–49.

Porter, Stanley E. "Scripture Justifies Mission: the Use of the Old Testament in Luke-Acts." In *Hearing the Old Testament in the New Testament*, edited by S. E. Porter, 104–26. Grand Rapids: Eerdmans, 2006.

Powell, C. A. "Religion and the Sicilian Expedition." *Historia: Zeitschrift für Alte Geschichte* 28 (1979) 15–31.

Praeder, Susan M. "Acts 27:1—28:16: Sea Voyages in Ancient Literature and the Theology of Luke-Acts." *CBQ* 46 (1984) 683–706.

Prior, M. "The Liberation Theology of the Lucan Jesus." *LASBF* 49 (1999) 79–99.

Rabinowitz, Peter. "Truth in Fiction: Reexamination of Audiences." *Critical Inquiry* 4 (1977) 121–42.

Reinhardt, Tobias. *Cicero's Topica*. Oxford: Oxford University Press, 2003.

Read-Heimerdinger, Jenny, and Josep Rius-Camps. "Emmaous or Oulammaous? Luke's use of the Jewish Scriptures in the Text of Luke 24 in Codex Bezae." *RCT* 27 (2002) 23–42.

Reinmuth, Eckart. "Beobachtungen zur Rezeption der Genesis bei Pseudo-Philo (LAB 1–8) und Lukas (Apg 7.2–17)." *NTS* 43 (1997) 552–69.

Reitzenstein, Richard. *Die Hellenistischen Mysterienreligionen*. 3rd ed. Leipzig: Teubner, 1927. Repr., Stuttgart: Teubner, 1956.

———. *Hellenistische Wundererzählungen*. 2nd ed. Darmstadt: Wissenschaftliche Buchgesellschaft, 1963.

Remer, Gary. *Humanism and the Rhetoric of Toleration*. University Park: Pennsylvania State University Press, 1996.

Rese, Martin. *Alttestamentliche Motive in der Christologie des Lukas*. Bonn: Rheinische Friedrich-Wilhelms-Universität Bonn, 1965.

———. "Die Funktion der alttestamentlichen Zitate und Anspielungen in den Reden der Apostelgeschichte." In *Les Actes des Apôtres: Traditions, redaction, théologie*, edited by J. Kremer, 61–79. BETL 48. Leuven: Leuven University Press, 1979.

Richard, Earl. *Acts 6:1—8:4: The Author's Method of Composition*. SBLDS 41. Missoula, MT: Scholars, 1978

———. "The Creative Use of Amos by the Author of Acts." *NovT* 24 (1982) 37–53.

Riesner, Rainer. "Versuchung und Verklärung (Lukas 4,1–13; 9,28–36; 10,17–20; 22,39–53 und Johannes 12,20–36)." *TBei* 33 (2002) 197–207.

Robbins, Vernon. "The Claims of the Prologues and Greco-Roman Rhetoric." In *Jesus and the Heritage of Israel*, edited by D. P. Moessner, 63–83. Harrisburg, PA: Trinity, 1999.

———. "Prefaces in Greco-Roman Biography and Luke-Acts." *PRSt* 6 (1979) 94–108.

Rothschild, Claire K. *Luke-Acts and the Rhetoric of History: An Investigation of Early Christian Historiography*. WUNT 2/175. Tübingen: Mohr/Siebeck, 2004.

Bibliography

Rudman, Dominic. "Authority and Right of Disposal in Luke 4.6." *NTS* 50 (2004) 77–86.
Rusam, Dietrich. *Das Alte Testament bei Lukas.* BZNW 112. Berlin: de Gruyter, 2003.
Russell, D. A. "On Reading Plutarch's *Lives.*" In *Essays on Plutarch's* Lives, edited by B. Scardigli, 75–94. Oxford: Clarendon, 1995.
———. *Plutarch.* New York: Scribner, 1973.
Rutz, Werner. "Zur Erzählkunst des Q. Curtius Rufus." *ANRW* 32/4:2329–57. Part 2, *Principat,* 32/4. Edited by H. Temporini and W. Haase. New York: de Gruyter, 1986.
Ryan, Eugene E. *Aristotle's Theory of Rhetorical Argumentation.* Montreal: Laboratoire de recherches sur la pensée antique d'Ottawa, 1984.
Salier, Willis H. *The Rhetorical Impact of the Sēmeia in the Gospel of John.* WUNT 2. Reihe 186. Tübingen: Mohr/Siebeck, 2004.
Sandt, Huub van de. "Acts 28,28: No Salvation for the People of Israel?" *ETL* 70 (1994) 341–58.
———. "The Quotations in Acts 13,32–52 as a Reflection of Luke's LXX Interpretation." *Bib* 75 (1994) 26–58.
Satterthwaite, Philip E. "Acts Against the Background of Classical Rhetoric." In *The Book of Acts in its First Century Setting,* edited by B. W. Winter, 1:337–79. Grand Rapids: Eerdmans, 1993.
Schiavo, Luigi. "The Temptation of Jesus: The Eschatological Battle and the New Ethic of the First Followers of Jesus in Q." *JSNT* 25 (2002) 141–64.
Schlosser, Jacques. "Moïse, Serviteur de Kérygme apostolique d'après Ac 3,22–26." *RevScRel* 61 (1987) 17–31.
———. "Les Tentations de Jésus et la Cause de Dieu." *RevScRel* 76 (2002) 403–25.
Schneider, Gerhard. *Das Evangelium nach Lukas: Kapitel 1–10.* Ökumenischer Taschenbuch-Kommentar 3/2. Würzburg: Gütersloher, 1984.
Schoedel, William R. *Polycarp, Martyrdom of Polycarp, Fragments of Papias.* The Apostolic Fathers. Vol. 5. Camden, UK: Nelson, 1967.
Schreiber, Stefan. "Die theologische Signifikanz der Pauluswunder in der Apostelgeschichte." SNTSU 24 (1999) 119–34.
———. "'Verstehst du denn, was du liest?' Beobachtungen zur Begegnung von Philippus und dem äthiopischen Eunuchen (Apg 8,26–40)." SNTSU 21 (1996) 42–72.
Schubert, Paul. "The Final Cycle of Speeches in the Book of Acts." *JBL* 87 (1968) 1–16.
———. "The Structure and Significance of Luke 24." In *Neutestamentliche Studien für Rudolf Bultmann zu seinem siebzigsten Geburtstag am 20. August 1954,* edited by W. Eltester, 165–86. Berlin: Töpelmann, 1954.
Schürmann, Heinz. *Das Lukasevangelium: Kommentar zu Kap. 1,1–9,50.* HTKNT 3. Freiburg: Herder, 1969.
Schütrumpf, Eckart. "Non–Logical Means of Persuasion in Aristotle's *Rhetoric* and Cicero's *De Oratore.*" In *Peripatetic Rhetoric after Aristotle,* edited by W. W. Fortenbaugh and D. C. Mirhady, 95–110. New Brunswick, NJ: Transaction, 1994.
Segal, Alan F. "Acts 15 as Jewish and Christian History." *Forum* 4 (2001) 63–87.
Seznec, Jean. *The Survival of the Pagan Gods: The Mythological Tradition and its Place in Renaissance Humanism and Art.* Translated by B. F. Sessions. New York: Harper & Brothers, 1953.
Sheeley, Steven M. *Narrative Asides in Luke-Acts.* JSNTSup 72. Sheffield: JSOT Press, 1992.

Sherman-White, A. N. *Roman Society and Roman Law in the New Testament*. Grand Rapids: Baker, 1963.
Shuler, Philip L. "The Rhetorical Character of Luke 1–2." In *Literary Studies in Luke-Acts: Essays in Honor of Joseph B. Tyson*, edited by R. P. Thompson and T. E. Phillips, 173–89. Macon, GA: Mercer University Press, 1998.
Smith, Abraham. "'Do You Understand What You are Reading?' A Literary Critical Reading of the Ethiopian (Kushite) Episode (Acts 8:26–40)." *Journal of the Interdenominational Theological Center* 22 (1994) 48–70.
Smith, Morton. "Prolegomena to a Discussion of Aretalogies, Divine Men, and the Gospels and Jesus." *JBL* 90 (1971) 174–99.
Soards, Marion L. *The Speeches in Acts: Their Content, Context, and Concerns*. Louisville: Westminster John Knox, 1994.
Squires, John T. "The Function of Acts 8.4—12.25." *NTS* 44 (1998) 608–17.
———. *The Plan of God in Luke-Acts*. SNTSMS 76. Cambridge: Cambridge University Press, 1993.
Stadter, Philip A. "The Rhetoric of Plutarch's Pericles." *Ancient Society* 18 (1987) 251–69.
Stamps, Dennis L. "The Use of the Old Testament in the New Testament as a Rhetorical Device: A Methodological Proposal." In *Hearing the Old Testament in the New Testament*, edited by S. E. Porter, 9–37. Grand Rapids: Eerdmans, 2006.
Stanley, Christopher D. "The Rhetoric of Quotations." In *Early Christian Interpretation of the Scriptures of Israel: Investigations and Proposals*, edited by C. A. Evans and J. A. Sanders, 44–58. JSNTSup 148. Sheffield: Sheffield Academic, 1997.
Sterling, Gregory E. "'Do You Understand What You are Reading?' The Understanding of the LXX in Luke-Acts." In *Die Apostelgeschichte im Kontext antiker und frühchristlicher Historiographie*, edited by J. Frey, C. K. Rothschild, and J. Schröter, 101–18. BZNW 162. Berlin: de Gruyter, 2009.
———. "Jesus as Exorcist: An Analysis of Mt 17:14–20; Mk 9:14–29; Lk 9:37–43a." *CBQ* 55 (1993) 467–93.
———. "*Mors Philosophi*: The Death of Jesus in Luke." *HTR* 94 (2001) 383–402.
———. "'Opening the Scriptures': The Legitimation of the Jewish Diaspora and the Early Christian Mission." In *Jesus and the Heritage of Israel*, edited by D. P. Moessner, 199–225. Harrisburg: Trinity Press International, 1999.
Steyn, Gert J. "ἐκχεῶ ἀπὸ τοῦ πνεύματός . . . (Ac 2:17, 18) What is Being Poured Out?" *Neot* 33 (1999) 365–71.
Stowasser, Martin. "Am 5,25–27; 9,11f. in der Qumranüberlieferung und in der Apostelgeschichte." *ZNW* 92 (2001) 47–63.
Strelan, Rick. *Strange Acts: Studies in the Cultural World of the Acts of the Apostles*. BZNW 126. Berlin: de Gruyter, 2004.
———. "Who Was Bar Jesus (Acts 13,6–12)?" *Bib* 85 (2004) 65–81.
Strobel, August. "Passa-Symbolik und Passa-Wunder in Act. XII. 3ff." *NTS* 4 (1958) 210–15.
Stump, Eleonore. *Boethius's De topicis differentiis*. Ithaca: Cornell University Press, 1978.
Swain, Simon. "Plutarch: Chance, Providence, and History." *AJP* 110 (1989) 272–302.
Sweeney, James P. "Stephen's Speech (Acts 7:2–53): Is it as 'Anti-Temple' as is Frequently Alleged?" *TJ* 23 (2002) 185–210.
Swinburne, Richard. *The Concept of Miracle*. London: Macmillan, 1970.
Sylva, Dennis D. "The Meaning and Function of Acts 7:46–50." *JBL* 106 (1987) 261–75.

Bibliography

Talbert, Charles H. "The Concept of Immortals in Mediterranean Antiquity." *JBL* 94 (1975) 419–36.

———. *Literary Patterns, Theological Themes, and the Genre of Luke-Acts*. Society of Biblical Literature Monograph Series 20. Missoula, MT: Scholars, 1974.

———. "Miraculous Conceptions and Births in Mediterranean Antiquity." In *The Historical Jesus in Context*, edited by A.-J. Levine, D. C. Allison, Jr., and J. D. Crossan, 79–86. Princeton: Princeton University Press, 2006.

———. "The Place of the Resurrection in the Theology of Luke." *Int* 46 (1992) 19–30.

———. "Promise and Fulfillment in Lucan Theology." In *Luke-Acts: New Perspectives from the Society of Biblical Literature*, edited by C. H. Talbert, 91–103. New York: Crossroad, 1984.

———. "Prophecies of Future Greatness: The Contribution of Greco-Roman Biographies to an Understanding of Luke 1:5–4:15." In *The Divine Helmsman: Studies on God's Control of Human Events, Presented to Lou H. Silberman*, edited by J. L. Crenshaw and S. Sandmel, 129–41. New York: Ktav, 1980.

———. *Reading Acts: A Literary and Theological Commentary*. Rev. ed. Macon, GA: Smyth & Helwys, 2005.

———. *Reading Luke: A Literary and Theological Commentary on the Third Gospel*. Rev. ed. Macon, GA: Smyth & Helwys, 2002.

———. *What is a Gospel?* Philadelphia: Fortress, 1977.

Talbert, Charles H., and J. H. Hayes. "A Theology of Sea Storms in Luke-Acts." In *Jesus and the Heritage of Israel*, edited by D. P. Moessner, 267–83. Harrisburg, PA: Trinity, 1999.

Tannehill, Robert C. "Israel in Luke-Acts: A Tragic Story." *JBL* 104 (1985) 69–85.

———. *The Narrative Unity of Luke-Acts: A Literary Interpretation*. 2 vols. Philadelphia: Fortress, 1986.

Tatum, W. Jeffrey. "Cicero's Opposition to the *Lex Clodia de Collegiis*." *CQ* 40 (1990) 187–94.

Taylor, N. H. "The Temptation of Jesus on the Mountain: A Palestinian Christian Polemic against Agrippa I." *JSNT* 83 (2001) 27–49.

Theissen, Gerd. *The Miracle Stories of the Early Christian Tradition*. Edited by J. Riches. Translated by F. McDonagh. Philadelphia: Fortress, 1983.

———. *Urchristliche Wundergeschichten: Ein Beitrag zur formgeschichtlichen Erforschung der synoptischen Evangelien*. Gütersloh: Gütersloher, 1974.

Thom, Johan C. "'The Mind is its Own Place': Defining the topos." In *Early Christianity and Classical Culture: Comparative Studies in Honor of Abraham J. Malherbe*, edited by J. T. Fitzgerald, T. H. Olbricht, and L. M. White, 555–73. NovTSup 110. Leiden: Brill, 2003.

Tiede, David L. *The Charismatic Figure as Miracle Worker*. SBLDS 1. Missoula, MT: SBL, 1972.

Trull, Gregory V. "Peter's Interpretation of Psalm 16:8–11 in Acts 2:25–32." *BSac* 161 (2004) 432–48.

Twelftree, Graham H. "The History of Miracles in the History of Jesus." In *The Face of New Testament Studies*, edited by S. McKnight and G. R. Osborne, 191–208. Grand Rapids: Baker, 2004.

———. *Jesus the Miracle Worker*. Downers Grove, IL: InterVarsity, 1999.

Uemura, Shizuka. "Isaiah 6:9–10: A Hardening Prophecy?" *AJBI* 27 (2001) 23–57.

Unnik, W. C. van. "Der Befehl an Philippus." In *Sparsa collecta: The Collected Essays of W. C. van Unnik*, 1:328–39. NovTSup 29. 3 vols. Leiden: Brill, 1973–1983.

Bibliography

Viviano, Benedict T. "The Least in the Kingdom: Matthew 11:11, Its Parallel in Luke 7:28 (Q), and Daniel 4:14." *CBQ* 62 (2000) 41–54.
Wahlde, Urban C. von. "Acts 4,24–31: The Prayer of the Apostles in Response to the Persecution of Peter and John—and its Consequences." *Bib* 77 (1996) 237–44.
———. "The Problems of Acts 4:25a: A New Proposal." *ZNW* 86 (1995) 265–67.
Wall, Robert W. "The Function of LXX Habbakkuk 1:5 in the Book of Acts." *BBR* 10 (2000) 247–58.
———. "Successors to 'the Twelve' According to Acts 12:1–17." *CBQ* 53 (1991) 628–43.
Wallace, Daniel B. *Greek Grammar Beyond the Basics: An Exegetical Syntax of the New Testament*. Grand Rapids: Zondervan, 1996.
Wansink, Craig S. *Chained in Christ: The Experience and Rhetoric of Paul's Imprisonments*. JSNTSup 130. Sheffield: Sheffield Academic, 1996.
Wardman, Alan. *Plutarch's Lives*. Berkeley: University of California Press, 1974.
Weaver, John B. *Plots of Epiphany: Prison-escape in Acts of the Apostles*. BZNW 131. Berlin: de Gruyter, 2004.
Weder, Hans. "Wunder Jesu und Wundergeschichten." *VF* 29 (1984) 25–49.
Weinreich, Otto. *Antike Heilungswunder: Untersuchungen zum Wunderglauben der Griechen und Römer*. Giessen: Töpelmann, 1909.
Weinstock, Stefan. "Clodius and the Lex Aelia Fufia." *JRS* 27. Part 2 (1937) 215–22.
Weiß, Wolfgang. *"Zeichen und Wunder": Eine Studie zu der Sprachtradition und ihrer Verwendung im Neuen Testament*. WMANT 67. Neukirchen-Vluyn: Neukirchener, 1995.
Wenkel, David H. "Imprecatory Speech-Acts in the Book of Acts." *Asbury Journal* 63 [2008]: 81–93.
Werline, Rodney A. *Pray Like This: Understanding Prayer in the Bible*. New York: T. & T. Clark, 2007.
Wikenhauser, Alfred. "Doppelträume." *Bib* 29 (1948) 100–111.
Williams, Stephen. "The Transfiguration of Jesus Christ." *Them* 28 (2002) 13–25.
———. "The Transfiguration of Jesus Christ (Part 2): Approaching Sonship." *Them* 28 (2003) 17–27.
Witherington, Ben. *The Acts of the Apostles: A Socio-Rhetorical Commentary*. Grand Rapids: Eerdmans, 1998.
Witherup, Ronald D. "Cornelius Over and Over and Over Again: 'Functional Redundancy' in the Acts of the Apostles." *JSNT* 49 (1993) 45–66.
———. "Functional Redundancy in the Acts of the Apostles: A Case Study." *JSNT* 48 (1992) 67–86.
Wright, N. T. "The Resurrection and the Postmodern Dilemma." *STRev* 41 (1998) 141–56.
Wuellner, Wilhelm H. "Toposforschung und Torahinterpretation bei Paulus und Jesus." *NTS* 24 (1978) 463–83.
Yamada, Kota. "The Preface to the Lukan Writings and Rhetorical Historiography." In *The Rhetorical Interpretation of Scripture: Essays from the 1996 Malibu Conference*, edited by S. E. Porter and D. L. Stamps, 154–72. JSNTSup 180. Sheffield: Sheffield Academic, 1999.

Scripture Index

Old Testament

Genesis

1:2	234n22
12:1	163
12:3	159, 159n180
15:13	163
15:14–16	163
18:18	159n180
22:18	159n180
26:4	159n180

Exodus

8:1	143n102
13:2	144
13:12	142n99
14:15	203n64
22:28	171
23:20	149, 149n132
23:20	

Leviticus

12:8	144
19:15	171n230
19:18	153n150, 270
23	160
23:29	159n179
25:23	143

Numbers

8	125n18
16	202
16:31–33	202
16:35	202
23:19	143n101

Deuteronomy

1:16–17	171n230
6:13	146n117
6:16	146n117
8:3	146n117
18	160
18:15–19	159n179
18:15–20	159, 159n179
25	152
25:5	151n141
25:5–10	151n141

1 Samuel

7	218
7:7–9	218
7:9b	218
7:10b	218

2 Samuel

7:12–14	152n148

2 Kings

1	236

Scripture Index

Psalms

2	161, 161n185
2:1–2	142n100
2:7	167
15	158n171
15:10	167
15:8–10	158n172
15:8–11	157
18:12–14	203n66
30:6	230
43	123n9
68:26	156
77:16–20	203n66
90	147n123, 147n124
90:11–12	146n117, 147, 269, 148n126
108:8	156
109:1	152, 153n149, 157, 158, 164n202

Isaiah

6	173, 173n236, 173n238
6:9–10	142n99, 172, 173n236, 275
6:10	173n236
40	145n112
40:3ff	145n112
40:3–5	145
42:21	170n224
49:6	273
53	165n204, 165n205, 166
53:7–8	165n204, 165n205, 166n208, 272
53:12	154n155
55:3	142n99, 167
58:6	148n128
66:1	163n196
61:1–2	148n128

Jeremiah

3:4	143
12:15–16	170n224

Ezekiel

1:7	122n9
14:17	135n69

Daniel

1–6	146n120
4:14	150n137
7:9–13	153n149
8	219
8:1	219
8:2	219
10:6	122n9

Joel

3:1–5	157

Amos

9:11–12	170, 170n225, 273

Habakkuk

1:5	168, 168n218, 273

Malachi

3	244n58
3:1	149, 149n132, 150n135
3:22–24	244n58

Deuterocanonical Books

2 Maccabees

5:2–4	183n17

4 Maccabees

4:1–14	248n74

New Testament

Matthew

27:45–55a	230n6
3:16–17	232

Mark

1:10	234n22

1:10–11	232	2:17–18	127
12:35–37	153n149	2:18	126n30, 269
15:33–40a	230n6	2:21–24	144, 269
		2:22	144

Luke

		2:22–23	144n107
		2:22a	144n107
1–9	3	2:22b	144n107
1:1–4	79, 81	2:23	142n99, 144, 144n107
1:4	277	2:24	264n136
1:5	243	2:24b	144
1:6	243n52	2:25	134
1:7	244	2:25–35	133, 269
1:8–9	243	2:26	135
1:8–23	243, 269	2:30	135
1:8–23, 26–38	243	2:35	135n69
1:10	243	3	239
1:16–17	145	3:4–6	145, 150, 150n134, 269
1:17	150, 150n134, 244, 245n61	3:15–16	150n134
1:18	244	3:16	134n63, 239
1:19–20	244	3:21–22	122n3, 123n12, 144n104, 146, 148n125, 191n43, 231n15, 232, 233n20, 269
1:26–38	269		
1:31	245		
1:32	245		
1:32–33	126		
1:33	245n61	3:23	269n7
1:34	246n66	3:23–38	146n118, 233n19
1:67	134	4:1–2	148n126
1:67–79	133, 269	4:1–13	146, 269
1:68	134n65	4:4	146n117
1:70	134n65	4:5–8	146n120
1:71	134n65	4:6	146n120
1:74	134n65	4:8	146n117
1:75	134n65	4:9	147n122
1:76	134n63, 150, 150n134	4:10–11	146n117, 148n126
1:76–77	135, 145	4:12	146n117
1:76–79	134n63	4:16	165n205
1:76a	134	4:16–30	122n5, 148, 270
1:76b–77	134	4:17	150n137
2	133	4:20	148
2:7	144n104	4:21	148
2:8–20	126, 269	7	270
2:9a	126n25	7:18–23	149
2:9b	126n25	7:22	1
2:10	126, 127n32	7:26	150
2:10–11	126n25	7:26–27	134n63
2:11	127n32	7:27	149, 150, 150n135
2:12	126, 126n25	7:28	150
2:13–14	126n28	7:29–30	151n139
2:16–17	126		

303

Scripture Index

Luke (continued)

7:30	150
8:5	232
8:22–25	241n48
8:25	180n6
8:25	241n48
8:28	260n126
8:47	260n126
8:48	260n125
9	122, 155n159, 270
9:7	122n5
9:9	122
9:16	122n7
9:20	122n6, 122n7
9:21–22	123
9:22	270, 270n8
9:22, 29ff, 44	122n7
9:28	122
9:28–36	122, 231n15, 270
9:29	122, 127n33
9:30	122
9:32	124n15
9:33	123, 124n15
9:33–47	124n14
9:35	122n7, 123
9:43	122n7, 180n6
9:51	235
9:51—10:24	235
9:51—19:44	235
9:52–56	235, 235n25, 270
9:57–62	235n25
9:58	232
10:1–24	235n25
10:25	153n150
10:25–37	153n150, 270
10:29	153n150
11:14	180n6
12:20–23	132
12:24	232
13:19	232
19:45–46	229n5
19:45—20:18	151n140, 229n5
19:47a	229n5
19:47—21:38	229n5
20:1–19	151n140, 229n5
20:1—21:4	229
20:16	229n5
20:20–26	151n140
20:27	151
20:27–33	151n140
20:27–40	151, 270
20:28–32	151
20:33	151
20:34–36	151
20:34–38	151
20:35	152
20:37	152, 152n146
20:37–38	152
20:39	153
20:41	152n147
20:41–47	151, 152, 270, 271
20:42–43	153
20:45	152n147
20:45–47	152n147, 153
21:6	228
21:7	228
21:10–24	228n2
21:11	228, 229
21:11, 25	228, 229n5, 271
21:25	228
22	156n167
22:37	154n155
22:54–62	156n161
23:4, 14, 22	231
23:13–25	231n10
23:15	231
23:40–41	231
23:44–45	230, 271
23:45	230n6
23:46	230
23:47	230, 275n9
24	3, 127, 127n33, 128, 128n35, 133, 155n157, 155n157, 165n205, 243n53
24:1–2	127
24:4	127n33, 127n34
24:5	127n34, 128n35
24:6–7	127n34
24:11	128
24:12	128, 128n36, 180n6
24:13–35	129n39
24:13–43	165n205
24:24	128n36
24:25–27	153
24:26	154n154

Scripture Index

24:26, 44	154	2:14–36	157, 238n33, 272
24:27	141, 154n152	2:16–36	157n168
24:44	156n162	2:17	142n99, 157, 157n170
24:44–45	158n176	2:17–21	157
24:44–49	153	2:22	276
24:44b–45	154n152	2:22–36	157n168
24:49	155n160, 239	2:24	158
		2:25–28	157, 158n172

John

12:28	88n50

Acts

1	127, 127n33, 133, 166, 264n137	2:29	158n171
		2:32	158n175
		2:33	158
		2:34	157
		2:37–40	157n168
1:1	1	2:41	159
1:1–14	127, 128, 271	3	157n170, 166
1:4	237	3–4	272
1:4–5	239	3–28	237
1:5, 8	155n160	3:12–16	159n178
1:7–11	128n37	3:1–11	136, 159, 161
1:8	128n37, 156, 237, 239, 242	3:12–18	159n178
1:10	127n33, 127n34	3:12–26	159
1:10b–11	128n37	3:14–15a	160n182
1:11	127n34, 128	3:15b	160n182
1:11a	128	3:16	160n182
1:11b	128	3:17–26	159n178
1:13	155	3:18	142n100, 159, 160
1:14	155, 237	3:19–26	159n178
1:15	156	3:21	142n100
1:15–16	155	3:22–23	159
1:16	142, 156, 156n166, 157	3:23	159n179
1:16, 21	156n166	3:25	159
1:20a	156	3:25–26	159n180
1:20b	156	4	1, 140, 166n210, 262, 272
1:21	155n160, 156n166	4:5–12	136, 272
1:26	264n137	4:5–6	136
2	125, 155n160, 156n167, 161n185, 166, 238, 246	4:8	133
		4:10	136n73
		4:13	136
2–12	237	4:16	136, 277
2:1–13	237, 238n32, 271	4:20	1
2:1–4	237, 246	4:22	136, 258
2:2	237	4:23	161n185
2:3	237	4:24	161, 258n116
2:5–12	238	4:24–26	142n100
2:14	159	4:24–30	259n118
2:14–15	157n168	4:25–26	161, 272
2:14–21	157n168	4:25a	161
		4:25b–26	161

305

Scripture Index

Acts (continued)

4:26c, 27	161n185
4:29	258
4:30	272, 277
4:31	136n75, 258, 259n118
4:31a	162, 258
4:31b	162, 258
5	132, 272, 273
5, 12	130
5:12–16	130
5:14	130
5:17	130
5:18	130
5:19	131
5:20	131, 131n49
5:21a	131
6	272
6:14	162
7	141, 162, 166, 272
7:1	162
7:2, 3	163
7:2–17	163n195
7:2–60	162
7:6	163
7:7	163
7:17	163
7:25	261
7:27	163
7:31	163
7:32	260
7:38	163
7:39	163
7:49	163n196
7:49–50	163n196
7:52	164
7:53	164
7:55a	164
7:55b	164
7:58	247n70
8	125n19, 272
8:1	247n70
8:1–3	129n41
8:1–25	129n41
8:3	247n70
8:4—12:25	129n39
8:26	129, 129n40
8:26, 29	129
8:26–28	129n40
8:26–30b	129n42
8:26–40	129n39
8:27a	129n40
8:27b–28	129n40
8:29	129, 129n40
8:29–30b	129n40
8:30a	129n40
8:30b	129n40
8:30c–35	130n42
8:32–33	165, 165n204
8:33	166n208
8:34	165n204
8:35	130n42, 166
8:36–40	129, 130n42
9	131n53, 169n220, 237, 237n31, 246, 247, 250
9:1	247
9:1–19a	246
9:1–31	249n77
9:3	247
9:6	248, 260n125
9:8b	248
9:8–9	248
9:10	247n71, 248n76
9:10–16	210n85, 249n79
9:12	247n71, 248
9:15	250
9:15–16	249, 249n77
9:18	249
9:29–30	250n82
9:32—11:18	251n85
9:32–35	251n85
9:36–43	251n85
10	125n19
10–11	81n26
10:1—11:18	166n209, 169, 210n85, 249n79, 250, 253n96, 273
10:2–3	251
10:3	251
10:3–6	251
10:4b	251
10:5	251
10:9	251
10:11	251
10:11–12	251
10:12	232
10:13	251

Scripture Index

10:14	251, 252n87	13:4	125n22
10:15	251	13:4–5	168n219
10:16	251	13:6–12	168n219, 248n73
10:19–20	251	13:7–8	137
10:23	252	13:9	137
10:28	252, 252n87	13:9–11	248n73
10:34	253n95	13:9–12	137, 273
10:34–43	252	13:11	138n83
10:39a	252n89	13:11a	138
10:41–42	252n89	13:13–43	165n205, 168n219
10:44	252	13:13–52	167n215
10:44–48	252	13:14	166
10:45	252	13:16b	167
11	253	13:16b–25	167n213
11:1–18	253n96	13:17–25	167, 167n213
11:3	253	13:22	167n212
11:5–10	253, 253n96	13:24	167n212
11:6	232	13:26	167
11:11–12a	253n96	13:26–31	167n213
11:12b	253n96	13:26–37	167n213
11:13–14	253, 253n96	13:27	168n216
11:15–17	253n96	13:27–37	167
11:16	253n96	13:32	142n99
11:27–28	139	13:32–33a	167
12	131, 131n50, 261n131, 273	13:32–37	167n213
12:1–5	132n54	13:33	167
12:3	131	13:33–35	273
12:6	131	13:33–35, 41	166
12:7	131n53, 132	13:34	142n99, 167
12:8a	131	13:35	167
12:8b	132	13:38–41	167, 167n213
12:8c	131	13:41	168, 169
12:9	132	13:42–43	168
12:12	132n56	13:44–45	168
12:17	132n57	13:44–47	168
12:18–19	260n123	13:44–52	168, 168n219, 273
13	124, 142n99, 273	13:45	169
13–14	254, 254n97	13:46	169
13–28	237n31, 246	13:47	168, 169, 171
13:1	124n17, 125n18	14:1–7	168n219
13:1–2a	124n16	14:8–18, 19–25	168n219
13:1–3	124, 124n16, 137, 171, 273	15	156n167, 166n209, 169n222, 273
13:1–14, 28	168n219		
13:2	124, 124n17	15–28	80
13:2a	124	15:1–5	169
13:2b	124n16, 125	15:7–11	169
13:2c	124n16	15:12	169, 170n226
13:3	124n16, 125	15:15	169

307

Acts (continued)

Reference	Page(s)
15:15–18	169
15:16	170n224
15:16–17a	170n225
15:16–18	170, 273
15:17	170n225
15:17b–18	170n225
15:18	170n224
15:36	254, 254n97
15:37–39	254
16	255n102, 261
16:5–8	254, 254n100
16:6	254n99
16:6—17:15	254
16:6–8	254
16:7	254n99
16:8–10	254n99
16:9–10	253, 254, 255n102
16:10	255, 260n121
16:11–15	255
16:16–18	255
16:19–40	255
16:24–40	259, 273
16:25	259
16:26a	259
16:26b	259
16:28	259n119
16:29	260
16:30	260
16:31	261
18:1–17	255
18:5–8	255
18:6	255, 256, 274
18:9	255, 256, 84n32
18:9–10	253, 255
18:11	256, 256n108
18:12–17	256, 256n108
18:18a	255n104
19:21	138n84, 139, 257, 274
19:23	139n89
20:1—21:26	138n84
20:23	139, 139n87, 139n89
21	139n87, 139n89, 181n12
21:1–6	139n85
21:4	138, 274
21:5–6	139
21:7–16	139n85
21:10–12	138, 139, 274
21:11	138
21:12	139
21:17—23:11	239
22	249
22:1–29	246
22:6–16	274
22:9	248n73
22:15	250
22:17	249
22:17–21	246, 274
22:30—23:10	256
23	171, 274
23–26	257n114
23:1	171
23:3	171
23:5	171
23:8	131n48
23:11	253, 256, 257, 274
23:11—26:32	256
23:11a	257
23:29	239n39
24:1–27	239
25:1–27	239
25:11	239
25:25	239n39
26	249, 250
26:1–23	246, 274
26:1–32	239
26:16	250
26:19	247n71
26:31	239
26:32	239
27	241n48
27:1—28:10	239
27:9	239, 240n42
27:10	240
27:12	240
27:13–44	240
27:20a	240
27:20b	240
27:23	240n43
27:24	240, 263
27:24–26	274
27:27–32	241
27:30–32	242
27:33–34	242
27:34	240n45, 261
27:42–43	241

27:43	242n50	28:24	172
28:4	241	28:25	142n99, 172
28:16	172	28:26	173n238
28:17–22	173n237	28:26–27	172
28:17–31	173n237	28:28	173
28:18	173n237	28:30–31	173n237
28:23	172		
28:23–28	173n237		

Ancient Writers Index

Aeschines

In Ctesiphonem

135–36	57n88
136	57n88

Anonymous Seguerianus

Art of Political Speech

145	44n58
181	51

Apsines

Art of Rhetoric

5.1	45
9.1	45
10.1	45
10.2	46n63
10.15	46n63
10.16	46

Aristides

Defense of Oratory

19	54
22	54n79
23–41	54
27–28	54n80
38	54n81
41	54n82
42	54n83
45	55n84
50–57	55
58–65	61
75	61
78–83	53n76, 55
81	55

Aristotle

Rhetorica

1.15.1–2	30n27
1.15.13–19	30
1.15.15–17	31
1.2.1	29
1.2.2	29
1.2.21	29, 37n43
1.2.21–22	30
1.2.3–6	29
1.2.8–9	29
2.2.13	37n43
2.23.1–29	30

Topica

1.1.18	28
1.18.33–35	29
1.1.25–31	28
2.2.34–36	29
2.3.29–30	29

Ancient Writers Index

CAESAR

Bellum civile

3.105	195n52

CICERO

Academicae quaestiones

1.4.16	52n75

De amicitia

2.7	52n75
2.10	52n75
4.13	52
4.14	60

In Catalinam

3.18	58
3.19	58n93
3.20–21	59
3.21	59n54
3.22	57

De oratore

1.8.30	34
1.8.32	34
1.13.56	39
1.31.138	68
2.29.127	40
2.34.146	34
2.35.147	34
2.35.149	34
2.35.151	35n38
2.36.152	35
2.39.162	35
2.42.178	70
2.54.146	34n38
2.91.174–75	35
3.55.210–12	68n114

De divinatione

1.5.9	68n117
1.43	205n71
1.45.101	85n37, 85n38
1.121	196n53

De domo suo

14.39–41	63n103

De haruspicum responso

9	65
9.18	71n124
9–10, 16	65
10	65
24	65n108
25	65
37	65, 65n107, 66
38–39	66n109
48	61n98
61	66
62	66
62–63	66

De inventione rhetorica

1.3.5	32n32
1.4.5	32
1.19.27–21.30	32n34
1.22.31–23.33	32n34
1.23.33–24.36	32
1.24.34	32, 34n34, 33, 80n22
1.24.34–41.77	33n34
1.26.38	33
1.29.44	33
1.30.49	33
1.42.78–51.47	34n34
1.52.98–56.109	34n34
2.14.47–15.48	40
2.45.132	70n121
2.50.111	31n31

De legibus

2.7.15	66
2.7.16	66
2.12.31	61n99, 62n99

Pro Ligario

2–17	64
19	64

Ancient Writers Index

Pro Milone

11	63
77–78	63
78	63n104
83–84	63
88	64n106

De officiis

2.14.51	70n121

Partitiones oratoriae

2.5	38, 50n70
2.6	50n70
2.7	38
3.8	38
9.31	80

Orationes philippicae

2.32.81–34.84	61n98
5.7	62

De republica

5.1	57n88

De senectute

21.78	52n75

Pro Sulla

40	58n91

Topica

1.2	36
2.7.8	36
2.8	37
2.8—4.23	38
2.9—4.23	37
4.24	38, 47
4.72	47n65
5.26—18.71	38
19.73	48, 48n66, 77, 137n75
20.76–77	2n3, 22, 50, 57, 83, 177, 266n3, 276

Tusculanae disputationes

1.22.52	53n76

In Vatinium

5.13	62
6.14	62
7.17	63n102
7.17–18	62n101
7.18	61n98

Demosthenes

In Midiam

47–55	55n86

Dio Cassius

Historia Romana

38.12.7	57n90
38.13.3–6	61n99

Dio Chrysostom

De servis

10.22	53n76

Ad Alexandrinos

32.9	59
32.12	59
32.79–80	59
32.80	60

Corinthiaca

37.5	60n95
37.6	53
37.7	53n78
37.9	60n95
37.12	60n95
37.13	60n95

De gloria ii

67.3	53n76

Ancient Writers Index

Diodorus Siculus

Bibliotheca historica

1.1.4	75
3.47.1–48.1	187n26
4.63.1–2	187n26
4.64.1–67.2	103n88
4.69.3	103
4.69.4	103
7.5.4–5	206
8.97	223
8.97.5	213
8.97.6	213
8.98.1	213
8.98.3	213
8.98.5	214
11.50.1	111
11.50.2–4	111
11.50.4	111
11.50.5	111n106
11.50.6	111
11.63.2–3	215
11.63.2–3	260
11.63.3	215, 216
12.10.4	105
12.10.5	105
12.10.6	106n93
12.11.1	106
12.11.2–3	106
12.11.3–4	106
12.12.1–19.3	106n94, 178
13.21.1	179
13.101–102	214
13.102.1	214n92
13.102.2	214n92
13.102.3	214n92
13.12.6	178
15.18.2	90
15.18.3	91n56
15.32.6	91
15.33.1	92
15.33.2	92
15.33.3	92n57
15.49.1	216n96
15.49.1–6	216, 260
15.49.3	216
15.49.4	217
15.51.1–56.4	92n57
15.54.2	92n57
15.80.1–6	180n9
15.80.3	181n11
16.9	141n93
16.66.3–5	194n49
16.91.2	100
16.91.3	100, 100n77, 100n78
16.92.2	100
16.92.4	100n79
16.92.5	101n80
16.93.2	101
16.93.3–94.4	101n81
22.6	213n91

Dionysius of Halicarinasus

Antiquitates romanae

1.1.2	76n3
1.2.1	76n3
1.23	95n63
1.55.1	96, 96n67
1.55.2	96n68
1.55.3	141n95, 96, 97
1.55.4	97n69
1.55.5	97
1.56.3	206n72
1.56.5	206n72
1.57.4	211, 249
1.59.1	211n86
3.35	200n60
3.35.1	199, 247n72
3.35.2	199
4.2.1	196, 197
4.2.2	196, 197, 238n35
5.15.1–4	84n35
5.16.1–3	84
5.16.2	84
5.16.2–3	84
5.46.2	198n59
7.68–69	207n78
14.9.3	92n58

De Thucydide

34.18	93n58

Ancient Writers Index

Florus

1.16.1	196n53

HOMER

Iliad

23.368–72, 448	59

ISOCRATES

Helenae encomium

4	28n23
38	28n23

JEROME

De viris illustribus

7	196n53

JOSEPHUS

Antiquitates judaicae

1.108	197n55
2.212ff	95n63
2.334–37	203
2.343–44	203
2.348	197n55
3.268	197n55
3.322	197n55
3.81	197n55
4.40–50	259n118
4.51	259n118
6.24	219n106
6.25	218, 219
6.27	219
10	262n132
10.269	219
10.271	220n108
10.272	220n109
11.326	211
11.327	211n87
11.330	212n89
11.332	212n89
11.334–35	212

Bellum judaicum

4.386	141n96
6.312	141n96
6.288	182
6.288–99	87n45, 182
6.292–96	182n16
6.299–300	87, 183
6.300	93
6.301–302	93
6.303	94
6.308	94n64
6.310	94

LIVY

Historiae (Ab urbe condita)

1.pr.10	75
1.pr.9	75
1.39.1–4	196n53
1.39.2	238n35
1.56.4	187n26
1.56.6–13	102n86
2.36	244
2.36.1	207
2.36.2	207
2.36.3–37.1	207
2.37.1	207n77
2.7.2	84n34, 84n36
3.36.3–6	187n28
5.15	137n76
5.15.2	118, 118n130
5.15.4	118
5.15.6–10	118
5.15.10	118n131
5.15.12	118n132
5.16.8	118
5.17.1	119n133
5.21.5	119n134
5.21.5, 17	119
5.32.6	85, 85n38
5.49.1	85n39
5.49.8	85
5.50.5	85, 85n38
5.52.2	85n40
7.26.3–5	184

Ancient Writers Index

Historiae (Ab urbe condita) (continued)

7.26.8	184
10.27.8–9	220
10.29.1	221n113
10.29.9	221n112
22.1–13	198n59
25.16	223
25.16.1	221
25.16.2–3	222
25.16.5–24	222
25.37.1–2	198
25.37.3–7	198
25.37.8	198
25.38.4	198n58
25.39.1–16	197
25.39.16	197, 198, 238n35
25.39.17	198
29.10.5	106
29.10.6	106
29.10.7	106n96
29.10.8	107n97
29.11.1–2	107
29.11.6	107
29.11.6–8	107
29.14.8	107

LONGINUS

De sublimitate

13.2.4	30n28

LUCIAN

How to Write History

55	237n31

LYCURGUS

Against Leocrates

83–89	53
92	57n88

OVID

Fasti

6.631–36	196n53

PAUSANIAS

Graeciae description

9.13.5	108n99
24.6	217n97

PHILO

De Abrahamo

262	143n103
270	143n103

De cherubim

49	143
51	143n101
108	143
124	143n103

De confusione linguarum

94	143, 143n103

Quod deterius potiori insidari soleat

46	143n101
74	143n101
86	143n101
126	143n101
166	143n103

Quod Deus sit immutabilis

62	143n101

De ebrietate

60	143n101
82	143n101

Ancient Writers Index

Legum allegoriae

3.129	143n103
3.142	143n101
3.215	143n101
3.245	143n101

De migratione Abrahami

115	143n103

De vita Mosis

1.66	123n9
2.68	123n9
2.284	202

De mutatione nominum

90	143n103

De opificio mundi

8	143n101

De plantatione

63	143n101

De posteritate Caini

169	143n101

De sacrificiis Abelis et Caini

57	143n101

De sobrietate

17	143n101

Plato

Alcibiades major

1.124a-b	53n76

Apologia

20e-21a	52

Charmides

164b-65b	53n76

Gorgias

463a–465c	54

Phaedrus

244b	91n55

Respublica

540c	54n82

Pliny the Elder

Naturalis historia

2.34.100	49n68
2.52.137	58n92
2.52.137–54.141	50n68
2.58.148	49n67, 49n68
2.86.200	66n110
2.181, 191–192	66n110

Plutarch

Agis et Cleomenes

5.2	114n112
5.3	114n112
6.2	114n114
6.4	114n113
8.1–9.1	114
9.1	114
9.2	114n115
9.3	114
10.1	114n116
11.1	115, 115n117

Agesilaus

2.2	112
3.1–2	112n108
3.3	218
3.3–4	112
3.3–5	218
3.4	112n107

Ancient Writers Index

Agesilaus (continued)

3.5	112n109
4.1	112

Alcibiades

39.1–4	179n5

Alexander

2.3–4	210
2.4–5	210
25	241n47
25.2	224
60.4	201

Caesar

38.4	202
38.5–6	202
43	223
43.3	194
43.4	194
43.5–6	195
47.1	195
47.1–2	195
48.4	195
69.3–6	179
69.5	180n7

Cato Minor

70.4–5	189

Comparatio Demosthenis et Ciceronis

2.1	57n90

Comparatio Lycurgi et Numae

1.1	87

Comparatio Pelopidae et Marcelli

3.1	102n85

Comparatio Agidis et Cleomenis cum Tiberio et Gaio Graccho

2.3	115

Comparatio Agesilai et Pompeii

1.2	112

Marcius Coriolanus

24.2	207n78

Demosthenes

3.2	142n97
17.1	109n102
17.2	109n102
17.3	109n102
18.3	109n102
19.1	109, 109n103
19.2	109n103
19.3	109n103
20.1	110
20.2	110
20.3	110
21.1	110
30.4	179n5

Titus Flamininus

20.1	102n83
20.2	102
20.3–4	101n82
21.1	102
21.1–2	102n84
21.4	102n84

De fortuna Romanorum

10	196n53

Galba

23.2	200
24.1	200, 224
24.2–3	224

Lycurgus

14	86
14.1	86n41
23.1	86
23.2	86
25.5	86

Ancient Writers Index

Nicias

23.6	178n2

Numa

6.1	185
7.1	185
7.2–3	185
22.4–5	179n5

Pelopidas

20.2	107n98
20.4	92n57, 108
21.1	107
21.2	108n100
22.1–2	108n100
23.4	108
31.2	180
31.3	180n10, 181n11
32.7	180
33–34	181
35.1	181

Pericles

1.3–4	76

Pompeius

68.1–3	195n52
68.2	195n52

Pyrrhus

1.4	99n73
2.6	99n73
3.4	99n73
3.5	99n73
8.1	99n73
8.4	99n73
26.1	99
29.1	99n74
30.1	99n74
30.2	99n74
31.2	99n75
31.4	99n75
32.4	98
34.1	98n72
34.2	98n72
34.3	98n72

De Pythiae oraculis

404e	91n55

Romulus

2.6	221
3.2	221
28.1–2	123n9

Solon

8.4–6	116n124
9.1	117, 117n125
9.2–3	117
9.4	117n126
10.1–3	117n127
10.3	117n127
10.4	117
11.1	117

De superstitione

165f-166a	71n125
168f-169a	71n125
169a-b	71n126

Themistocles

26.1	92, 207
26.2	134n62, 135n69, 208, 93
26.2–3	208
27.1	208n81
28.3	208
30	254
30.1–2	209

Theseus

3.3	142n97
36.1–2	179n5

Tiberius et Caius Gracchus

17.1	222n114
17.2	222, 225n116, 253n96
17.3	222n115
19.6	222
20.3	223
20.4	223

Ancient Writers Index

Tiberius et Caius Gracchus (continued)

21.1	223

Timoleon

1.1	76
8.2	193
8.3	193
8.4	194, 194n50
9.1	194

Polybius

Historiae

1.1.2	76n3

ps-Cicero

Rhetorica ad Herennium

2.30.47	41, 41n50
2.30.48	51
4.27.37	58n92
4.28.38	65n108
4.33–34	209n83
4.38.50	215n95

Quintilian

Institutio oratoria

1.5.6	68n113
2.15.3, 5	68
4.2.31	80
4.3.12	86n42
4.3.14	86n42
5.pr	42n51
5.1.1	42n52
5.9.1	42
5.10.20	51
5.10.20–21	42
5.10.22	42
5.11.36	51
5.11.36–37	51
5.11.42	51, 52, 57n89, 64
6.2.5	70
8.6.67–76	209n83
12.10.56	68n114

Quintus Curtius

History of Alexander

5.3.1–23	97
5.4	141n94
5.4.11	97
5.4.12	97
5.4.13	97n70
5.4.4	97
5.5.1	98n71
6.10.15	116
6.10.20–21	116
6.10.23	116
6.10.24	116
6.10.26	116
6.10.27	116
6.10.28–29	116
6.9.31–36	115n119
610.11–12	115
7.1.2	116n123

Seneca the Younger

Epistulae morales

34.19	27n18

Ad Marciam de consolatione

11.2–3	53

Naturales quaestiones

1.pr.17.2–3	49n68
1.15.5	49n68
2.12.2	49n68
2.21.1	49n68
2.32.1–51.1	49n68
2.41.1–46.1	49n68
2.46.1	50n68

Ancient Writers Index

SENECA THE ELDER

Controversiae

1.pr.8	56
1.pr.9	56

Suasoria

1.7.9	27n18

SERVIUS

ad Aeneid

2.683	196n53

SUETONIUS

Divus Augustus

2.92.1	190n38
2.94.1	186
2.94.10–11	187n27
2.94.2	186n22
2.94.3	186
2.94.4	186, 186n23
2.94.5	186
2.94.7	186, 187

Divus Claudius

5.2.1	188
5.6.1-2	188n32
5.6.2	188n33
5.7.1	187
5.7.2	188
5.8	188n31
5.9	188n31
5.66	200n60

Domitianus

8.15.2	200n60

Galba

1	200n60
7.9.2	209, 210
7.18.1	193n48, 217, 217n98
7.18.1–2	260
7.18.2	217
7.18.3	193n48
7.21.1	217n101
7.22.1	218n101

Divus Julius

81	223
81.1	189
81.3	190, 190n37
81.4	190
86–87	190
88	180n8

Otho

5.2	199
6.3	199
7.1	199
7.2	199

Vespasianus

8.5.1	104
8.5.2	104
8.5.3	104
8.5.4	104
8.5.5	104
8.5.6	104, 104n90
8.7.2–3	104
8.8.1	105
8.16	105n92
8.16.1	105n92
8.17.1	105n92

Vitellius

8.9.1	193n48

TACITUS

Annales

12.62	113, 113n110
12.63	113, 114
22	181
32	181

Ancient Writers Index

Historiae

1.27–41	217n99
1.38	200n61
2.50	189n36
5.13	87n46, 183n18, 228n3

Theon

Progymnasmata

22R	145n109
93	43
106	43
111	44n57, 198n57, 210n84
117–18	44n57
121	44n57
122	185n21, 51n73

Valerius Maximus

Memorable Doings and Sayings

3.4.ext	52n75

Xenophon

Cyropaedia

7.1.4	208n80

Zonarus

7.9	196n53

Apostolic Fathers

Martyrdom of Polycarp

5.2	191n42
8.2–3	88n48
9	191n42
9.1	88, 88n48
12.3	191n42
13	191
14	191
15	191
15.2	191n40
16.1	191, 191n41
16.1–2	192

Early Christian and Jewish Writings

Dead Sea Scrolls

4Q246	245n60

Old Testament Pseudepigrapha

Sibylline Oracles

3.316	135n69

Testament of Abraham

7.3–4	123n9
16.6	123n9

New Testament Apocrypha and Pseudepigrapha

Gospel of Peter

10.38	89n52
11.45	89
9.34—10.42	89